013621687

Plea
is p
one
duri
794

H.D. and Hellenism

H.D. and Hellenism: Classic Lines concerns a prominent aspect of the writing of the modern American poet H.D. (Hilda Doolittle): a lifelong engagement with hellenic literature, mythology, and art. H.D.'s hellenic intertextuality is examined in the context of classical fictions operative at the turn of the century: the war of words among literary critics establishing a new "classicism" in reaction to romanticism; the fictions of classical transmission and the problem of women within the classical line; nineteenth-century romantic hellenism, represented in the writing of Walter Pater; and the renewed interest in ancient religion brought about by anthropological studies, represented in the writing of Jane Ellen Harrison. Eileen Gregory explores at length H.D.'s intertextual engagement with specific classical writers: Sappho, Theocritus and the Greek Anthology, Homer, and Euripides. The concluding chapter sketches chronologically H.D.'s career-long study and reinvention of Euripidean texts. An appendix catalogues classical subtexts in *Collected Poems, 1912–1944*, edited by Louis Martz.

CAMBRIDGE STUDIES IN AMERICAN LITERATURE AND CULTURE

(Continued on page following index.)

H.D. and Hellenism

Classic Lines

EILEEN GREGORY
University of Dallas

CAMBRIDGE
UNIVERSITY PRESS

PUBLISHED BY THE PRESS SYNDICATE OF THE UNIVERSITY OF CAMBRIDGE
The Pitt Building, Trumpington Street, Cambridge CB2 1RP, United Kingdom

CAMBRIDGE UNIVERSITY PRESS
The Edinburgh Building, Cambridge CB2 2RU, United Kingdom
40 West 20th Street, New York, NY 10011-4211, USA
10 Stamford Road, Oakleigh, Melbourne 3166, Australia

First published 1997

Printed in the United States of America

Typeset in Bembo

Library of Congress Cataloging-in-Publication Data
Gregory, Eileen.
H.D. and Hellenism: classic lines / Eileen Gregory.
p. cm. – (Cambridge studies in American literature and culture; 111)
Includes bibliographical references (p.   ) and index.
ISBN 0-521-43025-9 (hardcover)
1. H.D. (Hilda Doolittle), 1886–1961 – Knowledge – Greece.
2. Women and literature – United States – History – 20th century.
3. Greek literature – Appreciation – United States.   4. American poetry – Greek
influences.   5. Hellenism – History – 20th century.
6. Greece – In litearture.   I. Title.   II. Series.
PS3507.O726Z675   1997
811'.52 – dc21

96-37393
CIP

A catalog record for this book is available from the British Library.

ISBN 0-521-43025-9 hardback

For Marie

Contents

Part II: Classical Intertextuality

Acknowledgments

―――――――――

This book had its origins in September 1986 during the centennial celebrations of H.D.'s birth held in Orono, Maine, and Bethlehem, Pennsylvania. I have vivid memories of those gatherings, the first assemblies of the many critics and poets who have seriously engaged in writing about H.D. I was struck then and still am by the originality and diversity of approach within this group, and also by a remarkable generosity and openness in their conception of professional exchanges. A desire to honor that spirit, so congruous with the kind of economy at work in H.D.'s writing, led me to undertake the *H.D. Newsletter*, where I had a means of continued exchange. The sense of a community of scholars, an imagined audience, has made my writing possible. Indeed, this study would have been inconceivable without the efforts of these critics over the past two decades to establish a climate in which H.D.'s writing could be considered respectfully and deliberately.

   Moreover, the professional support I have received during the conception, research, and composition of this book has been specific and steady. Susan Friedman has extended encouragement, keen criticism, advice, and advocacy. She has read and commented upon portions of this manuscript in many of its previous incarnations, in articles and proposals for grants and publications. Her openness to critical conversation and her responsiveness to new voices have certainly helped to create the hospitable quality of H.D. studies. Diana Collecott has shared many hours of animated conversation with me in the course of our common researches at Yale. She has been an important interlocutor in the conception and working through of my ideas, and she has steadily and enthusiastically encouraged me, especially in the efforts of the *H.D. Newsletter*. Special thanks must certainly go to Louis Silverstein for his unstinting generosity in facilitating research and in sharing his amalgamate "H.D. Chronology" and to Louis and Monty Montee for their warm hospitality at Silverleigh in New

Haven. Perdita Schaffner has been a generous and courteous executor of H.D.'s estate, and I have learned much from her keen insight into H.D.'s writing.

Many others have extended support and encouragement during the past few years. Rachel DuPlessis has repeatedly been a guide and an intelligent commentator. Al Gelpi helped in the formulation of the project at a crucial moment and has patiently inquired after its progress. Dee Morris in her unpredictable but clearly charmed paths of exploration has encouraged my own divagations. Alicia Ostriker, with whom I have spoken only briefly from time to time, has been an important presence within the imagination of this work. Donna Hollenberg has generously provided me with information from the H.D.–Pearson correspondence; Emily Mitchell Wallace has responded to my queries about H.D.'s studies at Bryn Mawr, spending time and effort in this additional research; and Cassandra Laity has shared with me some of her work in progress on H.D. and the Victorian fin de siècle. Others have also extended help or goodwill at important moments: Ann Ardis, Jane Augustine, David Bergman, Gary Burnett, Sylvia Dobson, Susan Howe, Charlotte Mandel, Judith Roche, David Roessel, Virginia Smyers, Robert Spoo, John Walsh, and Caroline Zilboorg. I am especially grateful to Ann Ashworth for her friendship and her perceptive and sympathetic reading of my manuscript.

This book would probably not have come to be without the Dallas Institute of Humanities and Culture, under the leadership of Gail Thomas, which has allowed me an ample arena for imaginative exploration and which generously sponsored the *H.D. Newsletter* for many years. Dona Gower has been a steadfast friend, showing implicit faith in the integrity of my direction even when it has seemed most dubious. I have counted on the fine judgment of another friend and colleague, Robert Dupree, to assess the early chapters at an insecure point in their development.

The University of Dallas has supported this project with released time, a leave, a sabbatical, and two grants for summer study from the King/Haggar Faculty Development Endowment. I am grateful as well for the support of three grants from the National Endowment for the Humanities that made possible my preliminary research and writing: a Summer Stipend award in 1985, a Travel to Collections grant in 1987, and a Fellowship for University Teachers in 1989–90.

My thanks go to the staff of the Beinecke Rare Book and Manuscript Library at Yale University for their courtesy and help, especially to Steve Jones and to Patricia Willis, the curator of the Collection of American Literature. Robert Babcock at the Beinecke, himself a classicist with an active interest in modern literature, has been especially supportive of this project. I have very much benefited from the efforts of Alice Puro, in charge of Interlibrary Loan at the University of Dallas, and of the Interlibrary Loan staff at the Dallas Public Library. The Dallas Public Library generously facilitated the last year of writing, which was undertaken during an extended appointment in the Frances Mossiker

Writer's Study Room. Very special thanks go to the all of the members of the humanities staff, whose courtesy, intelligence, and good-spiritedness have constantly sustained me. Frances Bell, the head of the humanities division, has helped me in many particular ways, and I have come to prize her keen literary acumen. Steve Housewright has been a remarkable presence both as a friend and as a knowledgeable classicist, a guide in my wanderings in the scholarly mazes of antiquity. I particularly thank him for his help with Greek translations, for reading portions of the manuscript with great care, and for having been moved at his first reading of "Sitalkas," thus reminding me of my own initial love of H.D. as lyricist.

Many intimate friends have contributed to a circulation of gifts that here comes to some sort of return: Angelyn Spignesi, who led me to see "the other-side of everything"; Rose Cleary, who has collaborated with me from the beginning in imagining H.D.; Esther Fischer-Homberger, who entered as angel at a crucial time; and Marie Basalone, who has served as critic, facilitator, generous realist, and unswerving friend.

Grateful acknowledgment is given to New Directions Publishing Corporation for permission to quote from the following copyrighted works of H.D.: *Bid Me to Live* (copyright © 1960 by Norman Holmes Pearson); *The Collected Poems, 1912– 1944* (copyright © 1925 by Hilda Doolittle; copyright © 1957, 1969 by Norman Holmes Pearson; copyright © 1982 by the Estate of Hilda Doolittle; copyright © 1983 by Perdita Schaffner); *End to Torment: A Memoir of Ezra Pound* (copyright © 1979 by New Directions Publishing Corporation); *The Gift* (copyright © 1969, 1982 by the Estate of Hilda Doolittle; copyright © 1988 by Perdita Schaffner); *Hedylus* (copyright © 1928, 1980 by the Estate of Hilda Doolittle); *Helen in Egypt* (copyright © 1961 by Norman Holmes Pearson); *Hermione* (copyright © 1981 by the Estate of Hilda Doolittle; copyright © 1981 by Perdita Schaffner); *Hippolytus Temporizes* (copyright © 1927 by Hilda Aldington; copyright © 1985 by Perdita Schaffner); *Ion* (copyright © 1937 by Hilda Aldington; copyright © 1986 by Perdita Schaffner); *Notes on Thought & Vision* (copyright © 1982 by the Estate of Hilda Doolittle); *Tribute to Freud* (copyright © 1956, 1974 by Norman Holmes Pearson).

All previously unpublished material by H.D. is copyright © 1996 by Perdita Schaffner; used by permission of New Directions Publishing Corporation, agents. Material by H.D. published in periodical form or out-of-print material is quoted by permission of New Directions Publishing Corporation, agents for Perdita Schaffner.

Quotations from unpublished manuscripts in the H.D. Archive at Yale ("Notes on Euripides, Pausanius, and Greek Lyric Poets," "Notes on Thought and Vision," and "Compassionate Friendship"), correspondence (H.D.'s letters to Norman Holmes Pearson and Bryher; letter from Pearson to Thomas Swann, letter from Bryher to H.D.), and notes (1912 Paris Diary, Notebook of 1932 Hellenic Cruise) are used by permission of Perdita Schaffner and the Collection of American Literature, Beinecke Rare Book and Manuscript Library, Yale University. Quotation from a letter from H.D. to John Cournos is made by permission of Perdita Schaffner and the Houghton Library, Harvard University. Quotation of a letter from H.D. to Francis Wolle is made by permission of Perdita Schaffner and the Special Collections Department, University of Colorado at Boulder Libraries.

Grateful acknowledgment is given to New Directions Publishing Corporation and Faber & Faber Ltd. for permission to quote from the following copyrighted works of Ezra Pound: *ABC of Reading* (all rights reserved); *The Cantos* (copyright © 1934, 1937, 1940, 1948, 1956, 1962, 1963, 1966, and 1968 by Ezra Pound); *Ezra Pound and Dorothy Shakespear* (copyright © 1976, 1984 by the Trustees of the Ezra Pound Literary Property Trust); *Guide to Kulchur* (copyright © 1970 by Ezra Pound); *Literary Essays* (copyright © 1918, 1920, 1935 by Ezra Pound); *Selected Letters, 1907–1941* (copyright © 1950 by Ezra Pound); *Selected Poems* (copyright © 1920, 1934, 1937 by Ezra Pound); *Selected Prose, 1909–1965* (copyright 1960, 1962 by Ezra Pound; copyright © 1973 by the Estate of Ezra Pound); and *The Spirit of Romance* (copyright © 1968 by Ezra Pound). Material by Pound published in periodical form is quoted by permission of New Directions Publishing Corporation.

Quotation from the copyrighted work of Robert Duncan is made by permission of the Literary Estate of Robert Duncan: *Selected Poems* (copyright © 1993 by the Literary Estate of Robert Duncan); and *A Great Admiration: H.D. / Robert Duncan, Correspondence, 1950–1961* (copyright © 1992 The Literary Estate of Robert Duncan). Materials by Duncan in periodical form are quoted by permission of New Directions Publishing Corporation.

Extracts from these published writings of T. S. Eliot are quoted by permission of Valerie Eliot and Faber and Faber Ltd.: *After Strange Gods*; *The Letters of T. S. Eliot, Volume 1: 1898–1922*; and *Selected Prose*. Materials by Eliot in periodical form are quoted by permission of Valerie Eliot and Faber and Faber Ltd.

Material in some chapters has previously appeared as essays in *Sagetrieb* and in *Contemporary Literature*.

Introduction

H.D.'s "classicism" – her lifelong engagement with classical texts, art, religion, and mythology – is an obvious feature of her writing. No other modern writer is more persistently engaged in classical literary exchange. Beyond incidental intertextualities, which are considerable, H.D. operates out of certain fictional constructs of the hellenic – partially articulated at one point or another – that overwhelmingly shape her conception of her vocation and of her personal affiliations. H.D.'s hellenism is the major trope or fiction within her writing, providing her orientation within historical, aesthetic, and psychological mappings.

Despite its centrality, however, H.D.'s hellenism possesses the same kind of strangeness, unpredictability, and obliquity that characterizes other aspects of her writing – her modernism, her Freudianism, her hermeticism. "For H.D. terms are either duplicit or complicit, the warp and woof of the loom," Robert Duncan remarks ("Part 2, Chapter 3"). So with her hellenism: it too is part of a large, lifelong fabrication, in which individual valences shift, alter, narrow, and enlarge. Her hellenism is more complex, intelligent, and subtle than critical readings – including perhaps her own late retrospective readings – have sufficiently accounted for.

H.D.'s classicism cannot be explained simply as a product of late-nineteenth-century decadence, or of modernist poetics. Nor is the current critical predilection adequate: to see her hellenism as a set of masks or personae, unreal disguises for a real, biographically or historically contextualized subject.[1] Though these critical models have undeniable validity, they do not sufficiently address the specific character of H.D.'s engagement with classical writers and with the complexities of classical transmission. It is necessary to approach the question of H.D.'s classical intertextuality with the primary assumption that she is a knowledgeable and insightful reader, translator, and interpreter, and not simply a projector of meanings, reconstituting symbolic texts according to personal urgencies. Thus I have tried to account for the specific nature of H.D.'s readings and interpretations, her engagement with classical writers at the level of language, image, and theme.

It is apparent as well that H.D.'s hellenism is not univocal in its emphases. There is not one hellenism, not one monologic "Greek persona," but very many: many *topoi*; many sites within an imagined geography; many historical moments; many focal writers or "generating masters," in Duncan's phrase ("Two Chapters" 86), each of whom has a distinct character as a surviving image, or *eidolon*, of the dead. Moreover, a consideration of H.D.'s hellenic intertextuality over decades of her career makes clear a large interpretative pattern with considerable historical, philosophical, and religious complexity.

The effort of this book is to define the nature of H.D.'s famous classicism, which entails as well a tracing of its genealogies. I have attempted to delineate accurately H.D.'s classical exchanges, and at the same time to contextualize her fictions of the classical not only within modernism but within precedent classicisms. What began as an effort to locate H.D.'s "sources" and "influences" has ended in being a reflection on the "lines" of Western classicism, in the context of H.D.'s idiosyncratic but finally coherent tracings.

In using words and phrases such as "line," "lineage," "transmission," "descent," "classical letters," and "survival of the classics," I adopt self-consciously a traditionally classic model of literary history, aristocratic and patrilineal, because this is undeniably the model in which classicisms have imagined themselves and which H.D. too had to negotiate. "Dissemination," in the sense suggested by Jacques Derrida, may be closer to H.D.'s apprehension of her nonlinear relation to ancient writers. According to Barbara Johnson, dissemination, for Derrida, "is what subverts all such recuperative gestures of mastery. It is what foils the attempt to progress in an orderly way toward meaning or knowledge, what breaks the circuit of intentions or expectations through some ungovernable excess or loss" (xxxii). H.D. consistently veers from the linearity, seminality, and totality of certain classical models, preferring in her affiliations and in her imagination of literary history something like an antimodel involving dissemination, dispersion, and diaspora.

Though H.D.'s hellenism spans the whole of her career, one may discern different phases in her engagement with it. First is the early, prewar project of imagism, conceived by Ezra Pound in terms of T. E. Hulme's modern classicism but envisioned by H.D. and by her husband, Richard Aldington, very much within hellenic terms, specifically in terms of late-nineteenth-century romantic hellenism. After the war and its attendant traumas, H.D. persists throughout the twenties in exploring imaginatively the sites of her early hellenic engagements – the Greek Anthology, Sappho, Theocritus, and Euripides. But just as in her poetry and narratives of this period she begins the process of figuring out and working through the psychological binds of her early years, so too she becomes increasingly self-conscious about the character and genealogy of her hellenism. Her narratives – in particular "Hipparchia" (*Palimpsest*) and *Hedylus*, in each of which she stages herself as a displaced hellenistic poet – constitute an intelligent reflection upon her early Greek orientation. Though she makes explicit attempts in essay form to explicate the hellenic, prominently in the unpublished "Notes on Euripides, Pausanius, and Greek Lyric Poets," the hellenistic narratives are a more successful effort. Here one sees H.D. engaged not simply in biographical projection but in a complex mode of historical and cultural analysis, as well as self-analysis, within which she holds her own hellenic models up to scrutiny and articulation and elaborates a theory of history in which they are situated. H.D. increasingly understands the character of her hellenism, serving as an elaborate trope for the amalgam of experiences – both personal and cultural – in her early years. Thus she comes to detach herself from identification with particular figures in order to reflect upon recurrent patterns of interrelationships.[2] That self-consciousness has an initial and premature climax in 1927 with the verse-drama *Hippolytus Temporizes*, in which H.D. enacts the death of the hellenic rhapsodist. It comes to a completion of sorts with her analysis with Freud in 1934 and 1935, when she places hellenic nostalgia in the context of her family history. In the aftermath of her Freudian analysis she returns to a project of the prewar years, a translation of Euripides' *Ion* (1937), which lays to rest some of the recurrent preoccupations, not to say obsessions, within H.D.'s hellenic iconography. After *Euripides' Ion*, H.D. does not significantly engage the hellenic again until her late career in *Helen in Egypt*, when she takes up Euripides' *Helen* and, through Euripides, attempts a kind of synthesis of her governing poetic and personal fictions.

If indeed H.D.'s self-consciousness about her hellenism increases, what does she come to see? The answer to this question is constituted in the recurrent emphases of this book. Hellenism seems for her always contextualized by war. This is not merely a matter of H.D.'s own biography, in which her early shared hellenic aspirations were shattered by her experience of World War I. Rather, hellenism itself seems intrinsically linked to and brought into definition by wars, and the classic as a concept is bound to the notion of recurrent cultural catastrophe.

H.D. also grows increasingly aware of her lineage as a hellenist. She never outgrows her affiliations with late-romantic hellenists of the French and English decadence and with the Alexandrian model in which they imagine themselves. Rather she takes that model more seriously than any precedent or modern writer, except her Alexandrian contemporary C. P. Cavafy. She imagines herself in a classical line descending from Alexandria. This model helps to situate some of H.D.'s semantic overlays: the association of hellenism with nostalgia, with heterodox eroticism, with hermeticism. This Alexandrian hellenism is not merely a local late-nineteenth-century obsession but indeed constitutes a strand within Western classicism, albeit one held in suspicion and contempt within normative Latin models of order.

Whether carried in the trope of Athens or of Alexandria, H.D.'s hellenic nostalgia is oriented toward the figure of the mother, who is occluded within father and hero worship. The recognition of this matrix of desire in her life and art comes to H.D. with increasing clarity over the course of decades. Shaped especially by Susan Friedman's writing, this study points to H.D.'s recurrent recognition of the significance of the maternal within psychological and cultural life. However, it also testifies, as has Friedman, to the power of paternal authority in H.D.'s imagination, especially as this is figured in hellenism and in the public appropriation of the ancients by what H.D. calls the "academic Grecians" ("Helios and Athene," *Collected Poems* 328). Much as H.D. appears at times to stand against these scholarly guardians of the truth in defense of female daimonic power, she never surrenders her fascination with and longing for the authoritative father-scientist.

Though this brief summary suggests a developmental reading based on the chronological sequence of H.D.'s writing, *H.D. and Hellenism* is not so arranged. The book is divided into two parts, the first examining some of the contexts in which H.D.'s hellenism may be situated, the second considering H.D.'s exchanges with individual classical writers. Because H.D.'s hellenism was constructed within fin-de-siècle and early modern contexts, and because her most intense exploration of hellenic fictions occurs before the thirties, this study is in large part an exploration of H.D.'s early career, spanning roughly the period from her first publication of poetry in 1912 to the publication of *Hippolytus Temporizes* in 1927. Only the concluding chapter on H.D.'s Euripidean texts attempts a chronological reading, because H.D.'s engagement with Euripides remains consistent throughout her career, resurfacing at crucial junctures in her life.

The first part of this volume describes the generative matrix of H.D.'s hellenism in the models, iconographies, and ideologies operative in the late nineteenth and early twentieth centuries. Many different fictions of the classical are in circulation at the time H.D. begins to write, and my attempt has been to differentiate the classical agendas that shaped early modernists like H.D., Pound, T. S. Eliot, and D. H. Lawrence. But this effort – far beyond my original intention – has entailed a regression in the hall of mirrors called classicism, taking me back through the nineteenth century, to the early Renaissance, and finally to Alexandria.

I begin with a consideration of the most immediate context of H.D.'s hellenic writing: the theater of war, the literal experience of war, but also the critical "war of words" that in large part initiated early modernism,[3] the polemical opposition of romantic and classic, and the call by T. E. Hulme, Eliot, Pound, and others for a new classicism. The synchronicity of these two wars is not accidental, and

H.D.'s war trauma, lived out over decades, is professional as well as personal. This debate has in pivotal ways shaped H.D.'s critical reputation – and indeed still shapes it – as it established norms of classical legitimacy that at first included then firmly excluded her poetic experiments.

Chapter Two examines the question of classical lineage and the problematic status of a woman within the traditionally male domain of classical letters. Because modernists imagine themselves in the fiction of classical recovery, they turn their attention to a definition of a "true" classical descent, differentiating the authentic from the deviant or decadent lines. H.D. too imagined herself in terms of classical recovery, but because true descent in modern classicism is imagined as patrilineal, H.D. is faced with a pressing necessity to delineate her classical affiliations in alternative terms. Thus she boldly situates herself within the contaminated and despised territories of literary decadence, and in *Palimpsest* attempts to work out a nonlinear mode of female transmission.

Chapters Three and Four attempt to articulate in some detail the ground of early modernist fascination with gods and with mystery religions. Aesthetic mysticism of the decadence provides a coherent language of "pagan mysteries," taking these emphases from dominant lines within romantic hellenism. In Chapter Three, I consider in some detail the writings of Walter Pater as they articulate the emphases and iconography of romantic hellenism. Another dimension of early modernist preoccupation with the gods is the revolution in archaeology and anthropology that necessitated a serious reflection upon the nature of religious cults and, in the discussion of ritual and drama, a renewal of the romantic claims for the relation between religion and art. In Chapter Four, I take Jane Ellen Harrison as a main point of reference in delineating aspects of this religious recovery. Neither Pater nor Harrison is explicitly prominent among H D.'s nineteenth-century star names, such as Wilde, Swinburne, and Frazer, and thus my emphasis here may seem odd. Nevertheless, each of these figures, ignored in explications of modernism until recently, represents a nexus within the dissemination of cross-cultural and cross-disciplinary ideas. Thus they allow a way of articulating features of hellenic iconography and religious language that are very much at play among early modernists.

The second part of this volume attempts to assess as specifically as possible the character of H.D.'s classical intertextuality. Chapter Five considers the classical figures most important in H.D.'s lyric writing, taking as its basis a catalogue of references to classical texts in *Collected Poems, 1912–1944*, given in the Appendix. Here I examine not only H.D.'s specific exchanges with Euripides, Sappho, Theocritus, the poets of the Greek Anthology, and Homer, but a more general intertextuality – the way in which each writer allows a certain technical experimentation and defines a fiction having its own themes and predominant voice or voices. Chapter Six constitutes an examination of H.D.'s lifelong engagement with the plays of Euripides. This writer is the central figure within H.D.'s hellenism, standing in her own formulation as a kind of double for her as a modernist, a lyricist, and a "mystic" ("Euripides" 1–2). As an ancient generating master – father, scientist, psychopomp – he has a place in her literary project analogous to that of Freud in her autobiographical project. Throughout her life, Euripides' texts become sites of psychic enactment and reflection, serving as do her narratives – as Friedman argues in *Penelope's Web* – as kinds of "dream work" and self-analysis.

What has seemed primary in this project is an account of H.D.'s hellenism as she herself figures and articulates it, an analysis of it – at least initially – in its own complex terms. Such a reconstruction has seemed necessary for efforts of more sophisticated interpretation. I have not approached this material within any specific theoretical construct, which might have coerced and excised the evidence even while it was being assembled. Thus the critical orientation here is fairly eclectic, and the interpretative models employed provisional and local.

Contemporary theoretical constructs allow remarkable access to H.D.'s writing, and I have benefited from many of these, especially from various feminist readings – the groundbreaking work of Friedman in particular, as well as other psychoanalytical and New Historicist approaches. H.D. certainly appears at times fundamentally deconstructive, and many recent critics have turned specifically to formulations of Julia Kristeva in attempting to locate H.D.'s modes of linguistic resistance. Sensing the limitation of such models, however, critics like Adalaide Morris have employed anthropological models that very differently illumine the social agenda of H.D.'s writing. Given clues by recent commentary, I have found myself surprisingly aware of H.D's rhetorical strategies in both poetry and prose, suspecting some of her postures and duplicities, but admiring the courage of her risky moves. Nevertheless, I have found myself resistant to aspects of the postmodern climate governing H.D.'s reclamation, resistant to its hierarchies of praise and blame, which often seem to recapitulate the modernist terms of invalidation that have so dominated the reception of her writing. At crucial points, in the spirit of H.D.'s instinctive heterodoxy, I have attempted an apology for dispositions currently considered unacceptable: a defense of nostalgia, for instance, so virulently despised by modernists and postmodernists alike, and of the lyric, the focus of special contempt in deconstruction.

H.D.'s classicism first attracted me to the study of her writing, but her keen-edged heterodoxy, rebelliousness, and surprising strangeness have sustained my fascination and compelled my labor. In this regard two poets are implicit and sometimes explicit guides within my critical orientation: William Blake the iconoclast, who kept reappearing with uncanny appropriateness in my musings on H.D.'s Greece; and Duncan, who profoundly and comprehensively articulates H.D.'s heretical edge, defending her against the "Historians of Opprobrium" and valuing in her writing precisely those qualities that "[rescue] the work from what is correct and invulnerable" (*Selected Poems* 115; "Beginnings" 10). If one acknowledges her kind of legitimacy, H.D. leads one inevitably into heterodoxies of many kinds. She is remarkably shameless. She has in the past incurred and she will continue to incur the censure of any critic who assumes an orthodoxy dictating the boundaries of the shameful.

PART I

Contexts

Chapter One

Modern Classicism and the Theater of War

_____

"The Classics, it is the Classics! & not Goths nor Monks, that Desolate Europe with Wars." William Blake's remark might be taken simply as a reaction to eighteenth-century neoclassicism or, in terms of his own work, as a charge against the "Classics" as instruments of Urizen in the suppression of Orc. However, one might consider Blake's words in a more immediate way: the classicism of early literary modernism in the context of a century desolated by wars. To consider the synchronicity of classicism and war, one must admit, with Blake, that art forcefully shapes the world, that wars, as Paul Fussell has argued, are matters of imagination and of language and, not in the sublime but in the specific, pragmatic sense, matters of literary training and common reading, of culturally assimilated tropes and poetic patterns (ix).

The "Classics" to which Blake here refers are the Greek and Roman texts, such as Homer and Virgil, favored in Renaissance humanism. However, in this short meditation ("On Homer's Poetry" 267), he charges not so much the ancient works themselves as their exegetes. The classics are agents of desolation as they are instrumented through the pedagogy of the learned schools. Blake here specifically attacks the folly of abstract neoclassical norms in assessing the character or quality of poetry. Unity and Morality, he says, are "secondary considerations & belong to Philosophy & not to Poetry, to Exception & not to Rule, to Accident & not to Substance." But more than this irrelevance, Unity and Morality, as critical laws governing the interpretation of literature, have a venomous resolution: "Those who will have Unity exclusively in Homer come out with a Moral like a sting in the tail." This vicious, scorpion-like turn of the tale might be taken as the unstated link (in Blake's thought) between the classics and war. One can only infer that he sees this classical exegesis to have pragmatic consequence in the training of the public men who conceive of wars and bring them to birth.

_____

In her early review of W. B. Yeats's *Responsibilities* (1916–18), H.D. reflects upon the destructiveness of her own generation in World War I: "Our generation did not stand against the enemy – it *was* the enemy" ("Responsibilities" 53). Here H.D. addresses, like Blake, the haunting correlation between art and violence. As Gary Burnett has argued,[1] H.D. recognized, within the turmoil surrounding World War I, the conjunction of mechanistic ideologies and images of war with avant-garde movements such as vorticism and cubism – genuflection, in H.D.'s words, to "some Juggernaut of planes and angles." Her review suggests the confusion of her own generation in summoning the powers they would ostensibly deny: "[I]ts cubes and angles seem a sort of incantation, a symbol for the forces that brought on this world calamity" (53). H.D. here elaborates that "masculomaniac" obsession, in John Cournos's words, laying the linguistic and imagistic ground of war ("Futurism" 6). Both H.D. and Cournos in their response to the avant-garde clearly recognize "the subterranean collusion of modernism with the myth of modernization," the paradoxical alliance of antiphilistine art with mechanical and material progress (Huyssen 56).

Recent critics of literary modernism would also see the relevance of Blake's remarks in assessing the turbulence of the first decades of the twentieth century. Modernist fictions, Frank Kermode suggests, "were related to others, which helped to shape the disastrous history of our time. Fictions . . . turn easily into myths; people will live by that which was designed only to know by" (112). Although conservative in character, Jeffrey Perl suggests, "classicism, in whatever guise, has been extraordinarily destabilizing as a cultural ideology" (10). As the implicit motive of modern classicism Perl points to the ideology of return to "authentic" cultural ground, whose paradigm is the homecoming of Odysseus. The modern imagines itself as classical, positing a need to return to what has been lost (20). But Perl recalls the violent potential within gestures of reclamation. To return to an imagined order "requires a certain amount of social engineering: nostalgia, throughout the poem [Homer's *Odyssey*], is equivalent to slaughtering Penelope's suitors" (256). This desire for political purification is the sting in the classic tale; and, as recent critics have suggested, such a desire is not unrelated to the fact that many modernist figures came to espouse authoritarian political ideals.[2]

Friedrich Nietzsche served as a progenitor of modern classicism when in *The Birth of Tragedy* (1877) he articulated his "faith in a yet-impending rebirth of Hellenic antiquity" (123). Ironically, as he later recalls in a preface, he wrote this exuberant early prophecy in the context of war, the dramatic excitement of which, he implies, leads one to muse upon the Greeks (17). German victory in the Franco-Prussian War, Nietzsche states, should serve as preparation for a cultural purgation of "everything Romantic," leading to a re-creation of the great tragic age of the Greeks (138–9).

Though few early modernists besides Yeats explicitly claimed allegiance to Nietzsche's ideas,[3] his call for cultural, specifically artistic, purgation was answered in a new critical consciousness emerging in the United States and England in the years immediately preceding World War I. Like the classicism attacked by Blake, modern classicism was largely articulated in the sphere of literary criticism and pedagogy. In 1911–12, T. E. Hulme announced a classical revival in literature at odds with the suppositions of a century of romantic poetry, thought, and belief. Though Hulme died in the war, the new classicism that he signaled became one of the leading idioms of modernism. Ezra Pound was one of Hulme's chief advocates in the realm of literary practice, building on his thought in the movements of imagism and vorticism from 1912 through 1915. Influenced by Hulme, Pound, and others, T. S. Eliot in 1916 declared, "The beginning of the twentieth century has witnessed a return to the ideals of classicism."[4] After the war Eliot, especially in the pages of the *Criterion*, extended the debate between romantic and classic.

The terms of the classical debate were large; its tone was portentous and its legacy enormous. "Classicism," Eliot says in 1924 in a note on Hulme, "is in a sense reactionary, but it must be in a profounder sense revolutionary." Criticism is its handmaiden: "A new classical age will be reached when the dogma, or *ideology*, of the critics is so modified by contact with creative writing, and when the creative writers are so permeated by the new dogma, that a state of equilibrium is reached" ("Commentary" 232). Though critics eventually abandoned the specific terms of the argument, Eliot's projected revolution was successful. The debate was instrumental in establishing a critical orthodoxy, wherein the qualities originally signified as "classic" came to be understood as definitive of poetry per se: classicism, as universalized by Eliot, is "a goal toward which all good literature strives, so far as it is good" (review of *Ulysses*, 1923; *Selected Prose* 176). Like the neoclassical norms of unity and morality attacked by Blake, these classical criteria, C. K. Stead proposes, generated critical confusion, as they substituted "various extra-literary tests of the worthiness of the work for that of literary authenticity" (*Modernist Movement* 202–3).

This classical orthodoxy relegated many poets besides H.D. to the periphery. However, H.D.'s very explicit, lifelong preoccupation with hellenism, seen in this critical context, presents considerable complexities. Although H.D. has been associated with the "classical" as much as any other modern poet, her hellenism is not situated within the range of variants propounded by Pound and Eliot. Indeed, this paradox offers a way of understanding her marginal status within literary modernism. Beginning her career by exemplifying the technical virtues of Hulme's classicism, H.D. initially met with critical acceptance. But her critical legitimacy in terms of the new classicism was short-lived. Soon after Pound declared her exemplary status in imagism, he saw her as abrogating her aesthetic principles.[5] By the time of the publication of her second volume of poems in

1921, both Pound and Eliot had dismissed H.D.'s hellenic preoccupation as narrow, false, and decadent.[6]

Moreover, within a climate of increasing critical consensus in the twenties and thirties, it eventually seemed important to nullify any remaining mystique surrounding the early poetry of H.D., as though the praise of her as classical were too great a provocation to let pass. Thus one finds in 1927 the gratuitously contemptuous correction of the record by Laura Riding and Robert Graves (118–23), singling out H.D. as the notorious but worthless exemplum of a "dead movement" essentially exploitative and romantic in nature: "[H]er work was so thin, so poor, that its emptiness seemed 'perfection,' its insipidity to be concealing a 'secret,' its superficiality so 'glacial' that it created a false 'classical' atmosphere" (122). And one finds in 1937 the deliberate and detailed refutation by Douglas Bush of each aspect of H.D.'s hellenism that had met with critical praise, a dismissal also based largely on the grounds of what he repeatedly asserts is a "female" romanticism (501–2).

Indeed, H.D.'s critical reputation has been strangely punctuated by repetitive gestures of getting the record straight, sizing her up in toto, putting her in her proper place – necessities generated to a large extent, I would claim, by the ambiguities of her classicism. Since Bush's assessment, there is the game of turning H.D.'s classicism against her, the recurrent practice of determining the exact nature of H.D.'s failure as a lyricist, measured by what are clearly the classicist criteria that her early poetry itself established.[7] Or if one acknowledges the quality of the early lyrics, one can resort to ad feminam judgments that see her poetic success as evidence of personal neurosis.[8]

The explanation for H.D.'s "burial" in modernist literary history lies not only, as Susan Friedman argues, in her problematic status as a woman poet ("Who Buried H.D.?"), but also in the character of her classicism. That H.D. encroaches upon the domain of the classic opens her to still other charges than those typically leveled at the woman poet – charges of "dubious . . . authenticity" (Bush 503), of pretentiousness and fakery (Riding and Graves 122), the perpetration, in Pound's phrase, of "Alexandrine Greek bunk" (Letters 157). What are the energized, dangerous boundaries of authenticity, discretion, and candor that H.D.'s hellenism transgresses? How can it be true, as Bush asserts, that H.D.'s hellenism is "un-Hellenic," her Greekness "un-Greek" (505)?

To understand what hellenism Bush assumes as normative and constant requires a certain linguistic excavation. This first chapter begins by establishing the contemporary surface of that excavation – the "fiction of classicism," or what Levenson would call the "consolidated" position of modern classicism, articulated most fully by Eliot (167).[9] In this context, H.D. clearly deviates from the classic line. To establish the character of that deviation, I consider the investment by Pound, Eliot, and H.D. in the matter of Troy, the use of classical analogues to describe cultural and aesthetic necessities within the context of war. In this regard H.D.'s musings lead her not (with Nietzsche) to Aeschylus, but (with Pater) to Euripides. Finally, in the twentieth-century war of words, the accusation of "nostalgia" – made with great effect by Bush in his critique of "H.D.'s Greece" – is particularly devastating. In H.D.'s response to Bush one can see the character of her resistance to and evasion of the perspective of modern classicism.

Romantic, Classic, Modern

To understand H.D.'s marginal status in literary modernism, we need to assess the early argument between romantic and classic, delineating the classical construct as precisely as possible.[10] Summarizing the nature of the hostilities as envisioned by the combatants, I here sketch the linguistic configuration of modern classicism, so as to sense the weight and charge of certain epithets and the pattern of their impact. The language of the modern classical argument implies philosophical, political, and religious discriminations. But it carries as well an eloquent imaginal content, a dramatic configuration, which I here emphasize in yet another rehearsal of this famous argument. That drama takes place in the classical "theater" of war. War (actual and figurative) is its matrix. Its configuration is consistently dialectical – each positive quality implying a negative, and each negative, a positive. One imagines what one is not (for instance, Rousseau, or Shelley, or Swinburne), and one lays claim to a long, continuous tradition – going back through the Renaissance, or through medieval Christianity, to the Latins and Greeks – within which tradition the unauthentic predecessors are invalidated.[11]

In his call for the rebirth of hellenism in *The Birth of Tragedy*, Nietzsche establishes valuations that provide an unacknowledged basis for later critics. The hellenic here is defined in terms of the spirit of tragedy, which is pessimistic rather than optimistic, figuring heroic strength in the confrontation with darkness, as opposed to bourgeois denial. In his original essay he identifies the rebirth of tragedy with Richard Wagner's "Dionysian" music, but in his later "Attempt at a Self-Criticism" he ridicules the earlier assessment, now identifying German music with romanticism: "a first-rate poison for the nerves," having "the double quality of a narcotic that both intoxicates and spreads a *fog*" (25).

Irving Babbitt, Eliot's teacher at Harvard, was one of the first in the twentieth century to enunciate the climate of classical discrimination. In his influential discussion of French literature, *The Masters of Modern French Criticism* (1912), he calls for a new critical disposition emphasizing "masculine" virtues (analysis, judgment) rather than the "feminine" ones (knowledge, sympathy) presently in vogue (339). This distinction between masculine and feminine critical attitudes is later associated with the distinctions between the scientific (emphasizing significance) and the impressionistic (emphasizing suggestiveness) (341), between the ascetic and the hedonistic (350), between the "humanistic or aristocratic" and the Rousseauistic or "pseudo-democratic" (352–3). Babbitt uses the term "human-ism" as an equivalent to "classicism" in describing this critical temper, based on "the [Aristotelian] appeal to the judgment of the keen-sighted few, as opposed to that of the many" (352).

Like Babbitt, T. E. Hulme was forcefully antiromantic, though he would disagree fundamentally with Babbitt's adoption of "humanism" as a model. "Romanticism and Classicism," Hulme's extravagant essay written in 1911–12, as Michael H. Levenson has argued (87–8), defines clearly the specific war of words later inherited by Eliot. More than an aesthetic matter, classicism for Hulme, as for the reactionary French intellectuals of *L'action française*, has a political (antidemocratic) and religious (Catholic) implication (114–15); its chief component is a belief in human limitation and fallibility. Aesthetically and morally the classicist – as either critic or poet – must keep his head, refuse to be seduced, hold back. He adopts irony rather than naive par-ticipation in the imagined moment, adopts a resistant versus a receptive attitude (126).

Hulme vividly evokes, as Eliot later does, the bare, empirical, and disillusioned landscape of the new classicism. The classical world is dry and hard; the romantic is damp and soft. "In the classic," moreover, "it is always the light of ordinary day," as opposed to the drugged, hallucinatory romantic light "that never was on land or sea" (127). The "sincerity" of the classical poet lies in the objectivity of his perception. He conveys only "the exact curve of what he sees," and classic excellence "has nothing to do with infinity, with mystery or with emotions" (132–3). In the new age of classical art, "wonder must cease to be wonder" – because wonder too long maintained is a matter of arrested development: "Won-der can only be the attitude of a man passing from one stage to another, it can never be a permanently fixed thing" (140). Thus Hulme presents classicism as an ascetic, antilibidinous stance. Though he takes his gaze at the moving backside of a woman's body as his example of proper "aesthetic emotion," of a "zest" to "get the exact curve of the thing" (136), we are to understand through this image nothing of illegitimate titillation – though we are thus apprised of the male coterie among whom such a classical gaze is understood.

For Pound, Hulme's philosophic argument and his interpretation of cultural history were contestable. Of greater consequence to him was Hulme's articula-tion of a new classical/modern poetic style in reaction to the poetry of the nineteenth century. Pound never joined the bandwagon of official modern classicism with its implications of normative and orthodox authority. Indeed, he deliberately provided irritants to orthodox usage. Nevertheless, Pound's early formulations of the classical style of imagism – directness, precision, concreteness, and economy of diction – echo the language of Hulme. He prophesies:

As to Twentieth century poetry, and the poetry which I expect to see written during the next decade or so, it will . . . be harder and saner, it will be what Mr Hewlett calls "nearer the bone." It will be as much like granite as it can be, its force will lie in its truth, its interpretative power . . . I mean it will not try to seem forcible by rhetorical din, and luxurious riot. . . . At least for myself, I want it so, austere, direct, free from emotional slither. (*Literary Essays* 12)

The classical quality of "hardness" is here amplified by reference to rock – a traditional association of the classical with stone. One notes that "hard" and "sane" go together, the latter having the implication not only of mental balance but of health, in accordance with the precepts of what Pound, in another 1912 essay, calls Greek "humanism" – *mens sana in corpore sano* ("Tagore's Poems" 93). Such health is associated with an ascetic ideal: austere, without "din," without "luxury"; "bone," not flesh. The tone of ascetic revulsion at the impure is suggested in "emotional slither" ("slither": slipping, sliding, or crawling like a snake), as in other references to the "slush," "mess," and "blur" of bad writing (*Literary Essays* 7, 11). The truth or "interpretative power" of poetry, associated with all these implicit and explicit qualities, is tied to "directness." Pound said to Harriet Monroe of H.D.'s poetry that it was "straight talk, straight as the Greek!" (*Letters* 11) – and again this "straight," like "sane," carries a moral import, implying not only "exact" or "candid," but also "true" and "right," that is, undeviant from the line.

Eliot follows the lead of these men,[12] though emphasizing more explicitly the correlation between theories of art, religion, and politics. In university lectures on modern French literature given in 1916, Eliot defines the "ideals of classicism" as "*form* and *restraint* in art, *discipline* and *authority* in religion, *centralization* in government (either as socialism or monarchy)" (Schuchard, "Extension" 165). After World War I Eliot further refined and extended his definition of classical norms. In the course of his comments in the *Criterion* between 1923 and 1927, he elaborated a set of corresponding polarities aligned with classic and romantic that served as points of orientation in his early criticism. Responding to an essay by John Middleton Murry, Eliot in "The Function of Criticism" (1923) proposes these linked contraries:

With Mr. Murry's recent formulation of Classicism and Romanticism I cannot agree; the difference seems to me rather the difference between the complete and the fragmentary, the adult and the immature, the orderly and the chaotic. (34)

Later in this essay he elaborates the character of the whole and ordered classicist in a set of norms reminiscent of Hulme's negatives. In contrast to the romantic's deficient "sense of fact," the "classicist, or adult mind, is thoroughly realist –

without illusions, without day-dreams, without hope, without bitterness, and with an abundant resignation" (39). The historical or ontological "facts," it would seem, are inevitably bad, and to confront them entails a heroic stoicism. Classicism for Eliot represents a *via negativa*, a denial of all untoward imaginative, emotional, spiritual stimulation that would give the lie to the tragic truth. These assertions in regard to the ambience of fact allude to the classical modernist norm of engagement (the accommodation of facts), a norm implied in the negative charge of escapism (avoidance of facts), leveled not only at H.D. but at many of her contemporaries, including Eliot himself.

Wholeness, order, adulthood, realistic sanity, all manifested in postures of abnegation – these recurring classical criteria are clearly linked to Eliot's idea of the poet's impersonality, to his ability to effect "a continual self-sacrifice, a continual extinction of personality" (*Selected Prose* 40). This ability clearly is seen in contrast to romantic formulas of expression, wherein such a selflessness is egoistically resisted (58). Eliot's language of "abjectness," as Andrew Ross suggests (85–92), points to final metaphysical terms. Apparently for Eliot, underlying these hierarchic couples is another, more urgent moral choice: "[T]here are at least two attitudes toward literature and toward everything," he says in 1923, "and . . . you cannot hold both" – one attitude (classicism) is founded on obedience to Outer Authority; another (romanticism) is founded on adherence to the Inner Voice ("Function of Criticism" 34–7). In *After Strange Gods* (1934), Eliot seems to admit the exaggeration and falsification of his earlier remarks on the classic and romantic (28–9), though at the same time he proposes yet another polarity subsuming the previous ones – the distinction between the orthodox (traditional, classical) and the heterodox or heretical (antitraditional, romantic), which resolves in its examples (Joyce and Lawrence) into a distinction between Catholic and Protestant. These charged terms suggest a plane of censure other than the merely literary, involving questions of blasphemy, diabolism, and spiritual sickness.[13]

One other strain within the argument of modern classicism might be emphasized. In *After Strange Gods*, Eliot's explication of orthodoxy and heresy involves three examples, one of which, a story by Katherine Mansfield, does not matter at all. Her fiction is introduced to give an example of a work in which "the moral implication is negligible." The story "Bliss," Eliot says, is "in the best sense, slight; . . . As the material is limited in this way – and indeed our satisfaction recognizes the skill with which the author has handled perfectly the *minimum* material – it is what I believe would be called feminine" (38). The circumlocution, "what I believe would be called," announces the presence of classical criteria in the act of naming the "other," the "feminine."

Indeed, among proponents of modern classicism, the classic view *is* the "masculine," and clearly, as Cassandra Laity argues, modernists' rebellion against romanticism is explicitly gendered ("Swinburne"). To confirm the equivalence of classicism and the masculine, one need only remark the mapping of Babbitt's critical distinctions, or notice the triangulated gaze passing between Hulme, his fraternal listeners, and the moving female body that is contemplated. One need only catch the repeated signals in a book like Bush's *Mythology & the Romantic Tradition in English Poetry*, where adherence to the true hellenic spirit, at no point explicitly defined, repeatedly gains the epithet "masculine," and where, among those poems that Bush names "un-Hellenic" or "un-Greek," the charge leveled with greatest contempt is that of "effeminacy,"[14] encompassing forms of deviance ranging from lush, self-indulgent language to moral perversity.

What can one say, then, about the imaginal configuration of this debate? It suggests a *nomos*, a widely accepted, largely unspoken code, an energized discursive field that modern writers could not ignore. (Those terms in brackets indicate opposites that are structurally implied but not explicitly named.)

CLASSIC	ROMANTIC
hard	soft
dry	wet
disciplined	hedonistic
daylight	narcotic light [dreamlight]
adult	child or adolescent
love of finite	love of infinite
beauty known by fixed standards	beauty as infinitude
exact rendering	blurred rendering
recognizing "fact"	confusing "fact" and "fancy"
realistic	[escapist, neurotic]
scientific [objective]	impressionistic [subjective]
sane, healthy	[insane, unsound, diseased]
straight	[oblique, deviant]
austere	luxurious
impersonal	personal
extinction [of personality]	expression [of personality]
resigned	[resistant or rebellious]
without bitterness	[bitter]
without wonder	[with continuous wonder]
without illusion	[illusioned]
pessimistic	optimistic
without hope	[hopeful]
guidance by reason or analysis	guidance by passion or sympathy
aristocratic	democratic
civilized	barbaric
guidance by Outer Authority	guidance by Inner Voice

CLASSIC	ROMANTIC
orthodox	heretical
whole	fragmentary
ordered	chaotic
masculine	feminine

If one imagines this set of positive qualities as suggesting not only aesthetic norms but an imagined locus (somatic, psychic, moral, political), the landscape of the new classicism is, as we have remarked, somewhat barren and harsh in character, deliberately dehumanized and antivital – hard, cold, dry, hierarchic and regulated, impersonal and emotionally constrained, brilliant with shadowless daylight. It suggests urban planning of the most ambitious kind, conjuring a complex fantasy of a city simultaneously archaic and futuristic. There hover within it the lineaments of an ideal city posited in the past and anticipated in the future – the "fine dreams of empire, of a universal empire," Pound said in 1912, that "set a model for emulation, a model of orderly procedure," and that have been "a spur through every awakening" of culture (*Patria Mia* 69). This is the telos of nostalgia, the imagined place in which the aesthetic, moral, political, and (Pound would add) economic are one. But this classical landscape simultaneously signifies the modern city seen through eyes stripped of illusions. This realistic vision suggests the futurist, utilitarian city Pound describes in 1928, engineered to follow the "stream line or speed line," to eliminate crossings and superfluous deviances, and to allow maximum "solar advantage," maximum light and energy (*Selected Prose* 194–6).

This modern landscape is the clear, astringent world that Virginia Woolf's *Orlando* encounters as she awakes into the present (1928) after her long metempsychosis within English literary history. Woolf renders here the phantasmic impression of modernism upon body and soul – how it might possibly seem if one experienced it suddenly in a dream:

> The sky itself, she could not help thinking had changed. It was no longer so thick, so watery, so prismatic. . . . The clouds had shrunk to a thin gauze; the sky seemed made of metal, . . . But it was now – . . . now, in the evening, that the change was most remarkable. . . . At a touch, the whole room was bright. And the sky was bright all night long; and the pavements were bright; everything was bright. . . . The dryness of the atmosphere brought out the colour in everything and seemed to stiffen the muscles of the cheeks. It was harder to cry now. . . . Curtains and covers had been frizzled up and the walls were bare so that new brilliantly coloured pictures of real things like streets, umbrellas, apples, were hung in frames, or painted upon the wood. There was something definite and distinct about the age, which reminded her of the eighteenth century, except that there was a distraction, a desperation – . . . (296–8)

Woolf describes here not only a change in the historical moment, but a change in the *nomos* of aesthetic discrimination. Dry, hard and metallic, clear and bright, shrunken, definite, bare and "real": Woolf clearly understands the tenets of this modern neoclassicism. It is a new "enlightenment" in a literal, bodily sense, accompanied by lack of privacy or retreat, with "none of those lingering shadows and odd corners that there used to be." And this is rational illumination without emotional ground, so that "her thoughts became mysteriously tightened and strung up as if a piano tuner had put his key in her back and stretched the nerves very taut" (298). Classicism, responding to the new empirical realities of the early twentieth century, imitates them in its aesthetic dictates. This mirroring suggests, as Andreas Huyssen notes, that the modernist aesthetic is "subliminally linked to [modernity's] insistence on instrumental rationality, teleological progress, fortified ego boundaries, discipline, and self-control" (58). Within such a mapping, certain imaginative and psychic spaces are obliterated.

Orlando's sense of the anxiety of this time points to another aspect of modern classicism. Many of its dialectically defined nouns share ground with those of Freudian psychology as commonly understood – and not surprisingly, because Freudian theories were widely current in intellectual circles in the early decades of the century. Both critical dispositions depend upon an empirical, scientific, "daylight" posture faithful to "facts" and inimical to illusion, daydream, escape; both suggest a normative approach categorizing imaginative or psychic phenomena in terms of sickness, deviation, arrested development. As Huyssen notes, the modernist aesthetic seems "in some fundamental way to be located . . . on the side of . . . society's reality principle, rather than on that of the pleasure principle," the latter firmly associated with the "feminine" (55).

H.D. knew the voice of Eliot's classicist: in fact, he is a constant interlocutor in her life and imagination in several incarnations, not the least of which is Freud himself. She recognized, too, the gravity of classicist ideological structures, their persuasiveness in relegating boundaries and determining conventional expectations. Her reputation as a poet was shaped by the violent climate of these dichotomies, by which measures she must be seen as a failure in homologous terms – as a romantic, as a neurotic and desperate female poet.[15]

H.D. refused the centripetal pull of modern classicism. As Friedman argues, her sense of vocation and of modernism was tied to the marginal or eccentric rather than centric, to the position of outsider rather than insider ("Exile"). In technical terms, her poetry was classical, though only briefly satisfying Pound's criteria of linguistic hygiene. H.D. shared with modern classicists an ascetic sense of poetic discipline and a belief in the impersonality of the poet, though unlike them she fully acknowledged nineteenth-century sources of these ideas. Moreover, H.D. in her early poetry, and recurrently throughout her career, evoked the dry, hard, harsh landscape of early modernism, though it signaled for her an aspect of the vital cosmos, not the antivital dynamism of the modern city.

Moreover, one can recognize in the qualities here attributed to the romantic something of that positive field that H.D. explored unhesitatingly throughout her career: the territory of dream (erotic, fragmentary, associational), of the child, of mystery, illusion, beauty; the claim for feeling and desire as the bitter alchemical salt to be constantly worked; the deliberate creation of liminal territories in which "wonder" can be "a permanent, fixed thing"; the inherited claim, through her Moravian past, of a heretical religious stance, depending upon vision and inspiration (Inner Voice) and resistant to dogma (Outer Authority); the firm conviction that poetry is hermetic, set apart from the world (escapist), a place of retreat and healing.

In terms, then, of the structural map of modern classicism, H.D. is undoubtedly situated with the romantic. But this oppositional grid of modern classicism, I have tried to suggest, concerns much more than literary history. Likewise, H.D.'s affiliation with the obverse goes far beyond her connection with romantic or Victorian writers: it represents a deliberate choice for an alternative perspective and tradition that she senses can address the realities of disillusion and loss yet evade the kind of authoritarian order given in modern classicism. In her hellenism, H.D. has little predilection for the Unities and the Moralities. She senses the violence arrayed along the classic line and firmly situates herself in oblique and marginal territory.

Aeschylus versus Euripides

These cultural mappings are necessarily extreme, one might argue, because the critics of early modernism shared a sense of political crisis and because in various ways, as Lucy McDiarmid proposes, modern poets agonized over their responsibilities in the labor of "saving civilization" (ix–xvi). Or one might understand this polarization, as do Sandra Gilbert and Susan Gubar, as part of the masculinist "reaction-formation" to the threat posed by the increasing visibility of women in political and intellectual life (*No Man's Land* 125–56). But this structure of opposites, in more or less refined forms, is very familiar. It is in any case quite purely classical, that is, Attic, resembling in many ways the patterns that structuralists have found operative in ancient Athens. Froma Zeitlin delineates a series of linked oppositions in Aeschylus's *Oresteia*, such as father/mother, center/limit, order/chaos, head/belly, phallos/womb, reason/unreason, clarity/obscurity, and others ("Misogyny" 181–2).

The field of play belonging to such opposition is the universe of tragedy, depicting a problematic social and psychic reality. Indeed, the *Oresteia* might be seen as an implicit model in the classicist's imagination of modern crisis. For Nietzsche, the first to announce his faith "in the imminent rebirth of classical antiquity," Aeschylus stands as the apex of the Greek spirit, manifest consummately in the form of tragedy and in the war of opposition it projects.[16] In the years surrounding World War I, the *Oresteia* is especially compelling as a paradigm: it is the story of the aftermath of a devastating war, in which military violence and the sacrifice of innocence are brought home with the hero, generating what is increasingly imagined in the course of the Orestean trilogy as a monstrous female problem that threatens the survival of civilization (semen/polis/logos). As Zeitlin points out, all life-threatening turmoil in the Aeschylean trilogy, "every issue, every action," is generated immediately by female figures, whose power must be thoroughly constrained ("Misogyny" 160). The psychological and civic problems are so apocalyptic in implication, according to Aeschylus, that only divine intervention and the establishment of divinely sanctioned political institutions – an overarching orthodoxy like that proposed by Eliot – can forestall the annihilation of human order threatened by the female.

Moreover, when the Aeschylean set of gendered oppositions is seen in conjunction with the map of modern classicism at war with romanticism, one sees an Orestean rather than an Oedipal pattern in understanding early modernist "anxiety of influence." Seen in terms of a mythic paradigm, what happens is not the slaying of the overbearing literary father, as in Harold Bloom's model of generational conflict (*Anxiety* 8–11), but rather an imagined need "to defend against a Romantic foremother," to "forge a male identity though severing [a] preoedipal attachment to the mother," as Laity suggests in her analysis of early modernists ("Swinburne" 468). Moreover, one might add, this slaying of the mother *restores* a paternal authority temporarily lost, unlike the slaying in the Oedipal paradigm, where the father's authority is displaced. Moreover, that paternal authority is not condemned, as in the Oedipal story, but rather *sanctioned* by the highest Apollonian, intellectual and moral, claims.

This ancient model of crisis is a significant subtext within the urgent arguments of modern classicists, operating subliminally in their political, psychological, and aesthetic assertions. The *Agamemnon* had a literal place in the war, and both Eliot and Pound were deeply engaged with the Aeschylean text at the initiation of their modernist experiments.

The matter of Troy was very much in the imagination of leaders, soldiers, and intellectuals before and during World War I, because a major engagement of the Allied forces was the attempt to seize the Dardanelles from Turkish forces. Bloody, stalemated, and finally unsuccessful fighting took place in the Hellespont and on "the Trojan plain" for almost a year, from February 1915 until January 1916.[17] In March 1915 the flagship *Agamemnon* was among the British fleet bound toward the shores of ancient Ilion in the land assault on Gallipoli. Not only did the *Agamemnon* evoke the continuity of British heroic tradition (five ships had borne the name, the most famous commanded by Horatio Nelson), but, as David Roessel has pointed out, it had obvious resonance in the assault at hand, adding to an already heightened consciousness of the Trojan War.[18]

After the war (1920), T. S. Eliot, commenting on Gilbert Murray's and H.D.'s translations of Euripides, again brings the *Agamemnon* to mind, though in the context of literary discrimination. Eliot implies through casual ironic comment – as Pound does too in his review of H.D. – that Euripides is the wrong (uncanonical) author to translate. Both Pound and Eliot set up Aeschylus as a contrasting criterion.[19] Eliot indicates that H.D. and others in the Poets' Translation Series have attempted an insufficient, unhellenic poetic labor, that efforts at translation must be measured by the task of translating the *Agamemnon* (*Selected Essays* 50). Eliot refused an immediate request by Richard Aldington to do such a translation (Aldington, *Life* 144). However, he did eventually attempt it, unsuccessfully. At Pound's instigation, Eliot apparently worked with the Greek text of the *Agamemnon* during a crucial generative period, sending portions to Pound for comment in January 1922, in the midst of their correspondence over revision of *The Waste Land*.[20] This conjunction suggests the presence of Aeschylus's tragedy as an implicit subtext in the foremost of modernist poetic experiments.

The play was important to Pound as well in a crucial period during and after the war, and he continued to admire it throughout his life.[21] Pound published a commentary on translations of the *Agamemnon* in the *Egoist* (January 1919), and along with Eliot he also unsuccessfully attempted a translation (*Guide to Kulchur* 92–3). Moreover, as Leon Surette points out, Pound in the early *Cantos* of 1919 began to echo the *Agamemnon* (27–8). Richard Reid has suggested that the *Agamemnon* may be present as well in *Hugh Selwyn Mauberly* (1922), in the allusion to a vicious postwar homecoming: "came home, home to a lie, / home to many deceits, / home to old lies and new infamy" (*Selected Poems* 64; Reid xi).

Pound's admiration for Aeschylus echoes that of Nietzsche, who praised in his plays the "glory of activity," the masculine audacity of sacrilege, and a dynamic conflict of opposites essential to the tragic cosmos (Nietzsche 69–71). As evoked by Pound in the early *Cantos*, Aeschylus's *Agamemnon* provides one of many "repeats in history," tragic episodes of erotic and political strife with woman at the center (*Letters* 210). Indeed, the *Agamemnon* conforms brilliantly to Pound's model of the dynamic vortex; Pound admires in it "the whole rush of the action," the "'last atom of force verging off into the first atom of matter'" (1919; *Instigations* 346). When he originally describes the vortex in *Blast*, Pound might indeed be describing the complex generational turmoil of the *Agamemnon*: "All experience rushes into this vortex. All the energized past, all the past that is living and worthy to live. All MOMENTUM, which is the past bearing upon us, RACE, RACE-MEMORY, instinct charging the PLACID, NON-ENERGIZED FUTURE" ("Vortex" 153).

The *Agamemnon* thus gives a classical paradigm of textual complexity, compression, and energy; it gives the paradigm of war, of generative conflict. Moreover, the teleology of the *Oresteia* is deeply appealing to classicist sensibilities: it signals the retributive ruin of cities and, in its politicized deus ex machina, the apotheosis of a mortal city immortally sustained. In its dramatic action it remembers and attempts to recover for Athens – as subsequent classical revivalists do for their cities – the epic totality given by Homer.[22]

H.D. too meditated on the war and on the character of modernity through the oblique images in Greek tragedy; yet, apparently never fond of Aeschylus or Sophocles, she chose alternative versions of war given through the plays of Euripides.[23] Months after the opening of the Gallipoli campaign in April 1915, the *Egoist* announced translations by H.D. from Euripides' *Rhesos* in the first, August advertisement of the Poets' Translation Series and again in a September advertisement. Evidently abandoning the *Rhesos*, she published in November 1915 translations from the *Iphigeneia in Aulis* as her first published volume. In January 1916, translations from Euripides' *Ion* were announced, though not published.[24] Translations from the *Hippolytus* were published in 1919. Thus during the war H.D. was engaged with at least four Euripidean plays.

H.D.'s early affiliation with Euripides signals her variance from the modernist classical line. Though the classical style of *Choruses from the Iphigeneia in Aulis of Euripides* gained immediate recognition – not only from Pound and Eliot but from the respected classicist and translator J. W. Mackail[25] – her choice of Euripides clearly constituted a demerit. Unlike the hellene of Matthew Arnold's ideal, Cedric Whitman says, "Euripides [of all poets] did not see life steadily, and his era provided him with little help in seeing it whole" (119). He was unfashionable in the new classical climate. The first generation of modernists had read Nietzsche's *Birth of Tragedy* – appearing in English in 1909 – and had absorbed his condemnation of Euripides and Socrates as the murderers of Greek tragedy, in their rationality dissipating the tragic world of energized opposition (76–81, 86–89). Euripides at the turn of the century was associated with the decadence of Pater and Wilde and, through advocates like Gilbert Murray and Jane Ellen Harrison, with enlightened rationalism and progressive heterodoxies such as pacifism and feminism (Jenkyns 109–10).

But for all his chancy reputation, Euripides informed H.D.'s imagination throughout her career more than did any other poet, ancient or modern. H.D. finds in Euripides – as Pound in Aeschylus and Homer – a mirror for the visceral and bewildering experience of war. "Euripides lived through almost a modern great-war period," H.D. notes, and in his "detachment," his "non-partisanship, non patriotism," he is "problematic" to his contemporaries and peculiarly "modern" to H.D.'s own generation ("Euripides" 2–3). Where Pound finds in Aeschylus a dynamic, agglutinative technique of signification, H.D. turns to Euripides precisely for his attempts to demobilize the Athenian vortex. He consistently disintegrates the intellectual and moral *nomos* of the heroic world and simultaneously reveals the intensity of isolated lyric moments and the loneliness of partial heroisms enacted within fragmented contexts.

As the *Agamemnon* was to Pound in his early career, so the *Iphigeneia in Aulis* was to H.D. If the *Agamemnon* speaks of the generative turmoil in the aftermath of war, the power swirling around the homecoming hero, *Iphigeneia in Aulis* recalls its bitter beginnings. Indeed, the bitterness of the play seems unrelieved – the shallowness and vanity of the heroes, the deceitfulness of the "official" oracles and prophets, the crude bloodthirstiness of the Greek mob. The *Iphigeneia*, George Dimock suggests, encourages its audience to resist the deterministic influence of the old myths, "to resist . . . the idea of mythological necessity" (19). One should not underestimate for H.D. the importance of Euripides' skepticism and iconoclasm in clearing the air of debilitating pieties and in allowing a pattern of cultural, iconographical resistance. Euripides, as Rachel Blau DuPlessis proposes, "may have been her largest inspiration for a revisionary stance" (*Career* 18).

Though his skepticism toward the motives operative in war served as an important orientation for H.D., Euripides is equally important for her in his characteristic pathos, a lyric entrance into intense subjective states, particularly surrounding loss and grief in war. Almost every one of the plays of Euripides with which H.D. was engaged during her career – twelve of them altogether – in some way concerns grief surrounding the figure of the mother.[26] Certainly this preoccupation has resonance in H.D.'s own life; yet just as certainly it pertains to a larger theater of mourning. One might consider, for instance, H.D.'s initial choice of a Euripidean play for translation in the summer of 1915 – his earliest play, *Rhesos*. No evidence survives of H.D.'s work on this play, but one can nevertheless contemplate the reasons she might have been drawn to it, as it provided her with interpretative, mediating figures for the devastation of war.

The play renders an episode from the eighth book of the *Iliad*. Greek and Trojan armies are encamped at night on the plains, within sight of each other's fires. The Trojan sentries, confused and frightened by evidence of activity in the Greek camp, come to wake Hector. Certain that the Greeks are retreating from his manifest strength, he wants to attack immediately, believing that dawn will show certain victory. Instead, he is persuaded by Aeneas to hold back and to send a spy, Dolon, to the Greek camp. Odysseus and Diomedes, sent as spies to the Trojans, meet Dolon and kill him. In the Trojan camp Athene instructs them, so that they are able to massacre in their sleep the newly arrived Thracian king, Rhesos, and his company, who, if they had lived to see the dawn, would have altered fate, turning the course of the war toward a Trojan victory. The play concludes with the entrance of an unnamed Muse, the mother of Rhesos, holding her dead son in her arms. She herself gives Rhesos's death dirge, curses his murderers, and declares her bitterness at Athene. She, her sisters, and Apollo have sent Athens the prophet Orpheus and the Orphic poet Musaeus to reveal sacred mysteries. But they will send no more such sages to Athene's city.

One can well imagine the grave appeal of this play for H.D. in the summer of 1915. Beginning in late April and early May, reports of the Gallipoli campaign began to appear in British newspapers. Battles were fought literally on the Trojan plain, with the enemy on the heights and with the armies locked front to front, just as in *Rhesos*. As the play depicts the maneuvers of war shrouded in confusion and misinformation and the leader Hector blind in the infatuation of imagined victory, so the reports of the Gallipoli campaign seemed increasingly bewildering. Official reports of the War Office were hearty in praise of the valiant forces and blandly assured of successful maneuvers to come; both sides claimed victory and disclaimed the reports of the enemy; and the list of the dead mounted day by day. By midsummer the question of the ineptitude of the campaign was raised in Parliament, with a request for clearer information from the War Office.[27]

Besides these reports in the late spring and summer of 1915, there were the ordinary reports of carnage in the European campaign; zeppelin bombings of London began on 1 June and continued throughout the summer. And other disasters were especially devastating to H.D. The British poet Rupert Brooke died on 23 April, on his way to the Dardanelles. H.D. and her associates were deeply grieved over Brooke's death, as well as the death in May of the sculptor Henri Gaudier-Brzeska.[28] Immediately following this news, on 7 May the *Lusitania* was torpedoed by a German submarine in the Irish Sea, with a loss of about 1,200. The survivors, brought to Liverpool, gave heartbreaking accounts of the catastrophe. On 21 May, after a lengthy confinement, H.D. gave birth to a stillborn daughter, an event that she continued throughout her life to link to the "shock and repercussions of war news [specifically the news of the *Lusitania*] broken to me in a rather brutal fashion" (*Tribute to Freud* 40). H.D. remained in the nursing home until 11 June.[29]

Why, then, should H.D. take up the *Rhesos* during the summer of 1915? Its relevance to the Gallipoli campaign, and more generally to the whole course of the war, may have seemed compelling, and likewise the image of the Mother-Muse mourning the lost son (Rupert Brooke and Gaudier-Brzeska). As so frequently happens in tragedy, mourning in the *Rhesos* moves from individual pain to a sense of shared grief, just as for H.D. – as indicated obliquely in her narratives of these years – the loss of a child is bound up with mourning for all the young wastefully slain in the war. In her final words the Muse unites her grief with that of Thetis and of all mothers, divine or mortal, uttering the bald wisdom that a mother learns in war: "If you live through the night of your lives / childless / you will never / bury boys" (981–82, trans. Braun). This translation captures the bitterness of grief in the "unfortunate making of children," in bearing the young to be buried. H.D. found here one of the pivotal images defining affinity with Euripides, the figure of maternal mourning.

H.D. in her Euripidean interplay, finally, suggests an alternative classical teleology of the city, distinct from the apotheosis of masculine public order implied in the divine event at the end of the *Oresteia*. Burnett says of H.D.'s early aesthetic desire for "some golden city" in the context of war: "[Her position] relies . . . on a particular sense of tradition to construct a poetics which is constructive rather than destructive – set against the war rather than defined by it" ("Poetics" 61). In regard to her imagination of the city, Burnett rightly places H.D. in a prophetic tradition, with its distinct understanding "of the sacred and the responsible" (62). What war devastates through its Gorgon-like paralysis is the possibility of genuine daimonic possession. The city at war, like the Athens criticized by Euripides, does not bring a healthy Nietzschean energy of conflict, but the loss, as in the *Rhesos*, of the "mysteries," of inspired vision.

Within H.D.'s teleology, Euripides gives one of the chief images of the lost city. H.D.'s translations from the *Iphigeneia*, acknowledging the ambivalent dimensions of war, are in part a lament for Troy: "Ancient Troy / Will be given up to its fate. / They will mark the stone-battlements / And the circle of them / With a bright stain" (*Collected Poems* 78).[30] Troy is the first of many images throughout H.D.'s writing of the devastated city of the past recovered through writing, echoed by and intertwined with other, recurrent devastations and recoveries: Troy, Athens, Thebes, Corinth, Karnak, Rome, Pompeii, Paris, London. The import of this historical awareness is not, as with Eliot and Pound, the decline and fall of civilizations through moral turpitude. It would seem, rather, to be the experience of cities as the containers of multifarious memories and desires, of multiple times and selves. "Troy town was down" – the lament (echoing Rossetti) running throughout one of H.D.'s narratives of the war years – expresses for her the obliterated sites of the past that must be recovered through a painful archaeology.

War and Nostalgia

H.D.'s hellenism comes under full attack in a highly influential assessment by Douglas Bush (1937). Here is Bush's much-quoted critique of "H.D.'s Greece":

> But the Greece she dwells in has no real connection with the Greece of historic actuality. Most of her poetry has the air of an exquisitely chiseled reproduction of something, though it is a reproduction of something that never existed. . . . H.D. is a poet of escape. Her refuge is a dream-world of ideal beauty which she calls Greece; her self-conscious, even agonized, pursuit of elusive beauty is quite un-Greek. . . . The fact is that the hard bright shell of H.D.'s poetry partly conceals a soft romantic nostalgia which, however altered and feminized, is that of the Victorian Hellenists. . . . Her Greece, . . . is essentially the Greece of Pater and Wilde (who were scholars), and of Isadora Duncan (who was not). (505–6)

Bush's remarks cut two ways. They confirm to his sympathetic audience, through a shared language of dispraise, the specific points of delusion and falsity in H.D.'s imagination. But from another vantage point, they reveal implicitly the contours of "Bush's Greece."

One may construe Bush's own construct by querying the language of censure. "H.D.'s Greece," Bush says, has nothing to do with "the Greece of historic actuality." But which Greece, and which historic actuality, does he mean? Thucydides' Athens? The ruined states of Pausanias's description? Schliemann's Mycenae? The demythologized, historical Greece of George Grote and J. B. Bury? Moreover, what is the significance of "historic actuality" in regard to lyric poetry? How does Milton's "Lycidas" or Tennyson's "Tithonis" relate to the "actuality" of Greece? This emphasis upon actuality is reemphasized in insisting on H.D.'s association with "escape," with flight to "a dream world of ideal beauty."

But Bush here implies his own idealized imagination of Greece – where true hellenic love is not "self-conscious [and] agonized," but presumably un-self-conscious and serene. One infers moreover a complex norm of mimesis. His preference is for poetry that is original and dynamic (not a "reproduction") and natural/immediate (not "chiseled"). Finally, in his last remark, Bush signals the presence of his own fraternal, homoerotic coterie of classicists in insisting that H.D.'s hellenism represents postured female enthusiasm – Isadora Duncan – rather than scholarly male engagement – Pater and Wilde.

"Bush's Greece," then, partakes of the same biases and contradictions within modern classicism as a whole. These can be most clearly seen in the accusation summing up his other comments: "The fact is that the hard bright shell of H.D.'s poetry partly conceals a soft romantic nostalgia." One notes the call to realistic authority ("The fact is"), the implication of female cunning in the metaphor of concealment, and the note of disgust in "soft nostalgia." In the climate of modernism, the charge of nostalgia is especially devastating, carrying a sense of shameful debility. Modern classicism clearly distinguishes itself from a previous romantic generation in its insistence on realism and historical consciousness. Moreover, "nostalgia" suggests not only imaginative weakness, but bad faith, cowardice, and self-delusion.

However, Bush himself is not free of such disease. In fact, his implicit aesthetic criteria (immediacy, un-self-consciousness, and expressiveness) them-selves partake of romanticism, and specifically of Winckelmann's romantic hellenism, "noble simplicity and quiet grandeur" (33). The canonical authority of Bush's judgment of H.D. disguises the fictionality of his own construct of Hellas. Like those of other modern classicists, it is itself built upon nostalgia, the longing for a lost world: manly, large, coherent, and noble.

Ironically, in the Marxist and Nietzschean climate of postmodern criticism, the same charge of "nostalgia" leveled by moderns against romantics resurfaces prominently in the assessment of modernism itself: its avoidance of historical and social realities, its deluded desire for "metaphysical comfort," its nostalgia for "presence."[31] Jacques Derrida signals a primary focus of deconstruction: to censure the nostalgic orientation toward "the lost or impossible presence of the absent origin," which he contrasts with "Nietzschean *affirmation*" (292). Following lines of contemporary theory, recent critics love to hate nostalgias of many kinds.

Moreover, true to the turns of puritan revolutions, postmodernism itself is now criticized for its nostalgias. Nietzsche, Marx, and Freud themselves project ideals in the past or future by which the present is to be judged. Likewise, according to some critics, their disciples Derrida, Adorno, Foucault, and others suggest their own versions of atemporal longing.[32] Current Marxist critical theories, some suggest, implicitly involve "a nostalgic appeal to the past" in their critique of mass culture (Stauth and Turner, "Nostalgia" 511). And Clément Rosset has pointed to the avoidance by deconstructionists of the "banal" real in favor of some imaginary meaning in the "elsewhere"; Derrida and Lacan represent for him an unhappy "Hegelian nostalgia" (85–6; 113–15). Deconstruction carries with it, according to Josué Harari, a "nostalgia for the real" and a dependence upon "a phantasm of totality" (192).

One is struck by the regularity of these sequent pogroms of nostalgia, and also by the disdain and moral censure they imply. In this hall of mirrors, why is nostalgia so virulently condemned? What fuels the indignation that would locate and triumphantly expose it? One might suggest that a Girardian dynamic of "mimetic rivalry" is at work here – a recurring contest of intellectual appropriation and usurpation.[33] The common term of this rivalry – that which each desires to display in competition with the rival – is enlightenment, a position of intellectual clarity purportedly free of illusions and hateful of false idols, from which point the past can be finally discriminated. In the dynamics of ever-enlightened modernity, nostalgia always belongs to the anterior, delegitimized generation that the present one would supplant.

Nostalgia is a particularly recurring theme among twentieth-century critics because it points to irresolvable issues within postromantic thought. It resides in the interstices of old romantic tensions that even now, in altered language, generate anxiety and controversy: art in relation to life, imagination or intellectual cultivation versus utility, avant-garde versus bourgeois, atemporality versus historical consciousness, withdrawal versus engagement, solitary illumination versus political revolution. Clearly nostalgia is a metaphorical sign of other more explicitly philosophical issues attendant upon romanticism – the wavering contours of "subjectivity" and "consciousness" – that neither modernism nor postmodernism has resolved.[34]

In tracing the powerful negative charge of this word, one should note that though longing for home and the desire for return (*nostos*) have been around for millennia, such desire becomes a "disease" (*nostos* + *algia*, pain) only in the context of modernity. The word "nostalgia," coined in the late seventeenth century by a Swiss military physician, entered into currency in medical handbooks in the late eighteenth and early nineteenth centuries, understood as a melancholic pathology and treated chiefly among soldiers during war. The transferred sense of "nostalgia," as yearning for a distant past, exists, in English, only in the twentieth century. The first edition of the *Oxford English Dictionary* (1933) gives nothing but a medical sense; the second edition (1989) gives the first occurrence in English as 1920, in D. H. Lawrence's *The Lost Girl*.[35]

Two things are especially remarkable in the historical origins of the word. The first is the somatic as well as psychic origin of this melancholy. "Nostalgia" is a desire largely manifest *as disease* in the context of war and economic displacement, because it arose in conjunction with actual deracination and disorientation, in political situations allowing no hope of substitutes for what is lost. The separation from maternal care, "maternal deprivation," played a prominent role in the imagination of sufferers, a longing for familiar food and native milk (Rosen 341; Starobinski 87). Nostalgia was also understood as "an emotional upheaval which is related to the workings of memory," and thus seen in the context of an associationist psychology emphasizing the impressions of bodily senses (Starobinski 89–91). The disease symptomizes the repercussive physical and emotional violence that has characterized the history of modernity.

Second, the desire for homecoming becomes pathologized at the cultural moment when rationality, empiricism, and progress gain ascendancy as the determinants in defining the "actual." Hegel first gives the disease a negative metaphysical cast in the context of a dialectic of development (Berthold-Bond 369), echoed in later Darwinian, Marxist, or Freudian models, all of which assume the fiction of scientific dogma. But there is no "regression" outside the powerful linear fiction of "progression," no "sickness" of this kind without a model of health predicated on pragmatic adaptation and virile will. There is no negative charge to *pothos*, the desire for what is absent, outside an empirical model that invalidates the invisible, the oblique, the anterior.

In its hidden linkage to war, nostalgia may be the most widespread of modern diseases and – in the spirit of intellectual disdain for the realm of the maternal, for bodily and affective life – the most uniformly suppressed. Does the modern desire to eradicate nostalgia come from the hatred of an innocence capable of disillusionment? Does it suggest as normative a resignation to the perpetual condition of war, which sees as weak any sentiment that seems to evade the necessity of existential violence? H.D. is deliberately resistant throughout her career to these attitudes, which she clearly recognized within twentieth-century intellectual life.

There is no way to save H.D. from the charge of nostalgia in order to accommodate her within contemporary critical tastes. She steadily declined purgations of the disease, and in this, as in so many other things, "H.D. had an affinity for heretical causes" (Duncan, "Nights and Days" 49). Though many major modernist writers, as Perl argues, are guided by nostalgia, exploiting mythic patterns of return and refounding (17–33), the importance of nostalgia for

H.D. seems even more central. Indeed, in a stunning coincidence, the first recorded nonmedical usage of "nostalgia" in English, in Lawrence's *The Lost Girl*, occurs in passages that very likely allude to H.D.[36] H.D.'s writing constitutes an uncanny excavation of the original dimensions of nostalgia: displacement in war, maternal deprivation, the primacy of the body and of memory, the resistance to enlightened arguments against affection and longing.

It is very possible that H.D. had seen Bush's remarks on her hellenism when, at the end of 1937, she replied to a request by Norman Holmes Pearson for a statement of her poetic stance, to be published along with a selection of poems in the *Oxford Anthology of American Poetry*.[37] With his insistence upon the unreality of her hellenism, Bush in any case conforms to the imagined adversarial interlocutor of H.D.'s letter to Pearson.[38] Furthermore, in terms of our discussion, H.D. in this letter reveals a remarkable cognizance of the cultural context surrounding the pathologizing of nostalgia.

H.D.'s attempt to explain her poetry to those who consider it unreal begins with anecdotes about the dislocations of World War I. H.D. remembers that she "had staggered home" from suffocating air-raid shelters, to find a letter from Harriet Monroe, the editor of *Poetry*, suggesting "that H.D. would do so well, maybe, finally, if she could get into 'life,' into the rythm [*sic*] of our time, in touch with events." Monroe, H.D. says, though one of the first to recognize her talent, was "strangely, farcically blind to our predicament" (71–2). For "[i]n order to speak adequately of my poetry and its aims," H.D. says, "I must you see, drag in a whole deracinated epoc [*sic*]." But she speaks of deracination and homelessness with ironic literalness. One "came home" to find bombed-out buildings (72).

In this displacement of physical, intimate space is a displacement of poetry as well. Her companion in this anecdote, probably war-embittered Aldington, kicks a book across the room, demanding, "What is the use of all this – now?"[39] War profoundly decenters "home" as a coherent imaginative life. One may reject this displacement by repudiating the intimacy of the lost life, or by affirming its primacy in the face of facts that seem to obliterate significance. Aldington chooses the former course, H.D. the latter. The old poems, she says, "answered by existing. They were in other space, other dimension, . . . The *'unexpected isle in the far seas'* remained. Remains" (72). One notes the layering of moments implicit in these last verbs. In 1937, at the onset of World War II, H.D. remembers the experience of World War I. But if war appears to be a continuum, even more clear is the continuum of what "remains" – a continuum, according to Duncan, in which poems themselves constitute "events in another dimension, a field of meanings in which consciousness [is] in process" ("Part 2, Chapter 3" 138).

In this specific context of war, H.D. locates the "nostalgia" of her early poetry. Speaking of two of her early hellenic poems, she says:

Lotus-land, all this. It is nostalgia for a lost land. I call it Hellas. I might, psychologically just as well, have listed the Casco Bay islands off the coast of Maine but I called my islands Rhodes, Samos and Cos. They are symbols. And symbolically, the first island of memory [Calypso's island in the Lehigh River] was dredged away or lost, like a miniature Atlantis. (72)

This quotation is often used as a means of collapsing H.D.'s hellenism into biographical and psychological matter – as though her early hellenic orientation were only a mask or shield for personal problems later cogently unraveled by Freud. Such a biographical interpretation misses the complexity of the hellenic fiction itself, reducible neither to biographical or Freudian allegory nor to literary conventions.

Seeing H.D.'s "nostalgia for a lost land" in the context of her fiction of Hellas, one finds several complexities. First of all, in H.D.'s writing, all lands are "lost." All cities are unstable, dispersed, and displaced. "The islands" are images of all the lost lands in personal memory, history, and myth – "the first island" of memory on the Lehigh River, connected with the mythical lost island Atlantis. A corollary to this sense of historical time is that there is no "first" island: there are only anterior islands, serving within an erotic economy to mediate and defer the desire.

The complex character of H.D.'s play with nostalgia is evident in her earliest poetry, but one poem in particular deserves attention, "The Islands" (written in 1916 or 1917),[40] which remained for H.D. somehow a sign of her early hellenic nostalgia. The question raised in this poem (*Collected Poems* 124–7) remains central yet elusive: "What are the islands to me?" If one hopes to find here a simple articulation of H.D.'s hellenic telos, one will be dismayed.

What indeed are the "islands" signaled in this pivotal poem? They are, first of all, names and outlines, serving like a mantra to focus a certain meditative state. The islands are evoked in part 1 of the poem in a catalogue, and indeed one is very much reminded of the catalogue in book 2 of the *Iliad*, the islands taking the place of the Achaean ships as containers of the Greek world:

> What are the islands to me,
> what is Greece,
> what is Rhodes, Samos, Chios,
> what is Paros facing west,
> what is Crete?
>
> what is Samothrace,
> rising like a ship,
> what is Imbros rending the storm-waves
> with its breast? (*Collected Poems* 124)

In the symbolist mode, the names themselves call something into being. Like the names, the quasi-Homeric epithets have a purely suggestive power, evoking the island outline as an image on a visual map: "Paros facing west"; "Samothrace, / rising like a ship"; "Imbros . . . with its breast"; "the Cyclades' white necklace." The islands stand for the magical power of the word within an eidetic mapping.

However, the islands are conjured within a complex fabric of interrogation. The poem consists of a series of urgent questions, which effectively dislocate rather than locate significance: "What is Euboia / with its island violets, / what is Euboia, spread with grass, / set with swift shoals?" Euboia is a potent name, conjoined with the question of its existence. Like the Greek *eidolon*, the faint, bodiless image of the dead in Hades, Euboia is ghostly, appearing at the epiphanic point of disappearance, in the context of its questionableness.

This questioning is compounded by more complex levels of interrogation. After the initial questions of import, one finds other questions of comparison ("What can love of land give to me / that you have not?") and of condition ("What are the islands to me / if you are lost?"). The conflicting vectors of these questions, transposed one on another, serve to disorient any attempt at linear thought at the same time that they raise the emotional stakes within a dialectic that has loss or annihilation as an implicit term.

The "island" landscape of the poem is as complex as its rhetorical structure. Just as there are questions within questions, so there are islands within islands. The "isles of Greece" are simply signs of the specific, exclusive domain indicated in part 5 of the poem: "But beauty is set apart, / beauty is cast by the sea, / a barren rock, . . . Beauty is set apart / from the islands / and from Greece" (126). This island/beauty is set apart from names, and its power is much less accessible. It is not an abstract ideal, but a highly charged space, like that of Sappho's Lesbos, which H.D. describes in an early essay entitled "The Island" ("The Wise Sappho"), or like the *temenos* of the goddess in "The Shrine," likewise treacherous and inaccessible, but at the same time "tender, enchanted / where wavelengths cut you / apart from all the rest" (8). These similar images suggest "beauty" as a female space and potency at once erotic and maternal. Moreover, within this second island "set apart" is yet another insular space, the intimate "sea garden" described in part 6, where wind and salt have devastated the blossoms. This island of salt suffering, like the imagined space in *Sea Garden*, signifies in some way an openness to the subjective experience of desire.

One other aspect of "The Islands" gives a clue to the character of H.D.'s hellenic fiction. The poet almost immediately introduces the rhetorical complexity of "you." The interrogation throughout the poem is mediated by another, whose quoted words apparently intrude in part 4 to echo a question already posed. The "you" is never identified or located in any way but, like the islands, is repetitively evoked. It is clear, however, that this other functions as a necessary part of a triangle: "What are the islands to me / if you are lost, / what is Paros to me / if your eyes draw back, . . . What are the islands to me if you hesitate, / what is Greece if you draw back" (127).

The triangulation of desire in this poem (I/you/islands) is only one instance of a persistent erotic configuration. If, as H.D. says in *Tribute to Freud*, "[t]here were two's and two's and two's in my life" (31), this means, erotically, that there were always three's. H.D.'s lyric poems speak constantly of the triangular character of desire. The "ruse of the triangle," Anne Carson notes in her meditations on Greek poetry, "is not a trivial mental maneuver. We see in it the radical constitution of desire. . . . The third component plays a paradoxical role for it both connects and separates, marking that two are not one, irradiating the absence whose presence is demanded by eros." The poem of triangular desire is not about eros directed at an "object," but "about the lover's mind in the act of constructing desire for itself" (16).

In this context, the radical question posed in H.D.'s poem – "What are the islands to me, / what is Greece" – never implies a determinative answer. Nor is there figured in H.D.'s writing finally any home to return to. The telos of nostalgia, Edward Casey suggests, is neither a particular place, remembered in sensuous details, nor a "meta-place" favored by romantic writers, a deliteralized landscape constructed within "a cosmic revery of return" to "metaphysical origins" (370). Rather, the locus of nostalgia is a "plenum-of-places," an "encompassing whole made up of particular places in dynamic interaction with each other." The world imagined in nostalgia serves as a "mediatrix" between the particular place of actual memory and the metaphysical place of origins (378).

In Casey's terms, H.D.'s Hellas mediates between "home" as the United States and her mother Helen, and "heaven-is-my-home" and her father. On the one hand are actual memories. H.D. herself associates the islands with places known in childhood, and many critics have emphasized Pearson's remarks identifying H.D.'s Greek landscapes with those in Pennsylvania and New Jersey (Dembo, "Interview" 437). Others have pointed to H.D.'s own discovery, made through Freud, that her longing for Greece was a longing for her mother Helen (*Tribute to Freud* 44). But on the other hand, valences no less "real" to H.D. are also present. That Hellas carries what Casey calls a "metaphysical landscape" is suggested in an interesting comment in H.D.'s late memoir "Compassionate Friendship." She says, concerning her early hellenic poetry: "I am surprised at the sadness in those poems. . . . It is hard to explain it. We say (old-fashioned people used to say) when someone dies, he or she has *gone home*. I was looking for home, I think. But a sort of heaven-is-my-home, I was looking for that – that super-ego – that father-lover – I don't know – How can I explain it?" (12–13). This spiritual significance of Hellas is also suggested in *Tribute to Freud* in allusion to Oliver Wendell Holmes's "The Chambered Nautilus," another favorite of H.D., in which the spiritual voyager builds one shell chamber after another, each one larger, fitting the enlarging dimensions of the soul, each the "last found home," moving toward the final threshold of death and the home of heaven.

It is tempting to critics to collapse H.D.'s hellenic nostalgia into a neurotic sublimation finally resolved through Freud. However, as H.D.'s remarks in 1937 suggest, Freud did not dissolve nostalgia but instead allowed H.D. a way to deepen and refine it, clarifying for her through the enactment of memory and dreams the centrality of maternal longing and of incestuous configurations, the controlling presence in her life of the phobia of war, and the spiritual longing associated with the father. In the poems of the *Trilogy*, longing for the "islands" becomes part of a rich, polyvalent spirituality *still* centered in the desire for home.

H.D. found the right master for this guidance; for, if nostalgia is deeply resonant throughout H.D.'s career, it is likewise resonant as a suppressed component of Freud's thought. At the same time that nostalgia as a psychosomatic disease disappears, Casey points out, another psychosomatic malady, hysteria, emerges. The valences of one are displaced upon the other. Casey argues that Freud thoroughly incorporates the language of the old disease of nostalgia – its topography of *place* – in his analysis of hysteria in terms of the mechanisms of memory. With Freud the old suppressed disease went underground, to emerge in another form in the language of fixation and regression (Casey 371–5). However, Freud's rewriting of the old disease of nostalgia denies the remedy of a return home to maternal care, except as part of a way forward oriented to identification with the father and with the rational and pragmatic categories he controls. As Friedman and others have emphasized, H.D. altered the plot of Freud's therapeutic scheme, seeing the affirmation of her bond with the mother as freeing her (*Psyche* 137). At the same time, *Tribute to Freud* and the memoir *The Gift* suggest that H.D. through Freud was also able to suppress her bond with the father in healing ways, mitigating its tyrannizing abstraction yet affirming its spirituality.

H.D. relates in closing her letter to Pearson that a friend had recently called to tell her: "'Your islands were on the air . . . and read beautifully.'" H.D. meditates:

> I should have liked, in time, in actuality to have heard my "islands on the air," here in this island, to have made that link with those other islands, Calypso's island . . . vanished Atlantis in a river in Pennsylvania, sea-islands of the coast of Maine, Aegean islands sensed in passing and the actual Ionian island of Corfu, the early Capri, Syren island of Magna Graeca, and specifically, that island, noted in Phoenician days for its tin . . . England. I should like to have heard my "islands on the air," here in this island, the latest in my phantasy of islands, final link and perhaps "clasp of the white necklace." (74)

The echo of island within island, all lost, all anterior, yet all remaining, recoverable in memory and affection, is continuous with H.D.'s conception of the islands throughout her life. Moreover, England, the final link, the chief location of her poetic labor, is also the place of recurrent war. In *The Gift*, written a few years later during the bombardment in London, England becomes associated with *Wunden Eiland*, Isle of Wounds, from her Moravian family's past: "Was that this island, England, pock-marked with formidable craters, with Death stalking one at every corner?" (*Gift* 140). H.D.'s "phantasy of islands" is tied from beginning to end to the experience of war, which throws into question the value of the intimate and makes, through its discontinuities, a human continuum.

Chapter Two

The Survival of the Classics

Why, in the context of war, do images of ancient cities arise, and in the West, recoveries of the Greeks? The very notion of the classics is bound to the question of "survival" – the literal preservation of texts within the recurrent catastrophes and collapses of cities and kingdoms, as well as, in a broader sense, the continuing vitality of ancient works as influences within subsequent generations (Lloyd-Jones 9). In the vicissitudes of their survival, the classics bring one, more vividly than does any literary study, to questions of transmission. Such questions become acute in recurrent times of war, in its violent discontinuities with the past, its apocalyptic fever, its ruin and dispersal.

When one attempts to understand H.D.'s place within modern classicism, issues surrounding classical transmission become extremely vexed. For one thing, H.D. as an innovative amateur translator made legitimate claims as a participant in classical transmission, especially at a moment, as Eliot claimed in 1916, when the survival of the classics depended greatly upon modern translation. Good translation for Eliot constitutes an "enrichment of English by contact with Greek, a criticism of one language by another, a fertilisation." Indeed, Eliot in his review of the first Poets' Translation Series gives H.D. uncontested supremacy among her fellow hellenists: "And often she does succeed in bringing something out of the Greek language into the English, in an immediate contact which gives life to both, the contact which makes it possible for the modern language perpetually to draw sustenance from the dead" ("Classics in English" 102–3).

Yet H.D. in her role of translator and interpreter of ancient texts nevertheless assumes a place within a precinct universally imagined as male. How can a woman partake in cultural preservation and regeneration other than in biological, economic, or iconic roles? To entrust her with textual transmission is to invite contamination of the line. The misogyny traditionally prevalent within the learned schools and the general detestation of the "feminine" in classical parlance must be understood as factors in negative assessments of H.D.'s hellenism.[1]

H.D.'s place within modern classicism is further complicated by a war of hellenisms taking place within it. The survival of the classics is imagined within recurrent reformulations of the classic line. The issue of H.D.'s hellenism is clouded by a confusion within modern classicism itself regarding the authentic classic lineage. Upon what grounds, within what historical fiction, is this graphing of the line to be made? Hulme, Pound, Babbitt, and Eliot, for instance, propose different reconstructions of the authentic tradition. However, as we have seen, they all agree in defining themselves against the romantic hellenism of the preceding century.

This chapter traces H.D.'s own delineation of the classic line and her conception of her role within the survival of the classics. To do so, however, requires a larger mapping of the fictions of classicism available to writers in the early twentieth century. I would suggest that the critical efforts of Eliot, Pound, and Hulme may be understood as a battle not only between late romanticism and modernism, or between romantic and classic, but between two distinct classical traditions operative since the Renaissance, and particularly two distinct hellenisms operative in the nineteenth century.

The vagaries of the classical model in the nineteenth century are remarkably complex – as Frank M. Turner, Richard Jenkyns, and, recently, Martin Bernal have shown. Greek rather than Roman classicism predominates throughout the nineteenth century, and reverence for Latin models generally declines. However, hellenism here has its own permutations. The revolutionary political agenda of Shelley's "Hellas" (1822) is at the opposite pole from the moral agenda of Arnold's "sweetness and light" in *Culture and Anarchy* (1869). Descending from the first broad enthusiasm of romantic hellenism, the Victorians domesticate the Greeks according to the outlines of prevalent political positions – discussing the merits of Athenian democracy versus Spartan oligarchy, of Sophocles or Aeschylus versus Euripides, of the erotic Plato of the *Symposium* versus the authoritarian Plato of the *Republic* and the *Laws*.[2]

Walter Pater, in *Greek Studies* (1897), allows terms by which to locate the strains of hellenism operative in the late nineteenth and early twentieth centuries. Pater reads back into Greek culture itself two different tendencies: the "centrifugal" (the Ionian or Asian) and the "centripetal" tendency (the Dorian or European). The centrifugal or Ionian tendency suggests a "flying from the centre, working with little forethought straight before it, ... throwing itself forth in endless play of undirected imagination; delighting in brightness and colour, ... in changeful form everywhere." This Ionian tendency in political affairs is characterized by diversity rather than unity, by "the assertion of the principles of separatism, of individualism, – the separation of state from state, the maintenance of local religions" (267–8). It would be manifest in Athenian democratic institutions. In contrast, the centripetal is an "enemy everywhere to *Variegation*, to what is cunning or 'myriad-minded.'" This Dorian/European mode finds the "human mind the most absolutely real and precious thing in the world, enforces everywhere the impress of its sanity, its profound reflexions upon things as they really are, its sense of proportion." Politically the centripetal or Dorian is concerned with "the reign of a composed, rational, self-conscious order" – with the Spartan military model suggested in Plato's *Republic*, for instance (268).

Pater's division here mirrors a fairly serious tension within the hellenism of the nineteenth century. Turner echoes this contrast in delineating the sometimes virulent conflict within Victorian hellenism between "dynamic and evolutionary humanism" and traditional English Augustan humanism (16–17), the former generally allied with Athens, the latter with Sparta. Clearly Hulme and Eliot in their polemic of romantic versus classic are negotiating this same hellenic territory – severely reasserting the Dorian over the Ionian, the rational masculine over the "myriad-minded," effeminate traditions. Their rhetorical strategy in doing so, however, is to dismiss the inherited complexity of the classical model. The Dorian alone represents authentic classicism.

Though it represents a peculiarly Victorian viewpoint, Pater's distinction may also serve to describe a persistent tension within classical humanism as a whole. One way of imagining the classical ideal might be considered centripetal in Pater's terms. It emphasizes centrality, wholeness, and rational coherence. It reiterates certain moral and political virtues – aristocratic or oligarchic, rather than democratic – coincident with the teaching of the ancients, with right reason, with the sublimity of perfect form. It is prescriptive, affiliating itself with reasoned pragmatism. According to Jeffrey Perl, this interpretative tradition is fairly pessimistic in its historiography, seeing anterior periods of classical wholeness as radically discontinuous with the present and positing cultural dissociations or decadence to explain the loss (22–5). This model is represented in the Christian humanism of Erasmus and More, in eighteenth-century neoclassicism, and in Arnold's late version of hellenism. Greek and Latin texts authenticate the given sense of "right practice" (Arnold's phrase), of standards of virtue and aesthetic judgment; they allow "criteria" for discrimination (Eliot's term).

However, the centrifugal imagination of the classical – specifically associated with the Greek and not the Roman – is very much alive within Western traditions. It is eccentric in its focus, drawn to the discrete, the fragmentary, and the rationally obscure. It emphasizes the erotic and the visionary, and it is affiliated politically with democracy and freedom. This tradition of interpretation, as Perl has suggested (26–7), focuses upon the continuity rather than the discontinuity of hellenism in history, seeing it, as does Pater, as an underground stream, "from time to time [starting] to the surface," so that culture may be "drawn back to its sources" (*Renaissance* 210). This centrifugal classicism flourishes in the Greece of the "dispersion," in hellenistic Alexandria, nourished with

Neoplatonism, literary survivals, and syncretic religions. It survives only vestigially in Latin and Christian Europe, but it enters into late history in the Renaissance. Some (like Pater and later Pound) see this hellenism in the efflorescence of troubadour poetry in the twelfth century in Provence (Pater, *Renaissance* 2). But it surfaces consciously in the efforts of Marsilio Ficino and Pico della Mirandola to reconcile pagan and Christian belief through the recovery of classical Greek and hellenistic texts – Plato, Plotinus, and syncretic texts like the *Corpus Hermeticum*, the first of the ancient texts commissioned for translation by Cosimo de Medici.

Moreover, as Ernest Tuveson argues, this hellenistic strain, submerged for a while after the Renaissance, resurfaces with great force in romanticism. In a study tracing the vicissitudes of hermeticism, Tuveson articulates the character of hermeticism as revealed in the *Hermetica*, and traces the presence of this occult worldview not only in the Renaissance but, paradoxically, in the Enlightenment, in the forms of Freemasonry and Rosicrucianism. Finally, he studies the full-fledged resurgence of hermetic cosmology as the basic model within romantic metaphysical preoccupations, the attempt in romantic writing to describe and enact a *gnosis*, made possible through participation in the mysteries of Nature and Spirit. Stephen McKnight has argued indeed that this occult tradition informs not only romanticism but modernity itself to a degree not sufficiently acknowledged.[3]

Romanticism may thus be understood as the arena in which a complex inheritance from hellenistic traditions is made manifest. In the phenomenon of Philhellenism emerging in the late eighteenth century – the craze for Greece and its artifacts – the hermeticism embedded in the Enlightenment found a fortuitous imagistic ground. The Philhellenes of the Society of the Dilettanti, bringing back drawings of ancient monuments from Greece, may indeed have been Freemasons, participating in a fashionable hermeticism of gentlemanly circles; or at the least they were affected by the Enlightenment climate in which "rationalism was tinged with illuminism" (Yates, *Rosicrucian* 233).[4] What could be so natural as to see the Greece of beautiful, white marble and of perfect forms in terms of a tradition of spiritual illumination, itself distinctly linked (through Egypt) to the Greeks? Writers like Blake, Byron, and Shelley draw upon this tradition of interpretation when they speak of Greek art. For them, statues do not so much exemplify sublimity and nobility of form as they convey revelations of the invisible and eternal. In Blake's words, they are "representations of spiritual existences of God's immortal, to the mortal perishing organ of sight" ("Descriptive Catalogue" 532).

In romantic hellenism, "Hellas" itself becomes conflated imaginatively – though unconsciously – with the "pagan mysteries" of Alexandrian hellenism. In terms more pertinent to H.D., Greece undergoes a mystical transference with Egypt. This moment in classical dissemination is paradoxical. Among nineteenth-century classical scholars, as Bernal has shown, the "Aryan" model of Greece becomes dominant – Greece imagined as an ideal exclusively European and white. But at the same time this pure hellenism, in its popular assimilation by poets, may be seen as participating in corrupt Alexandrian spirituality, with its amalgamation of religious traditions from many races. For instance, Shelley's "Hellas," rightly cited by Bernal as evidence of the racist agenda of European hellenism (290–1), has as its focal figure Ahasuerus, the "Wandering Jew" or hermetic mage, "whose spirit is a chronicle / Of strange and secret and forgotten things" (456). Indeed, the romantic figure of the outcast who carries millennial wisdom (the Wandering Jew, Manfred) is explicitly related to the hermetic mage personified in Pico and Giordano Bruno, participating in Egyptian traditions. In the complex heterodoxy of the romantics, Greece carries not only the weight of radical political, erotic, and aesthetic agendas, but also the sense of a continuous, though hidden, visionary tradition. There is, in other words, an important, unacknowledged link between romantic hellenism and hermeticism.[5]

The hermetic bases of romantic hellenism become increasingly explicit toward the end of the nineteenth century, for several reasons. At midcentury Pater establishes the Renaissance as the precursor to the modern, at the same time seeing it as continuous with hellenism – and very much a centrifugal hellenism, at that. Pater explicitly treats prominent Renaissance figures within the context of the hermeticism of Pico and other Renaissance writers, who imagined themselves to be in the mainstream of hellenic spiritual tradition. Following from this fascination with pagany, the heterodox spirituality of late-nineteenth-century art becomes one of its most remarkable features. Pre-Raphaelites attempt to reclaim this aura of pagan mystery. Moreover, by the time H.D. and others of her generation came to learn their aesthetics, the Victorian intellectual context had been thoroughly modified by hermetic infusions from France. The "rêve hellénique" in France begins with the Parnassians,[6] such as Théophile Gautier and Leconte de Lisle, who turn to Greece in part because of its strangeness, its exoticism, removed in time and space from the present. Hellenism provides a code for "pastoral otherness," the dream of an erotic, artificial elsewhere (Knight 173). In particular the Parnassians find in hellenism the supremacy of plastic art, which becomes a model for the precision, objectivity, and detachment to which art should aspire. The idolatry of marble carries a strain of visionary mysticism essential to romantic hellenism, originating in Winckelmann's studies of Greek sculpture and permeating all romantic discussions of Greek art.

French symbolism is more explicitly allied with strains of hermeticism or Orphism, as it emphasizes the evocation of mystery through the mediation of the creative Word. Gerard de Nerval, Baudelaire, Mallarmé, and Rimbaud, for instance, are deliberate in evoking occult systems as the basis of their imaginative explorations; and the language of the occult is central in symbolist descriptions of the nature and aims of the poem. But throughout the poetry of the symbolists, the language of hellenism derived from the Parnassians remains a persistent medium of this visionary intent (Knight 188–213).

The hellenism that H.D. came to know in the first years of the twentieth century draws from this whole range of influences. Cassandra Laity treats H.D.'s explicit ties with the English romantics and decadents. Moreover, in her formative years in association with Pound and later with Richard Aldington in London and Paris, H.D. came to know the French poets who were at that time shaping the consciousness of a generation of modernists. They read Gautier and de Regnier together (Swann 10), and her early correspondence indicates that she was reading Mallarmé, Rimbaud, Villiers de l'Isle Adam, among many other French writers, during the time of her first publication of poetry.

It is not sufficient to see H.D. merely as a "Victorian hellenist," a derivative and imitative late romantic. Hellenism for H.D. is a serious and reflectively explored fiction, taking her beyond her own literary moment and beyond the romantics, affiliating her with the alternative "centrifugal" classicism delineated here. The site of her hellenic excursions is not classical or preclassical Greece, but rather hellenistic Alexandria. A participant in the "survival of the classics" as translator, H.D. imagined her role in visionary terms, in the context of recurrent catastrophes and vestigial remains, a priestess in a religious tradition in which clairvoyance and service to poetry were one and the same.

The Alexandrian Project

Within modern classicism both Eliot and Pound – albeit in greatly differing ways – assumed foremost roles of textual guardianship. They were alike in their self-chosen exile from academic life, but alike as well in their longing to influence the learned community, to affect education at a fundamental level. In recognizing an urgent need to think again about the survival of the classics in a modern context, Eliot and Pound turned their energies to pedagogy, not to say propaganda.

Eliot set out to clarify the truly classical, establishing his very influential concept of "tradition" (1919), a line of literary descent ostensibly providing a fiction of continuity within the discontinuity of modern culture. His delineation of the classic line is itself fairly eclectic – late French symbolists (LaForge), Jacobean poets and dramatists, Dante, Virgil – the basis of which appears to be a "metaphysical" tradition. He also develops the corollary notion of "dissociation of sensibility" (1921), initiating a language of psychological malaise in discussing deviance from the tradition. And finally he proposes the idea of the "mythic method" (1923), giving paradigmatic status to classical configurations of action.

Pound's efforts at constituting a tradition of descent, at "[condensing] the story of literature" and determining its "main line" ("On Criticism" 147–8), were no less strenuous than Eliot's, no less idiosyncratic, and no less dictated by models of historical crisis and fictions of dissociation.[7] However, they were anti-institutional in nature and iconoclastic in tone. Unlike Eliot, Pound did not attempt a systematic theory of formative tradition. Rather he was preoccupied from the beginning of his critical writing with complex details of textual transmission, with the cultural reception of ancient texts through the medium of specific scholars, editors, translators, and commentators. Moreover, he was brought early in his career, through his understanding of the troubadours in the context of the Albigensian Crusade, to acknowledge the sometimes violent discontinuities within transmission and the presence of repressed traditions.[8]

Pound, more than Eliot, embraced the complexity of classicism as a recurrent, mutable critical fiction. European civilization, he said, consists of "a mediaeval trunk with wash after wash of classicism going over it." These overlays exist simultaneously with presumably "real" classicism, which he roughly defines as "anything that has existed or subsisted unbroken from antiquity" (*ABC of Reading* 56). Pound's discerning comment indicates the problematic position of any new classicism: that another classicism is always anterior and that the location of "true" classicism depends on one's definition of the "unbroken" line.

Modern classicism saw itself at odds with an anterior (unauthentic, decadent, contaminated) hellenism that it sought to displace. In her early career H.D. was immediately caught in this confusing crossfire of hellenisms. Figuratively, H.D. was caught between Pound and her poet-husband Aldington. The imagism formulated by Pound and exemplified in H.D. was in part a response to Hulme's dictates for a new classicism, at odds with romanticism. Pound's explicitly hellenic efforts follow the same paths. The hellenism, for instance, implicit in two "Hellenist" series of essays in the *Egoist* (1917–19),[9] is imagined as a recovery, through Renaissance translations, of the main line in the transmission of ancient texts, overpassing the deviancy of romanticism. However, though participating in Pound's classicist efforts, H.D. shares ground as well with Aldington, who seems in his poetry and criticism never to have gone beyond late-nineteenth-century conceptions of hellenism. In an early issue of the *Egoist* (January 1914), Aldington identifies the "Hellenic ideal of art" with late-romantic positions (Rossetti and Pater) and attacks imagism as one of many modern reactionary movements essentially "unHellenic, and, . . . unhealthy" ("Anti-Hellenism" 35). Remarks similar to these met with Pound's scorn in the subsequent issue of the *Egoist* (February 1914), where he dismissed criticism by an anonymous reader directed at his own aesthetic pronouncements as "Paterine sentimentalesque Hellenism" ("Caressibility" 117).

Situated within this intellectual and linguistic confusion, shared by readers of the early literary magazines like the *Egoist* and *Poetry*, H.D.'s hellenism may have seemed slightly tainted, even though it met with initial praise. Explicitly Greek matter seemed increasingly suspect. One should note, for instance, that Pound's famous letter to Harriet Monroe in 1912, though declaring H.D.'s poetry to be "modern" and "straight as the Greek," also apologizes for its classical subject: "At least," Pound says, "H.D. has lived with these things since childhood, and knew them before she had any book-knowledge of them" (*Letters* 11). The locution "at least" is to signify the "real" (that is, biographical) basis of the poems, suggesting the air of bookish unreality that Pound associates with classical themes. By the end of World War I Pound had dismissed H.D.'s hellenic preoccupation (*Letters* 157), and Eliot wrote with disapproval to Aldington about H.D.'s second volume of poems, *Hymen* (1921), likewise indicating that "the Hellenism lacks vitality" (*Letters* 488). Clearly for Pound and Eliot H.D.'s hellenism was in the "flow-contamination" – Pound's phrase for bad influence (*Letters* 114) – of late romantics like Wilde or Swinburne.

But Pound's hellenism is itself none too pure, and its impurity points remarkably to the common ground Pound shared with H.D. – for in crucial ways they are alike in their interpretation of the unbroken line of classical transmission. One kind of hellenism seems central to Pound's program, the other marginal; but differentiating between the pure and the impure is tricky. Writing to Margaret Anderson in 1917, Pound elliptically asserts a working distinction: "You advertise 'new Hellenism.' It's all right if you mean humanism, Pico's *De Dignitate*, the *Odyssey*, the Moscophoros. Not so good if you mean Alexandria, and worse if you mean the Munich-sham-Greek 'Hellas' with a good swabian brogue" (*Letters* 107).

What is the true hellenism? One should note first that it is defined in antithesis to various decadences. Alexandria seems be here as elsewhere in Pound's writing a code word for decadence – conflating the decadence of hellenistic culture with the recent literary decadences in England and France. An extreme decadence, too, is represented in German romanticism, in which neohellenism, beginning with Winckelmann, became identified with German nationalism.[10]

"Decadence" is a falling away, but from what? Pound's examples in this letter would indicate his conception of a fall from a pristine, ephemeral state of predecadence. Pound here seems to locate "humanism" or hellenism at a certain cultural threshold, the moment of archaic beginnings, after which all is decadent. Homer of course is at the origins of all literature and art in the West. Pico della Mirandola would seem to represent the earliest (purest) Renaissance humanism, at the "dawn" of the dawning age, at least such is his exemplary status in Pater's *Renaissance* (34, 51). The Moscophoros, a sixth century B.C. Greek statue, is named by Pound in another 1917 letter as an example of pre-Phidian Greek sculpture, one of a few early worthwhile things within the "continuous decadence" of Greek art (*Letters* 104).

One can understand the connection Pound makes between Homer and the archaic Greek statue: both represent "geometric" as opposed to "vital" art, terms propounded by Hulme in 1914 in his increasing primitivism or archaism, and echoed, also in 1914, by Pound's friend, the sculptor Gaudier-Brzeska.[11] But the exemplary status accorded by Pound to the Renaissance hermeticist and magician

Pico della Mirandola is puzzling. The humanism of Pico's *De Dignitate* not only depends upon the despised Alexandria – in the form of the hellenistic philosophical and hermetic texts from which it draws – but in fact disseminates it.

In taking Pico as a guide, Pound signals his affiliation with the centrifugal classicism we have delineated. Clearly this marginal hellenic tradition remains a constant source in Pound's work, from his earliest essays (1912) in which he speaks of the visionary inheritance of the "hellenistic mysteries" surviving in Provence, until his mature career and his late *Cantos*, where he repeatedly evokes the language of the mysteries and speaks of the "light from Eleusis" as the unbroken line from the ancients, surviving "to set beauty in the song of Provence and of Italy."[12]

Like Pound, H.D. takes the hermetic or visionary lineage deriving from Alexandria as the "unbroken line" surviving from antiquity. Unlike him, however, she does not appear to have accepted the negative valence of decadence, the evocation of a primal purity as a measure of degrees of decline.[13] H.D., along with the early generation of modernists, begins her career by assuming the late-nineteenth-century fascination with Alexandria as the image of the decadent city. However, where Pound and most other modernists firmly reject Alexandrine literary decadence, H.D. deliberately embraces it. Laity has persuasively argued that H.D. and other early modern women writers identified with late romantic decadence not only because its writers were considered "effeminate" in the modernist debates, thus offering them literary "foremothers," but also because it presented a range of erotic exploration, especially homoeroticism ("Swinburne"; "Trangressive Sexualities" 53–4). But going beyond H.D.'s initial decadent affiliations, I would claim, Alexandria remains with H.D. throughout her career and becomes for her, as for C. P. Cavafy, what Florence is for Dante.

What, precisely, are the valences of decadent Alexandria in the late nineteenth century? Its evocation carries sometimes negative, not to say apocalyptic, implications, such as in Nietzsche's famous definition in *The Case of Wagner*. The "sign of every *literary decadence*," Nietzsche says, is linguistic dissolution: "every time, the anarchy of atoms, disintegration of the will" (170). As Linda Dowling has indicated, some Victorian intellectuals were gravely troubled by their perceived likeness to the Alexandrian, but other critics, notably Pater, defended stylistic Alexandrianism (Dowling, *Decadence* 107–8, 141–2). Often the comparison of the contemporary age to the Alexandrian suggested no censure, but simply a recognition of the particular literary and cultural gifts of both epochs.[14] The decadents themselves cultivated the ambiguity of this model. In his important essay, "The Decadent Movement in Literature," Arthur Symons asserts that decadent (symbolist/impressionist) poetry "has all the qualities that mark the end of great periods, the qualities that we find in the Greek, the Latin, decadence: an intense self-consciousness, a restless curiosity in research, an over-subtilizing refinement upon refinement, a spiritual and moral perversity" (858–9). But even in these comments decadence is understood not simply as a declension from greatness or as a disease of language but as a distinct poetic mode with its own possibilities.

In the deliberate iconographical reversals of the decadents, Alexandria gains prominence over other ancient cities. Oscar Wilde, for example, displaces the primacy of Athens with that of Alexandria as the foundation of Western art: "There is really not a single form that art now uses that does not come to us from the critical spirit of Alexandria, where these forms were either stereotyped, or invented, or made perfect. I say Alexandria . . . because it was to that city, and not to Athens, that Rome turned for her models, and it was through the survival, such as it was, of the Latin language that culture lived at all" (72).

No modern poet more obviously bears out the decadent implications of Alexandria than Cavafy, the Greek Alexandrian, who spent his early years in England, absorbing the currents of symbolism and decadence. Remarks like those of Wilde, which Cavafy surely knew, only clarified his intention in constructing a mythical city of Alexandria in the years between 1911 and 1921. Cavafy's Alexandria, going beyond late-nineteenth-century predecessors, in some ways represents decadence not as a local phenomenon or as a literary fashion, but as a universal, recurrent perspective within human history and experience.[15]

H.D.'s fabrication of Alexandria is roughly synchronic with that of Cavafy, whose poetry first became known in England, through E. M. Forster, beginning in 1919.[16] Her reference in a 1916 review to "our present-day literary Alexandria" with its concern for "originality" ("Review of *The Farmer's Bride*" 135) does not carry the negative weight of Nietzsche's model of decline. In this reference to Alexandria, H.D. specifically alludes to the aesthetic principles of Callimachus, a scholar and poet in the third century B.C. affiliated with the library at Alexandria. He urges poets to avoid a "road that carries many hither and thither." He prefers the narrow to the large, the short to the long, the small to the great, the lyric to the epic (*Palatine Anthology* 12.43, trans. Mackail, *Select Epigrams* 187; Wright, *Poets* 66–7).

As Robert Babcock has suggested,[17] H.D. clearly takes these Alexandrian principles as analogous to modernist aesthetics. Indeed, one might make a case for such a parallel. Hulme's early articulations of the doctrine of the image (1912) do indeed reflect his sense of an aesthetic retreat from "big things" (Levenson 46), though Pound in his adoption of Hulme's ideas never shared this conception of modest limitation. "The Dryad [H.D.]," Pound wrote to Dorothy Shakespear in 1913, "with no sense of modernity has writ a poem to Tycho the god of little things" (Pound and Shakespear 238). H.D.'s "poem to Tycho," which has not survived, was probably a translation or adaptation of an epigram from the Greek Anthology: "Even me the little god of small things if thou call upon in due season thou shalt find; but ask not for great things" (9.334, trans. Mackail). Clearly at odds with Pound's conception of the tragic/epic potency of modernity, the order governed by this "little god of small things" is nevertheless crucial to H.D.'s early lyric endeavors, and it has the authority of Alexandria behind it.

Moreover, as Robert Duncan was the first to note, H.D. in her hellenic writing privileges Alexandria, or the hellenistic and Roman period of its prominence, thriving as a literary and scientific center from the third to the first century B.C. and as a spiritual center from the first to the fourth century A.D.[18] "Her classicism," Duncan says, "is like that of Plutarch and Philo Judaeus" ("Two Chapters" 86). We have already noted the centrality in H.D.'s hellenism of Euripides, who for Nietzsche is consummately Alexandrian in spirit, that is, synonymous with Socratic or theoretical man (109). Moreover, most of H.D.'s translations of and allusions to Greek lyric poetry in her early career concern hellenistic poets – Theocritus, Callimachus, and other poets of the Greek Anthology, particularly those collected in Meleager's original *Garland* (Plato, Moero, Nossis, Anyte, Antipater of Sidon, and Meleager himself). Likewise the bulk of H.D.'s unpublished "Notes on Euripides, Pausanius, and Greek Lyric Poets" might also be considered Alexandrian in cultural terms. Apart from Euripides and Sappho, the other writers she treats here in separate chapters – Theocritus, Meleager, Anacreon, and Pausanias – are situated within the broad period of Alexandria's prominence as a cultural center in hellenistic and Roman times.[19]

Though it may seem strained to gather writers from Euripides to Pausanias under this Alexandrian rubric, it is nevertheless helpful in clarifying a crucial locus within H.D.'s imaginative geography. Classical fifth-century Greece has centrality in H.D.'s writing as a fiction of brilliant, inexorable perfection, illuminated by the supreme and absolute presences of the gods. H.D. constantly invokes as well images of pre-Periclean religion and art. However, one should note that she usually approaches these territories obliquely: she approaches Greece by way of Egypt, Athens by way of Alexandria, archaic Greece by way of vestigial remains.

Just as Martin Aske has argued with regard to the hellenism of Keats, H.D.'s writing also suggests "the very difficulty and uncertainty of antiquity's representation in a modern text" (1). As we have seen, the "isles of Greece," representing a kind of dream of anteriority, are fragmentary and inaccessible. Greece for H.D., as for Keats, "is something more than a text or collection of texts; as a fiction it is finally, unrepresentable, unimaginable" (Aske 4). H.D. comes to Greece imaginatively through the late, "decadent" Athenians Euripides and Plato,[20] through the hellenistic anthology (Meleager), through the hellenistic travel guide (Pausanias), and even through late hellenistic historians (Appian, Arrian, Plutarch, Diogenes Laertius). The "islands" exist always in the context of loss; they are constantly invoked in the context of a later era, through the medium of longing and memory. H.D. engages not Athens but Alexandria, which, like Cavafy's city, is "the marginal culture of the Greek diaspora, or centrifugal Greece" (Clay 160).

Three of H.D.'s fictional narratives of the twenties and early thirties deliberately take the Alexandrian period as a setting – "Hipparchia" in *Palimpsest* (1926), *Hedylus* (1928), and the unpublished "Pilate's Wife" (1934). Two of them have hellenistic poets as central figures, each of whom is an Alexandrian scholar of sorts, translating or writing poetry in the spirit of the Alexandrians – that is, within an imagined recovery of the "lost islands" of Greece. After the lyric exploration of hellenism concluding in her *Collected Poems* (1925), these narratives constitute a second, reflective stage in H.D.'s awareness of her fiction of Greece. They represent to some extent analyses of the geographical and psychic boundaries of her early hellenic obsession.

That H.D. was conscious of the temporal and geographical displacement of her hellenism is suggested in *Hedylus*, which, besides its autobiographical and psychological content, dramatizes a central intellectual and poetic conflict between Athens and Alexandria. Set on the island of Samos immediately following the Macedonian conquest of Greece, its central figures of mother-poet and son-poet, Hedyle and Hedylus, play out the imaginative exigencies of the two cities. Hedyle is trapped in adoration of the beauty of lost Athens, in the context of whose inexorable perfection nothing in life seems worthwhile. The narcissism of her love is suggested in the image of the mirror, wherein Hedyle fixedly contemplates her own beauty, identified with the lost but still mesmerizing beauty of Athens. Moreover, like Lais of Plato's epigram (translated by H.D., *Collected Poems* 149–50), Hedyle uses her beauty and the beauty of lost Greece to "tyrannize" her son, putting before him constantly the absolute poetic measures of Athens.

The young poet Hedylus, however, from the beginning contemplates escape, not only from his mother, but from the fixed Athenian perfection she represents. In fact, all Hedylus knows of Athens is that it has wounded him, both physically and psychically. As a child he fell on the Acropolis, cutting his head; and he bears a scar of that event, a sign both of his impure, marred beauty and of his impotence to match the intellectual grandeur of Sophocles (20). "Why Sophocles, anyway?" the boy thinks to himself. He feels little affinity with Sophoclean, Periclean totality. Hedylus is and is not Athenian: he is profoundly and irrevocably displaced. In terms of his own poetic motives, it is not, as his mother thinks, that Hedylus wants to *become* an Alexandrian – that is, to follow this latest poetic fashion – but that he *is*, "adequately," Alexandrian (111).

Hedylus concludes with the young poet's decision to "leave with Sikeledes and Posidippus for Alexandria" (116), separating himself from the imperious Athenian standards of his mother, because "it is necessary for the Muse's garland to be rewoven" (34). Likewise, the story "Hipparchia" in *Palimpsest* ends with Hipparchia's decision to go to Alexandria (not Delphi or Athens) with Julia Augusta; for, as a poet in another section of the novel asserts, "the formula [the orders of song] must be re-formulated," especially after the violent devastation of

49

war (155). Both figures, too, find sanction in this choice at the level of their daimonic motive, carried in the figure of Helios/Apollo. In *Hedylus* this figure is represented in the strange visitor, Demion, apparently Hedyle's lover and the father of Hedylus; it is the mysterious Demion/daimon who somehow releases Hedylus to leave for Alexandria. Hipparchia, too, finally recognizes that Helios/Apollo, the god of poets, is also "a god of colonists," a god of the dispossessed (93).

The significance of Alexandria in H.D.'s writing may be further unraveled in contemplating the figure of Meleager as H.D. interprets him.[21] Though he never saw the great Egyptian city, this poet for H.D. is "Meleager of Alexandria" (*Paint It Today* 70). Meleager represents what I would call the "Alexandrian project" of H.D.'s early career: an imagination of textual recovery and transmission. In terms of cultural history Alexandria is a city of heterogeneous texts and artifacts, of scholars and poets gathered in library and museum. And in this respect it is hard not to recall that the London of H.D.'s early years had the British Museum as a crucial focus, its reading room, as well as its galleries of artifacts, and that H.D. knew these places as part of the collaboration of a group of writers. Moreover, the record of H.D.'s early European tours, given in her 1912 Paris diary, in *Paint It Today*, and in *Asphodel*, consists largely of her visits to museums. In a very literal way, then, H.D.'s early European intellectual landscape was a "literary Alexandria," the place of regathered, fragmentary artifacts. Alexandria is the place essentially identified with the legible and the scriptable, with manuscript, palimpsest, marginalia, epitome, compilation, commentary, and anthology: the city of textual recovery and transmission. For H.D. Meleager's anthology represents the consummate instance of preservation and reinscription. His *Garland* indeed *is* Alexandria, the city of fragmentary, numinous script and transcript.

Meleager is profoundly Alexandrian as well in his peculiar historical and cultural context: he is a Greek Jew roughly contemporary with Christ, born in Gadara (where Christ drove demons into swine), continuing a Graeco-Egyptian poetic tradition in the context of Roman domination ("Garland" 1, 4; *Notes on Thought and Vision* 33–7). Meleager thus represents a central aspect of Alexandria; it is, in Jane Pinchin's words, a "city of assimilation" (19) where distinct racial, cultural, and religious currents come together. In this context H.D. appears to vary from what Martin Bernal describes as the "Aryan model" of the Greeks, with its denial of Afro-Asiatic contamination in the imagination of Greece.[22]

In terms of its accessibility to the poet, Alexandria is the *residual* city, where, as in Cavafy, the voices speak from within layers of historical memory. In his writing, mingled with scenes from modern Alexandria are figures from its Syrian, Egyptian, Arabic, and Roman histories, figures caught in the sensual and yet intellectual charm of the city. In Cavafy's poetry, Edmund Keely argues, "Alexandria" comprises this polyphonic and fragmentary testimony of human desire, in which planes of the ancient and the contemporary converge (71). Like other mythically imagined cities – Dante's Florence, Virgil's Rome, Thucydides' Athens – this Alexandria makes claims as a human paradigm, though it reveals, unlike these others, an intimate and erotic underlife, essentially lyric, unheroic, and unmonumental. Alexandria is not simply another ruined city of ancient history, but, for Cavafy, the ruined city of one's own history: "Wherever I turn, wherever I happen to look, / I see the black ruins of my life, here, / where I've spent so many years, wasted them, destroyed them totally." And though one desires escape from this city, "You won't find a new country, won't find another shore. / This city will always pursue you. . . . You will always end up in this city" ("The City" 28). But paradoxically, though it is inescapable (always present), Alexandria is the city that is always being lost, always at the point of oblivion ("The God Abandons Antony" 33).

For H.D., Meleager's syncretism is linked essentially with his eroticism. Indeed, Alexandria, like Babylon and Sodom, is traditionally seen as the erotic or "Sensual City" par excellence (Keely, chap. 3) and Alexandrian eroticism is multivalent. H.D. is fascinated in particular with Meleager's bisexuality, his passionate engagement both with women and with men ("Garland" 2–4). Homoeroticism figures predominantly in Alexandrian poetry as a whole, from the first generation of its founding, with Callimachus and Theocritus, to its incarnations in the twentieth century in the writing of Cavafy, Forster, Durrell, and, most recently, the poet Mark Doty, in *My Alexandria* (1993). As suggested in Doty's volume, Alexandria is clearly a code word in male gay culture. This aspect of its configuration, Richard Jenkyns argues, explains a great deal of its appeal in the late nineteenth century among homosexual poets and writers (281 92).

In Alexandria the sensuality of hellenistic and Roman religion mingles with the spirituality of gnostic and Christian cults. This mixed passion is the aspect of Alexandria preferred in late-nineteenth-century hellenism, especially in popular novels taking hellenistic or Roman settings in order to situate extremes of sensual and spiritual desire. This eroticism is frequently rendered through female figures of hetaeras and priestesses, images with which H.D. clearly identified (both Hipparchia and Hedyle, for instance, are hetaeras). Several of these stories are mentioned in H.D.'s writing: Pierre Louÿs's *Aphrodité*, set in pre-Christian Alexandria, concerning the courtesan Chrysis; Gustave Flaubert's *Salammbô*, set in Carthage of the third century B.C., concerning Salammbô, a pure priestess of the goddess Tanith who falls into sensuality; Edward Bulwer-Lytton's *The Last Days of Pompeii*, set in the first century B.C., featuring Ione, a Greek poet, whose brother, a priest of Isis, is converted to Christianity; Anatole France's *Thaïs*, set in Alexandria of the second century A.D., concerning a courtesan who falls in love with a Christian monk.[23] H.D. is clearly fascinated by the mixed eroticism that these stories dramatize.

The centrality of Alexandria in H.D.'s writing may be suggested by a simple though somewhat occluded fact. H.D. locates "Helen" in this geographical locus – this shore where the river meets the sea, where the island of Proteus/Pharos guards the harbor, where (Strabo says) the ibis gather at every crossing (17.1.6–8). In H.D.'s writing Helen is never immediately located in Greece or in Troy, but only indirectly, through memory or legend. She is proto-Alexandrian, located mythically at the junctures that define historical Alexandria. In H.D.'s poem "Leda," Helen is conceived through Zeus's union with Leda at the boundary "[w]here the slow river / meets the tide" (*Collected Poems* 120). Likewise, in her essay on Euripides' *Helen*, H.D. describes Helen upon an Egyptian shore, where "[t]here are two sounds of water. The sea at lowest tide and the Nile flowing over the sand." Birdlike, such as a daughter of the swan would be, Helen waits near the temple tomb of Proteus by the sea – presumably on the island of Pharos ("Helen in Egypt" 1–2). In her late *Helen in Egypt* H.D. returns to this same landscape. In the opening section, "Pallinode," Helen contemplates her fate within a temple of Amen/Proteus; however, she has her erotic encounter with Achilles on a salt shore, after Isis flies at them in the form of an ibis. Indeed, Achilles as well as Helen is essentially affiliated with this confluent Egyptian territory through his mother, Thetis, a figure of Isis and a female counterpart of the metamorphic Proteus. The narrator in *Helen in Egypt* says that after their encounter Helen and Achilles *"are both occupied with the thought of reconstruction, he 'to re-claim the coast with the Pharos, the light-house,' she to establish or re-establish the ancient Mysteries"* (16–17, 63). With these efforts of recovery and preservation Helen and Achilles are, in a sense, first citizens of Alexandria.

H.D.'s "Alexandria" is the liminal city par excellence, the place and time *between* – between East and West, Troy and Greece; between ancient and modern, Athens and Rome; between body and spirit; between male and female; between intellect and desire; between past and future; between inscription and transcription; between dead and living; between the lost and the recovered. This locus is crucial within H.D.'s imaginative geography of the ancient world as it represents – in relation to "Hellas" – a state of perpetual displacement from origins, of absence and loss, within which one explores to its full limits the power of nostalgia.

Transmission and the Female Line

If the classics, by definition, are those ancient works of "enduring value," remaining to authorize present thought and action, by what means do they survive? Texts of the earliest writers have survived in large part through canonical lists, or *classici*, which probably at crucial points of transmission in part determined those writers considered worth preserving. They also shaped academic curricula and thus dictated the further culling of authors in the creation of "epitomes" (literally "incisions" or cuttings: abridgments or selections) of received learning.[24] Classical survival, then, represents as much a curtailment as a continuance of inherited lines.

Moreover, the survival and authority of the classics are to some extent allied with the needs of political order. What survives and what does not has a great deal to do with its perceived importance to public life and political interests. The first references to the "classic" writer (classicus, "of the highest class") by Cicero and other Latin commentators are borrowed from usage in political and military hierarchy. But the word as we use it, as synonymous with the authority of the ancients, dates from the Renaissance, whose scholars imagined themselves as snatching learning from oblivion.[25] Thus in the Renaissance the "classical" is homologous with "the enduring," and the recovery of ancient texts is thereby a sign of one's participation in the conquest of time.

Classical transmission operates within a seminal (patrilineal/fraternal) order. There are only a few extant women writers from antiquity, and a similar few who have participated as scholars and commentators – as transcribers, translators, transmitters – within the classic line.[26] Indeed, what is the "classic," in rough parlance, but a "seminal text" within literary generation? And if the generator or transmitter (writer/scholar) is imagined as male, operating within a fraternal community of traditional discourse, one might imagine the body of generation – bound to time, chance, error, and material vicissitude – as female.

One recent scholar betrays such a fantasy in defining the pattern of textual transmission "from Antiquity to the end of the Renaissance": "In its crude and essential form it appears to the imagination to follow the traditional lines of the hourglass, . . . or the simplified shape in which the female form is often represented – broad shoulders, tiny waist, full skirt." The scholar elaborates the "vital statistics" of this figure. The top half, representing "[o]ur knowledge of the transmission of texts in Antiquity," is "sketched in hazily or not at all; it disappears thinly into the mists of time, a ghost from the waist up." The bottom half, however, representing scholarly knowledge since A.D. 800, increases in girth until it "billow[s] out into the Renaissance" (Reynolds xiii–xiv). Embracing this "crude and essential" figure, one might say that the modern (post-Renaissance) scholar is in the typical position of male lover/spectator in relation to the icon of woman: he enjoys the diaphanous intimacy of the billowing skirts, representing his own knowledge, while drawn yearningly to the numinous, blurred face, the "ghost from the waist up," the unknown Other. Moreover, the icon of woman as the body of transmission does not signify a female presence within it, no more than the troubadour's narcissistic fixation on the icon of the Lady implies an actual female. It rather implies male proprietorship of the tradition itself and a community of poets within which the icon has accepted significance as the Beloved Other.

After the Renaissance, when the survival of most major classical texts had been relatively assured,[27] transmission increasingly involves translation. If authenticity is crucial within the fiction of textual transmission, marital language of fidelity and betrayal infuses discussions of translation, combined with Pauline overlays (the "letter" and "spirit" of the text), suggesting the sacrosanct domain of classical intercourse, where the marriage of scholar to the body of generation cum Holy Temple is enacted. This temple needs priests or presbyters. Matthew Arnold says in *On Translating Homer* that in fulfilling his charge of fidelity to the text, the translator should address himself to an imagined ideal scholar, a final arbiter of faithfulness, such as, say, the "Provost of Eton" or the Professor of Cambridge or Oxford – for, with a masterful knowledge of Greek combined with consummate literary sensitivity, "he alone knows [Homer] at all" (36, 60).

"To enter the classics," Rachel Blau DuPlessis says, "is to confront the issue of cultural authority, for knowledge of Greek and Latin . . . [has been the] main portal of the liberal humanist hegemony" (*Career* 17). In contemplating H.D.'s place within the fiction of classicism, one immediately encounters the exclusive determinants of a male tradition, access to which is a knowledge of ancient languages, exercised within institutions that authorize certain forms of ritual display – allusion, quotation in the original, mastery of scholarship.[28] How much knowledge is sufficient in order to participate legitimately in classical transmission?

Specifically, how much knowledge, and how displayed, allows a woman, in the gentleman's judgment, to seem more than "a queen who played at classicism," as H.D. imagined Pound's early attitude toward her (*Hermione* 172). The question of "knowing or not knowing Greek" surfaces continually with regard to H.D. "How much Greek did she know?" I have been consistently asked by scholars, colleagues, and students, as though an accurate answer to this question would resolve the issue of H.D.'s pretensions to legitimacy, as though, indeed, it were *the* question with regard to H.D. and classicism. The corollary remark to this question is often that "Pound [or Aldington, or X] clearly knew Greek better than she." This question of H.D.'s specialized knowledge, in other words, is bound to the spirit of gentlemen's competitive games, a model deeply implicated in the display of classical learning.

But the question of "knowing Greek" is a very ambiguous and loaded one, presuming as it does some tangible key to authority. How much is "enough," and how much is "more" or "less" – and by whose standards? Certainly by professional classicists' standards, or by the standards of British public school education at the turn of the century, H.D.'s knowledge of classical languages was not profound – nor, indeed, was that of Pound or Aldington or of any of the writers who contributed to the Poets' Translation Series. H.D. studied Latin formally in high school and at Bryn Mawr, and she studied Greek independently beginning in her high school years and throughout her early years in Europe.[29]

She never had, and never aspired to, any but an amateur knowledge of these languages. A study of the extant books of her library housed at Yale indicates that she apparently translated with no little effort, using standard German editions (with Latin translations, notes, and commentary), with the consistent help of dictionaries and with the mediation of French and English translations. H.D. told Thomas Swann in a letter late in her life, "Yes, I read a very little Greek and what possible translations there were" (Swann 10).

That H.D. considered herself an amateur is not to say, however, that she did not have considerable knowledge of primary and secondary sources. Her intimacy and complex interplay with texts have been obscured in criticism of her work for several reasons, not the least of which is the unreflective dismissal of the pretensions of the "poetess." H.D. was habitually self-effacing in public contexts about her own efforts – though, as her autobiographical fictions make clear, privately self-assured, if not arrogant, about her particular gifts. Moreover, H.D. was deferential to those with whom she shared her poetic ambitions, giving tributes to many male associates as her intellectual guides, and, as a result, critics credit any mark of her knowledge or sophistication to others.

H.D.'s generosity toward the gifts of others is connected with another misleading aspect of her literary interaction with the classics: that she does not join in the gentlemen's game of pyrotechnic display. She frequently disguises allusion to her sources, because in her conception of her poetic role, this privileged knowledge (traditionally set apart by signs of status) must be made common knowledge in order to work as it should. It may, indeed, have been Pound or Harriet Monroe, not H.D., who entitled her earliest published poems "Verses, Translations and Reflections from 'The Anthology'" and who, in particular, named the poems themselves "Hermes of the Ways," "Priapus, Keeper of Orchards" (consistently referred to by H.D. as "Orchard"), and "Epigram: After the Greek" (never later collected by H.D.).[30] These titles represent the kind of fussy erudition much loved by Aldington and by Pound in his early career, but never preferred by H.D. She had very little to do with marketing her erudition.

The question of a woman's "knowing Greek," as R. Fowler has shown, has always haunted women with pretensions to "letters." But the Provost's assessment of this knowledge, for women at any point on a sliding scale of expectations, will be correspondingly negative. Virginia Woolf negotiates the question wisely – arguing that "it is vain and foolish to talk of Knowing Greek," because no one can really know it with sufficient intimacy ("Not Knowing" 24). But behind this rhetorical assertion is the fact of her exclusion from the ranks of those who could even pretend to know it.[31] And along with ignorance of Greek come other "feminine" deficiencies. "Unlike her fellow-pioneers . . . she did not know Greek well; her judgment was erratic, and . . . she made many errors," the classicist Hugh Lloyd-Jones says of Jane Ellen Harrison, the leader of the

Cambridge anthropologists (202). In his study of classical transmission in the nineteenth and twentieth centuries, Lloyd-Jones omits Harrison from the lineage of twenty-five male scholars, though including Gilbert Murray, who popularized and diluted her ideas.[32] In the same way Eliot, in his brief mention of H.D.'s translations from Euripides in the context of a discussion of Murray, disparages H.D.'s seriousness as a scholar – "allowing for errors and even occasional omission of difficult passages" – while praising the effect of her translation (*Selected Essays* 50).

Douglas Bush stands firmly within this gentlemanly tradition of evaluation. In his analysis of her translations, he faults H.D. for violating the letter of the text, in misconstruing, altering, adding to, overemotionalizing, modernizing the original, and for violating the spirit of the text, in making Euripides a modern [woman] imagist (497–501). When these criteria of authenticity are applied to the larger body of H.D.'s lyric poetry, one senses the more visceral partiality traditionally associated with the learned schools. What Bush really faults is "the feminine" – associated implicitly with the trivial, precious, overinflated, turbid, narcissistic. He finds in the lyrics "pictures and emotional symbols, the 'Greek' world of the feminine eye and the feminine heart." These, though lovely, are insubstantial: "[W]hat is one to say of a kind of beauty which vanishes the moment one's eye leaves the page?" They are likewise shallow: "H.D.'s clear bright light plays over surfaces, it seldom strikes into the depths" (501–2). Unlike the male organ of sight, the "feminine eye" does not master; it does not penetrate. And the "feminine heart" – unlike the masculine seat of courage and spirit – does not engage in decent public intercourse; rather it dissipates itself in the repetitive theme of love, "the love that is woman's whole existence" (502). One notes as well his association of the feminine with the ephemeral. For Bush, a "kind of beauty that vanishes" – that disappears elusively in the peripheral vision of the diverted eye, or that refuses to monumentalize or stabilize its meanings – is unworthy of comment.

H.D. unquestionably recognized what she was up against in entering, even as an amateur, the domain of traditional classicism. She certainly understood herself to be engaged in the "survival of the classics"; she had real ambitions as a translator. Such a motive is clear enough in the Poets' Translation Series, with which she assisted her husband in 1915–16 and again in 1918–19, and to which she contributed translations of Euripides.[33] It is clear as well in her fictional rehearsals of her early career, particularly in *Palimpsest*, *Asphodel*, and *Bid Me to Live*, in which H.D. renders the seriousness of her early engagement in translation: "She was self-effacing in her attack on those Greek words, she was flamboyantly ambitious" (*Bid Me to Live* 162). Her aspirations as an amateur in classical precincts are shown as well in a series of essays on Greek writers somewhat in the manner of Pater's *Greek Studies* (written 1919–25), which she made some effort to have published.

As H.D. consciously shaped her role in the survival of the classics, however, she envisioned it as clearly marginal to the life of letters as traditionally conceived and practiced, even by her fellow imagist rebels, with their scorn for traditional scholarship. She saw her role in terms of a subversive, erotic, and visionary endeavor fundamentally challenging the assumptions of classical transmission; or, in Pater's terms, she saw herself as speaking from the "centrifugal" margins, against the Germanic dominance of classical learning:

> The mind, in its effort to disregard the truth, has built up through the centuries, a mass of polyglot literature explanatory of Grecian myth and culture.
> But the time has come for men and women of intelligence to build up a new standard, a new approach to Hellenic literature and art.
> Let daemons possess us! Let us terrify like Erynnes [sic], the whole tribe of academic Grecians!
> Because (I state it inspired and calm and daemonaical) they know nothing! ("Helios and Athene," *Collected Poems* 328)

In these words, from a short prose piece written in 1920 during her first voyage to Greece, H.D. refers specifically to the scholars whose *Wissenschaft* diverts attention from the essential, who oversee and sabotage the transmission of Greek texts. She fully understood the violent discontinuities within classical transmission, coming in part from political and religious biases: the gradual removal, even deliberate destruction, of manuscripts (lyric/erotic poetry) thought to be indecent or heretical, the haunting loss of all but a few poems and fragments from what appear to have been vital female poetic traditions ("Garland" 5–8). As DuPlessis has argued, H.D. deliberately affiliated herself with just this broken and largely irrecoverable line of transmission (*Career* 17–30).

In this allusion to the Furies, H.D. imagines an ancient, forgotten power, avenging transgressions by the "tribe of academic Grecians." What are the congenital crimes of this tribe? A Penthean blindness to the ecstatic is only part of its problem. A more fundamental sin is economic and, implicitly, spiritual – a false imagination of possession. In one of H.D.'s novels drawn from her early years as a poet, *Bid Me to Live*, a young poet-translator comments: "Anyone can translate the meaning of a word. She wanted the shape, the feel of it, the character of it, as if it had been freshly minted. She felt that the old manner of approach was as toward hoarded treasure, but treasure that had passed through too many hands, had been too carefully assessed by the grammarians" (163). In this metaphor the ancient words are coins too long fingered and handled, weighed and counted, by their tutelary possessors, so that the imprint has become vague and dull. Authoritative transmission, though preserving them, has taken them out of circulation, confining them to the meticulous brokers. The crime of the academy is a kind of greed within an imagination of proprietorship.

Reminting words puts them into free circulation once more, though, to the hoarders, this act is no less than counterfeiting.

As Morris has argued, H.D. returns throughout her career to issues of economy – the vision of commodities dominating Western thought in contrast to the sense of a "gift economy" emphasizing not possession but circulation of goods in a community of exchange ("A Relay of Power"). H.D. understood the act of translation in this sense – not, as the Provost would have it, a bartering of word for word before a tribunal of literary guardians, but rather a reciprocation and tribute to the word's original gift. H.D.'s stance in regard to tradition, influence, and transmission, though revisionary and even vengeful, is also generous in its commitment to common circulation within a spiritual economy.

This sense of transmission is commonly configured in H.D.'s writing as a matrilineal one, and it is not without its peculiar torture and bewilderment for the female poet. An autobiographical rendering of gift exchange within the generational line occurs in *The Gift* (written 1941), where H.D. the poet receives her inspiration from the imagined child, Hilda, who comes to understand her artistic and visionary gift as inherited from her mother and grandmother. In terms of classical transmission H.D. much earlier in her career imagined continuities and complexities within a female line (DuPlessis *Career* 18–26). Clearly for H.D. "Sappho" is the begetter of the classical line of erotic poetry. However, though many critics have pointed to H.D.'s literary engagements with Sappho, one should emphasize, in the context of transmission, that H.D. avoided any but prose transliterations of Sappho. In her adaptations of Sapphic fragments, even the quoted fragment heading each of the poems is always from W. H. Wharton's translation.[34] For H.D. a direct female transmission from Sappho is highly problematic.

H.D. delineates the "distaff" or "sinister" side obliquely, as DuPlessis has suggested (*Career* 18). H.D. points to the "feminine" character of Euripides (*Notes on Thought and Vision* 32). She emphasizes that Meleager's *Garland* – a nexus of classical lyric transmission – begins "with the names of women" ("Garland" 6). Moreover, she may have understood Meleager himself in terms of a distaff descent, as this thought is suggested in F. A. Wright's *Poets of the Greek Anthology*, the source work for H.D.'s essay on Meleager as well as for details of hellenistic history incorporated into fictional narratives.[35] Wright emphasizes that Meleager was born of a Jewish mother, who bequeathed to him the "Eastern fervour of her imagination," And, he says, "[i]t is from his mother that his unique gifts come."[36] Wright in fact imagines an early imaginative symbiosis between child and mother, "the child roaming by his mother's side through the meadows about the town, gay with wild lilies, yellow and white" (*Poets* 124).

The complexity of transmission is emphasized as well in two narratives of the twenties set in hellenistic times, *Hedylus* and "Hipparchia" (in *Palimpsest*), whose leading characters, as we have seen, are each engaged in a scholarly as well as poetic task of classical transmission. Moreover, both write in a crucial, transitional time of literary transmission, when the preservation of texts depends upon their activity, in each case made possible by patronage. Hedylus is in the literary circle surrounding the ruler and historian Douris of Samos (300 B.C.), after the conquest of Greek cities by Philip and Alexander of Macedon. During the lifetime of Hedylus, hellenic literary activity shifts from Athens to Alexandria. Hipparchia lives in preimperialistic Rome (75 B.C.), after the Roman subjugation of Greece and Egypt. She is affiliated with exiled Greeks who have access to the significant library of Greek manuscripts gathered by the Consul Lucullus,[37] and she is engaged in the translation of Greek texts into Latin.

These imaginative projections of ancient life are in fact fascinating meditations on the complexity of matrilineal transmission. In *Hedylus* the central character, Hedylus, represents an actual poet in the Alexandrian school (early third century B.C.), the son of another actual poet, Hedyle, whose mother, Moschine, in turn was also a poet. In *Palimpsest* the young poet Hipparchia is imagined as the daughter of a historical figure, the Greek Cynic philosopher Hipparchia. The young Hipparchia's most intimate male companion in the story is her uncle, Philip, a rival of Theophrastus engaged in a botanical catalogue of flowers. But Philip is imagined within a complex genealogy in which patrilineal descent is blurred by assimilation into psychic matrilineality. Philip is her "father's younger brother," whom she calls at one point her "young foster-father" (10). He is so young in fact that he serves effectively as a brother to her, but he "might have been a sort of son even to young Hipparchia" (14). From the many accounts of the lives of ancient poets, H.D. is drawn to these complex familial configurations not only, as critics have pointed out, as a mirror of her own familial and erotic complexes, but also as a meditation on distaff transmission – transmission not as legitimate patrimony (Hedylus is illegitimate) or as proprietary exchange among guardians (Hipparchia is a Greek slave among Romans), but as a circulation of gifts between the dead and the living.

The story "Hipparchia" from *Palimpsest* renders imaginatively through its main character H.D.'s conception of her own activities – as scholar, poet, translator – within classical transmission. The psychological dimension of female transmission as rendered in this story – the relation of Hipparchia to her philosopher-mother – has been perceptively explored by Deborah Kelly Kloepfer and Susan Friedman.[38] In the context of this study, however, I will rather emphasize the specific conception of historical transmission and poetic transmutation rendered here.

The story contains continuous references to historical events, specifically to the events of many different wars, interwoven with the citation of Hipparchia's translations of actual Greek poetry. The complexity of the historical and literary textuality in "Hipparchia" is suggested by the following chronological mapping of texts and events alluded to and implied in the story:

ca. 75 B.C.: Present time: Hipparchia in "War Rome," in the Third Mithridatic War

ca. 76–75 B.C.: Hipparchia captured and her uncle, Philip, killed in Roman incursions into Macedonia preceding the Third Mithridatic War

fl. 75 B.C.: Meleager of Gadara, *Garland*[39]

80 B.C.: Alexandria officially put under Roman jurisdiction

86 B.C.: Athens conquered and plundered by Romans in the First Mithridatic War, the Piraeus destroyed

fl. 110 B.C.: Antipater of Sidon in Rome, author of epigrams, "Where, Corinth, charm incarnate" (fall of Corinth) and "I cast my lot with cynics" (Hipparchia)

146 B.C.: The brutal destruction of Corinth by Rome after the defeat of the Achaean League; the razing of Carthage by Rome

fl. 250 B.C.: Moero of Byzantium flourishes; two lyrics collected in Meleager's *Garland*

332 B.C.: Alexander founds Alexandria

336 B.C.: The brutal destruction of Thebes by Alexander after a rebellion

338 B.C.: Athens and Thebes fall to Philip of Macedon

ca. 345–325 B.C.: The Cynic philosopher Crates of Thebes and his wife, Hipparchia, flourish; Hipparchia knows Philip of Macedon; Crates entertains Alexander of Macedon

ca. 335–300 B.C.: Theophrastus, *Inquiry into Plants*; Theophrastus in Athens, student of Plato and Aristotle, successor to Aristotle at the Peripatos; Hipparchia's brother studies with him

404 B.C.: Athens defeated by Sparta in the Peloponnesian War

425 B.C.: Euripides, *Hecuba*, about the aftermath of the fall of Troy

480 B.C.: Athens taken and the Acropolis destroyed by invading Persians

ca. 800–750 B.C.: Homer, *Iliad* and *Odyssey*, about the fall of Troy to Greeks and its aftermath

ca. 1200 B.C.: Troy falls

As this chronology suggests, the narrative alludes to a long history of wars, devastations, dispersals – and particularly a sequence of repercussive falls of cities in Greek history. Clearly this layering of wars gives a simulacrum of the palimpsest in the title of the novel as a whole.

In exploring this scribal trope in relation to war, one might note, H.D. is far from arcane and idiosyncratic. Rather, she seems remarkably faithful to the European experience of World War I. Here are remarks, entitled "The Palimpsest of War," from an anonymous correspondent in the London *Times* for 17 April 1915, in the midst of the disastrous Gallipoli campaign:

Graved and scored with characters through all recorded time, [the map of Europe] is being graved and scored once more, by a pen of iron and with ink of blood, in characters that seem indelible. . . . Are our hearts, then, also palimpsests, like the earth on which we dwell? Are our minds the same abiding stuff, on which a God who is only a God of battles eternally writes his crimson script, only erasing the message of one age to write it in the next with a direr pen, dipped still more deep, a message still more charged with the ancient woe? (9, cols. 4–5)

This recurrently reengraved map, appearing day after day in European newspapers, is an image from the early days of the war in the Dardanelles, "in that odd spring [1915], never to come again," as Hermione remarks in *Asphodel*. It is the icon that Hermione regards during the disastrous last interview with her husband: "map of the Balkans, difficulties, marked off in dark lines, cut into dark thick lines, political, meaning nothing . . . and the map was a map of Greece, all distorted by political black lines and dotted lines" (200).

In this context of the ravaged map of Greece, simultaneously a palimpsest of the heart, H.D.'s autobiographical narratives take place. "Hipparchia" is a survivor's story, though Hipparchia is the survivor not of a single war but of a chain of catastrophes spanning centuries. The task of transmission is defined in the context of this network of destructions. Within this radically foreshortened and palimpsestic conception of the past, poetic transmission takes on a haunting, ghostly character; the dead have daimonic, hallucinatory presence within the dispersion and fevered disorientation of the present. The poet is the medium of spiritual exchange and, as well, a kind of Hermes at the boundary of the underworld.

As the historical mapping should also make clear, "Hipparchia" is based on a glaring chronological inconsistency. The young poet of the story is a Greek woman captured in Macedonia by Roman soldiers making incursions there in a war against the armies of Mithridates, immediately before the Third Mithridatic War (75–65 B.C.); young Hipparchia is presently in "War Rome (circa 75 B.C.)," and her Roman lover, Marius, under the command of Lucullus, becomes engaged in the fighting.[40] However, Hipparchia herself claims to be the daughter of the Cynic Crates and of his follower and wife, Hipparchia.[41] But the historical Hipparchia flourished (along with Crates) in the late fourth century B.C.[42] Thus, in terms of chronology, a gap of about two and a half centuries separates mother and daughter (75–325 B.C.).[43]

Adding to this chronological complexity, the Hipparchia of the story seems to place her mother and her uncle, Philip, within the period immediately following the late Macedonian empire, which ended with the fall of Corinth to the Romans in 146 B.C.[44] In other words, the elder Hipparchia is imagined to be roughly contemporary with Antipater of Sidon (flourishing in Rome around 130–110 B.C.), whose epigrams on the historical Hipparchia and on the fall of Corinth (*Palatine Anthology* 7.413, 9.151) are translated in this story by the young Hipparchia.

These inconsistencies may simply be mistakes on H.D.'s part. But if they are, they are all the more incongruous because the narrative itself calls attention to historical contexts and to historical writing. H.D. studied Greek and Roman historians,[45] and in establishing the historical context of "Hipparchia" she certainly draws upon Diogenes Laertius and Plutarch, and perhaps also upon Pausanias, Appian, and Arrian.[46] Hipparchia is herself a scholar – not only a poet but a historian, a bibliophile, and a compiler. She is engaged in "revising certain lives of writers, poets" from the Greek past (91). She possesses manuscripts of an "unfinished history of the Macedonian conquest" (34, 91) that the young historian Julia Augusta comes to seek at the end of the story. She also has many poetic manuscripts, including some of the "new Alexandrians" (77, 34), perhaps, indeed, Meleager's *Garland* itself, since Hipparchia is translating Moero, an early hellenistic poet (third century B.C.) included in his anthology.

With all the emphasis in the story upon history and the clear distinction between present and past – for instance, the contemporary Roman wars of the first century B.C. with the Macedonian conquest of Greece in the fourth century B.C. – it seems strange to encounter historical confusion in Hipparchia's own lineage. One might surmise, indeed, that the narrative represents H.D. as author, like Hipparchia, in the process of "revising certain lives of writers" according to esoteric correspondences. The link between the two Hipparchias is (in the fiction of the story) memorially and psychologically "real" but nevertheless impossible according to an ordinary conception of time and history. Through this fiction of matrilineal descent, H.D. has deliberately conflated three eras of the hellenistic world, each predicated on the subjugation of Greece – Philip and Alexander's conquest in the fourth century B.C. (the destruction of Thebes); superimposed upon it, the Roman conquest in the second century B.C. (the destruction of Corinth); and, finally, the exploitation of Greek language and art in the present Rome of young Hipparchia.

These superpositions occur as well *within* Hipparchia on the level of memory. Details from her remembered past are mingled and transposed with details of her mother's legendary story: that young Hipparchia is with her uncle, Philip, in Macedon at the time of her capture (ca. 76 B.C.) and that the elder Hipparchia once entertained Philip of Macedon (ca. 330 B.C.); that the young Hipparchia and Philip follow the work of Theophrastus, as did the brother of the historical Hipparchia. At least two epochs and two histories inhabit Hipparchia simultaneously. When she looks far in the past to remember the moment of Philip's death in the fields of Macedon when the Romans suddenly attacked, she takes on the vision of her mother more than two centuries earlier foreseeing the coming of the Roman barbarians in the distant future: "Far and far and far like some prophesying sound apprehended in a trance, she had heard bugles, . . . Far and far and far as in some Pythian trance (presaging future happenings) Hipparchia had heard . . . the odd speech that presently accosted her" (70).

If indeed Hipparchia cannot be the daughter of a mother more than two centuries dead, who or what is she? Might she be a ghost or revenant or fury coming from the past with a diabolical enchantment, a "Phantom," as Marius accuses her of being?

> What proof, he asked himself, had he that Hipparchia was Hipparchia the daughter of Crates, the cynic, and of his wife the woman of whom . . . Antipater the late Roman favourite had once written, . . . Why hadn't Olivia told him, as was most obvious, that Hipparchia was simply that lost Hipparchia who took "the beggar's stick," . . . Phantom. Wraith. . . . Hipparchia was simply that Hipparchia. . . . Involving him, of all people, with death and with illusion. (15–16)

She may indeed be, as Marius says, "one risen from the very realms of Acheron" (31). Hipparchia herself seems to confirm this possibility later: "She was a dear phantom and another one had come to reinstate her Iu the realm of the Acheron. Osiris in Acheron" (84).

This ghostly foreshortening of time and this confusion of occurrences from one generation to another makes of classical history an attenuated memory, subject to the same lapses and substitutions as personal memory and dream. One can remember in vision what one has never experienced, as Mamalie in *The Gift* remembers episodes involving the Moravians on Wunden Eiland occurring generations in the past. In this novel, as in *The Gift*, H.D. foregrounds the figure of the poet, who works within this palimpsestic sense of history to render condensations of personal and cultural memory. Indeed, the prominence of textual and poetic transmission in "Hipparchia" points to the crucial role of texts in actually constituting history.

It would appear, for instance, that Hipparchia's mother is actually not a woman but a text – Antipater's poem commemorating the dead Hipparchia. Young Hipparchia obsessively reiterates this poem in place of any palpable, concretely affective memory of her mother. In the whole of the narrative there are no details of the mother's appearance, no images or words given to her, other than those of Antipater's poem. Hipparchia loves and battles with the presence signified in the poem, its absolute and arrogant assertions: "*I cast my lot with cynics, not / with women seated at the distaff, . . . I kept no tunic with bright gem, / nor shoes the Asiatics wear, / nor the myrrh-scented diadem*" (8). She battles with the concomitant absence evoked through the poem – the mother's gesture of renunciation, which means, for the daughter, abandonment. She battles as well with the mother's flamboyant heroic challenge: that she possesses a Wisdom whose "*fame exceeds . . . Atalanta's*" (15).

But besides the absence of the body of the mother in memory, the story suggests yet another level of aggravated absence: Antipater's poem on Hipparchia, a memorial epigram, is itself predicated upon absence, defined not only by death but by a temporal void of almost two centuries. Moreover, young Hipparchia locates this evanescent maternal *eidolon* in the context of another poetic evocation of the dead, Antipater's epigram on the destruction of Corinth, "*Where, Corinth, charm incarnate, are your shrines?*" signaling the final loss of the Greek world to the Romans: "*War wreaked on you his hideous ravishment, / we, we alone, Neriads inviolate, / remain to weep, . . . Corinth is lost, Corinth is desolate*" (5).

One increasingly understands the profundity of this loss as Hipparchia, caught in betrayal, erotic mésalliance, and finally illness, is feverishly exposed to the power of the dead. These losses – of the mother, of the city – are wounds repeatedly opened. And they are somehow summarized in the vividly remembered image of the death of her beloved uncle/brother/lover, Philip, by a Roman arrow. Hipparchia is transfixed and twinned with Philip in his moment of sudden death. In understanding this twinship in death, one is compelled, as with the hyacinth flower, to "[read] across [the] wide brow the letters of allusion" (12). Both Hipparchia and Philip are like Apollo's doomed lover, Hyacinth, and like the Niobids, all youths fatally wounded by Apollo.[47] The Niobids, in particular, are wounded, as is Philip, by arrows: "She saw the arrow that exactly pinned him and his arms flung outward and the very spray of the wild flower he had stooped to gather. The arms were widespread, the head back bent. O vanquished Niobid. Philip. Philip" (70). Hipparchia too is a "vanquished Niobid" (29, 56), and her identity with Philip signals the sexual ambiguity already present in the myths – the homoeroticism of the Hyacinth figure, the brother/sister equivalence in the Niobe story.[48] On another level it suggests the incestuous and spiritual completion she desires, "intimacy without intercourse" (67). To Marius, gazing upon her as she sleeps, Hipparchia seems at once boy and girl: "Was she, . . . about to run the gamut of those children of proud Niobe? Was she patently beneath his eyes to become sister to herself and brother and changing and interchanging brother, sister, ringing the changes" (30).

Moreover, Hipparchia's twinship with Philip as "victim of the sun-god" (29) indicates that loss in its many catastrophic layers is imagined as a wound of vision, a wound to the clairvoyant eye and intellect, belonging especially to those too intimate with Apollo/Helios. Echoing this image, in *Hedylus* both Sikeledes and Hedylus bear the scar of Helios on the forehead (29, 39) – representing both a gift from and a betrayal by the god of vision. Hipparchia's transmission of ancient texts into the present – like Cassandra's unheeded witness – occurs as an exercise of a visionary gift within a bitterness that includes the experience of betrayal, the betrayal not only of human lovers, but of the god himself.

As a clairvoyant of Helios, Hipparchia is an inspired translator. She receives and transmits ancient Greek texts in abrupt and intense snatches, with always imperfect but inspired correlation with the original. Words come to her – "written in authentic metre in the air above me" (79) – as do the voices and images of the dead Hipparchia and Philip. "She saw her Greek poets as images not as intellects," and her art as translator is to convey that ghostly *eidolon* of the dead poet, guided by a mind "so diabolic in its cunning that long dead poems could yet remake a universe" (73). In this interchange with the dead, as in her visionary exchange with her ghostly mother, Hipparchia is a conduit in the circulation of spirit.

The poems translated by Hipparchia suggest a line of transmission at once textual and spiritual, and that transmission takes place in the context of destruction. In her act of translation she contributes to an already complex palimpsest of poetic response spanning eight centuries, beginning with the Trojan War and its dispersal of peoples. In fact, the line of transmission suggested in Hipparchia's translations coincides with a sequence of cities destroyed through war but surviving through the testimony of poetic texts.

The line of those cities might be drawn like this, in order from present to archaic past: Rome – Alexandria – Corinth – Thebes - Athens – Troy. The present Roman city at war receives as slaves the dispersed scholars and poets from destroyed or conquered cities. Lucullus patronizes these exiles and gives them access to manuscripts. Hipparchia translates Moero of Byzantium from the third century B.C., whose poetry undoubtedly comes through conquered Alexandria to Rome, surviving through the witness of something like Meleager's *Garland*. Hipparchia also translates epigrams from Antipater of Sidon, who lived in Rome but represented the poetic inheritance of Greek Alexandria and who bears witness in his poem to the final destruction of the Greek world in the conquest of Corinth. Hipparchia also renders Antipater's epigram on the historical Hipparchia, who with her husband, Crates, chose a life of homelessness during the time when ancient Greece was finally lost to Macedonia, in the brutal destruction of Thebes first by Philip and then by Alexander (Diogenes 6.93). Finally, the poet Hipparchia translates from the choruses of the Euripidean plays *Hecuba*, *Hippolytus*, and *Helen*, plays contemporary with the Athenian wars of the fifth century B.C. *Hecuba* in particular recalls Homer in the depiction of a mother's mourning for lost Troy and the desolate homelessness of the dispossessed.

These poetic translations carry with them in the narrative something of the miracle of their survival through time and of their somewhat accidental transmission to the poet through intermediaries. Poems, manuscripts, and "letters" belong in Hipparchia's mind to the ephemeral but timeless realm of flowers, associated with Philip, gathering flowers in the meadow; with anthologies, gatherings of flower/poems; with the hyacinth, carrying in its "mysterious script" the sign of the duplicitous love of the god: "Manuscript, manuscript. Letters written on the leaf" (81). It is no accident that both Hipparchia and Philip seek to rival the botanist Theophrastus, whose name means "marked by god."

H.D.'s conception of the realm of letters stands outside the ordinary notion of literary properties and exchange, based on mastery of information, acquisition and possession of knowledge. In *Hermione*, Hermione says to her erudite mentor and fiancé: "'George, I am so unlettered.' She used the word advisedly wondering if he could possibly not know she was thinking of the lettered hyacinth" (172). But her lover, though learned, is surprisingly ignorant of her allusion to Theocritus.[49] The significance of "letters" here suggests the subtlety of H.D.'s sense of her role in classical transmission. To be lettered is not, as Eliot would have it, to be conscribed by the tradition, but rather to be marked by the god: it is this mark for which the young poet longs, for all its painful potential. And likewise, for H.D., the poetic activities of transmission involve an awareness of violence and suffering within the classical line and a clairvoyant apprehension of ghostly letters and images incising the mind.

Touring with Father: H.D. and Pausanias

When H.D. extravagantly pits herself as Fury against the "whole tribe of Academic Grecians," she engages in a complex battle – not only institutional or official but also quite intimate. In traversing the domain of the classical world, one's scholarly guide or chaperon is likely to be a paternal gentleman sounding very like father or grandfather. H.D. made many such scholarly journeys through classical lands, guided by ancient writers like Herodotus, Strabo, and Pausanias; by Victorian humanists like John Addington Symonds and F. A. Wright; by scientifically oriented classicists like Gilbert Murray and Lewis Richard Farnell; by Sigmund Freud, himself a guide to his miniature museum of Mediterranean antiquities and a Pausanias of the psyche. Baedeker in hand, she also made literal journeys to these lands accompanied by distinguished gentlemen: in 1912 in Italy with her father, Charles Doolittle, during her early intimacy with Richard Aldington; in 1920 in Greece with Havelock Ellis, during her early intimacy with Bryher; in 1932 on a hellenic cruise with her daughter, Perdita, guided intellectually, if not by the provost of Eton, then by the canon of Malta and the dean of St. Paul's.[50] Despite her matrilinear model of classical transmission, and despite her erotic and poetic rebelliousness, H.D. has habitual awe for scholarly paternal authorities, for their intelligence, their breadth of learning, their impersonality. Herself unscholarly, she nevertheless took her scholars very seriously.

In her essays, fiction, and letters, H.D. reveals considerable struggle with an internal, authoritative censor-editor who would dismiss her writing as trivial, inconsequential, and illegitimate. An early typescript draft of her *Notes on Thought and Vision*,[51] written in 1919 with Ellis as an imagined interlocutor, reveals that one portion, entitled "Conversation," originated as a dialogue with someone – sounding much like Aldington – hostile to and contemptuous of her ideas. In a segment of the text marked out in pencil, the "I" of the essay addresses "you" in an imaginary dialogue:

I have been trying to tell you about it. I have wrought from myself an image that can easily be turned to ridicule – the jelly fish I mean, I have plodded along wearily excavating, digging out sentences or thoughts. . . . I tell you I have been endeavoring to phrase my answer for some time. I began this talk with you by saying that the body corresponds to the limbs of a tree – to the branches of a fruit tree –

At this point the interlocutor interrupts with disgust: "For heavens sake be human for once – keep away from jellyfish and fruit-trees" (TS 57–8). In the course of this omitted dialogue the interlocutor charges the "I" of the essay with pretentiousness and arrogance, preciosity, obscurity, and banality. This other voice concludes with a patronizing remark to the charming [female] pretender: "I don't understand a bit what you'r [sic] talking about. But my dear poet, you speak eloquently about this and with uncommon charm and I like to hear you talk even when you talk about nothing at all and almost thou persuadest me to be a poet" (TS 60). H.D.'s conscious formulation of this dialogue indicates a fairly accurate awareness of adversarial voices, not merely literal (biographical) but imaginary.

However, other early instances of this internal dialogue – particularly in "Notes on Euripides, Pausanius, and Greek Lyric Poets" – are sometimes raw and unresolved. This unpublished typescript, composed of fourteen essays, was probably begun in 1920 during a trip with Bryher to California, after the birth of H.D.'s child, the breakup of her marriage, and her trip to Greece with Bryher and Havelock Ellis. She wrote at least some of the five essays on Pausanias in California, and probably also the essays on Sappho, Anacreon, and Theocritus. The essay on Meleager and the four essays on Euripides (including consideration of the *Helen*, the *Ion*, and the *Bacchae*) were written at undetermined times.[52] Upon her return to England H.D. made some efforts to place the "Notes" as a complete manuscript.[53]

Why did H.D. write these Greek essays? What did she hope to accomplish? Does she imagine herself doing "criticism," or prose-poetry, or lyrical meditations after the style of Pater or Wilde? Who is her imagined audience – the young Bryher, the "isolate and adolescent soul" to whom she refers at one point ("Pausanius" 5), an initiate whom she addresses as wiser mystagogue; or the amateur hellenist of the prewar literary journals; or the professional humanist, like Ellis? Why did she choose these authors and works for comment? Does the selection reflect design, or arbitrariness? Her ambivalence about this literary effort reveals itself throughout as an overt or covert dialogue between a knowing scholar-guide and a meditative poet-hierophant.

Indeed, it is difficult to approach the essays without first acknowledging the prominence of this conversation, which often makes its turns suddenly, not only from passage to passage but from sentence to sentence. This conflict may explain some of the peculiarities of tone in the essays, a sometimes odd colloquial breeziness in the essay-paraphrase of the *Bacchae*; or a recurrent defensiveness, such as that in the essay on Anacreon ("I am not fleeing for sanctuary across dead lintels of the past" [3]). Many of the essays in "Notes on Euripides" are constituted by the evocation of scholarly authority against which another voice rebels in daydream, romance, and free association.

In embarking on a series of essays on Greek subjects, H.D. follows a line of prestigious humanists like Arnold, Pater, Symonds, F. A. Wright, Andrew Lang, J. A. Mackail, even Ellis himself. Inevitably, then, she puts herself in danger from the censor. That this writing pretends to be no more than "notes," rather than essays, shows his first trace, and his authority surfaces continually as a viewpoint to take into account, as evidence to be admitted or avoided, as disdainful dismissal, as a stolid presence that banishes children from the library and to the playground.

H.D.'s essay on Euripides' *Helen* strikingly illustrates these tensions. Indeed, it is reasonable to claim that Euripides here serves as a poetic double to H.D. and that her judgments of his work serve as a mirror of her conflicted self-evaluation. After beginning with an articulate and compelling narrative projecting the opening of the play in visual terms, the poet-essayist pulls back from her daydream:

> Perhaps in the opening of this study of Helen, I have been carried away too much by my own imagination, been unbalanced, intoxicated a little with my own idea, my own game, my toy, my discovery that the lines of this Greek poet . . . are to-day as vivid and as fresh as they ever were, but vivid and fresh not as literature . . . but as portals, as windows, as portholes. . . . These words are to me portals, gates. (8–9)

The initial apology for excess slides in the very course of a sentence into another enthusiastic trope; self-depreciation ("my own game, my toy") careens surprisingly into affirmation ("my discovery"). But this extravagance in turn immediately brings to mind the critic, in the sentence following the passage above: "I know that we need scholars to decipher and interpret the Greek, but we also need poets and mystics and children to re-discover this Hellenic world, to see *through* the words" (9).

For a few more pages the poet-essayist follows the path of poetic evocation. But then in the last portion of the essay the scholar-censor gains control, parroting then-current critical authorities (probably A. W. Verrall and Gilbert Murray):[54]

> It is true as critics assert, this play, one of the poet's worst, is full of artificialities, is cold in tone, is meaningless. It is this, but through all the tedious dialogue, through the crude mechanism of discovery and

recognition, through the trite and appallingly dull repetitions, Helen the Helen of the world of poetic reality remains the same, remote, electric, white, smiling, goddess, bird. The story is silly, wilful almost, as if the poet mocked himself. But what does it matter? Helen is there – she is standing on the shore. (12–13)

The one who finds Helen vivid and compelling must bow to the one who sees the play as bad art, meaningless and trivial. The poet must willfully assert the evocative power of the text – the words as gates to vision – while consenting to the nullification of the text. This leaves the writer in a symbolist *néant* worthy of Mallarmé. Moreover, this critical dynamic is finally self-referential, an assessment indeed of the very essay here being written. On the one hand, it is visionary, evoking the "poetic reality" of Helen; on the other hand, it is "full of artificialities," meaningless, trite, repetitious, silly, willful – the very terms of the self-censor in *Notes on Thought and Vision*.

The voice of the art police continues to disparage the play for the remainder of the essay: "[It] is no doubt trivial. . . . Certainly this play is bad" (12–13). The locutions "no doubt" and "certainly" serve as obeisance to authority. However, in a further dimension of this imaginary conversation, marginal comments reflect H.D.'s rereading of the typescript in 1958. The old poet is distressed by the young poet's capitulation to the censor. Next to her earlier dismissals of the play, she has written: "Must read deeper . . . Superficial judgment. . . . O, *No*. . . . No, No. . . . O, O! . . . No –" (8–13). This older writer clearly grasps the drama of authority enacted within the early discourse.

A more complex dialogue takes place in H.D.'s essays on Pausanias, where she exploits this double voice, acknowledging that she is "romancing in [the] midst of would-be criticism of a ponderous, historical work" ("Those Near the Sea" 5). Here the censorious pedants, the "professional grammarians" ("Pausanius" 5), remain a target of animosity, but Pausanias himself, as father-scientist, gains grudging admiration. The distinction between the petty and the honorable scholar is to some extent a spurious one. Both are in a way tyrannical; both would insist on laborious, meticulous, and comprehensive mastery; both would insist on directing one's education (like Charles Doolittle), on choosing one's canon of reading (like Pound and Aldington). And H.D. in these essays appears to be recklessly hostile to such direction: "Choose unreservedly and don't be tyrannized by what you think others think you ought to like" ("Pausanius" 6). She is proud of her "discovery" of Pausanias because "[a]t least no one has helped me in this" (4a).

Indeed, the centermost essay of the group, "God or Hero," carries metonymically the burden of this textual drama of tyranny and rebellion. In it H.D. tells the romantic story of enslaved Messina in its struggle against the authoritarian rule of Sparta. Much like the subversive voice in these essays, the Messinian hero Aristomenes wages guerrilla warfare, ambushing, attacking, retreating, repeatedly escaping from captivity to fight again. With each new rebellion and defeat, however, he brings upon his people still greater repression from Sparta, "untold misery and years of hopeless exile" (9). Though H.D. emphasizes that the Messinians retain their integrity as a people, the repressors here really win the day – as indeed they do, on the whole, in this group of essays.

H.D. in her writing on Pausanias establishes a kind of triangulation between seeker, petty scholar, and genuine researcher in order to deflect fury from the father-censor, even though the weight of his plodding science is almost overbearing to the poet. Indeed, she turns his "astute [little] meticulous consciousness," his "dry-as-dust museum catalogue," into a visionary theater ("Pausanius" 3). His unimaginative, factual observations become outlines or hieroglyphs in a sometimes untrammeled associative play. In this way, H.D. attempts to legitimize the father-censor as part of an imaginative labor.

One can see clear traces in H.D.'s Pausanias of her astronomer father or her biologist grandfather; of the archaeologist Heinrich Schliemann or Arthur Evans; of the sexual pathologist Ellis. This antiquarian traveler is in a way the forerunner of Freud. The first essay on Pausanias begins with resistance and resentment, for his "Teutonic . . . intention" of comprehensiveness, his facticity and ignorance of nuance. He is mechanical and flat like a "little recording-machine," like a collector of little toy models; he is a "dried-up mummy of a traveller." In other words, "his impersonality is colossal" and to some extent repulsive (1–3). However, in the very accumulation of negative qualities, the admirable scientific laborer emerges. Pausanias is like an archaeologist, "digging down into the sources of walls and out-lying heaps of odd stones." He gives one names of Greek cities and temples that affect the visionary as do the "names of minute star-clusters" presented by the astronomer in professional journals (3–4). One finally comes to admire "his fortitude, his discrimination, his real antiquarian love of these things" (3). Like the true scientist, he is noble in his "determination to be led aside nowhere." He is "a true guide and a specific and grim protector. He states a thing scientifically and without sentiment" (4).

This scientific impersonality somehow for H.D. makes possible a counteractivity – "romancing," tale telling, or, at times, a nonlinear, arbitrary association of images. She repeatedly characterizes this mode in terms of child-likeness, thus conjuring not only the spirituality of the gospels, but, more immediately, the implicit presence of the parent. This associative play – as a self-allowed release from conscious control – is at times very revealing. The mystic that pursues these associations is like a dream ego, selectively indulging and censoring evoked images. Within this field of dangerously ricocheting signs, she confesses at times to almost unbearable stimulation. Passages show not only H.D.'s inevitable emphases within hellenic cosmology (Athens and

Sparta, Athene and Apollo), but also some of her avoidances, aversions, and displacements.

For instance, one is immediately confronted in "From Megara to Corinth" with issues of visceral importance in H.D.'s immediate history surrounding World War I: terror and insanity.

> Pausanias tells us simply that in the statues of The Venerable Ones, the Erinnys [sic], "there is nothing horrible." . . . None of the statues of the infernal deities, he says, suggests anything terrible or malignant. Poignant tribute to the sanity of the Athenian sculptor and the Athenian people. . . .
>
> The God in the infernal regions was as sane as the God in heaven or on earth. The serpent at her feet and the Nike, . . . are subject alike to the mind of Athene. . . . Even the Medusa, the Gorgon, Pausanias writes, . . . appeals in line and moderation of expression, not to superstition and realms of hidden terror but to the intellect, and it is "wrought in gold." (1–?)

The repetitive insistences in these remarks – nothing horrible in the underworld, nothing uncontrollable or crazy-making in the serpent or Gorgon, nothing uncanny in the golden realm of intellect – seem transparent when understood in the context of H.D.'s experiences during the previous three or four years. H.D. refers in her autobiographical writing to her terror of death and violence during World War I and to her own borderline psychosis during the breakup of her marriage and the birth of her child in 1919. Projecting Pausanias as an authoritative guide and Athens as a therapeutic sanctuary, H.D. here attempts to deny or avoid that history, rather insisting that all is sane and reasonable within the protection of an imagined Athene.

This willful assertion belies the emphasis in another essay, "People of Sparta," where H.D. struggles with an unreconcilable aspect of the Greek dream – the Spartans' love of violence, their bloody savagery, enacted under the aegis of the god of reason himself: "the boys sacrificing outside the city, under the patronage of Apollo, young dogs to the god of war" (418). Thus, if Athens represents the rule of moderation and sanity, H.D. here at least acknowledges within the imaginary context of Sparta the terror and insanity affiliated with war and with the Greeks: "But beyond Athens, . . . beyond the consciousness, be-yond the intellect, is the terror of the unexpressed, the fear that rages, tearing us like the young men each other, inchoate, undefined, or the beauty unexpressed and dying to be worshipped dead" (418–19). This last phrase – "beauty unexpressed and dying to be worshipped dead" – touches on some private code for the poetic vocation, associated here and elsewhere with the Hyacinthia, the Spartan ritual memorializing the slaying of Hyacinth by Apollo. H.D., however, does not sustain the focus on this unspeakable, terrible beauty, but rather dissipates attention, ending the essay with a lyrical catalogue of scattered pearl names and jewel images from Pausanias, concluding with "our Athene again" (420).

One may also note in "From Megara to Corinth" H.D.'s reluctance to address the Corinthian Aphrodite, whose notorious temple prostitutes are far removed from virginal sanctuaries such as those of Athene, Hera, or Artemis. Again, this aversion may be situated in the context of the erotic experience of H.D.'s recent past – her sequent and always triangulated entanglements in the preceding decade with Pound, Frances Gregg, Aldington, John Cournos, D. H. Lawrence, Cecil Gray, and Bryher.

Provoked by images from Pausanias's narrative, the writer approaches these Aphroditic precincts, then rhetorically veers away. She notes an inscription in an Athenian garden: "Celestial Aphrodite is the oldest of those that are called Fates." But she elides completely the gravity of these words, instead taking the appearance of Aphrodite in Athens as a sign that Athene somehow will protect one from fatal attractions and murky sensuality. As one approaches Aphroditic Corinth, she says, "we need not lose the patronage of the Grey-Eyed Athenian because we wander in gardens over-run with myrtle, dark with roses" (2). At another point she quotes Pausanias: "On the ascent to Arcocorinthos there is also a temple to Aphrodite." This is the famous temple at Corinth, as well known and well visited as the Parthenon. But here the writer displays a remarkable failure of imagination and a bald gesture of aversion: "I cannot at the moment visualize this temple nor the many others sacred to the goddess, but rather, just across the border, in Argolis, . . . the shrine of another queen, . . . Here of Heaven" (3). Happily deflected to the heavenly queen for a few pages, her attention returns at the end of the essay to the chief goddess of Corinth, but she is still insufficiently prepared to approach her: "I am a pilgrim, worn, travel-stained, fervid yet not ready to enter the porches of the holiest Aphrodite" (7).

In this essay as in others, Athene serves as the buffer, the focus of displaced eros, just as she also serves to mitigate the image of the Medusa and the serpent. The last essay on Attica, "Those Near the Sea," concludes with an ecstatic paean to Athene, who here carries the greatest part of the erotic burden in this hellenic daydream:

> Athene the Diviner, Athene, healing peril and diseases of fear and mania and depression, Paeonian Athene, Athene, lover of craftsmen and architect, . . . Athene the Worker, Athene Itonia, . . . Athene, standing beside Hephaistos by the Royal Portico, Athene, with arms outstretched toward the shaft, straight as her spear, silver and bright with leaves, her olive-tree. (6–7)

The incantatory quality of this concluding quasi-prayer has the effect of overriding ambiguities and instabilities; it enacts rhetorically the victorious flight of Athene Nike, overcoming the sinister darkness.

The complex drama of paternal authority enacted in H.D.'s essays on Pausanias may be summarized by contextualizing a well-known remark in the introductory essay, wherein H.D. invokes but seriously misconstrues a scholar-father in order to sanction her visionary enterprise:

"Ghosts to speak must have sacrifice," I remember reading long ago in a critique by a great German scholar, "and we must give them the blood of our hearts." The great German, Willamowitz-Müllendorf [*sic*] meant the ghosts of Greek beauty, the glory that lives in every page of Pausanius, for instance. Ghosts to speak must have sacrifice. The odd thing is that the sacrifice is so exquisite a finding of oneself that one is willing to let everything go, friends, society, wealth or position in the pursuit of this Spirit ... so one feels, one is convinced ... then things break across, we grow older, we come to realize ... that we must live too in life. ("Pausanius" 6)

Ulrich von Wilamowitz-Moellendorff, the twice-great ("great German scholar," "great German"), is the consummate Teutonic classicist, the scholarly rival in Germany of the inspired young Nietzsche (Lloyd-Jones 172). As an "academic Grecian," none more weighty might be imagined. In quoting him, H.D. refers to the conclusion of a published Oxford lecture, "On Greek Historical Writing." There Wilamowitz argues that in the study of history scientific research is paramount and that only after satisfying the demands of the scholar "Dryasdust" may one indulge the "free formative imagination." In this context, and in speaking of the scholar's desire to revivify the dead past, he makes the remarks quoted by H.D.:

We know that ghosts cannot speak until they have drunk blood; and the spirits which we evoke demand the blood of our hearts. We give it to them gladly; but if they then abide our question, something from us has entered into them; something alien, that must be cast out, cast out in the name of truth! For Truth is a stern goddess; she knows no respect of persons, and her handmaid, Science, strides ever onward. (25)

In his Homeric figure of "blood for the ghosts," Wilamowitz suggests the passion of the scholar. But the necessary blood sacrifice for him is finally *not* (as H.D. would have it) to the "ghosts of Greek beauty," to the "Spirit" of vision that demands the sacrifice of the "real" world. Rather, it is to the goddesses Truth and Science, who demand a total casting out of subjective apprehension. H.D. effectively reverses the scholar's "Teutonic intention" in order to find sanction for a brave, extravagant, and risky abandonment of actuality. But his insistence upon the Goddesses of Fact nevertheless may serve subliminally to curb H.D.'s visionary flight, because she here – as in the later apotheosis of Attic Athene –

admits the inevitability, if not the sanity, of the contingent (things break across, we grow older, we come to realize).

H.D.'s visionary, idiosyncratic meditations are articulated in spite of, in arduous resistance to, the voice of the censor – but also, strangely, in alliance with it. She very much admires and needs this authoritative presence. This erotic engagement with the father-scholar is perhaps another variation of the dynamic of "thralldom" that Rachel Blau DuPlessis has delineated in H.D.'s writing, wherein H.D. appears to court relationships that simultaneously undermine and stimulate her work ("Thralldom" 412). However, to some degree all writers, women writers in particular, know such interlocutors. Deborah Kelly Kloepfer has suggested that H.D.'s thralldom and self-censorship represent indeed a recurrent "interplay between the semiotic and the symbolic," in Julia Kristeva's terms, between the inexpressible babble associated with the mother's body and the language of the father (118). In any case it would seem fruitless simply to refuse this voice in fury. As H.D. more or less recognizes, it is one's own, though ventriloquized by others. Moreover, there is the chance that its criticism *might* be accurate. The trick, rather, is to allay its animosity by listening to it and, gradually, to claim it consciously as an element of one's own authority.

H.D. in her essays, fiction, and poetry accomplishes this strategy – but through painstaking engagement over the course of a lifetime. Recurrently in her essays and autobiographical fiction she shows a remarkably canny awareness of the aesthetic, moral, and psychopathological charges to be laid against her. Her narrative experimentations allow her to explore an interior polyphony, and she refines in her poetry too a dialogic sense of voice. The essay form itself, as DuPlessis has emphasized, becomes in *Tribute to Freud* and in her late meditations a subtle and complex instrument (*Career* 85–6). Eventually in *The Walls Do Not Fall*, as Robert Duncan has pointed out, she puts the censor in his place by brilliantly laying bare her dialogue with him: "The poem takes as its condition of being its liabilities, . . . where the poet lets the voice of the adversary play and list against her work just those qualities that rescue the work from what is correct and invulnerable" ("Part II, Chapter 5" [*Credences*] 89).

Chapter Three

Pagan Mysteries: Walter Pater and Romantic Hellenism

The consistent early attacks upon H.D. as a "Victorian hellenist" have been in recent years countered by an apology for her writing in terms of its modernism. However, recent studies by Cassandra Laity have attempted to give nineteenth-century contexts their due. In a series of essays Laity has explored H.D.'s appropriation of decadent writers like Swinburne and Wilde, who offer an antidote to the masculininst poetics of early modernism and who provide her with codes of "transgressive sexuality" within which she may express homoerotic desire. The treatment of romantic and decadent writers in this chapter is indebted to Laity's groundbreaking work in delineating fin-de-siècle models of gender operative in early modernism and in H.D.'s writing. Though our conclusions about H.D.'s decadent eroticism coincide in many ways, my focus here is specific and limited: to trace nineteenth-century models of hellenism and their impact on H.D.'s writing.

H.D., as we have suggested, draws explicitly upon decadent hellenism, which represents for her a last flowering of a continuous tradition descending from hellenistic Alexandria. In H.D.'s literary reception of "hellenic mysteries," Pater is arguably the most significant figure among nineteenth-century writers. Pater shaped the literary generation of the nineties within which H.D.'s early formation took place, but he is an especially crucial figure in the delineation of hellenism. The historian Frank Turner asserts that among the many late-Victorian commentators on the Greeks, such as Ruskin, Arnold, and Swinburne, "only Walter Pater attempted to provide an integrated interpretation of the Greek experience" (68). His concepts, emphases, and concerns with regard to the Greeks are architectonic, reaching H.D. not only directly through her reading but indirectly through widespread dissemination.

As many have recently observed, Pater's influence among the early generation of modernists is in inverse ratio to their declared indebtedness. They claim to owe him little, when they owe him too much to admit.[1] H.D., however, in contrast to some of her literary friends, never publicly disavowed the earlier generations of writers, among whom Swinburne is perhaps the most prominent.[2] But Pater is also a significant precursor, whom H.D. acknowledges often.[3]

Taken together, H.D.'s direct and oblique allusions to Pater establish a relation to him at least as great as that to any other predecessor. In prose writing, especially in a 1912 Paris diary and in autobiographical accounts of her early career in London and Paris (1911–19), H.D. frequently refers to Pater, with the suggestion that specific and often obscure phrases from *The Renaissance* were common parlance in literary circles, especially among "les jeunes hellenists." There is sufficient evidence in H.D.'s writing to indicate her awareness especially of *The Renaissance* but also of some of Pater's other writing, notably essays in *Greek Studies* and in *Plato and Platonism, Marius the Epicurean*, and well-known "imaginary portraits" such as "The Child in the House," "Apollo in Picardy," and "Denys L'Auxerrois."[4]

As Eliot does for modern classicism (Levenson 167), Pater in a way presents the "consolidated" position of romantic hellenism. In his broad erudition, he brings together versions of English and continental hellenism as well as currents of classical scholarship. He was aware of hellenic strains within English romanticism, and he shows fluency as well with German romantic hellenism in Winckelmann, Goethe, Heine, and Hegel;[5] and he was influenced by the speculations of Karl Otfried Müller, one of the chief architects of the "Aryan model" of Greek culture described by Martin Bernal.[6] Moreover, Pater provided a conduit in England for French literary traditions. As John J. Conlon has shown, Pater reveals in his writing a thorough critical awareness of French literature, especially emphasizing the line of hellenic transmission in the troubadours and in the poets of Renaissance France. He manifests a broad knowledge of French romantic literature, and he clearly learned from the hellenism of the Parnassians and symbolists, particularly Gautier and Baudelaire.[7] He knew of the strains of illuminist and Swedenborgian mysticism among the French writers, which, as Philip Knight has shown, merged with a language of hellenism in French romanticism and postromanticism.[8] Moreover, Pater's influence upon H.D.'s generation is amplified in that he significantly shaped writers of the younger generation of English decadents, especially protégés like Arthur Symons, Vernon Lee, and Oscar Wilde, all of whose writings H.D. certainly knew. His influence, moreover, doubles back upon English decadents from French writers like Verlaine, Mallarmé, and Rimbaud, who acknowledge his importance to their symbolist agenda.

Through direct and oblique transmission Pater gave writers of the late nineteenth and early twentieth centuries a fairly consistent metaphorical language of pagan mysteries – a specifically *literary* language, remaining distinguishable, even within the spiritualist overlays of Madame Blavatsky's theosophical invasions in the eighties and nineties.[9] Though the distinctive eroticized spirituality of the Pre-Raphaelite group preceded him, "it was Pater who most sensitively delineated its ideals" (Preminger and Brogan, s.v. "Preraphaelite Brotherhood"). Much of the language of the "religion of beauty" or the "religion of art" in late-nineteenth-century England is affected by Pater's complex religious explorations. Indeed, Pater represents the discursive voice in England of the popular religion of beauty.

In large part through Pater's writing, particularly the essays of *The Renaissance*, hellenism at the turn of the century becomes associated with the language of the occult, and art with the language of vision and clairvoyance. The mysteries of art are secret, discerned only by the initiate, who prepares for them through ascetic discipline. Moreover, those mysteries involve an erotic engagement of an essentially subversive kind. It should be noted that Pater's associations of art with religious mysteries are not arbitrary or invented; on the contrary, they are in part derived from genuine Renaissance traditions of which Pater was thoroughly aware. They are consistent with the "poetic theology" of Renaissance philosophers and artists, who, as Edgar Wind has made clear, borrowed from the Alexandrian *Hermetica* a metaphorical language of the pagan mysteries, suggesting manifestations to initiates of the God hidden within appearances, revelations instrumented through the god Eros.[10]

Pater's metaphorical play with the language of pagan mysteries and sacred initiation is Renaissance in spirit, in that it respects no dogmatic boundaries; yet it is of course less naive in its ecumenism. In this heterodox evangelism, Linda Dowling has shown, Pater follows his mentor at Oxford, Benjamin Jowett, whose attempt to supplant the legitimacy of conventional Christianity with Platonic wisdom was part of a large agenda of cultural renewal. Jowett "repeatedly sought to naturalize and make vitally relevant the unfamiliar or alien turns of Platonic thought by presenting them in terms of Christian and English parallels" (*Hellenism* 71). Likewise, Pater deliberately subverts the language of Christian evangelism, describing aesthetic epicureans in terms borrowed from the New Testament – as initiates, moved by "love" into "a new kingdom of feeling and sensation and thought" (*Renaissance* 26). He thus posits a strictly antinomian sanction to the pursuit of beauty, a religious legitimacy "beyond and independent of the spiritual system then actually prevailing" (*Renaissance* 7). The aesthetic mysteries to Pater are a kind of worship in exile, an access to ancient deities now displaced, to which absent presences the artist, through the rites of craft, seeks to witness. Thus the artistic act itself – as well as the critical act of discernment – takes on hieratic status. Pater distinguishes different kinds and gradations of craft, more or less approaching the holiest mystery – full revelation in the Apollonian art of marble sculpture.

The erotic configurations of Pater's writing help to shape H.D.'s fiction of Greece. This chapter explores some of the elements of that configuration: Pater's association of hellenism with the hermetic tradition; his sense of hellenic mysteries in terms of an alchemical language of *ascesis* and purification, associated with the imagery of crystal; his elaboration of the model of Dorian hellenism, which determines the valences of a "white eroticism" associated with Hellas. However, the very eroticism that makes Pater's hellenism a viable model for H.D. also presents hazards. It is highly rarefied and, for all its "effeminacy," it is inexorably male in orientation. One witnesses throughout H.D.'s early hellenism the way in which the main strains of Greek classicism, wedded as they seem to be to manly athletic and military strength, conceal or negate the female erotic body, replacing Aphroditic power with the male eros governing love between men. H.D. in her early poetry and prose shares Pater's figural dispositions, though at the same time she constantly struggles with them.

Hermeticism and the Exiled Gods

In Pater's early writing, the associations surrounding the "hellenic spirit" are implicitly and explicitly hermetic. The artist in the hellenic tradition for Pater is engaged, like the alchemist or mage, in a hermetic *opus*: his work is an intuition of unseen correspondences, in relation to a process of *gnosis*, or momentary, ecstatic illumination. This sense of hellenic aesthetics is associated in Pater with a notion borrowed from Heinrich Heine, perhaps by way of Gautier (J. S. Harrison 655–6). Heine in an essay, "The Gods in Exile," imagines that the Olympian gods, after the coming of Christianity, were "exiled" from their homeland and forced to assume the guise of humble, ordinary people, manifesting themselves occasionally in disturbing ways. Pater's lyric insinuation of the link between hellenism and hermeticism certainly has its place in H.D.'s early writing. She knew of Pater's and Heine's fiction of the gods in hiding – if one is to believe John Cournos's fictional portrait of her[11] – and envisioned poetry as a means of their recovery.

Pater begins and ends his career with essays on two of the most important Renaissance hermetic mages – "Pico della Mirandola" (1871), republished in *The Renaissance*, and "Giordano Bruno" (1889), revised as the concluding chapter to *Gaston de Latour*. These two essays, which fairly accurately summarize the Renaissance assimilation of hermetic teachings, suggest the centrality of hermeticism in Pater's interpretation of Renaissance humanism as a continuation of the hellenic spirit. In neither of these essays does Pater refer to "hermeticism" as such, but this silence with regard to Hermes is not unusual, since scholarly recognition of the centrality of hermetic teaching in the Renaissance is fairly recent.[12] Pater always signals this tradition by reference to a cluster of Greek philosophers like Pythagoras, Plato, Plotinus, and Dionysius the Aeropagite, or to the "secret wisdom of Moses," the cabala. But certainly the original authority of Hermes Trismegistus, the amalgamation of these and other traditions, is known to Pater through primary Renaissance texts, such as Pico's *De Dignitate*. Pater indeed hints at such a knowledge in "Denys L'Auxerrois," one of Pater's stories of a god in exile, where "the sage monk Hermes, devoted to study and experiment," is the only one able to recognize the omens surrounding the god Dionysos (*Imaginary Portraits* 60). For Pater, Hermes and hermeticism are linked not only to the recovery of the ancient gods but, as critics like Francis A. Yates have confirmed, to the Renaissance humanism inspiring the scientific enlightenment.[13]

Pater's essay on Pico begins with a long quotation from Heine describing the Olympian "Gods in Exile" (*Renaissance* 32–4). This theme recurs throughout the essays of *The Renaissance*, as well as in two actual "imaginary portraits" of gods in exile ("Denys L'Auxerrois" and "Apollo in Picardy"). Heine's idea is especially important in *The Renaissance*, because this period is for Pater predominantly the time when "the older gods had rehabilitated themselves, and men's allegiance was divided" (32). Pico della Mirandola is significant to Pater in representing the "initiatory idea" of that age, the recovery of antiquity, particularly the "reconciliation of the gods of Greece with the Christian religion" (34, 37). Never forgetting the old gods, Pater says, Pico is one of the last to take pagan religions seriously (45).

It is not entirely clear what Pater means by the "rehabilitation" of the old gods or how he sees the importance of the old religions. In his essay on Pico he seems deliberately coy about the import of this agenda.[14] However, this recovery seems to serve as a chief metaphor for the revival of the hellenic spirit in philosophy and art, manifest as a return of the sense of the sacred to the whole sphere of human experience, to intellect, to erotic and bodily life, and to the things of the world. This sense of a unitary and inclusive cosmos animated by spirit is echoed for Pater in the Dominican preacher Giordano Bruno, coming near the close of the Italian Renaissance. Bruno, Pater says, returns to the "ancient 'pantheism,' after the long reign of a seemingly opposite faith" (142). Pater refers to Bruno's reading of Plato, Plotinus, and other philosophers, and his attempt to discern "the real purpose of thinkers older still, surviving in glimpses only in the books of others" – Empedocles, Pythagoras, and Parmenides, "who had been nearer the original sense of things" (*Gaston de Latour* 141).

Besides this recovery of the spiritualized cosmos, the teaching of Pico's *De Dignitate* and of Bruno's treatises also opens nature to the seeking mind. That hermetic teaching revolves around the idea of correspondences, as Pater summarizes in the essay on Pico:

> Everywhere there is an unbroken system of correspondences. Every object in the terrestrial world is an analogue, a symbol or counterpart, of some higher reality in the starry heavens, and this again of some law of the

angelic life in the world beyond the stars. . . . There are oracles in every tree and mountain-top, and a significance in every accidental combination of the events of life. (*Renaissance* 47–8)

Bruno recapitulates this model, though in more highly mystical and eroticized language. "The Spirit of God," so Pater paraphrases Bruno's *antica filosofia*, "in countless variety of forms, neither above, nor in any way without, but intimately within, all things, is really present, with equal integrity and fulness, in the sunbeam ninety millions of miles long, and the wandering drop of water as it evaporates therein" (*Gaston de Latour* 142). This sense of an immanent rather than a transcendent spirit, known through the fullness of human experience, according to Ernest Tuveson, precisely distinguishes hermeticism from forms of dualistic gnosticism (4–7).

The mysteries of the higher mind are accessible through disciplined initiation into a certain mode of attentive perception, which is at once mystical and empirical, focused on the particulars of sense perception. For though these writers give allegiance to the divine, the emphasis clearly falls on the divine capacity of the perceiving human mind. Things are divinized, as is the mind itself, which acts in likeness to the creating mind of God. In this way, then, the particular phenomena of nature are opened to the freely speculating intellect, initiating scientific enlightenment, imagined as identical with spiritual illumination.

Pater in his essay on Leonardo da Vinci in *The Renaissance* speculates on the way in which this hermeticism is played out in one of the chief artists of the revival of the ancient wisdom. Pater here gives a lyric portrait of the artist as mage, "possessing an unsanctified and secret wisdom." Accepting the occult doctrine to "follow nature," Pater says, Leonardo

> plunged, then, into the study of nature. And in doing this he followed the manner of the older students; he brooded over the hidden virtues of plants and crystals, the lines traced by the stars as they moved in the sky, over the correspondences which exist between the different orders of living things, through which, to eyes opened, they interpret each other; and for years he seemed to those about him as one listening to a voice, silent for other men. (108–9)

In this brooding attentiveness to things of the world, Leonardo in both his science and his art participates in hermetic magic. "The science of that age," Pater says, "was all divination, clairvoyance, . . . seeking in an instant of vision to concentrate a thousand experiences." In this search for *gnosis* Leonardo is the alchemist par excellence: "Pouring over his crucibles, making experiments with colour, trying, by a strange variation of the alchemist's dream, to discover the secret, not of an elixir to make man's natural life immortal, but of giving immortality to the subtlest and most delicate effects of painting, he seemed to them rather the sorcerer or the magician" (112).

Pater represents this intense aesthetic/empirical perception as a kind of "double sight, . . . clairvoyant of occult gifts in common or uncommon things, in the reed at the brook-side, or the star which draws near to us but once in a century" (113). Indeed, the theme of clairvoyant or visionary art runs throughout the essays of *The Renaissance*. Pater's description in this essay of "Leonardo's type of womanly beauty," the Daughters of Herodias, clearly establishes a pivotal figure of the oracular priestess:

> They are the clairvoyants, through whom, . . . one becomes aware of the subtler forces of nature, . . . all those finer conditions wherein material things rise to that subtlety of operation which constitutes them spiritual, . . . Nervous, electric, faint always with some inexplicable faintness, these people seem to be subject to exceptional conditions, to feel powers at work in the common air unfelt by others, to become, as it were, the receptacle of them, and pass them on to us in a chain of secret influences. (121–2)

In seeking out cultural icons for H.D.'s conception of the visionary female artist, one need look for nothing more esoteric than this provocative, well-known passage. Pater gives broad cultural legitimacy to an ancient tradition of daimonic female possession and oracular gifts – though at the same time, one might add, he marks that divinatory female as neurotic and languishing, confirming aspects of Victorian iconography.[15]

H.D. responds most overtly to Pater's delineation of hermetic hellenism in *Notes on Thought and Vision* (1919). She has Pater's essay on Leonardo in mind when she takes this artist, in the tradition of hellenic art, as representative of "over-mind consciousness," possessing "the secret of dots and dashes" (27), the code, in other words, of imaginative interpenetration with the *nous*. H.D. also grasps Pater's emphasis on the conjunction of the mystical and the scientific in Renaissance magic. Leonardo is empirical and technical, at the same time that he is visionary and erotic. The scientific precision, the eroticism, and the mystical clairvoyance are one. Indeed, this conjunction is a basic principle for H.D. The mystical and the scientific are always inextricably bound together and contained within each other: thus her clairvoyant and subliminal interplay with father-scientists such as Pausanias and Freud; thus her psychological play between "my father's science and my mother's art" (*Tribute to Freud* 145).

Moreover, H.D. picks up on other implications of Pater's general antinomian argument when she identifies the "secret of dots and dashes" with the mind animated by love, and thus with the "secret" taught by Christ. Leonardo "went mad" in the vision of passionately loved particulars, "because those lines of the bird's back or the boy's shoulder or the child's hair acted on him directly" as the reception of a hidden code of significance (26–7). In the same way, the Galilean "was a great artist, like da Vinci": "The Galilean fell in love with things as well as people," responsive to lines and inferences that brought him in touch with "over-mind thought" (27–8). The erotic/visionary efforts of Leonardo and Christ represent for H.D. activities of the fully engaged hermetic mage, who both responds to and generates the animation of spirit in things, and who does so through senses and bodily desire.

Such a visionary intensity as Leonardo's is implied in Pater's own mysticism, with its ideal of electric consciousness, "present always at the focus where the greatest number of vital forces unite in their purest energy" (*Renaissance* 251). "Art," Pater says, is "always striving to be independent of the mere intelligence, to become a matter of pure perception" (*Renaissance* 145). The famous "Conclusion" to *The Renaissance*, ostensibly derived from epicureanism or hedonism, but in fact thoroughly empirical,[16] clearly gains its force through a metaphorical evocation of mysticism, through its claim for an exclusively visionary, epiphanic access to truth, a *gnosis* of a sort. This Paterian mysticism is suggested as well by the young Pound in *The Spirit of Romance* (1908), when he speaks of an "ecstasy" that "is not a whirl or a madness of the senses, but a glow arising from the exact nature of the perception" (*Spirit of Romance* 91).

Likewise, in a review of *Sea Garden*, John Gould Fletcher suggests that H.D.'s poetry must be read within a mystical or visionary tradition. Though it appears to refer to ordinary natural things, Fletcher says, "it is really about the soul, or the primal intelligence, or the *Nous*, or whatever we choose to call that link that binds us to the unseen and uncreated" (267). Indeed, to confirm the sense of H.D.'s visionary quality, Fletcher here quotes at length one of the strangest poems in *Sea Garden*, "The Gift." It speaks well for Fletcher that he recognizes the importance of this poem, which explores the ambiguity of the gift of clairvoyance; Pound, in contrast, finds it an "incomprehensible thing" (*Letters* 71).

The modern clairvoyant suffers in being profoundly displaced from any religious context. Pater reads back into Renaissance paintings (and later into Greek art) his own melancholic, modern sense of alienation and eccentricity. Even in the Renaissance, an age of fortuitous convergences, the spirituality of the clairvoyants for Pater is tenuous and disturbing. They are "[n]ervous, electric, faint with some inexplicable faintness," perhaps because like Pater's their spiritual seizures have no apparent ground, no *temenos*, no oracular tripod. H.D.'s poem in *Sea Garden* points to this same modern displacement of the clairvoyant gift. One might, during "[s]leepless nights, . . . remember the initiates, / their gesture, their calm glance." But here there are no "rites," no "mysteries," but those enacted interiorly in solitary compulsion, in an endless because uncontained liminality:

> I have lived as they
> in their inmost rites –
> they endure the tense nerves
> through the moment of ritual.
> I endure from moment to moment –
> days pass all alike,
> tortured, intense. (*Collected Poems* 17)

The almost unsustainable burden of clairvoyant intensity indicated here is echoed elsewhere in H.D.'s poetry, essays, and fiction through the recurrent image of figures elected by Apollo, who are marked usually, like Hyacinthus, with a wound to the head. Such a role is obviously a dangerous one, and in assuming it H.D. risked taking on the associated images of neurosis and fragility, and risked, too, the danger of megalomania, which Pound in the early years and later Freud found in her.[17]

H.D. like Pater imagined this clairvoyance in the context of the effort to rehabilitate the ancient gods. In emphasizing this theme, Pater is continuous with a predominant tradition of romantic hellenism. As Lawrence Kramer has argued, "[T]he returning gods are an essential element in the phenomenology of the Romantic imagination" (484). H.D.'s recovery of the exiled gods in her early poetry comes in part through the simple act of literary transmission, like that of the artists Pater describes in *The Renaissance*. Her translations from the Greek Anthology, from Ovid, Homer, and Euripides, like her efforts in the Poets' Translation Series, were envisioned as serving a continuous renewal of the hellenic spirit.[18] More essentially, for instance in the poems of *Sea Garden*, this recovery comes through a reinvention of the Orphic prayer, the persistent use of apostrophe within a sense of the magical power of words. The apostrophe establishes the illusion of sudden epiphany in the presence of a mysterious other.

Moreover, many of H.D.'s early poems – such as "Sea Gods," "The Shrine," "Cliff Temple," "Hermes of the Ways," "The God," "Hymen" – participate in a romantic tradition, the "theophanic poem," described brilliantly by Kramer. In this broad and continuous genre exercised by poets in the romantic tradition, the poem is the locus in which "the return of the gods takes place" (484). Pater would seem to be an important link in the transmission of this poetic tradition, by giving articulation to an imaginative enterprise of great cultural urgency.

"When they appear in theophany," Kramer says, "the gods embody the assertion of imaginative power"; they are "reflections of the strong imagination that is lifting experience into vision" (484–5). What the poet calls upon in summoning the gods is her own power, through the poem, to transfigure the ordinary. As Kramer elaborates it, the theophanic poem, as a kind of mirror of the poet's summoning of creative power, begins with "the first act of naming" that is "always a recognition of the gods' absence," followed by self-doubt projected as the impossibility of the gods' return. Then, in compensation for this barrenness,

> the poet's doubt leads away from itself by assuming blindly the burden of its desire and bringing forward a series of images for the theophany that may be denied it. These images are not images of the gods alone, and sometimes not images of the gods at all; they give central place to a number of metonyms of divine presence, which embody the transfigurations that the gods would bring if they came. (486)

The emergence of these images out of absence and self-doubt "create[s] the illusion that the sought-for theophany is in the process of taking place" (487). When that theophany does appear, the god is often manifest not directly but invisibly in terms of altered vision, receding namelessly again into an animated landscape (498–9).

"Sea Gods," for instance, is remarkably illumined when understood in terms of Kramer's model. The first part of the poem posits the gods' absence and the impossibility of their return; the second gives an incantatory catalogue of flowers serving as "metonyms of divine presence"; the third announces the imminent return of the gods, to be signaled by barely discernible traces of their presence in the ordinary but transformed landscape. In an aspect of this poetic form not emphasized by Kramer, the prosody of the poem itself becomes a metonym of the gods' absence or presence and, correlatively, of the poet's strength: it begins with irregularity, the lines, like the gods, "ragged ... cut apart ... misshapen ... broken"; then it increases in regularity and repetition, ending in the strong, willful assertions of the concluding part. The affirmation of the desired, absent gods is also an affirmation of the strength of the desiring poet, a hoped-for reanimation of nature that constitutes a reanimation of vision through the language of the poem.

It seems clear that, as L. S. Dembo has argued, H.D. in her early career imagined herself in terms of Pater's "aesthetic mysticism," as a receptor of the code hidden in things, as a priestess or clairvoyant like Pater's Daughters of Herodias, as a scholar-poet attempting the recovery of the exiled gods ("Imagism"). However, whereas Dembo sees this aestheticism in terms of literary history, for H.D. it pointed to a genuine religious tradition, which she continued to pursue and to deepen throughout her career. Indeed, as I have tried to indicate here, Pater does convey with some accuracy the outlines and the implications of Renaissance hermeticism. These eventually lead H.D. back to Alexandria and to the "lost gods" of the diaspora, and then, not coincidentally, to a Leonardo-like Sigmund Freud and to the mystically inspired religion of her Moravian ancestors. H.D. in her midcareer gains some distance from the aesthetic "early H.D." But she really never abandons the religious territory and the oracular necessities shaped under Pater's spell.

Ascesis: *Crystal and Salt*

Through his essays on the hellenic tradition, H.D. and her generation also received from Pater an overarching notion of the discipline of art, associated with *ascesis*, a regimen of austere restraint that the artist, like the athlete, must cultivate.[19] That habit of asceticism is associated, as in Orphic cults, with a process of purification, indicated often in Pater's writing, especially in *The Renaissance*, through the chemical metaphor of crystallization. Unquestionably, H.D. understood her labors in the context of this notion of *ascesis*, as it implies both the discipline of craft and the religious consecration of life.

In the preface to *The Renaissance*, Pater says: "Few artists, . . . work quite cleanly, casting off all *débris*, and leaving us only what the heat of their imagination has wholly fused and transformed." When, for instance in Wordsworth, such clean fusion occurs, one finds the deposit of "a fine crystal here or there" (xii–xiii). As Perry Meisel has demonstrated,[20] this chemical metaphor appears throughout Pater's writing. It seems to refer chiefly to the chemical processes of distillation, the crystal being the final refined sublimate after evaporation. The purgation of everything inessential in the artist's expression of personality occurs through *ascesis*, "a regimen of self-curtailment" (Meisel, *Absent* 56). This discipline is most often associated in Pater with that of the young male athlete: the *ascesis* of the Spartan youth (*Plato and Platonism* 222), or the young horsemen on the Panathenaic frieze, "with their level glances, their proud, patient lips, their chastened reins" (*Renaissance* 231), or the implied athletic figure in the famous phrase describing the early periods of artistic flourishing, "the charm of *ascêsis*, of the austere and serious girding of the loins in youth" (*Renaissance* xiv).

The crystal, achieved through *ascesis*, signifies the transparency and brilliant refractiveness of the realized work of art, associated, as Meisel says, with "the quality of luminous whiteness," a focusing of disparate rays of light into a single clear intensity (*Absent* 57–8). This is the refractive character, for instance, belonging to the artists and philosophers in Renaissance Florence, who "catch light and heat from each other's thoughts" (*Renaissance* xvi), and the character of the "diamond" of Plato's aesthetics (*Plato and Platonism* 281–2; Meisel, *Absent* 57). The brilliance of the crystal pertains to the perfection not only of art and thought but of life and character, such as that of the enigmatic figure described in Pater's earliest essay, "Diaphaneitè": "It does not take the eye by breadth of colour; rather it is that fine edge of light, when the elements of our moral nature refine themselves to the burning point" (*Miscellaneous Studies* 248). One notes the association of *burning*, *refinement*, and the crystal *edge of light*.

This configuration of images is especially pertinent to H.D.'s early writing. She assumes this demanding and severe sense of artistic discipline, and like Pater she associates it with the male figure of the athlete and with a Spartan austerity, feminized to some extent by association with the chaste goddesses Artemis and

Athene. H.D. shares with Pater's aesthetics of crystal — and also, as we shall see, of marble — the Apollonian emphasis of artistic perfection associated with purity, whiteness, and brilliance. Moreover, H.D. explores the moral and religious urgency implied in Pater's discussion of the artist. As Pater himself suggests at several points (Meisel, *Absent* 57), the chemical metaphor of purgation/ crystallization is really an *alchemical* one — pertaining to processes of spiritual transformation — issuing in a purified apprehension susceptible to visionary epiphany. The mystical/alchemical implications of this metaphor are suggested tellingly by the famous image in the "Conclusion" to *The Renaissance*: "To burn always with this hard, gem-like flame, to maintain this ecstasy, is success in life" (251). This burning ecstasy — a self-conscious, relentless attention to ephemera — suggests the blue, clear flame after the "débris" has been burned away, but at the same time it evokes obliquely an image of the crystallizing jewel. H.D. was aware of both the chemical and alchemical dimensions of crystal, its pertinence as a metaphor both for aesthetics and for spiritual mysteries.

The Paterian configuration of *ascesis*, athlete, and illumination is suggested repeatedly in H.D.'s early poetry and prose. "The Contest," for instance, one of the first poems in *Sea Garden*, speaks of the athlete as an object of art, the sharply defined lines of his body associated with light, whiteness, and fire (*Collected Poems* 12–14). In *Notes on Thought and Vision* (24–7), the lines of the taut body of the Charioteer at Delphi convey the code known to the clairvoyant. A similar visionary association of the athlete's *ascesis* is given in the early (1920) prose piece "Helios and Athene": "The naked Greek, the youth in athletic contest, has set, accurately prescribed movement and posture," which makes of him a kind of quasi-artifact. "We gaze upon this living naked embodiment of grace and decorum. We are enflamed by its beauty. . . . Its beauty is a charm or definite talisman" (*Collected Poems* 327–8).

The image of the athlete here, as in Pater, suggests the physical discipline of the body that creates an illuminating form, that gives off light and fire; but it also mirrors the moral/aesthetic *ascesis* of the artist's craft. In "The Contest" it is needless to differentiate between the sharp lines of the athlete's body and the hard lines of the poem. Both "are chiselled like rocks / that are eaten into by the sea" (12), the sharpness and rigidity suggesting granite, the movement suggesting light and fire. The athlete's body functions as a poem, and the poem as an athlete's body. The same aesthetic is suggested in "Charioteer" (*Collected Poems* 190–7) as well as in "Red Roses for Bronze" (*Collected Poems* 211–15), each a dramatic monologue by the maker of an athlete's statue. The eroticism directed at the spare, codified male body becomes one with the austere eroticism propelling the creation of the artifact.

This set of images works obliquely in H.D.'s association of artistic craft with the guardianship of Athene. In this role Athene strangely keeps her military image of helmet and armor, such as in the Phidian statue in the Parthenon, rather than the alternative classical image as the calm, dignified maiden that she often takes as patroness of artisans.[21] This goddess of craft, H.D. suggests, grants the strength and compulsion of artistic *ascesis*. She gives "glamour to [the] will" ("Prayer," *Collected Poems* 142), and her helmet suggests the strenuousness of mental effort, "riven steel, / caught over the white skull" ("Helios," *Collected Poems* 143). In the same way, in "Helios and Athene," the image of Athene "with silver line between eye-brow and ridge of helmet," gazing "with all the concentrated power of her eyes," suggests the austerely disciplined vision of the artist (*Collected Poems* 329). As Deborah Kelly Kloepfer has pointed out, in *Palimpsest* this image of the helmet with its "icy glamour" is associated with the intensity of poetic creation in the two poets Hipparchia and Ray Bart, who both experience its hard restraint and concentration as a kind of tyranny (*Palimpsest* 35, 147–8; Kloepfer 104–5).

Moreover, this Paterian configuration of *ascesis* is suggested in H.D.'s early preoccupation with two supremely chaste male figures from Euripides, both emphasized in Pater's writing: Hippolytus, a young man obsessively devoted to the austere Artemis; and Ion, Apollo's own son, serving as a pure attendant at his Delphic shrine.[22] These two figures remain pivotal for H.D. throughout the first half of her career, beginning in the traumatic years of World War I and culminating in the aftermath of her analysis with Freud, immediately before World War II.[23]

Artemis and Apollo, the patron gods of Hippolytus and of Ion, respectively, are, like Athene, associated with the life of discipline. They are both predominant at Dorian Sparta, where, as Pater describes, the life of *ascesis* is the norm, and all the gods are modified within the Lacedaemonian aura, a kind of intellectualized virility (*Plato and Platonism* 228). Hippolytus and Ion fascinate H.D. in her early years precisely because they serve as an image of the consecrated ascetic life, and the Euripidean choruses mirror astringent, Orphic ecstasy of her early poetry.

This compelling process of *ascesis* and crystallization is indicated in H.D.'s early writing, as we have seen, in a poetry of *ecphrasis*, a fascination with the visionary power imparted by works of art, very much corresponding to Pater's lines of emphasis. In a way, this fascination is misguided, leading sometimes in H.D.'s poetry to a kind of fetishism, a repetitive fixity upon artifact. Those poems in which that fixity appears – such as "The Contest," "Prayer," or "Red Roses for Bronze" – are by no means her best. The Paterian sense of aesthetic *ascesis* presents real problems for the female poet. It is consistently male in its orientation and eroticism, connected exclusively with a sense of male beauty, which for Pater consummately expresses the Greek spirit. And, despite Pater's emphasis on body and sensuousness, his "gem-like flame" is very rarefied and spiritualized, suggesting a consummation beyond the debris of the body and a longing for light far removed from its shadows.

What appears to be missing from Pater's aesthetics of the crystal, missing from both his chemistry and his alchemy, is a sufficient sense of the *matrix*: the material ground out of which the crystal is projected; the *prima materia* worked in the alchemical *opus*; the maternal ground, accessible through memory. Though, as we shall see, Pater acknowledges a place in feeling for the virginal mother, he has consistent difficulty in confronting the dark aspects of feeling and desire. However, even in her early poetry, H.D. comprehends the matrix – rocky ground, occluded and shadowy body, visceral feeling – the matter out of which desire comes, from which it never escapes.

By the mid-twenties H.D. began her own critique of "the early H.D.," as Susan Friedman has emphasized,[24] and she eventually came to be especially annoyed with the epithet of "crystalline" applied by critics to her poetry, certainly recognizing its negative connotations – fixity, rigidity, prettiness, superficiality. But she was irritated as well by the sense that the stock epithet missed the distinctiveness of the writing: "[P]erhaps I did not see, did not dare see any further than my critics. Perhaps my annoyance with them was annoyance with myself. For what is crystal or any gem but the concentrated essence of the rough matrix, or the energy, either of over-intense heat or over-intense cold that projects it?" (*H.D. by Delia Alton* 184).

H.D. here shows a keen awareness of the chemical metaphor of crystallization, emphasizing what Pater elides – the matrix – as containing a hidden dynamic. The power of the crystal is not, as with Pater's Spartan athletes, an exclusively male power. Even in "The Contest," the hard-shaped male body of the athlete is transformed by the end of the poem into the intimate, recursive lines of blossoms: "your feet are citron-flowers, / your knees, cut from white-ash, / your thighs are rock-cistus" (*Collected Poems* 13).

The convergence of crystal and flower, and the sense of the ominousness of the crystal matrix, is seen clearly in "Garden":

> You are clear
> O rose, cut in rock,
> hard as the descent of hail.
>
> I could scrape the colour
> from the petals
> like spilt dye from a rock.
>
> If I could break you
> I could break a tree.
>
> If I could stir
> I could break a tree –
> I could break you.
> (*Collected Poems* 24–5)

Evoking the Paterian crystal through apostrophe – *clear, cut in rock, hard, hail* (*ice/crystal*) – the language constitutes a rock rose, as elsewhere it makes a statue – the austere encoded lines of the rose indistinguishable from the poetic line. But here the effort of the poet to appropriate an "object" through fascinated gaze and coercive rhythm, to celebrate her own power through *ecphrasis*, breaks down. The rock rose, unlike the statue, refuses or evades appropriation. The evoked rose remains other, unbreakable and untouchable, having a power apart from the evoking poet so great as to render her impotent. After beginning in the first stanza with hammer-stroke assertion, the language of the rest is increasingly conditional. Perhaps this dynamic comes from the fact that the rock rose belongs not to male but to female iconography, not to surface but to an interiority associated with the matrix of desire. The poem in a kind of *via negativa* reveals the hidden virtue of the crystal/flower.

H.D. explores poetically another more genuinely alchemical dimension of the theme of crystallizing – the matter of "salt." Her early poems and translations evoke seawater, biting frigid wind, and burning sand, a configuration composed of crystals – seasalt, ice, silicon. Though, as we have seen, these elements evoke the austerity of *ascesis*, they evoke as well a kind of impurity and suffering generally alien to Pater, the "over-intense heat or over-intense cold" belonging to the projecting matrix. In alchemy sea/salt is the arcane substance tied to a certain necessary bitterness. "Without salt," it is said, "the work [the alchemical *opus*] has no success" (Jung 246). To experience sea/salt is to be within the visceral elements of bodily life, the "common salts" (Hillman 117).

In other words, for H.D. crystal is not simply (as for Pater) the sublimate of the last stages of purification by fire. Rather it suggests the by-product of primary corrosions and saltings of the alchemical process – *nigredo*, or blackening. This dark dimension of the alchemical process – crystal suddenly projected from the "rough matrix" – is suggested in one of the recurrent patterns in the poems of *Sea Garden* – a sudden movement from disintegration to momentary transfiguration. In "Sea Lily," for example, the flower is "slashed and torn"; "scales are dashed / from your stem, / sand cuts your petal, / furrows it with hard edge." But this image, subjected to a salt astringency, is crystallized in a flash of light: "Yet though the whole wind / slash at your bark, / you are *lifted up*, / aye – though it hiss / to cover you with froth" (*Collected Poems* 14; emphasis added). This astringent alteration in the wash of waves is repeated in many poems, especially in "Storm" and in the flower poems, frequently ending, as this one does, with an exalted moment, an ascension. In "Sea Rose," the flower is "caught . . . flung . . . *lifted* / in the crisp sand / that drives in the wind" (5; emphasis added). In "Storm" a leaf is "broken off . . . hurled out, / *whirls up and sinks*" (36; emphasis added). The ecstatic image at the end of "Sea Violet" is even clearer: "Violet / your grasp is frail . . . but you catch the light – / frost, a star edges with its fire" (26).

This exaltation belongs to a "virginal" ecstasy, to the "fervor of salt" associated, James Hillman suggests, with *ascesis* and with a psychological desire for purification *through* the impure element of salt, through the intensity of subjective experience. Though salt is necessary to the alchemical process, Hillman emphasizes, *dosage* is the crucial matter (130–6). One of the psychological dangers of Paterian asceticism, especially as voiced in its most radical version in the "Conclusion" to *The Renaissance*, is the urgency and limitlessness of its moral demand, to "burn *always*" with the purifying flame, to "maintain this ecstasy," or else to fail in one's obligation to beauty.

H.D. very early recognized the danger of ascetic crystallization – a kind of oversalting of the soul: "I had drawn away into the salt, / myself, a shell / emptied of life" ("The God" [1917], *Collected Poems* 46). One notes the identity between "salt, / myself," indicating the crystal as a too-fixed "self." Like other psychic consequences of her early career, this threat of fixity took many years to sort out. H.D. says of the poetry of *Trilogy*, written during World War II, that it is not in the early crystalline mode: "It is no pillar of salt nor yet of hewn rock-crystal. It is the pillar of fire by night, the pillar of cloud by day" (*H.D. by Delia Alton* 193). The retrospective poet of *Trilogy* sees more clearly the danger of petrification, as Lot's wife was crystallized in fixation on grief and loss. She also sees how the crystal is lost – "Splintered the crystal of identity" – and how regained, in the "bitter jewel / in the heart of the bowl" (*Collected Poems* 526, 552).

The Dorian Model and White Eroticism

Pater participates in a scholarly tradition, initiated by German classicists following Winckelmann, which Joan DeJean has described in some detail.[25] These critics and editors, with Winckelmann, insist on the "absolute privileging of the athletic young male body as the measure of the Greek aesthetic ideal," which was implicitly too an ethical ideal carrying a nationalistic agenda (206). At the same time, they locate the very essence of hellenism in institutions of male homoeroticism, "privileging of the erotic gaze of male upon male, *pederastia*" (207). These German scholars, DeJean has indicated, make the claim that male love represents a higher eros that is, according to one scholar, "if not completely devoid of sensuality, at least blameless," whereas women are capable only of a "baser, sensual eros and never its higher form" (DeJean 208). Female corporeality and female desire are outside the range of serious regard. Thus, while presenting an apology for male homoeroticism, DeJean argues, these same scholars find the possibility of female homoeroticism in the great Sappho literally unthinkable, a prospect that would taint the male homoerotic ideal forming the basis of their entire hellenic edifice (210).

Among English writers, Pater and John Addington Symonds adapt this German tradition, reinforced through their Oxford education; they decisively link hellenism and male homoeroticism, thus giving their own culturally marginal erotic practice legitimacy and centrality. As Dowling has shown (*Hellenism* 67–103), Pater and Symonds at Oxford were writing within an intellectual fraternity that largely accepted this association. Dowling traces the increasing public visibility of male love in late-nineteenth-century England to educational reforms at Oxford under Jowett, who helped in 1853 to establish the curriculum of *Literae humanitores* (the "Greats"), at the center of which was Plato, and who made central to Oxford education the importance of "Socratic eros" in the dialectics between tutor and student. This Platonic love, according to Dowling, is consistently portrayed under Jowett's influence as an elevated andro-generative power, a "spiritual procreancy" within philial intercourse between men, and specifically within the bond between older man and youth. Pater and Symonds, in the first "spiritual generation" of Jowett, themselves attempt to bring about in their writing a revolutionary cultural awakening inspired by consciousness of this spiritualized masculine love.

Because in fact late-nineteenth-century hellenism legitimizes homoeroticism and imagines it in the context of a tradition of Platonic spirituality having historical continuity and metaphysical significance, the language of hellenism becomes part of a general homoerotic code available to both male and female writers. However, the model finally poses serious constraints to the woman writer. If hellenic beauty is quintessentially male and a realized spiritual wholeness accessible only through purified male or quasi-male images, what territory can the female hellenic artist negotiate?

The implications of this identification of hellenism with male homoeroticism can best be seen by examining the Dorian model of Greek art that Pater shared with other Victorian intellectuals and the Dorian eroticism that it accommodated for him. In *Greek Studies*, Pater draws out the distinction between Ionian and Dorian proposed by K. O. Müller's *Die Dorier* (*The History and Antiquities of the Doric Race*). He wholly adopts Müller's interpretation of hellenic art, as well as his larger argument concerning the autochthony and racial purity of genuine hellenic culture, what Martin Bernal calls the "Aryan model" of Greek origins. For Müller, the Ionian, associated with decadent Athens, represents a racially impure strain, associated with Asiatic influence. In contrast, the Dorian, represented prominently by Sparta, defines the hellenic spirit per se; it is European and northern in origin, racially pure, giving the Ionian strain its strength, austerity, and nobility.[26] In *Greek Studies*, Pater, for instance, identifies Troy with the Ionian, the Achaeans with the Dorian: Trojans were "weaker on the practical or moral side, and with an element of languid Ionian voluptuousness in them, . . . an element which the austere, more strictly European influence of the Dorian Apollo will one day correct in all genuine Greeks" (228). The Ionian, clearly, is Aphroditic and effeminate, luxurious and morally weak, "corrected" by union with the austere Dorian, the Apollonian masculine.

In applying this model to the history of Greek art, Pater names the early age, under Asiatic/Ionian influence, *"the period of graven images"* (250), carrying metaphorically the biblical injunction of false or unenlightened worship. It is characterized by detailed, "Hephaestean" craft in metalwork, jewelry, and ivory and gold (chryselephantine), which altogether comes out of an Aphroditic sensibility, the love of an exquisitely textured life. Ionian art for Pater is indeed a wedding of Hephaestus and Aphrodite. The Cyprian goddess, in particular, is the channel to Greece of Asiatic influence, the "decrepit Eastern civilization, itself long since surfeited with [its] splendour" (231). In contrast to this detailed handiwork is marble sculpture, the consummate, "revealed religion" of Greek art. Dorian or European in influence, it is governed by Apollo in its clarity, intelligibility, and luminescence, in its "energetic striving after truth in organic form" (252).

There is no question that H.D. knew the imaginal lines of this pervasive model and engaged in continual conversation with it. What are its consequences for her as a woman writer? The following sections will briefly deal with three aspects of the Dorian/Ionian model as played out in H.D.'s early hellenism: the centrality of an aesthetic of statues and marble; the prominence of the figure of the white virgin/mother; and H.D.'s self-censorship associated with the Ionian style and with Aphroditic necessities.

Marble and the Apollonian Code

Dowling establishes the way in which Müller's study allowed the Oxonians nurtured on Socratic eros to reverse a traditional censure of male homoeroticism. The dominant "classical republican tradition" in England, Dowling argues, is based on a warrior ideal, an association of *vir* and *virtue*, so that virtue is essentially "manliness," and its opposite "effeminacy." In terms of this ideal, Sparta with its severe military discipline is clearly the ideal Greek state.[27] But in elevating the Dorian ideal, Müller also recovers in detail the Spartan institution of *pederastia*, publicly sanctioned homoerotic unions between older and younger men (2:300–6). Thus Müller establishes, as Dowling states, that pederasty was "martial in origin, closely related to that inspiring warrior ideal" of the republican tradition. Advocates of Platonic eros, then, through the model of Sparta as recovered by historians, could evade the charge of effeminacy and appropriate the virtue of a higher manliness (*Hellenism* 78–9). Thus when Pater eulogizes the Dorian in his late essays, especially in "Lacedaemon," he engages in homoerotic "double talk," in Wayne Koestenbaum's phrase, an evasive language that at once "obscures [its] erotic burden" yet "give[s] the taboo subject some liberty to roam" (3).[28]

This Dorian eroticism is thoroughly assimilated by decadent writers and it is still alive and well in the milieu of early modernism.[29] It is therefore valuable to define its markings in some detail, in particular its identification with sculpture. Sculpture, like crystal, is figured by Pater in terms of *ascesis*. The sculptor must "purge from the individual all that belongs only to him, all the accidents, the feelings and actions of a special moment." This purity of sculptural art is associated, as Richard Jenkyns has shown, with white light (146–9) and at the same time with a traditional Neoplatonic "theory of color."[30] Pater in his discussion of sculpture in *The Renaissance* says, "That white light, purged from the angry, bloodlike stains of action and passion, reveals, not what is accidental in man, but the tranquil godship in him, as opposed to the restless accidents of life" (225). Color here seems associated with the impurity of contingent, mortal life; and white, with the immortal. Pater emphasizes repeatedly this white colorlessness, representing, it seems clear, a participation in the "divine forms," the "supreme and colourless abstraction" of essences (237, 232).

Part of the stain from which the statues are removed would appear to be that of sexuality. Pater emphasizes that "the beauty of the Greek statues was a sexless beauty: the statues of the gods had the least traces of sex," and that the lover of hellenic statues, like Winckelmann, has a commensurate "moral sexlessness," his spiritual eros toward young men having a natural and untainted quality (*Renaissance* 234). Yet at the same time, Winckelmann in a letter quoted by Pater asserts that "the supreme beauty [of Greek art] is rather male than female" (*Renaissance* 203), and likewise Pater, following the German scholarly tradition, at another point identifies the Greek ideal with "a male beauty, far remote from feminine tenderness" (*Plato and Platonism* 222). One may infer from this apparent contradiction that for Pater, as for his confreres in the Platonic aura of Oxford, male eros is sexless in that its white spirituality transcends the colors of mere sexuality, bound to the tainted (female) body.

Beyond its association here with male homoeroticism, the sexlessness or transcendent sexuality of the Greek statue is a persistent romantic theme. The logic behind it is essentially Platonic. Sculpture, as Winckelmann says, gives us "something beyond nature, namely certain ideal forms of its beauty, which, as an ancient interpreter of Plato [Proclus] teaches us, come from images created by the mind alone" (7). Thus sculpture, as we have seen, reflects the white light of the eternal forms, abstracted from finite bodily particulars, such as sexuality. Sculpture is also, thus, associated with perfection and with unity. One can see why, then, the marble statue represents a transcendent *asexuality*, but also why it comes to be associated with *bisexuality* – with the figure of the hermaphrodite or androgyne, representing an original unity of being, or signifying the mysterious *conjunctio* of alchemy, a unity of opposites attained through transformative process.[31]

The mysticism of classical marble defines one among many converging strains of the nineteenth-century obsession with the androgyne, fueled by the proliferation of hermeticist and especially alchemical doctrines and symbols.[32] It is this figure, as Stephen A. Larrabee points out, that Shelley, for instance, most associates with sculpture, "a perfect hermaphrodite being of an ideal sexless beauty"; "an ideal being of mixed or bisexual nature" (192, 196). Similarly one finds in Balzac's *Seraphità*, a book that fascinated H.D. in her formative years,[33] the same esoteric association of marble statue, spiritual perfection, and androgyny: "that face of purest marble [Seraphitus/Seraphità] expressed in all things strength and peace" (21).[34] Indeed, the configuration is ubiquitous among decadent writers, serving as part of a code for idealized, heterodox eroticism. In *Althea* by Vernon Lee (Violet Paget), for instance, one finds a "statuesque" androgynous woman, reincarnated later in the Althea[35] of H.D.'s *Paint It Today*: "Althea stopped and turned her head, less like a woman's, in its large placid beauty and intellectual candour, than like that of some antique youth's in whose marble effigy we fancy we recognize one of the speakers of the *Phaedo* or the *Euthydemus*" (6–7).

This complex spiritualized eroticism surrounding marble sculpture is associated by Pater exclusively with Phoebus Apollo, who virtually embodies "hellenism" as Pater defines it, "the principle pre-eminently of intellectual light" (*Renaissance* 201). In *Greek Studies* Pater elaborates the Apollonian as it signifies the Dorian: "He represents all those specially European ideas, of a reasonable, personal freedom, as understood in Greece; of a reasonable polity; of the sanity of soul and body, through the cure of disease and of the sense of sin; of the perfecting of both by reasonable exercise or *ascêsis*" (270). These qualities of Pater's paean define an exalted spirituality manifest particularly, as we have seen, in the statue of the naked male athlete, "the purged and perfected essence, the ideal soul" of the Diadumenos or the Discobolos or the Jason (299).

This Dorian model is fundamental to H.D.'s early hellenism. H.D. imagined her own hellenism in terms of a Dorian ideal. In her early autobiographical narrative, *Hermione*, H.D. figures her own poetic gift as "Laconian" (Spartan/ Lacedaemonian):[36] "[George] wanted fire to answer his fire and it was the tall sapling, the cold Laconian birch tree, the runner and the fearless explorer (my mind was) that drew spark from him" (219). In this same passage Hermione reiterates the epigraph by Simonides to the Spartan soldiers at Thermopylae to signify her sense of fidelity to Apollonian "orders": "[T]ell the Lacedaemonians that we lie here obeying their orders" (221). Moreover, H.D. persistently emphasizes the fact that Helen, the icon of hellenic beauty, is "queen of Sparta"; and in her essay on Euripides' *Helen* she associates her not with Aphrodite but with Artemis, "the goddess of ecstasy," alluding to the Brauronia, the primitive ritual for young girls dedicated to the goddess of the wilderness (6, 10–11). Helen belongs for the early H.D. to the white ecstasy of Lacedaemon, along with her brothers, the Dioscuri, who for Pater are a mythic figuration of perfect Dorian friendship (*Plato and Platonism* 230–2).

Moreover, as Laity has shown, H.D.'s early poetry and her autobiographical fiction are filled with Paterian adoration of the male statue, and with much the same implication of white eroticism ("Lesbian Romanticism" xxviii–ix; "Trangressive Sexualities" 54–8). "We should be able, more easily, to fall in love with a statue than with any other work of art," the narrator of *Paint It Today* says (61). Young Midget in the Louvre gazes clairvoyantly and worshipfully at the Discobolos and the Jason, two of the statues of "Athletic Prizemen" especially meriting Pater's study (62–4; *Greek Studies* 299–316). These two statues, the narrator says, "brought to my soul the uttermost calm of utmost friendship, the delight of a vision of perfect understanding, without the deep fear of that friendship broken or ever being broken, the deep fear and the deep delight that comes only with infatuation" (64). Thus, as with Pater, the male athletic statue represents a dream of perfect fraternity.

Further, as Diana Collecott has argued, this Dorian statuary whiteness seems associated by H.D. with a sense of self, a "scene of recognition" that is also a "self-recognition" ("Images" 363). H.D. arrives at this trope perhaps in connection with Apollo's *gnothi seauton*, his "revelation of the soul and body," or with the Dorian ideal of fulfillment as Pater sums it up, that one may become "himself as a work of art" (*Plato and Platonism* 232–3). Hermione of *Hermione* imagines herself – her self – as marble, and specifically as a statue of Artemis:

> Keep Parthian quiver strapped to a stalwart marble shoulder, don't let any go. Don't let any single shaft escape you. Wily and divine, keep it all, keep it all. Save yourself and offer them a sort of water creature. Keep marble for yourself and keep marble for marble. Keep a marble self for a marble self, Her for Her, Her for Fayne exactly. (176–7)

Marble here carries the sense, as it does traditionally, of the changeless and the durable – a hidden "real" self, known in the homoerotic/autoerotic mirroring of self, as opposed to a pliable and duplicitous social self.

As Laity and Collecott have indicated, H.D. in her autobiographical narratives makes use of this Dorian figural model to define female homoeroticism. She situates it within classical images of Artemis, Athena, and Apollo, and ironically not in terms of Aphrodite, the goddess of Ionian/Lesbian Sappho; and she consistently associates that Dorian quality with marble. Collecott explores this encoding of desire in terms of statues in her rich study of H.D.'s scrapbook of photomontages dating from the late twenties. In these images, juxtaposing photographs of H.D.'s naked body with pictures of Greek statues and architecture, Collecott emphasizes H.D.'s conception of "the statue . . . as a site of transformation" (325). These "images at the crossroads," she argues, encode H.D.'s bisexuality (323–8).

But for Midget in *Paint It Today* and Hermione in *Hermione*, statues at the same time carry great ambivalence. Some experiences of stone are not so happy, because they indicate a conflicted and dark territory that cannot be subsumed under the spiritualized fiction of male homoeroticism. The actual experience of desire – such as H.D.'s infatuation for Frances Gregg – is often quite painful (Laity, "Lesbian Romanticism" xxv). Midget is disturbed by a statue of the Hermaphrodite: "There is no white friendship in this statue" (64). The Hermaphroditus is different from the male statue in calling attention to the puzzle of sexuality rather than ostensibly transcending it.

Another problem of Dorian accommodation surrounds the statues of women, which are very far from the Paterian ideal of "white friendship." This is, in particular, the problem of the Venus de Milo, the representation of the Aphroditic female body. Discovered in 1820 and placed in the Louvre in 1821, the Venus de Milo was a central icon within romantic hellenism, and a long line of male poets – Leconte de Lisle and Heine among them – recorded their ineffably aroused gazing (Haskell and Penny 328–30). H.D. recalls these tributes when in 1912, during her visit to Paris, she and Richard Aldington spend long hours "beneath the Venus" and Aldington buys her a little replica to place on her writing table (Paris diary 9, 15–18, 51). Thus H.D. finds herself within the complex triangulations of the male gaze, wherein the white female body with its blank eyes carries the projection of male erotic fantasy.

One last aspect of Pater's Dorian eroticism is supremely important to H.D. in the first half of her career – the primacy of Phoebus Apollo. He is at first the Paterian god of statues, to whom, in her 1912 diary of her visits to the Louvre, H.D. prays in committing herself to her craft (64); and this early Apollonian rapture of museums is replayed in *Asphodel* (19–20). Apollo is for H.D. not only Phoebus ("shining") but Helios (the sun) itself: light to the eyes, illumination to the mind, inspiration to the spirit. In effect, Helios/Apollo governs the whole domain of clairvoyance as well as the dedicated, ascetic life, the process of purification or transformation.

In terms of H.D.'s conversation with Dorian eroticism, one aspect of Pater's Apollonian configuration is especially significant: his persistent interest in the story of Hyacinthus or Hyacinth, a young lover of Apollo whom the god accidentally kills in a game of quoits. Pater repeatedly mentions Hyacinth throughout his writing, with increasing elaboration of the story.[37] The last and most complex of these is "Apollo in Picardy" (*Miscellaneous Studies* 142–71). It is a disturbing version of the traditional story, in part because it emphasizes homoeroticism and the "homophobia" aroused by it;[38] and also because it points to the ambivalent effects of Apollonian possession, resulting here in violent death and in mania. For H.D. too the story of Hyacinth is a primary locus of significance, as Laity has been the first to observe.[39] H.D. refers to Hyacinth in poetry, fiction, and essays; and she often signed herself Hyacinth in correspondence with Bryher and with Havelock Ellis.[40] Moreover, the often coded reference to the flower hyacinth is ubiquitous in H.D.'s writing. "Apollo in Picardy," to which H.D. alludes in one of her early narratives (*Asphodel* 155), is the chief text in her conception of the myth, and it carries for her the implications not only of Dorian homoeroticism but also of sacrifice and daimonic possession associated with the ascetic life of the poet.

In Pater's story, set in medieval France in the context of a monastic community, the god manifests himself in a secluded valley as a shepherd, called by the community Apollyon, the name of a malignant spirit in the Bible. The narrator of the story describes two figures – the prior Saint-Jean and his young, beautiful companion, Hyacinthus – each of whom falls in love under the spell of Apollyon. The god in disguise confronts each with "the power of untutored natural impulse, of natural inspiration" (156). The consequences of this inspiration are distinct for each of them, but together they describe the complexity, for Pater, of the Dorian ideal as lived out in the mundane world.

For the boy Hyacinthus this natural impulse means a release of physical exuberance and gaiety in the constant company of Apollyon. This erotic and aesthetic fullness of the body climaxes in a game of quoits, after Hyacinthus finds an ancient discus in a grave. Apollyon and Hyacinthus shed their clothes, and, naked in the moonlight together, they re-create for an instant the immortal images of Greek sculpture. Apollyon becomes the Discobolos: "[C]rouching, right foot foremost, and with face turned backwards to the disk in his right hand, . . . he seemed – beautiful pale spectre – to shine from within with a light of his own" (167). But then a stormy darkness comes, along with the turn of the solar year to winter (the coming of the north wind), and Hyacinthus is struck brutally in the face with the discus: "His shout of laughter is turned in an instant to a cry of pain, of reproach" (168). In this interpretation of the myth, the Apollonian perfection of white friendship carries with it a terrible shadow – betrayal, wounding, and disaster.

Prior Saint-Jean is an old monk engaged in the last volume of a magnum opus on "mathematics, applied, . . . to astronomy and music" (143). The "natural inspiration" of the god to him is not so much physical as intellectual and visionary: "It was a veritable 'solar storm' – this illumination, which had burst at the last moment upon the strenuous, self-possessed, much-honoured monastic student" (144). The crushing blow to the brain delivered to Hyacinthus at Apollo's hand is a literal image of the prior's spiritual wound, "burst[ing] at the last moment" upon his ascetic life.

After the brilliant Apollyon becomes his scribe, the prior gradually senses that he has forgotten his carefully learned formulas and that he now possesses clairvoyant perception of celestial matters: "Did he not *see* the angle of the earth's axis with the ecliptic, . . . and the earth – wicked, unscriptural truth! – moving round the sun, and those flashes of the eternal and unorbed light. . . . The singing of the planets: he could hear it" (164). However, his clairvoyance and clairaudience manifest themselves in ecstatic seizures – episodes of divine mania – that in their hallucinatory intensity begin to destroy the prior:

> ... that astounding white light! – rising steadily in the cup, the mental receptacle, till it overflowed, and he lay faint and drowning in it. Or he rose above it, as above a great liquid surface, and hung giddily over it – light, simple, and absolute – ere he fell. Or there was a battle between light and darkness around him, with no way of escape from the baffling strokes, the lightning flashes; flashes of blindness one might rather call them. (164–5)

This ecstasy of light is recorded in the visionary illuminations with which the prior adorns his manuscript. Instead of the rational mathematical diagrams of the earlier volumes, one finds here "winged flowers, or stars with human limbs and faces, still intruding themselves" (165). Eventually, after the death of Hyacinthus, Apollyon departs, leaving the prior under suspicion of murdering the boy "in a fit of mania" (169–70). He is taken away and sequestered, to live the rest of his life in longing to return to the place of his ecstasies (170). For Pater the price to be paid for the visionary gift of the god – conflated in the story with a triangular homoeroticism – is madness and displacement. In one way or another, the lover of Apollo suffers a wound to the head.

H.D. appears to have seen in this story an analogue for the vicissitudes of her own dedication as a poet. The Hyacinth story is one of H.D.'s classical metafictions, pertaining not to a single aspect of her life but to its whole career. Her autobiographical narratives cover again and again the same ground, reiterating the crucial events of the approximately ten years comprising her initial relationships with Pound, Frances Gregg, Aldington, Lawrence, and Bryher (1909–19). The biographical basis of those fictions – much rehearsed by critics – involves complex betrayals and catastrophes, in the context of both heterosexual and homosexual bonds. But throughout H.D.'s early writing there are persistent traces of the themes of Pater's story and its overarching puzzle concerning the god who exacts a terrible price for his favors: the dream of white friendship, homoerotic, Dorian, fraternal, carrying the promise of some intimate self-knowledge; the betrayal of that spiritualized erotic bond; and in the context of those psychic wounds, clairvoyant and hallucinatory episodes.

Beyond H.D.'s fixity upon incidents of personal betrayal is a more urgent need, to map the failed trajectory of her brilliant career, to understand Apollo's betrayal. If I am right about the centrality of this fiction within H.D.'s self-conception as an artist, it would explain the pivotal place of her translation of Euripides' *Ion* following her analysis with Freud – an attempt to complete a fiction, begun in the terrible years of World War I, pertaining to a woman's betrayal by Apollo and her subsequent history of bitterness and infertility. This fiction is especially important for H.D. because it situates Apollo in relation not to the male but to the female. It pertains not to the idealizations of male homoeroticism, but to the recovery of a figure notably absent in Pater's late myth of a wholly male community – the bitter, "black" mother.

Demeter's White Hands

As we have seen, the Dorian model of male homoeroticism that Pater shares can allow, even celebrate, the body of the androgyne. It can allow, further, the "white" female body – the virgin and the milky mother. Because both mother and virgin stand in melancholy proximity to loss and death, they comprise a whiteness with shades of "blues." The white eroticism surrounding these female figures merges with the chaste aura of hellenic homoeroticism, governed, as Plato says, by a heavenly or "Uranian" Venus, distinct from the base, sensual Venus of ordinary worship (*Symposium* 180d–e; *Dialogues* 1:538).

Pater elaborates for H.D. some of the chief aspects of an Eleusinian desire, or, in Deborah Kelly Kloepfer's phrase, a "maternally connoted homoeroticism" (122). Pater's writings return to the "whiteness" of the virgin mother, persistently seen in relation to the child and home and in the context of sanctuary. In Pater's early imaginary portrait, "The Child in the House," the "quiet of the child's soul [was] one with the quiet of its home, a place 'inclosed' and 'sealed'" (*Miscellaneous Studies* 181). A central point in this locus of unified consciousness is "that little white room," where, under the bright window, his mother teaches him to read. There "things without thus [minister] to him," figuring themselves "on the white paper, the smooth wax," of the soul (177–8). This figural model is repeated later in Pater's treatment of Demeter and Persephone. The dual goddess is associated with a range of colors, or rather light and shade – resolving predominantly into white and shades of blue. In the Eleusinian ritual quoted by Pater, she "bring[s] us a *white* spring, a *white* summer" (*Greek Studies* 127; Pater's emphasis). However, the traditional sign of the mournful Demeter is her "robe of dark blue . . . the blue robe of the earth in shadow" (116). Persephone is for Pater ambiguous and sinister, representing the freshness of new life in its intrinsic proximity to death (140). Pater's treatment of this composite figure – sublime, grave, and chaste – reflects not only his scholarly interest in mythology, but the "feeling for maternity" that he projects upon Leonardo (*Renaissance* 120; *Greek Studies* 151).

In *Marius the Epicurean* Marius's mother is identified by the boy with "White-nights," the name of his childhood home, and with "the mystery of so-called *white* things," that seem to be "the doubles, or seconds, of real things" (1:13). Thus the aura of whiteness from the beginning is like that of shadowy waking dreams, and his mother is likewise "languid and shadowy" in her pious and regretful worship of the dead (1:17). Thus she suggests the duality of the great goddess, an image of the *mater dolorosa* but also of the goddess at the threshold of the underworld. The quiet house, "cloistral or monastic," is a Demetrian vessel, a "*sacellum*, the peculiar sanctuary of his mother" (1:20). Marius comes to associate religious awe and sorrow with the mother's presence: "And Marius . . . even thus early, came to think of women's tears, of women's hands to lay one to rest, in death as in the sleep of childhood, as a sort of natural want. The soft lines of the white hands and face, set among the many folds of the veil and stole of the Roman widow, . . . defined themselves for him as the typical expression of maternity" (1:21). The "white hands and face" of the mother here echo Pater's earlier description of a statue of Demeter in the sanctuary at Eleusis, "with face and hands of ivory," in "likeness to women's flesh" (*Greek Studies* 142–3). Pater's emphasis in these passages is remarkably coincident with aspects of Victorian iconography delineated by Nina Auerbach – the dissociation of the female body into fetishized parts, and the particular focus upon the image of women's hands, suggesting a binding, mobile, and unifying power (47–52). However, what is also striking here is the identification of the fragmented signs of the female body with "natural want." This ambiguous phrase suggests at once some "want" or absence in nature (grief, sleep, death), but at the same time, on the part of the child, some natural "want" or craving. This duality of want – absence and craving – is moreover associated particularly with the whiteness of the mother.

Pater most fully elaborates this figural model in a late essay, "Hippolytus Veiled" (1889), an imaginary portrait based on a lost version of Euripides' *Hippolytus*. He presents in Hippolytus his most complete portrait of the virgin, with "immaculate body and soul" (*Greek Studies* 175), in relation to the virgin mother. His modulation of the Eleusinian myth in this study is particularly striking, as Gerald Monsman has observed (*Portraits* 166–8). Through his Amazon mother the young Hippolytus comes to worship the goddess Artemis, who has a shrine near their home off a road to Eleusis. But in a kind of personal revelation, Hippolytus comes to understand that this Artemis is really the child of Demeter, the virginal Persephone. Hippolytus thus comes in an Eleusinian worship to fuse in the figure of Artemis the attributes of the dual goddess, emphasizing especially her maternity:

> [T]he goddess reveals herself to the lad, . . . as at once a virgin, necessarily therefore the creature of solitude, yet also as the assiduous nurse of children, and patroness of the young. Her friendly intervention at the act of birth everywhere, her claim upon the nursling, among tame and wild creatures equally, among men as among gods, nay! among the stars . . . gave her a breadth of influence seemingly co-extensive with the sum of things. Yes! his great mother was in touch with everything. (*Greek Studies* 174)

The Attic Artemis, with her narrow sphere of the hunt, comes in Pater's retelling to have the significance of the Magna Mater herself. Pater's Artemis/Persephone is also clearly associated with chaste whiteness and with blues. To Hippolytus she is "sweet as the flowers he offered her gathered at dawn, setting daily their purple and white frost against her ancient marbles" (177).

In elevating this cluster of associations surrounding the virgin mother, Pater also recurrently emphasizes an incestuous eroticism between mother and son – precisely that implied in Marius's "want." This concern is signaled in Pater's attention in *The Renaissance* to the iconography of Virgin and Christ child, a traditional locus of figural play on the theme of incest (Layard 173). Moreover, this bond between mother and son is amplified in certain mythological emphases. In his essays on Dionysos (1876, 1878), sequent to the essay on Demeter and Persephone (1875), Pater rhetorically overlays and even displaces the Eleusinian with the Dionysian mysteries, the latter having shadows of Asiatic worship of the Magna Mater and her son-consort (*Greek Studies* 6, 38–9). Dionysian religion effectively appropriates as well the matri-centrality of the Eleusinian mysteries, because Dionysos according to Pater is chiefly governed by mother-love, "found[ing] a new religion" in "vindication of the memory of his mother," revealing himself "out of tenderness for her." It is fairly easy to find an erotic shading in Pater's conception of this tenderness: Dionysos possesses a "yearning affection [for the mother], the affection with which [on an Etruscan mirror] we see him lifting up his arms about her, satisfied at last" (57–8). With regard to the Eleusinian mysteries themselves, Pater insists upon the equality of Dionysos with Persephone as the lost child of the mother. Dionysos interrupts and complicates the dyad of mother and daughter, becoming finally the "[s]on or brother of Persephone," in an erotic triangulation (39–40).

Pater nowhere more deliberately exploits the theme of incest than in "Hippolytus Veiled." In this story, Hippolytus has three mothers, all in rivalry for his love. The first is his biological mother, Antiope, an Amazon dedicated to Artemis, who is raped and impregnated by Theseus. Her Artemisian chastity is surrendered in love for the child in the womb: "In the wild Amazon's soul, to her surprise, and at first against her will, the maternal sense had quickened from the moment of his conception, . . . kindling more eagerly at every token of his manly growth" (*Greek Studies* 169–70). Antiope's kindled love issues in jealousy, for as the boy matures, he cultivates increasingly a rival love for an absent, transcendent mother, Antiope's patroness Artemis (175–8). Finally, Hippolytus comes in contact with his stepmother, Phaedra, "a fiery soul with wild strange blood in her veins," who tries to initiate him into the erotic rites of "the divine courtesan" Aphrodite, thus competing both with Antiope and with Artemis (185–7). Out of all this erotic complication comes a version of the familiar tragic calamity.

H.D.'s conversation with Pater with regard to Demetrian images is at times quite specific. For instance, one finds Demeter's "blues" in H.D.'s description of Kreousa,[41] the mother of Ion; in Hedyle, the mother of Hedylus; and in Thetis, the mother of Achilles. H.D. unquestionably echoes Pater's essay on Hippolytus in "She Contrasts with Herself Hippolyta," a poem imagining the awakening of maternal eros in Hippolyta,[42] and this essay is a chief source in her configuration of the Hippolytus myth in *Hippolytus Temporizes*.

Though Pater is not unique in his emphasis on Demetrian nostalgia, his presence as a literary precursor is distinctly recognizable in H.D.'s treatment of the Hippolytus story. A unique figural marker in Pater's essay is his transmutation of Artemis into the virgin mother of the child's longing. This chaste Dorian goddess and the other virgin goddess, Athene, stand for "mothers" in the psychological and spiritual world of H.D.'s early hellenism. They take the place of Demeter as images of maternal comfort and protection and of Persephone as images of austere and even ruthless virginity. In *Paint It Today*, as we have seen, Midget/H.D. refers to the "maid of Delos" who protects Josepha and herself: "Her face was like our mother's face. She was sister to our mother. She culled us close to her, more loving than a mother, because her arms were hungry" (57).[43]

Thus H.D.'s Dorian affiliations privilege the "white body" of male homoeroticism, as Laity has shown ("Trangressive Sexualities" 54–8). In Pater that whiteness alludes not only to marble luminescence, thus to androgynous intercourse, but to the milkiness of the virgin mother. The mother-goddess brings "a *white* summer, a *white* spring," not only in the whiteness of blossoms, but in the calm aura of sensuous satiety.

The link between whiteness and female homoeroticism in H.D.'s writing is hidden, encoded, thus finally undemonstrable. But one might consider in the context of Paterian whiteness this passage from *Asphodel*, Hermione's internal monologue when first encountering Beryl (Bryher):

> [W]hen she looked into two blue eyes . . . Hermione remembered her own name, . . . Hermione was the mother of Helen, or was Hermione the daughter of Helen? Hermione, Helen and Harmonia. Hymen and Heliodora. Names that began with H and H was a white letter. H was the snow on mountains and Hermione (who now remembered that her name was Hermione) remembered snow on mountains, sensed the strong pull-forward of sea-breakers, sensing the foam that was white and the white steed of some race chariot. And white steeds, white flowers, white rocks looked at her out of enormous eyes. (168)

Whiteness and H here serve as symbolist signs – like the linguistic essences in Arthur Rimbaud's "Vowels" or the color essence in Henri de Regnier's "Symphonie en blanc majeur." They are associated in Hermione/H.D.'s catalogue with mother-daughter (Helen/Hermione), with "harmony," with poetry (*Hymen* and *Heliodora* are H.D.'s second and third volumes of poetry), and with an Artemisian ecstasy like that of Hippolytus (white sea foam and white steeds).

This gestalt of whiteness, moreover, is coincidental with self-remembrance, occurring within the mirroring eyes of Beryl.

One also finds a Demetrian, Paterian whiteness in *Hermione*. The white hands of Marius's mother, and of Demeter's statue, are suggested to Hermione in the "Demeter hand[s]" of her mother, Eugenia, as Hermione watches her knitting in the dark: "[T]his hypnotic movement of hands, of hands in darkness, of hands in half-light, of hands crossing hands and making a pattern like moonlight across the black leaves of swamp, of March lilies." This description suggests the Isis-like mother in Marius's home, an eternal, liminal attendant upon the dead husband. These hands, like those of Marius's mother, also evoke some "natural want," want as absence (darkness, half-light, moonlight) and also want as desire. "Your throat looks so pretty coming out of that ruffle," Hermione says, "like a moonflower. You're soft like a moonflower" (80–1).

These overlays of whiteness may give clues to many of H.D.'s lyrics, where often erotic intimacy is not sexually determined. Some critics point to certain of H.D.'s lyrics as homoerotic, when no explicit signal of gender exists.[44] This is perhaps because they are cognizant of her codes. In "At Baia," from *Hymen*, for instance, erotic valences are suggested as an "I" addresses an imagined other, in a subjunctive and subliminal fantasy of a gift of white orchids, touched by white hands. The speech conflates flowers and hands of giver and receiver in an evocation of fragility, gentleness, and delicate touch: "Flower sent to flower; / for white hands, the lesser white, / less lovely of flower leaf, // or // Lover to lover, no kiss, / no touch, but forever and ever this" (*Collected Poems* 128). In "White World," another lyric from *Hymen*, one finds something close to Pater's Eleusinian whiteness. "The whole white world is ours," the poem begins, though it continues not by cataloguing white things but by discriminating muted shades of color:

> and the world, purple with rose-bays,
> bays, bush on bush,
> group, thicket, hedge and tree,
> dark islands in a sea
> of grey-green olive or wild white-olive, . . .

The "whole white world," it seems, is not an empirical but an erotic entity, tied to the unspecified intimacy signaled in "ours." The whiteness here, as in Pater's "*white* summer, *white* spring," does not refer to light or color in itself but to a sensuous consummation: "[O]urs is the wind-breath / at the hot noon-hour, / ours is the bee's soft belly / and the blush of the rose-petal, / lifted, of the flower" (*Collected Poems* 134–5). The eroticism of these images, depending on oblique allusion to intimate touch (soft belly, blush, lifted rose-petal), suggests that the "white world" with its felt discriminations signifies the white body itself.

H.D. would seem also to have taken seriously the figural possibilities of incest that Pater deliberately explores. She is fascinated in all her hellenic texts with the dyad of son and mother – Rhesos/Muse, Ion/Kreousa, Hippolytus/Hippolyta, Philip/Hipparchia, Hedylus/Hedyle, Achilles/Thetis, Memnon/Eos, and others – increasingly summed up in the Egyptian mother–brother–son triad of Isis/Osiris/Horus. Critics of H.D. have reflected on the psychological aspects of this preoccupation. However, no one, to my knowledge, has amplified the specifically literary contexts of the theme, particularly in Pater's writing. Undoubtedly, Pater's most provocative exploration of incest, "Hippolytus Veiled," provided an impetus to H.D.'s prolonged attention to that myth, issuing, in *Hippolytus Temporizing*, in a complex erotic fantasy surrounding the absent body of the mother. Moreover, H.D. took Pater's suggestion – specifically noted and amplified by Freud – that Leonardo's Mona Lisa is the transformation of the image of the desired mother, "[f]rom childhood defining itself on the fabric of his dreams."[45] Such a "[fixation] to the mnemic image of his mother" (Freud 100) is played out in H.D's treatment of Achilles and Thetis in *Helen in Egypt*, wherein Achilles comes to see the childhood image of Thetis as the root of all his desire.

The predominance of this theme reflects the "matrisexuality" of H.D.'s poetics, which has received amplification from critics.[46] But at the same time, as Kloepfer has emphasized, the motif of mother–son incest displaces the exploration of a forbidden or inaccessible eros – the daughter's desire for the mother. In *Tribute to Freud* the brother/son mediates the daughter's intimacy with the mother: "If I stay with my brother, become part almost of my brother, perhaps I can get nearer to *her*" (33). Thus one can detect in H.D.'s early hellenic writing certain areas of self-censorship, corresponding to the male iconographies represented in Pater and at the same time reflecting these psychologically forbidden territories.

One finds in H.D.'s writing, as in Pater, a submergence of the original Eleusinian bond between mother and daughter and a displacement of emphasis upon Dionysos as the child of Demeter. One sees this displacement, for instance, in "Demeter," a poem in *Hymen* (*Collected Poems* 111–15), where H.D. presents an interior monologue of the Cnidian Demeter, a statue in the British Museum, commented on at length by Pater (*Greek Studies* 150–2). The goddess, imprisoned in stone, follows an associative and obscure line of meditation. At two points (parts 1 and 4) she broods upon an unnamed "she," who at first appears to be an object of rivalry: "[S]he is slender of waist, / slight of breast, made of many fashions; / they have set *her* small feet / on many a plinth" (111; emphasis added). The second she is "*mistress of Death*," evoked in erotic terms of the kiss and embrace of Hades (114). At least subliminally, these two "shes" are conflated (Aphrodite/Persephone/Hecate) and disposed to the margins of the poem. However, at the center, in the middle parts 2 and 3, is the other child, Dionysos:

"Many the children of gods / but first I take / Bromios" (113). Whereas in H.D.'s hellenic writing the mother–son dyad is persistently evoked, the Demeter–Persephone bond has only a shadowy presence, though a more pronounced presence in the autobiographical fiction, wherein H.D. confronts the matter of her actual erotic ties with her mother and with other women.

The Dorian Censor

The iconography of Dorian hellenism, while providing a way of figuring the homoerotic, presents some serious constraints for the woman writer, issuing finally in forms of self-censorship. Most obviously, it presents H.D. with a predicament of style. Situated within heavily weighted dichotomies, the Dorian model of art leaves a treacherous territory of the obverse to be negotiated – qualities of the Ionian, Asiatic, or Aphroditic, and the centrifugal. We come back, in other words, to the issue of decadence. H.D. was thoroughly aware of the Ionian and Dorian categories. Imagism can be seen as a new articulation of Dorian art, with its call to discipline, hardness, and brilliance, and its move away from the luxuriousness and dissipation of fin-de-siècle poetry. But like Pater, even at her most Dorian or imagist H.D. was also very much Ionian in disposition. She indicates a predilection for the sensuous and "centrifugal" in an early review of poetry by John Gould Fletcher (1916), in which she exults in the luxury of color: "[H]ow much more than the direct image to [the lover of beauty] are the images suggested by shadow and light, the flicker of the purple wine, the glint across the yellow, the depth of the crimson and red" (183).

H.D. seems to have deliberately cultivated this Aphroditic style in *Hymen*, after the Dorian astringency of *Sea Garden*. The volume is highly "colored" and explicitly erotic.[47] Precisely this sensuousness – what Eliot called "neurotic carnality" – displeased many of her early male readers.[48] Moreover, the volume as a whole makes continual allusion to classical artifacts, and in this domain of the "museum" H.D. locates herself with the Ionian. In the title poem, she refers to a series of artifacts – chryselephantine (images of ivory and gold), medallions, bas-relief, Tanagra statuettes – that are precisely those marked by Pater as the minor Ionian art of "graven images" (*Greek Studies* 250–5). This Ionian tendency – her "best purple pseudo-classic style," she called it[49] – is apparently for H.D. something a little shameful, associated with "Asiatic abandon."[50]

H.D.'s 1920 essay on Sappho has received much attention since its first publication in 1982, having been discussed in terms of H.D's imagination of Sappho as a female literary precursor and of Lesbos as a site of female-directed desire.[51] However, in light of the hellenic iconography we have delineated here, another emphasis becomes clear. H.D. feels compelled in this essay to apologize for her own poetic and erotic dispositions, to redeem a too-Ionian, too-Aphroditic, and Eastern Sappho.

Such a rehabilitation is not easy, because Sappho's poetry is in fact nothing if not Aphroditic, and Aphrodite is the goddess that she chiefly celebrates. But H.D.'s essay may indeed be read as an apology for her literary foremother in the context of decadent exploitations. H.D. treats Sappho as much as possible in the acceptable terms of a Dorian aesthetic. "[T]rue," H.D. says, "there is a tint of rich colour . . . violets, purple woof of cloth, scarlet garments, dyed fastening of a sandal, the lurid, crushed and perished hyacinth, stains on cloth and flesh and parchment" ("The Wise Sappho" 57). The operative rhetorical construction here − "True . . . but" − is necessary because the *tinted, dyed, lurid,* and *stained* belong to a prurient iconography of Sappho, exemplified in Gautier's *Mademoiselle de Maupin,* in Baudelaire's and Swinburne's "lesbian," and in Pierre Louÿs's *Chansons de Bilitis.* But H.D. redeems Sappho's color-taint, the deep "stains . . . on the red and scarlet cushions" (57), by indicating that the words of Sappho are themselves "states" of color, "transcending colour yet containing . . . all colour" (58). This is, as we have seen, the traditional color iconography of white marble. Likewise "burning Sappho," in H.D.'s apology, burns not with the ordinary heat of passion, but with a fire like lightning, "white, inhuman element . . . as if the brittle crescent-moon gave heat to us" (57–8). Color thus is transformed to white light, heat to white heat, even to Artemisian moon heat.

One notes also in this essay H.D.'s avoidance or displacement of Aphrodite as Sappho's goddess. For instance, she at one point downplays Aphrodite by naming her as only one among other deities mentioned in Sappho's poems − "Aphrodite, Hermes, Ares, Hephaistos, Adonis, . . . the Graces, Zeus himself, Eros" (60) − when in the Sapphic fragments all other deities *but* Aphrodite are marginal. At another point, she indicates that Eros, not Aphrodite, determines Sappho's "bitterness" (59) − though the most famous of Sappho's poems, the only complete one, locates female Aphrodite and not male Eros at the center of erotic suffering. Finally, in Dorian/Aryan fashion, H.D. must qualify *Eastern* Aphroditic sensuousness by placing her in proximity to the *Western* chaste Athene: "[T]hough she stood in the heavy Graeco-Asiatic sunlight, the wind from Asia, heavy with ardent myrrh and Persian spices, was yet tempered with a Western gale, bearing in its strength and salt sting, the image of another, tall, with eyes shadowed by the helmet rim, the goddess, indomitable" (63). Thus Sappho in her temperate "Greekness" is saved from the "danger of overpowering sensuousness," from "Oriental [sexual] realism," from "Asiatic riot of colour" (63). This apology for a tainted Sappho indicates tellingly the inevitable self-conflict in H.D.'s poetics and in her conception of herself as a poet.

The ambivalence toward an Aphroditic Sappho also reflects a conflict with regard to H.D.'s attempts to represent female homoeroticism. In this respect the diminution of Aphrodite and the elevation of male eros within Dorian hellenism has undeniable effect. The hellenic cosmos that H.D. assimilates from this dominant classical homoeros can be summed up in her early prose piece, "Helios and Athene" (*Collected Poems* 326–30), written in 1920, near the time of her essays on Sappho and other Greek writers. The cosmos in that prose meditation is triangulated in power, between Helios/Apollo at Delphi, the visionary god of statues; Athene, the "Parthanos" [*sic*] of Athens; and Demeter of the mysteries, with Dionysos as their focus. Where are the female body and female desire in this configuration? Apollo's love is for the male; helmeted Athene's love, first for the male; Demeter's love, strangely, for the male. One finds a virgin (male-born) and a mother, but no female-directed desire, no daughter Persephone, no Aphrodite. Instead, as we have seen in Pater, there is an emphasis on "Dorian eroticism," centered in the mysticism of the male athletic statue; on the asceticism belonging to the Androgyne Athene, who combines attributes of Apollo and Demeter; and on the incestuous dyad of mother and son.

These emphases, though providing H.D. with an erotically and spiritually charged language, nevertheless determine vacancy and confusion with regard to the representation of female desire. As we have seen, female homoeroticism is predominantly figured in H.D. within models borrowed from Dorian hellenism – marble sensuousness, intimacy with the Eleusinian or Artemisian mother. However, the Artemisian model, fully articulated, for instance, in the last part of *Paint It Today*, has limits that H.D. clearly discerns. Midget is speaking to Althea, an imaginary projection of an ideal Artemisian companion. She mentions the fact that even in London, which Althea scorns,

> "[t]hey have made a statue, . . . of the deity, the goddess of shaft and bow, . . ."
> "Who is this goddess?"
> Midget answered, "Artemis."
> Althea yawned. She asked, "And Aphrodite?"
> Midget knew she was defeated. She said, "There is no Aphrodite." (87)

Why is she "defeated"? Because, in the context of the dialogue between Midget and Althea, if Midget is to apologize for the value of the "visible world," she cannot avoid Aphrodite. Yet the Artemisian ideal of female desire at the same time cannot include her. Midget clearly alludes here to the famous epigraph of Alcman: "There is no Aphrodite. Hungry Love / Plays boy-like with light feet upon the flowers."[52] Her dismay at catching herself in this denial may indeed suggest her recognition of the dominance of male eros within the Artemisian model and the tragic exclusion of Aphrodite, the female erotic body.

Chapter Four

Anthropology and the Return of the Gods: Jane Ellen Harrison

In tracing the contexts of H.D.'s hellenic spirituality, the first question in Pound's early pagan catechism remains central: "What is a god?" ("Religio," *Selected Prose* 47–8). Pound, H.D., and other modernists invoke the ancient gods not as figurative markers within genteel discourse, but as psychological markers within the creative process itself. In this they follow main lines of romantic mythography, as Lawrence Kramer has made particularly clear in his exploration of the theophanic poem in romantic and modern poetry. Indeed, early modernist assumptions about gods and myths derive immediately from theoretical debates among Victorian intellectuals at the turn of the century.[1] Moreover, as Hugh Kenner has argued, modernists also take for granted a scholarly renaissance occurring in the last part of the nineteenth century, generated by discoveries of archaeology and anthropology (41–75).

No modern writer takes the "gods" more seriously than does H.D. Her early poetry makes references to herms, shrines, temples, altars, to prayers and offerings, pillar worship, daimonic possession, and *hieros gamos*. Moreover, the gods do not diminish but increase in significance in the course of her career. In her prose writing H.D. makes clear that the gods are part of a psychological and occult symbology, figured within a heroic imaginative project. As Hipparchia of *Palimpsest* says, "The very names . . . of the Greek gods still held virtue" (72), functioning as binding charms. The gods become ciphers for H.D. in an increasingly elaborate mapping of her history.[2]

Thus it seems important to recover the specific character of H.D.'s fascination with ancient deities and cults. Jane Ellen Harrison and the Cambridge ritualists are especially important in establishing the terms of the discussion about ancient religions in the first decades of the twentieth century. Like Pater, Harrison is a facilitator and disseminator of ideas, but also an original scholar and theoretician in her own right. She is remarkably ecumenical in her acceptance of literary, scientific, and theoretical discourse. As a classicist she was steeped in romantic hellenism, but she was also actively engaged in archaeological excavations. She embraced and promoted many theoretical currents of the first decades of the twentieth century – the ideas not only of Frazer and other ethnologists, but of Marcel Mauss, Emile Durkheim, and Arnold van Gennup, and the writing of Nietzsche, Henri Bergson, Sigmund Freud, and Carl Jung. However, again like Pater, Harrison is little acknowledged among modernists as a significant intellectual figure. She meets with condescension in the pretentious climate of early modernism – for instance, in the pages of the *Egoist* – on the same grounds that Pater and, later, H.D. are dismissed: for female enthusiasm, lack of intellectual rigor, "Specialised Unintelligence," and "brain-fuddle" (Carter 114, 115).

Nevertheless, I turn primarily to Harrison in explicating H.D.'s sense of Greek religion, and I deal only slightly with two figures that are more commonly cited in relation to H.D.'s sense of gods and rituals: Frazer and Nietzsche. Harrison's formulations best suggest the amalgam of thought about Greek religion prevalent in the early twentieth century. Further, H.D. herself assumes positions in contrast with some of the assumptions and conclusions of Frazer and Nietzsche; conversely, she has remarkable affinities with Harrison.

Both Frazer and Nietzsche had a powerful general effect upon intellectual life in the early decades of the twentieth century, and H.D. absorbed their ideas, as she did those of Freud, not only directly but indirectly. The publication of the third edition of *The Golden Bough* between 1911 and 1915 caused great excitement among intellectuals. In an unpublished 1920 essay, H.D. mentions Frazer with admiration in the context of his classical scholarship, as an editor of Pausanias ("Pausanius" 4a). Later, in the thirties, Frazer is a subject of conversation between H.D. and Freud (*Tribute to Freud* 182). With regard to Nietzsche, both Aldington and Pound wrote for the *New Age*, edited by A. C. Orage, one of the leading advocates of Nietzsche in England; and Havelock Ellis, one of H.D.'s earliest psychological counselors, wrote a pivotal series of essays explaining Nietzsche's thought to the English public.[3]

As a rationalist and a scientist, one of many professor figures in H.D.'s intellectual theater, Frazer holds a place of awe for H.D., especially because he substantiates some of Freud's theories of psychological life and of civilization. In terms of myth and religion *The Golden Bough* is important to H.D. for the same general reasons that it is important to other modernists like Eliot and Joyce.[4] The figure of the dying god and the idea of the cyclic recurrence of the enactment of death and rebirth were especially significant for H.D. At the same time, Frazer's aesthetic as well as conceptual importance to H.D.'s writing is limited. She steadily resists Frazer's rationalist, enlightenment perspective.

Further, critics naturally think of Nietzsche's *The Birth of Tragedy* in relation to H.D.'s figuration of Apollo and Dionysos. A Nietzschean Dionysos is often foregrounded in discussions of H.D.'s writing in relation to such men as Lawrence and Pound (Hall 65–9; Gardiner). However, the assumption of the prominence of Nietzsche for H.D. needs qualification. There is little in Nietzsche's formulation of the Apollonian and Dionysian that is not common in German romantic hellenism, which saturates discussions of Greek art and culture in the late nineteenth century. Nietzsche's originality lies in his emphasis on the chthonic aspect of the Dionysian, in his theory of the origins of tragedy and of its Periclean perfection as the enactment of violent dichotomies analogous to sexual strife, and in his interpretation of the death of tragedy at the hands of Socrates and Euripides.

Nietzsche's study, translated into English in 1908, had a powerful but largely unacknowledged effect upon H.D.'s generation. But, as I have suggested, H.D. resists some of its basic terms. Though Yeats, Pound, vorticists, and futurists call in the years surrounding the war for the re-creation of a cosmos of tragic oppositions, H.D. stands with the accused in Nietzsche's scenario: Socrates/ Plato, Euripides, and their Alexandrianism. Plato's *Phaedrus*, for instance, is very probably an immediate source for H.D.'s understanding of divine possession. Further, H.D. herself suffers in personal relations from the Nietzschean worldview that sees male and female strife as the root of (male) creativity, the violent struggle between man and woman that is so much a part of Lawrence's imagination.

In other words, H.D.'s working of the territory of Greek mysteries is in many ways antithetical to the approach of Nietzsche and of Frazer. At the same time, one finds an uncanny parallelism between Harrison and H.D. in terms of their intellectual affinities and imaginative emphases. This likeness apparently cannot be explained as direct influence, such as exists between Harrison and Virginia Woolf, as Patricia Maika has shown (6–15). Rather, it suggests a broad and diffused intertextuality. Harrison and H.D. share ground undoubtedly in the ambiguous cultural role that each chose to perform in entering the male domain of the classics. Both are constitutionally poised between intellect and emotion, science and art. In their orientation toward the Greek world, one finds in each a similar mixture of romanticism and rationality, enthusiasm and facticity. Indeed, each lives out this tension in her life and projects it in her hellenic iconography: an instinctive affiliation with the mother and with art and thus a rebelliousness toward Olympian rational totality, and at the same time a compulsive affiliation with Apollonian paternal authority.[5]

H.D. never directly refers to Harrison in her writing. It is very likely true, as Robert Duncan has suggested, that H.D. followed the biases of her early intellectual associates.[6] However, H.D. could not have remained ignorant of Harrison's widely diffused ideas. Indeed, Eliot, in his 1920 review of Gilbert Murray's and H.D.'s translations, praises the Cambridge anthropologists as though they were familiar intellectual presences (*Selected Essays* 49). Harrison's

Prolegomena to the Study of Greek Religion (1903), in particular, permanently shifted conceptions of Greek religion. Robert Ackerman describes the *Prolegomena* as one of the rare works of scholarship that "alter[s] an intellectual landscape so profoundly that everyone is required to re-examine normally unexamined assumptions" ("Introduction" xiii). Murray, in an essay of appreciation after Harrison's death, gives the same judgment: "It is a book which . . . made an epoch" ("Harrison" 568).

Members of the group surrounding Harrison focused attention on the origins of Greek drama in sacred ritual. Their scholarly explorations, climaxing in major publications during the few years before World War I (1910–14), established a climate of eager discovery about Greek religion. "[W]hen you can," D. H. Lawrence writes to a friend in late 1913, "lend me books about Greek religions and rise of Greek Drama, or Egyptian influences – or things like that – I love them" (*Letters* 114). Lawrence's interest in these subjects is not arbitrary or unique; rather it shares in the contemporary interest generated not only by the mammoth third edition of Frazer's *The Golden Bough*, but also by publications specifically on Greek religion and drama coming from the Cambridge group or those responding to them with corrective theories.[7]

It is hard to believe that H.D. did not read at least *Ancient Art and Ritual*, published in the popular Home University Library in 1913 and discussed in the *New Freewoman* and in the *Egoist*.[8] She could have learned about it through Lawrence, who read it a few months before his acquaintance with H.D. began and who was strongly taken with its insight, "to see art coming out of religious yearning" (*Letters* 90, 114). Textual evidence in H.D.'s early and later commentaries on Euripides' *Ion* strongly suggests her reading of this book. There she seems to echo Harrison's text, taking for granted a conception of drama uniquely articulated by Harrison – the play as an enactment mediating between life and art.[9]

In any case, H.D. would have felt Harrison's influence, if not directly, then indirectly, through Gilbert Murray, whose critical writing and translations she read extensively during her early career and whom she very much respected.[10] Murray in his frequent discussions of Greek religion explicitly states his indebtedness to Harrison, his close friend and collaborator. Indeed, in his popular studies of Greek religion and of Euripides, both of which H.D. certainly read, he summarizes arguments given in Harrison's *Prolegomena* and *Themis*.[11]

Along with romantic hellenism, then, anthropology at the turn of the century provided a context in which H.D., along with Pound and other modernists, could take "the mysteries" seriously as a poetic fiction having the authority both of spiritual tradition and of scientific discovery. The following brief discussion of Harrison's *Prolegomena* in relation to H.D.'s early hellenic writing attempts, then, to delineate not literal influence but intertextuality, to suggest H.D.'s working of a widely disseminated set of ideas prominently articulated in Harrison's writing.

Keres

One of the most provocative and influential arguments of *Prolegomena*, like that of Nietzsche in *The Birth of Tragedy*, is directed against the ideality of Olympian religion and the entrenched classical tradition perpetuating the fiction of Greek serenity. Harrison asserts, through an analysis of specific festivals and cults, that Olympian religion is everywhere overlaid upon an older, precedent stratum of worship involving "snakes and ghosts and underworld beings" (28). She opens the *Prolegomena* with a frontal attack on Olympian bastions, considering the Diasia, a festival in honor of Zeus – not Zeus in his Homeric splendor, however, but Zeus Meilichios ("easy-to-be-entreated"), "figured by his worshippers as a snake" (18). This god is "Zeus in his underworld aspect – Zeus-Hades," the "male double of Erinys [the Fury]" (17, 23).

The dual character of the chief of the Olympians suggests that each of the major Olympian cults has hidden chthonic roots. In this light Harrison considers some of the other major festivals of the Attic calendar, notably the Attic feasts of Demeter, with the intent of illustrating an older stratum of ritual practice, not entirely subsumed by the newer cults. She then gives a "demonology" of chthonic spirits propitiated in older rites, variations of the Ker, or evil daimon, manifested in various images – as disease, death, or fate, as gorgon, wind daimon, siren, harpy, or fury. Harrison's very detailed consideration of these spirits, based on evidence from literature, art, and archaeology, establishes a pervasive dimension of Greek worship oriented toward the uncanny and the daimonic, subsisting vigorously within Olympian cults.

This irrational aspect of the Greeks, though highly apparent in Greek literature, is largely elided in romantic hellenism, but opened anew through anthropology. An emphasis on the chthonic figuration of ancient gods clearly distinguishes the moderns from the literary generation preceding them. Lawrence's poem "Snake," recounting a momentary recognition of the chthonic power of a snake, and Pound's figuration of violent divine metamorphoses in *The Cantos* both characterize a new fascination with darkness in the casting of the gods. Though, as we have seen, H.D. participates in romantic idealizations, this chthonic awareness is ubiquitous in her early hellenic writing – in the sense of a haunted and ominous landscape, in the awareness of death and disintegration as a facet of experience, and in persistent allusion to the duality of the Olympians as both kindly and destructive.

The poems of *Sea Garden* are haunted by unnamed daimonic presences compelling responses at once erotic and fearful. That gods are everywhere addressed in this volume but deliberately unnamed establishes a sense of their ur-status, like the original undifferentiated Pelasgian *theoi* mentioned by Herodotus, or like Harrison's Keres, ghosts, genii, and daimons. The Wind Sleepers resemble even more pointedly the wind daimons described in Harrison's *Prolegomena*,

Keres not gentle but imperious in their demand for propitiation (179–83). Poems like "Orchard" and "Pursuit" also indicate a kind of seizure and compulsion in relation to an unnamed god.[12] The offering to the god of the orchard is made in "prostration," in the anxiety of some unbearable fecundity; in "Pursuit" the pursuer is erotically bound in a desperate chase in which the pursued is known only through traces, always escaping, perhaps with the assistance of "wood-daemons." "The Helmsman" specifically alludes to the sophisticated daimon of Plato's *Phaedrus*, the erotic guide of the individual soul (247c–d; *Dialogues* 3:154), while in "Hermes of the Ways," at the other extreme, a worshiper enters within the *mana* of a primitive "standing stone." In the estranging light of this landscape, even ordinary moments – in "Mid-day," "Evening," and "Night" – have the hallucinatory quality of ghostly visitations, like those of the "midday daimon" or the "Keres of all mortal things" that Harrison describes (203, 173–4).

One of these last poems, "Night," points to the chthonic aspect of the gods that H.D. often emphasizes. This lyric traces the destruction of a flower in an inexorable process instrumented by night: "The night has cut / each from each / and curled the petals / back from the stalk." Night indeed becomes like a god in the apostrophe at the end of the poem, taking in its hand as placatory offering the "petals / of the roses," but leaving "the stark core / of the rose / to perish on the branch" (*Collected Poems* 33). The poem in simple lyric terms indicates the "grave pace" of time and death in relation to the perishable. But in other terms it might be seen to figure the *kathodos*, or descent, of Persephone into darkness.

H.D. alludes often to this descent into the underworld, as a devastation not only inevitable but also necessary, as an initiation into mysteries. The title poem of her second volume, *Hymen*, constitutes an epithalamion, figuring the sexual initiation of the bride in the bridal chamber in language suggesting both sensuality and violation. H.D. through Euripides' *Iphigeneia in Aulis* knew something of the homologies in Greek ritual between the bride's preparation for marriage, the preparation of a victim for sacrifice, and the preparation of the dead for burial. All brides are brides of Hades and all the dead are brides. Moreover, the pattern of many of H.D.'s autobiographical narratives alludes explicitly to Persephone's descent, often signaled by a mania or illness – at the end of *Hermione*, for instance, and of "Hipparchia" in *Palimpsest*, and of *Asphodel*. In this last novel Hermione during her pregnancy muses about the coming of winter: "[S]un lies heavy on the rough brambles, berries are almost over, frost makes a veil, the bride of God, the dead bride, Persephone veil over the bushes, over me, Persephone in Hell" (168).

One may see *Notes on Thought and Vision*, H.D.'s essay written in 1919 in the immediate aftermath of her "great-war" catastrophes, as a kind of apology, or self-consolation, for this necessary *kathodos*. The large argument in this essay is a familiar romantic one – that if one accepts physical and spiritual desire, one also accepts pain and death. H.D.'s meditation, however, takes account of the chthonic dimension of the gods themselves:

> Zeus Endendros – God in a tree; Dionysius Anthios, God in a flower; Zeus Melios, God in the black earth, death, disruption, disintegration; Dionysius Zagreus, the flower torn, broken by chemical process of death, vein, leaf, texture – white luminous lily surface, veined with black – white lily flesh bruised, withered. (32)

These epithets of the gods[13] give figures for the process of life itself, having intrinsically both a vital and a disintegrative aspect. God is in tree or flower, god is in its dissolution. That H.D. here chooses Zeus and Dionysos-Zagreus is not accidental; she thus acknowledges a traditional identification of the two. Both have the titles of Meilichios and Chthonios, and they form part of a triad with Hades, as the "great god" who is also the "black" god of the underworld.

The gods for H.D. are master tropes for the necessities of bodily, erotic, and spiritual life. As signs of necessity, they take on the dual aspect that Harrison explores: while they bestow their gifts, they at the same time compel painful initiation and service. More particularly, the gifts of the gods often bring mania, as Plato describes in the *Phaedrus*: Apollo the mania of prophecy, Dionysos maenadic frenzy, the Muses the mania of poetry, and Aphrodite the mania of desire (265b; *Dialogues* 3:173). Undoubtedly consoled by Plato's legitimization of irrational seizure, H.D. figures her own episodes of psychic breakdown in terms of divine mania.

The double edge of the gods' gifts is especially shown in H.D.'s allusions to Apollo/Helios and to Artemis, the chaste gods of her ascetic and crystalline hellenism. Their spiritual exaltation has a dangerous edge. Like the sharp edge of the discus that wounds Hyacinth, Apollo's casual but inexorable love wounds Cassandra, Kreousa, Hipparchia, and Hermione. Artemis, chaste and detached, is also associated with savage and bloody rites, which H.D. often emphasizes. Moreover, for H.D. the Greek world as a whole is associated with this precipitous danger. Projections have their sharp edges. "Greece is a thing of rocks that jag into you," Hermione in *Asphodel* muses, "every Greek line of poetry breaks you, jags into you, Hellenes the supreme masochists, *hurting* – how did they manage it?" (167). For all of H.D.'s intense idealization – or *because* of it – the sublime islands are also the "Cthonian [*sic*] Cyclades" (*Hermione* 210).

Korai

Another aspect of the *Prolegomena* has received much critical attention in recent years: Harrison's argument in a chapter called "The Making of a Goddess" that patriarchal Olympian religion suppresses an earlier matriarchal religion and that vestiges of this earlier worship can be found in the iconography of extant artifacts. She attempts to establish a lineage from archaic, pre-Homeric images of one Great Goddess, to the later, fragmented and specialized Olympian deities. Her insistence throughout is that the development of cults – the "articulation and separation" of the early "undifferentiated" images – has entailed significant loss (313).

Harrison's argument in this chapter relies not on philology or abstract theory but on imaginal association. She establishes a network of interrelated and recurring images from artifacts suggesting the survival in memory and tradition of an archaic theology. An example from the discussion of the Kourotrophos, or Great Goddess as child carrier, gives a sense of this mode of argument (263–321). The continual recurrence of a single image in metamorphic form suggests to Harrison increasingly diversified and distant strains of the old unitary and encompassing image. She presents a sequence of these primary images of the goddess from iconographical evidence: the prehellenic image of the Great Mother as the Lady of Wild Things, surrounded by fierce animals; the Kourotrophos; the dyad of Mother and Maid, or Kore; the image of the *anodos* of the Kore, a head emerging from the earth as from a womb, with attendant gods as midwives; the ubiquitous trinities of Korai in Greek cult, finally crystallizing in the goddesses of the "Judgment of Paris," Hera, Athene, and Aphrodite. This trinity especially makes clear the argument that the Great Goddess is finally reduced and compartmentalized in official Olympian religion into distinct and largely exclusive functions.

Harrison suggests the fullest echo of an original goddess in the figure of Aphrodite, who is also, like Persephone and Pandora, figured in terms of the *anodos*, the rising Kore. She is thus not only the *nymphe* or bride, but the virgin, and later, in connection with the Orphic cult of Eros, the mother as well. Moreover, Aphrodite is associated not only with earth but prominently with the sea (as Aphrogenia or Anodymene), and imagery suggests as well her affiliation with air. Thus Aphrodite more than any other Olympian retains vitality in popular worship and even increases in dimension. When "the mystery and the godhead of things natural faded into science," Harrison says, "[o]nly the mystery of life, and love that begets life, remained, . . . hence Aphrodite keeps her godhead to the end." In the late image of Venus Geneatrix, Harrison proposes,

> we have the old radiance of Aphrodite, but sobered somehow, grave with
> the hauntings of earlier godheads, with shadows about her cast by Ourania,
> by Harmonia, by Kourotrophos, by Eirene, by each and every various form
> of the ancient Mother of Earth and Heaven. (314–15)

Until very recently, Harrison has been alone among classicists and anthropologists in ascribing this fundamental importance to Aphrodite and in seeing her kinship with a unitary Great Mother.[14]

These related themes in Harrison's work have remarkable resonance in H.D.'s writing: H.D.'s fascination with the figure of the Greek Kore; her continual associative play with configurations from Greek myth; her grouping of multiple images of the Korai, as virgin, bride, and mother; her gradual recognition of a matriarchal stratum preceding Greek patriarchal religion or, more specifically, of a unitary figure within the fragmented images of the hellenic Korai.

H.D. in her early writing appears to follow a traditional differentiation in her iconography of Artemis, Athene, Demeter/Persephone, Hera, and Aphrodite, each appearing to have distinct functions. Athene, the projected image of Athens, represents the intelligence, discipline, and courageous will necessary to the craftsman. The domain of Artemis is the wilderness and the un-self-conscious release of the young girls who belong to her *thiasos*. Both of these figures of the virgin, as Susan Friedman has emphasized, are signs for H.D. of a freedom from patriarchal mastery and from societal constraint – though, as I have suggested, they also function effectively within the androcentric agenda of Dorian hellenism. In H.D.'s writing Athene or Artemis, in "daring to be herself" (*Asphodel* 11), stands in contrast to the essentially domestic sphere of female generation represented in Demeter and Persephone, as well as to the erotic sphere of Aphrodite, thoroughly appropriated and exploited within patriarchy. The whole range of these differentiated Attic Korai is shown clearly in "Hymen," a series of songs interspersed with dramatic narration. Here each stage of a woman's life – young child, girl, adolescent, virgin, bride, young and mature matron – is represented in a hieratic procession of Korai, each bringing offerings of distinct flowers and each associated with artifacts and rituals of Hera, Artemis, Athene, and Aphrodite.

This essentially Dorian impulse toward differentiation, however, is countered in H.D.'s writing by an equally strong Ionian instinct toward confluence and amalgamation. In H.D.'s *Hippolytus Temporizes* (1927), a complex meditation on her early hellenism, the Cretan Phaedra hates the Greek tyranny of spirit manifested in its insistence on separate gods "differing each from each, / yet each complete." Instead, she asks, "is there no merging, / no hint of the east? / no carelessness / nor impetuousness of speech?" (48). Though H.D. often names the goddesses, demarcating limited signs, she also deliberately refrains from naming, thus blurring distinctions and deferring final significance.

H.D. suggests from the beginning in her poetry an undifferentiated goddess latent not only in these fragmented images but in the landscape of the islands itself. In *Sea Garden* the goddess of "The Shrine" and of "Huntress" goes unnamed, as does the goddess in the opening and closing poems of *Hymen*, "They Said" and "Prayer." In iconographical terms Artemis is fairly easily identified with the huntress, and Athene with the goddess of the craftsman in "Prayer." But the figure in "They Said," for instance, is amalgamate, a goddess who is distant and detached, *"high and far and blind / in her high pride,"* but at the same time "*most kind*," gentle and comforting. She could then be Demeter in her phase of rage and coldness, or Artemis or Athene in a maternal aspect. She seems in the second stanza to be associated with the dead, and in the last stanza, she merges with Persephone, in the image of flowers springing up "*gold and purple and red / where her feet tread*" (*Collected Poems* 101). However, these passionate colors as well as the image of the *anodos* of the Kore associate her also with Aphrodite. A rejected title of this poem, "Daemon" (*Collected Poems* 616), suggests a primary female figure, a muse or erotic inner guide. Beyond the images of Athene, Artemis, Demeter and Persephone, Aphrodite, and Hera is a powerful figure who remains finally unnamable.

More than in any other figure, this subliminal goddess for H.D. is found not in Aphrodite but in Thetis, the mother of Achilles, a figure frequently appearing in her early poetry. In *Choruses from Iphigeneia in Aulis* (1915) she first appears unnamed, as the "sea-woman" who is mother of Achilles. She is suggested as well in the figure on the prow of Achilles' ships: "A goddess sheds gold: / Sea-spirits are cut in tiers of gold" (*Collected Poems* 74) – the goddess-masthead later appearing in *Helen in Egypt*. In her translation from Euripides H.D. omits the names of Thetis and of the Nereids occurring in the text, to allow an indeterminate significance. Thetis appears again in *Hymen* (1921), in a poem describing a *kathodos* of the goddess into the sea (*Collected Poems* 116–18). The unmistakable allusion to a passage from Ovid's *Metamorphoses*, amounting almost to translation, locates this descent immediately before the violent rape of Thetis by Peleus (Gregory, "Ovid"). In another poem in H.D.'s next volume, *Heliodora* (1923), Thetis, having put away her husband, Peleus, as an old man, now seeks her son, Achilles (*Collected Poems* 159–63). In an *anodos* from the sea, she rises seductively adorned as a bride with "pearl and agate and pearl" wound at her throat, but at the same time she wears a blue cloak, the sign of Demeter. Thus H.D. in her play with the figure of Thetis alludes to the virgin Persephone, to Demeter, to the hetaera and bride Aphrodite. Moreover, H.D.'s early as well as late preoccupation with Thetis suggests that this syncretic sea goddess belongs to mysteries surrounding the son-consort. Her allusion to this figure becomes increasingly explicit, as H.D. takes in the implications of archaeological discoveries of prehellenic matriarchal civilization.

In H.D.'s awareness of a figure of the divine mother it is difficult to find a direct link with Harrison's writing. Friedman has noted that many scholars whom H.D. read accepted the general premise of an original matriarchy first proposed by Bachofen (*Psyche* 266). But Harrison's work was pivotal in establishing widely accepted arguments about Greek religion, and her ideas were in circulation in H.D.'s intellectual milieu, though remarkably unacknowledged. For instance, H.D. wrote with excitement to Bryher in 1932 during a hellenic cruise: "[T]he Wigram states there were *mother*-cults under *all* the Zeus cults, from Dodona, down the coast!"[15] The Reverend W. A. Wigram, canon of Malta, gave lectures aboard ship during this cruise, whose select, intellectual participants included the Very Reverend William Inge, dean of St. Paul's.[16] H.D. assiduously took notes on some of these lectures, which can be found in a little travel daybook in the Beinecke Rare Book and Manuscript Library at Yale. A study of these notes indicates that Rev. Wigram in his comments on Greek religion and worship paraphrased Harrison's *Prolegomena*. His remark about the mother cults under-lying Zeus cults summarizes the argument of concluding chapters in *Themis*. Wigram himself in a later travel guide credits Harrison explicitly.[17] H.D. was excited by Wigram's remark, which she repeated later in the post-Freudian memoir, *The Gift* (quoted in Friedman, *Penelope's Web* 329), because it confirmed conclusions that she had already grasped in working through the psychological territory of her Greek pantheon.

Like Harrison, H.D. attempts to reassemble from its refractive facets in Greek cults the occluded image of the divine mother. H.D.'s hellenic landscape throughout her career is linked to this absent or vestigial figure; and within that landscape one can see signs, even in the earliest poetry, of the "maternal quest" that Friedman has consistently explored in H.D.'s late writing and in her fiction. Speaking of H.D.'s recognition at midcareer through her work with Freud, Friedman says, "To recover the mother, H.D. felt, is to reach the foundation of the psyche" (*Psyche* 144–5). Harrison is an early initiator in an increasing scholarly recovery of prehellenic images of the Great Mother, possessing a full range of attributes and functions.

Dionysos at Eleusis: Sacred Marriage and Sacred Child

The treatment of the Eleusinian festival in *Prolegomena* possesses a distinctive set of emphases. Harrison gives little prominence to the Eleusinian rites themselves, the feasts surrounding Mother and Maid, seeing them as basic harvest ceremonies based on magical propitiation. But she returns to the Eleusinian mysteries in the context of a discussion of Dionysian and Orphic religion, claiming that "nearly all their spiritual significance, was due to elements borrowed from the cult of Dionysos" as influenced by Orphism (539).

Dionysos, according to Harrison, represents intoxication, both physical intoxi-cation associated with wine and spiritual ecstasy associated with music and song (449–53). The worshipers are possessed by the god, and through that possession they become the god. The spiritual dimension within Dionysian worship is magnified through the influence of Orphism, which clearly has Apollonian elements in its primary emphasis on the sun god Helios and which can probably be traced to Egyptian rites of Osiris (461–2). The Orphic doctrine emphasizes not physical but spiritual ecstasy in the context of an ascetic discipline of purification, the end of which is "the possibility of attaining divine life" or immortality (474–7). Thus Orphism spiritualizes some of the bloody aspects of Dionysian orgies, and it spiritualizes as well the simple harvest festival of the Mother and Maid. In this nuanced Orphic form, as Harrison says in a later book, Dionysos "is the god of the ecstasy of the worshipper; he *is* the ecstasy projected" (*Mythology* 135).

Harrison in *Prolegomena* argues forcibly two controversial issues – the place of Dionysos within Eleusinian worship and the nature of the climactic mystical revelation. Following tradition, she finds Dionysian influence at Eleusis first in the literary identification of Dionysos with the god called Iacchos, who leads the Lesser Mysteries. But more significantly and originally, she argues the presence of Dionysos in elements of the Eleusinian ritual that correspond to those in Dionysian and Orphic ritual: the Liknophoria, or the carrying of the harvest basket, and the Sacred Marriage and Sacred Birth.

For this latter ritual there is evidence from accounts of the Eleusinian rites and analogous evidence from rituals belonging to Dionysos and to Cybele. One early Christian commentator says: "Is there not there performed [at Eleusis] the descent into darkness, the venerated congress of the Hierophant with the priest-ess, of him alone with her alone? Are not the torches extinguished and does not the vast and countless assemblage believe *that in what is done by the two in darkness is their salvation?*" (563). Harrison is to my knowledge alone among her contemporaries in arguing that the sacred marriage and the sacred birth are "*the* central mystery" at Eleusis (563). The *hieros gamos* is symbolically, not literally, performed, she claims; and in this rite the initiate through the enactment of the hierophant as goddess has symbolic union with a god and witnesses the birth of a divine child from that union: "Holy Brimo has borne a sacred Child, Brimos." In this ritual the Goddess as Mother and Virgin is the bride; Dionysos is both bridegroom and, by the name of Iacchos, also the child (548–9). Thus in Harrison's interpretation the rites at Eleusis participate in Eastern patterns of the worship of the Great Mother and the son-consort. As Plutarch was the first to note, they also echo the rites of the Egyptian Isis and Osiris, Demeter being Isis and Dionysos Osiris.[18]

Dionysos figures often in H.D.'s writing, and in a way very close to that in Harrison, as Nor Hall has suggested (54–6) – closer indeed to Harrison than to Nietzsche. As we have seen, H.D. understands his chthonic nature, stressed by Nietzsche, as a god of irrational shattering and disintegration, and like Nietzsche she also considers him to be the god of sensuous, bodily life. The iconography of vine and grape suggest that Dionysos is the dark figure supplicated in "The God"; he is manifested in an erotic possession, a sensual intoxication bringing one from the "bare rocks / where salt lay" into the compulsion of the sea itself: "[N]ow I am powerless / to draw back / for the sea is cyclamen-purple, / cyclamen-red, colour of the last grapes, . . . cyclamen-coloured and dark" (*Collected Poems* 46–7).

However, Dionysian ecstasy generally has another tonality for H.D., reflecting to some extent an Orphic spirituality; and that spirituality is associated for her with the Eleusinian rites. In "Demeter" and also in "At Eleusis" the focus of the mysteries would appear to be Dionysos, not the bond between mother and daughter. This latter poem, from *Heliodora* (*Collected Poems* 179–80), suggests H.D.'s sense of the Eleusinian mysteries and of Dionysos's place within them. It is composed of a refrain, with stanzas that appear to be the interior monologue of a hierophant "set in the goddess' place," who watches the initiates approach and assesses their readiness in terms of a necessary purification. They participate, apparently, in the festival of Liknophoria (the carrying of the harvest basket), preliminary to the final stage of the mysteries.

The refrain is unequivocal about the "matter" of the mysteries: "*What they did, / they did for Dionysos, / for ecstasy's sake.*" Curiously, this assertion is in the past tense, and it is set apart in italics from the stanzas of monologue. These demarcations suggest a critical, detached reflection, in opposition to the immediate drama of the hierophant. It collapses all the gossip and theory about the mysteries to a single point. "*What they did,*" the "things done," or *dromena*, of the mysteries, pertains to Dionysos, and Dionysos *is* ecstasy, "the god of the ecstasy of the worshipper," as Harrison bluntly puts it.

However, this ecstasy certainly appears different from the sensual intoxication of "The God." As in Orphic rites, it is rather predicated upon an ascetic restraint and a desire for purification. The hierophant speaks to herself: "[N]ow take the basket, / think; / think of the moment you count / most foul in your life; / conjure it, / supplicate, / pray to it." The one whom she addresses is unable to solicit and confront that dark image, and thus cannot continue to the final revelation, or *epopteia*, of the mysteries. H.D.'s sense of the mysteries in these spiritual terms is suggested in a later narrative, *Bid Me to Live*, where the H.D. figure muses about her ascetic hypersensitivity during World War I: "Purified. Exactly, they practised these things in temples, Yogi, Tibet, Eleusinian Mysteries, but here they got that sort of psychic initiation all the same, every day" (42). H.D. here clearly interprets the "psychic initiation" of the mysteries in terms of *ascesis* and purification.

That H.D. makes allusion to the basket of the Liknophoria indicates her knowledge of the *sacra*; and the poem suggests the specific interpretation given to this object in *Prolegomena*, the basket of fruits doubling as a cradle in signifying the new birth or resurrection (526). The hierophant stresses the necessity for the childlikeness of the initiate, which is associated with the mystery of the mother: "[F]or each that fares onward / is my child," she says. In other words, for H.D. as for Harrison, the end of the mysteries is the birth of the child Dionysos, which the initiates undergo in themselves in the climactic vision.

The poem thus confirms Harrison's Orphic reading of the Eleusinian mysteries, as well as her distinctive interpretation of Dionysos as a god of spiritual intoxication. An even more significant element of her reading is the emphasis upon the *hieros gamos* and the birth of the child as the center of the mysteries. As

Peter Makin has indicated in tracing Pound's Eleusinian theme, Harrison appears alone among early-twentieth-century commentators in giving this emphasis (244–5 n132 and n133), as well as in seeing Dionysos as the pivotal figure in this rite.[19]

Pound appears to interpret the mystery of Eleusis as the *hieros gamos* understood as sexual coitus simply, as Leon Surette has shown. Moreover, that union is represented in *The Cantos* with a phallic orientation, in terms of a male initiate "entering" the dark goddess (Odysseus entering Circe) as a way of entering the underworld (Surette 63–5). The focus for H.D. is understandably different. It is, first of all, oriented to female and not male fertility and creation. The poem "Hymen" deliberately evokes dignified ritual processions leading to the bride's entrance to the bridal chamber and the *hieros gamos*. As May Sinclair says, it evokes "the slow, magical movement of figures in some festival of Demeter or Dionysos, carrying the *sacra*" ("The Poems of H.D." 207). However, this ritual focuses not on the bridegroom but, like Sappho's poetry, on distinct subjective moments within the female cycle of life.

The *hieros gamos* and the birth of the child for H.D. pertain more specifically to the consecration of the poetic and visionary gift. In her copy of Lewis Farnell's *Cults of the Greek States*, H.D. underlines *hieros gamos* and notes to the side, "Corfu," the location of the visionary episode in 1920, the "writing on the wall," that she later unraveled in analysis with Freud. She seems to have seen this vision at Corfu as itself a sign of her union with Helios, whose image she interpreted in the configuration of signs appearing to her. In a poem published in 1923, "Cassandra / O Hymen king" (*Collected Poems* 169–71), Cassandra fuses "Hymen King" and Helios/Apollo in her prayer to that nameless power of "white fire" possessing her as virgin priestess. Union with Apollo alienates the visionary from all other intercourse, from communication and from ordinary marriage and generation; and his gift paradoxically brings darkness: "[W]hy do you dart and pulse / till all the dark is home, / then find my soul / and ruthless draw it back? / scaling the scaleless, / opening the dark?" In other words, the union with Helios/Apollo is also an entrance into Hades, and thus a version of the union with the dark god Dionysos.

Nietzsche made commonplace the idea of an absolute polarity between Apollo and Dionysos, but this is not at all H.D.'s dominant emphasis. Indeed, in her affiliation with Euripides as well as with Plato, H.D. must part ways with Nietzsche's general interpretation in *The Birth of Tragedy*. The two gods – jointly worshiped at Delphi – merge in the syncretism of Orphic spirituality: "Zeus the same as Hades, Hades as Helios, Helios the same as Dionysus" (a hellenistic commentator, quoted in Murray, *Four Stages* 84). Just as Zeus and Dionysos-Zagreus merge, so one can see similarity between the spiritualized Zeus-Dionysos of the mysteries and Helios, the Orphic god of enlightenment, of *gnosis* itself.[20] Though possession by dark and by light have different valences in H.D., they are intimately connected. Helios as he possesses the clairvoyant becomes a dark god, and initiation by Helios/Apollo leads into an underworld darkness and into the realm of the dead. Conversely, the Dionysos of the mysteries and of the choral songs in Euripides' *Bacchae* is a god of light.

The sacred marriage and the divine child become prominent in H.D.'s late writing – *Trilogy, Helen in Egypt, Vale Ave, Hermetic Definition* – as these mythic images are deliberately subsumed in hermetic patterns. They resolve themselves predominantly in the myth of Isis, Osiris, and Horus – the sister-bride who is also mother, whose union with a dark god issues in a divine child. I have suggested elsewhere ("Falling") that in her syncretism of the mysteries surrounding the mother/virgin, mate, and son H.D. traces a solar configuration. It is echoed in late versions of Egyptian myth, where Osiris and Ra are identified, one the underworld and the other the upperworld sun, and also echoed vestigially in Greek myth surrounding Aphrodite, where Phaon/Phaethon is an image of the dying and rising sun, and Aphrodite as Hesperus and Phosphorus is the mate and mother of the sun. These patterns, though amplified in H.D.'s hermetic reading, have their early Greek source in an interpretation of the Eleusinian mysteries shaped directly or indirectly by the new fascination with Greek religion opened with Frazer and Harrison.

Dromenon *and* Drama

Harrison's argument throughout *Prolegomena* is predicated on an assumption made increasingly articulate in later works: that the precedence in the study of religion should be given to "things done," *dromena*, or ritual, rather than "things said," *epe*, explanations given in cultic formulas or myth (283). To understand the motives of religious worship, one must take the primary clues from actual practice: thus the study of major Greek festivals in revealing an older stratum of chthonic worship.

Harrison's focus in *Prolegomena* on ritual and on Dionysian cult leads to the question of the origin of Greek drama in Dionysian worship, the link between *dromenon* and drama, ritual and art. Why, she asks, does the ritual of Dionysos lead to drama, while the ritual of Athene or Zeus or Poseidon does not? Because of "the cardinal, the essentially dramatic, conviction of the religion of Dionysos, that the worshipper can not only worship, but can become, can *be*, the god." Only in an orgiastic religion, focusing on mortal cycles of change and ecstatic possession, could such "splendid moments of conviction" arise; thus it is the source of drama (567–8).

In later writing Harrison elaborates more fully the movement from Dionysian ritual to Greek tragedy, leading her to more complex questions about the nature of religious worship itself and the relation of religious belief and practice to art. The Dionysian *thiasos*, or attendant group of followers, becomes a clue to

Harrison of the collective nature of all religious worship. Following the theories of Emile Durkheim, she states in *Epilegomena to the Study of Greek Religion* that "the function of religion is to conserve the common life physical and spiritual" and that the god is a projection arising out of a collective consciousness (xxii). That "common life," she goes on to argue in *Epilegomena*, is preserved in primitive religion through fertility rituals marking the passage of the seasons and in initiation ceremonies – in Van Gennup's term, rites of passage – marking the movement from one stage of life to another, such as birth, maturity, marriage, and death (xxx–xxxiv). Primitive ritual thus is essentially "liminal," in the term coined by Van Gennup, signifying threshold states celebrated collectively.

In *Ancient Art and Ritual*, Harrison again emphasizes this collective religious impulse in speaking of the relation of Greek drama to ancient ritual. Of all the survivals in tragedy of religious ritual, "one . . . the chorus, strangest and most beautiful of all," is essential to understand. However odd it seems to a modern audience, she says, the chorus is at the heart of the drama, giving to the tragedies "their incommunicable beauty" (122). It is central, she argues, because tragedy has its primitive source in the collective song and dance in honor of the god. Thus the chorus, enacting in language and gesture a finally inexpressible religious desire, is a key to understanding the way in which "ritual and art have, in emotion towards life, a common root" (168).

These concepts – summarized and amplified in Murray's treatment of Greek drama[21] – shape H.D.'s early poetry in fundamental ways, giving it some of its most distinctive character. The idea of a poem as enactment or rite issuing in a transformation of vision certainly has its roots in romanticism. Anthropological discussions of ritual and drama by the Cambridge ritualists confirm this belief in the efficacy of art. However, some of H.D.'s early lyric experimentation specifically shows its effect. She conceives of the lyric as *dramatic* not in the traditional sense of emphasizing individuality and character – as in Browning's dramatic monologue – but precisely in the sense suggested by Harrison: drama as associated with *dromenon*, with liminal passage, with "common life."

I have argued elsewhere that in arranging poems within volumes and in sequences H.D. has a ritual intent, the poems in contextual amplification suggesting thematic and imagistic movement. The "contextural architecture" (Fraistat 5) of *Sea Garden* and of *Hymen* establishes a contained space wherein poems echo and interplay in a complex intertextuality. The poetic sequence for H.D., as for many other moderns,[22] serves as a shadow drama figured in the pattern or procession of individual lyrics. Moreover, H.D.'s early lyrics demand from the reader a distinct, dramatic form of attention and participation. Jeanne Kammer has seen early imagist poems – such as "Oread" and "Storm" – as resting in a poetic mode that does not, like other forms of metaphor, move from concrete to abstract, but rather rests in juxtaposition and suspension of concrete elements in a configuration. Kammer says that the "conspicuous absence of a named feeling or quality or abstraction to make up for the lack of connectives, force[s] us to search for other, less rational entries into the poem." This form of speech turns the metaphoric activity inward, so that "the reader is forced *through* the singular experience of the poem" (158).

Some of H.D.'s well-known imagist lyrics employ this dramatic or ritual mode established through juxtaposition. Other poems, however, are explicitly cast as processual enactments, in which some movement toward epiphany, some dramatic "happening," is indicated. We have already pointed to the theophanic poem, exemplified in "Sea Gods" or in "The God," wherein one solicits a god in a self-fulfilling verbal gesture, the god becoming manifest in language and cadence. In "The God," the first part asks whether the absent god can appear; the second part redeems the doubt in immediate erotic/linguistic presence: "And in a moment you have altered this; // beneath my feet, the rocks / have no weight" (*Collected Poems* 45). Three other more complex processual poems establish structural points in *Sea Garden*: "The Shrine" at the beginning, "Cliff Temple" in the middle, and "Hermes of the Ways" at the end. These are theophanic poems, but with a difference – here are specific *dromena*, things done, mini-narratives within which the presence of the god becomes gradually intensified almost to the point of epiphany. "Hymen," in H.D.'s second volume, is even more explicit in presenting lyrics within the dramatic context of a rite of passage. In other words, in many of these early poems H.D. finds technical means to create the illusion of the poem as a liminal passage.

H.D.'s emphasis on the Greek chorus and the choral voice is coincident with this emphasis. H.D. was translating Euripidean choruses from the beginning of her career, and this effort remains for her a sign of primary imaginative intercourse with the Greeks. In the first part of her career, she translated choruses from six Euripidean plays. The form that H.D. came to call the "Choros Sequence" – represented most fully in *Choruses from the Iphigeneia in Aulis* and in *Choruses from the Hippolytus* – is, as Melvin Lyon has suggested (58), another form of the poetic sequence used in larger scale elsewhere. It is a condensed lyric drama, the action and images of the play interiorized, the impact of the distinct characters and conflicts absorbed in a collective lyric voice.

H.D.'s interest in the Euripidean chorus is tied to her deliberate lyric experimentation, an effort to find polyphony in lyric voice and complexity in lyric temporality and spatiality. Murray in *Euripides and His Age* speaks of the function of the chorus as expressing an emotion "that tends quickly to get beyond words: religious emotions of all kinds, helpless desire, ineffectual regret and all feelings about the past." The chorus, he says, expresses a "residue" of emotion generated but not expressed in the "ordinary language of dialogue" (228–9). Many of H.D.'s early poems, especially those of *Sea Garden*, may be understood as fragments of choral songs. Though few of the poems speak of "we," the collective voice in *Sea Garden* is almost always suggested; the "I" dissolves within the pervasive sense of generalized suffering and exaltation, like the single voice in the chorus of tragedy that is really multiple.

H.D.'s conversation with anthropology in terms of ritual and drama finally points to the same concern voiced in Harrison's *Ancient Art and Ritual*: how art, as a form of mediation between religion and life, can serve collective spiritual needs. Though H.D.'s early lyrics have been faulted for their avoidance of the temporal circumstances of a world at war, she certainly saw her engagement with the lyric as a socially responsible gesture, a form of spiritual mediation. Adalaide Morris, reading H.D.'s *Trilogy* in terms of Victor Turner's model of liminality and communitas, returns us to the territory explored by Harrison – an insistence on the collective nature of religion and art, on "art as cultural work" in service to the life of the tribe ("Signalling" 124). In this model, art functions culturally like a rite of passage; it allows participants or initiates to move from ordinary social "structure" into a liminal space of "anti-structure." In this liminal space the tribe as a whole renews itself in recollection of common dramas (V. Turner 94–130). The poet in this scheme, Morris emphasizes, is like a threshold or liminal person within a tribe: "Whether those who undertook these tasks were initiates in momentary seclusion or permanently designated seers or sayers, their work exposed them to great peril and entitled them, in return, the support of the tribe" (124).

Turner's model – based on Van Gennup and Durkheim – has natural relevance to H.D.'s early poems, as well as to the more socially and historically contextualized poems of *Trilogy*; indeed, I have elsewhere read H.D.'s *Sea Garden* in these terms ("Rose"). These lyrics establish a liminal space set apart from the ordinary, requiring nonrational and nonhierarchical participation, in which one is made aware of longing, vulnerability, and poverty.

H.D.'s heterodox courage from the beginning comes from a religious sense of her role as a liminal figure, serving a domain of inexpressible, ancient knowledge otherwise lost to the tribe engaged in brutal self-destruction. With the benefit of the understanding of religion surfacing with Harrison and others, H.D. was able then as later to imagine her artistic role in an affirmative way.

PART II

Classical Intertextuality

Chapter Five

H.D. and the Classical Lyric

Earlier chapters have attempted to trace the complexities of the classical fictions that contextualize H.D.'s writing. The last two chapters address more particularly her literary engagement with classical writers. This consideration of H.D.'s relation to specific precedents should add dimension to an understanding of her achievement as a lyric poet in the first half of her career. Several commentaries on the early poetry in recent years have opened reflection on its stylistic and intellectual complexity and on the importance to H.D.'s lyric project of classical poets like Sappho and Meleager.[1] However, a fresh assessment of the early poems, based among other things on a more detailed recognition of their intertextuality, is very much needed. For H.D.'s reputation as lyricist has been and still is an issue debated with surprising virulence, subject recurrently to various critical fictions within which it is either promoted or condemned. Reading of the early poetry has been confined largely within interpretative constructs reflecting violent swings in critical fashion.

That H.D.'s lyric writing is a site of a critical battle on many fronts is an insufficiently acknowledged fact – one pertaining not only to the history of academic criteria but to the nature of the poetry itself. As we have seen, in the context of modern classicism, represented in Hulme, Eliot, and Pound, H.D.'s imagist experimentation was applauded and promoted. At the same time, however, it was advocated by Richard Aldington for opposite virtues, as a continuation of late-romantic hellenism. But in any case, it has long been recognized that imagism was for H.D. effectively a "critical cage," in Susan Friedman's phrase (*Psyche* xi), a theoretical category that never satisfactorily described even her earliest poetry, but within which her reputation was constrained and distorted.

Moreover, very soon after H.D.'s initiation as a poet, and increasingly throughout the twenties and thirties – notably in critiques by Laura Riding and

Robert Graves (1927) and by Douglas Bush (1937) – her lyric achievement was dismissed as romantic in the context of postromantic critical assumptions. This modernist version of dismissal has had several avatars, each occurring at a pivotal point in the recent recovery of H.D.'s writing – Bernard Engel (1969), in the first commemorative issue on H.D. (*Contemporary Literature*); Brendan Jackson (1984), near the time of the publication of Martz's edition of the *Collected Poems* (1983); and, most recently, Lawrence S. Rainey (1991), at the point when H.D.'s writing, becoming widely available for use in universities, has gained increasing recognition. Each of these critics assumes normative criteria of high modernism.[2] Each feels compelled to discriminate the good poem from the bad and to make a lesson of H.D.'s failures. All of them, along with Graves, Riding, and Bush, set out to prove that H.D.'s early reputation as a poet has been overrated. Some of these modernist critics share Rainey's essentially ad hominem argument and his condescension in summing up the early career – consisting, he judges, in the merit of "a few poems with astringent charm" (118).

H.D.'s current reputation as a writer owes enormously to her consideration within two frameworks – within the religious, visionary context represented in Robert Duncan's *The H.D. Book*, segments of which began to be published in the early sixties, and within feminist literary recovery, beginning with Susan Friedman's essay in 1975, "Who Buried H.D.?" and her *Psyche Reborn* (1981), considering the occult and Freudian contexts of the writing. However, much as these architectonic studies have laid the lines for a reconsideration of H.D., it is not primarily as a lyric poet that either Duncan or Friedman attends to her; rather, both are finally concerned with the "long poem" or with narrative – forms that can claim epic status in parallel with the writing of male modernist counterparts.

Duncan's passionate and intellectually complex advocacy – as an accomplished male poet speaking generously for a female mentor – has helped to establish respect for H.D.'s lyrics, long poems, and prose among contemporary practicing poets. However, with regard to the lyric, feminist approaches to some extent share ground with other postmodern critical stances, within which the traditional claims of lyric are regarded with skepticism. Both romanticism and modernism accept the lyric as a paradigmatic genre, and New Critical theory supports this bias. For these reasons, as Elisa New has emphasized, the lyric has been the special focus of deconstructive analysis (8). Postmodern theory rather holds narrative in primary place. It generally legitimates the lyric poem only when it can be shown to "disbelieve itself," in New's phrase (8), qualifying or subverting its apparent claims to transcendence or closure, or when it can be read in the interpretative context of narrative – for instance, as "dialogic" rather than "monologic," in Bakhtin's terms, or as part of a cultural or biographical intertextuality.[3] As Jonathan Culler and Jonathan Arac have pointed out, postmodern theory presents only a negative critique of the lyric, without having arrived at positive constructs beyond New Critical poetic theory (Culler, "Lyric" 43–4; Arac 346–8).

The turn against the lyric in contemporary theory gained a major impetus beginning around 1970 with the publication of several essays by Paul de Man on the rhetorical strategies of the romantic lyric.[4] In this commentary, the word "lyric" comes to carry decidedly negative connotations. In the latest of these essays, de Man concludes, "The lyric is not a genre, but one name among several to designate the defensive motion of understanding" (261). It signifies, in other words, a duplicitous avoidance of historical contingency. The concluding passage of "Anthropomorphism and Trope in the Lyric" suggests the negative valences surrounding the lyric within postmodern theory:

> Generic terms such as "lyric" . . . as well as pseudo-historical period terms such as "romanticism" or "classicism" are always terms of resistance and nostalgia, at the furthest remove from the materiality of actual history. If mourning is called [in Baudelaire's "Obsession"] a "chambre d'éternel deuil où vibrent de vieux râles," then this pathos of terror states in fact the desired consciousness of eternity and of temporal harmony as voice and as song. True "mourning" is less deluded. The most *it* can do is to allow for non-comprehension and enumerate non-anthropomorphic, non-elegiac, non-celebratory, non-lyrical, non-poetic, that is to say, prosaic, or, better, *historical* modes of language power. (262)

The concluding catalogue of "nons," signaling de Man's refusal of deluded gestures toward presence, is rhetorically closed with his underlining of "historical" and the metric weight of "language power." The lyric or poetic is disdained as a willful gesture of evasion, through voice or song creating a deluded "consciousness of eternity and temporal harmony" in the face of rupture and indeterminacy; both its "elegy" and its "celebration" are cowardly gestures of nostalgia and essentialism (anthropomorphism). The "true" alternative to this mode – which would be historical and prosaic – is clearly narrative. Though de Man's essays ostensibly address the phenomenon of the romantic lyric, they propose in effect a moral censure of the genre itself.

Paradoxically, then, the energetic and revisionary critical climate allowing the recovery of H.D.'s published and unpublished writing is also one remarkably skeptical of, if not hostile to, the lyric – the genre wherein H.D. first made her mark, wherein her achievement is as remarkable and durable as any other aspect of her career. The new edition of *Selected Poems* by Louis Martz (1988) reflects these current emphases. The selection itself is a revisionary one – weighted against the best-known early poetry. A majority of the lyric poems chosen in collaboration with H.D. for the first *Selected Poems* (1957) are here omitted.[5] Martz as editor of a widely distributed text that substitutes for the original selection is in the position to confirm and perhaps determine a new emphasis –

upon "her longer, more powerful, more personal poems" (viii). Many of these, as Martz points out, H.D. herself chose not to publish or collect – though one cannot assume, as he implicitly does,[6] that self-censorship alone, and not aesthetic judgment, determined these choices. Martz's canonizing gesture links together *longer, powerful, personal*, implying aesthetic criteria very much open to debate. His emphases are coincident with concerns of feminist criticism, revealing "woman's struggle for liberation and equality" as "the essential struggle that lies deep within her poetry" (viii).

Feminist critics of H.D. have made a persuasive case for reading the whole body of her writing in these terms, using a variety of theoretical approaches in order to illumine her consistently revisionary relation to received literary and religious traditions and cultural iconographies. This study is itself centrally indebted to such conversation and is imagined as participating in it. But the fact remains that the early lyric poetry – precisely because it radically eschews the local, historical, and personal – is not of primary concern in such an interpretation.

Among feminist critics Susan Friedman has most deliberately engaged postmodern critical approaches to the lyric genre. In *Penelope's Web*, she situates H.D.'s early lyric experimentation in relation to her parallel narrative engagements (46–68). Within a many-faceted discussion of "the early H.D.," Friedman sees the lyric quality of the poems of *Sea Garden* – impersonal, genderless, ahistorical, apolitical – in general opposition to H.D.'s narrative project, explicitly situated in historical and autobiographical contexts: "H.D.'s artistic self, the depersonalized self projected into and by the poem, was removed from not only her personal history, but also the history of her times" (50).

The terms cumulatively associated by Friedman with the "transcendental discourse" of "the early H.D." – disembodiment, depersonalization, repression, flight, stasis, fixity of marble and crystal – are alike in having negative valence. They stand in necessary relation to positive opposites manifest in narrative. Just as H.D.'s impersonalization represents a flight from oppressive social contingencies, so the narrative represents for Friedman a "flight from the lyric poet" (67). Friedman's reading here would seem to locate in the early poetry the kind of willfulness implied by de Man, a "resistance and nostalgia" in the face of the "materiality of actual history." Thus, in the context of Marxist and Freudian theories, Friedman reads *Sea Garden* in terms of its repression and encoding of historical and autobiographical content (50–62). She insists, at the same time, that the poems may be approached in other terms, that such a decoding as she presents to some extent belies the "impersonal poetics" informing them; and she acknowledges the radical and visionary nature of that poetics. Nevertheless, Friedman's preference for narrative contexts represents a wide consensus in readings of H.D.'s lyrics – manifest in the current emphasis upon the early protonarrative poems and the poems amplifying Sapphic fragments, read as masks for a biographically contextualized female subject.[7]

Indeed, this emphasis is continuous with contemporary readings of lyric poetry in general, but especially in the criticism of women lyricists like Emily Dickinson and Louise Bogan, whose poetry is read in terms of self-limiting textual strategies and postures, serving as a means of negotiating a fraught territory of gendered poetic and religious conventions.[8] In its emphasis on repressed biography, conflicted identity, and self-limitation, this criticism of the lyric strangely confirms familiar censure of female lyric poets, who, as Mary Lefkowitz remarks about Sappho and Dickinson, are traditionally assumed to be neurotic or "*emotionally disturbed*" and their poems to be "*psychological outpourings*" (113).

Contemporary aversion to the "lyrical" H.D. shares ground with an aversion to the "mystical." Adalaide Morris has pointed out how a representative feminist reading of *Trilogy* "emphasizes discourse, not disclosure" and "privileges power, not presence." Her remarks about *Trilogy* are pertinent to some readings of H.D.'s lyrics: "[F]eminists who have examined *Trilogy*'s visionary moments tend to mute the mysticism of H.D.'s practice by turning it back to the material realm and using it to reshape social definitions of gender" ("Signaling" 130). The lyrical is like the mystical, as Morris describes it, in presuming the status of "immaterial essence[s]" like "soul" (130), as well as "presence," "beauty," "mystery," and "union." Moreover, they are alike in being associated with stereotypes that still uncomfortably haunt discussions of women poets – ghosts of the Poetess, whose "lyric or religious posturing" Theodore Roethke so viciously ridicules.[9]

In these aversions one returns to an issue raised in Duncan's early comments on H.D.: the problem of shame. "The way the poet H.D. admitted, let-in, to her self through the poem, and then, in a double sense, admitted to the listener or reader, . . . let life use you this way – this was not shameful." Writing "O wind, rend open the heat," Duncan says, "being intense about trivial things like pears, threatened the composure of household, gang, school and city or state, and was shamed, as one must put away childish things" ("Beginnings" 10). Shame is an interiorized sense of socially censured boundaries, an impingement of public orthodoxy that sets the limits of acceptable utterance and behavior. It is a function of institutions – family, gang, school, city. For Duncan, H.D. and his teacher Miss Keough, who first read this poem to him, offered an intensity and vulnerability that took courage and that rather called the illusory composure of institutions into question.

Academic institutions prominently assume the role of naming the intellectually and aesthetically shameful. The remarkable edge of contempt and anger with which critics sometimes dismiss H.D. speaks to the fact that her poetry often touches on shameful matters, igniting a public-spirited urgency to demarcate limits. One may put Duncan's remarks about H.D.'s courage beside Rainey's claim that the poetic voice in H.D.'s *Trilogy* plays to readers' prejudices, assuring them of "insight that demands nothing and threatens no one" (114). Is it that she demands or threatens nothing, or, like the traditional prophet, everything? It may be that Rainey is simply limited in his imagination of challenge or danger – which must for him be violent "alterity," not H.D.'s consistent liminality or dissolution of boundaries (111). H.D.'s sometimes shameless poetic voices, Duncan would insist, are often threatening in ways difficult to acknowledge or negotiate within academic contexts.

Even H.D.'s most sympathetic readers are chary of the vulnerable voice that so engages Duncan. The Blakean "active desire" that Alicia Ostriker rightly sees as governing the early poetry (13) inevitably, as in Blake's *Songs of Innocence and of Experience*, entails erotic and spiritual suffering. Active desire is manifest in passion of many kinds. But in the case of a woman writer, openness and vulnerability to such suffering raises the specter of complicit victimization or "romantic thralldom," in Rachel DuPlessis's phrase, disgraceful postures from which enlightened readers want to distance themselves. Thus there has been a certain disposition among critics to read active desire heroically, that is, in terms of will and freedom from constraints, rather than psychically, in terms of suffering and necessity. One focuses in *Sea Garden*, for instance, on "the theme of fearlessness and the anti-inland, antisocietal, antisafety elation" (Ostriker 13); the "I" of the poems engaging in "pursuit with female power as stalker" (Duplessis, *Career* 13); the poet, "like a skilled tracker, [moving] from sign to sign in rapt, sagacious pursuit" (Morris, "Projection" 277). To find in H.D.'s sea rose primarily an image of stoic "triumph over the elements" (Laity, "Romantic Landscapes" 115) or an assertion of "gendered rebellion" against conventions of femininity (Friedman, *Penelope's Web* 57) mutes the sense of necessity, the unprotected openness, the passion/passivity – *all* the verbs designating the rose are passive – that also determine the valence of this allegorical sign for the seer.[10] It is difficult in the heroic terms governing the academy to engage the exposed fragility, the unstable and ephemeral sublimity, the vocative, optative, risky, and intimate voices of the early poems.

With regard to the problematic character of these voices, one might point to the overwhelming predominance of apostrophe in H.D.'s early lyrics. Addresses to natural objects, for instance, occur in more than a third of the poems of *Sea Garden* (10). Akin to apostrophe are addresses to an absent, imaginary "you" (god or lover), occurring in as great a number (11).[11] Jonathan Culler's exploration of the claims of apostrophe allows an approach to the often unnamed and ambiguous I–you constituting the axis of desire in H.D.'s lyrics.

Culler points out that critics uniformly repress mention of apostrophe in commentary on lyric poetry, because, he suggests, it is a peculiarly embarrassing trope in its insistence on the largest possible claims for poetic speech: "Indeed, one might be justified in taking the apostrophe as the figure of all that is most radical, embarrassing, pretentious, and mystificatory in the lyric, even seeking to identify apostrophe with the lyric itself" ("Apostrophe" 137). Apostrophe cannot be adequately explained, as rhetoricians attempt to do, simply as reflecting intensity of feeling. "What is really in question," he says, "is the power of poetry to make something happen" (140). What happens is on one level the constitution of poetic voice itself: the vocative establishes a relation between two subjects, with the reader forming a third (141). Within this triangular dynamic of voicing, the "poet makes himself a poetic presence": voicing is a figure of vocation. Apostrophe "emphasizes that voice calls in order to be calling, to dramatize its calling, to summon images of its power so as to establish its identity as poetical and prophetic voice" (142).

What also happens in the apostrophic poem, according to Culler, has to do with the implicit optatives within it – "Be thou me," as Shelley says to the wind. The apostrophe comes with "impossible imperatives . . . which in their explicit impossibility figure events in and of fiction" (146). Apostrophe announces the happening of the poem as a grandly fictional moment. The apostrophic element within poetry, Culler claims, is at the opposite pole from a narrative element within it; apostrophe insists on itself not in terms of "temporal sequence" but as "a *now* of discourse, of writing" (152). Apostrophe, he concludes, "is not the representation of an event; if it works, it produces a fiction, a discursive event" (153).

This embarrassing, critically repressed apostrophic voice marks H.D.'s lyricality in a decided way. This trope is at the heart of H.D.'s lyric project, as the extreme instance of a kind of dual erotic address establishing a triangular play with a reader. Critics have not sufficiently addressed the rhetorical complexity of voice in the lyrics as it determines erotic valences. The opening of "The Helmsman" (*Collected Poems* 5–6), for instance – "O be swift – / we have always known you wanted us" – combines the optative/imperative voice with the choral "we." The apostrophe here urges an immediate daimonic possession, which the voice enacts in the language of the poem. The urgent first assertion establishes a Platonic teleology, in which knowledge ("we have always known") and desire ("you [have always] wanted us") work in inevitable, reciprocal concert. Its strong subliminal claim – manifest in the present perfect tense and made emphatic with "always" – is an inescapable necessity working through time. The vocative here clearly announces vocation, suggesting the intimacy of a long-known erotic bondage. "Adonis" (*Collected Poems* 47–8) establishes a similarly intimate triangular discourse in the repetition of its disquieting refrain, "Each of us like you / has died once." The tonality of this voice is deliberate and contemplative rather than ecstatic, but like that of "The Helmsman" it makes complex claims with regard to temporality and knowledge. The address to the god Adonis is quietly intimate, as though the speaker – like Aphrodite in the traditional lament – can claim knowledge of his body. The repeated "each of us," linked steadily and minutely to images of the natural process of dying, as well as to divinization, makes no trivial demands upon the reader. Establishing an imaginary, figural circuit between [I], "we," and "you," the poem explores what it means to participate in the dying body of the god.

These rhetorical modes of H.D.'s early lyric poetry are coincident with, contextualized by, her hellenism. Sappho's fragments teach her the radicals of intimacy in the erotic address to an imagined other; the Greek Anthology presents countless contextless prayers in which, in Culler's words, "presence and absence [are] governed not by time but by poetic powers" ("Apostrophe" 150); Euripides' choruses give a model of communal voice erotically refracted and complicated within a sublimated context of drama. The "discursive event" of the apostrophic poem in H.D.'s writing is a performance within her spiritualized Alexandrian project of textual recovery and transmission. Apostrophe for H.D. is the lyric version of the epic prophetic voice, in which the poet claims that "[she] is not merely an empirical poet, . . . but the embodiment of poetic tradition and of the spirit of poesy. . . . Devoid of semantic reference, the O of apostrophe refers to other apostrophes and thus to the lineage and conventions of sublime poetry" (Culler, "Apostrophe" 143).

"[O] Rose, harsh rose," "[O] Reed, / slashed and torn," "O rose, cut in rock," "[O] Weed, moss-weed, / root tangled in sand" "O silver . . . O white pear": regarded in Culler's terms the O of flowers in *Sea Garden* represents a cipher more risky and radical than the ordinary vocables of romantic sentiment, which, in comparison, are like the packaged pears so disdained in "Sheltered Garden." The sea rose is a sign in terms of which a poetic voice presumes power and opens a circuit with the reader, who is thus implicated in a transtemporal project – making the rose out of language, interiorizing the rose in an allegory of desire, within this fiction invoking the rose in a lineage of invocations – Yeats's Rosicrucian rose, Browning's rose tree, Blake's sick rose, Waller's lovely rose, Meleager's anthology/garland with Sappho's roses.

But for all its presumption, H.D.'s O is the mark not of perfection and finality, but of initiation and process. If, as Culler's remarks suggest, "Sea Rose" might be about the power of poetic voicing, one may take the uttered, lettered flower, like the O, as an "image of voice" ("Apostrophe" 142). If the flower figures voice, then the voice of "Sea Rose" is not static, frigid, or "crystalline," but rather harsh, marred, meager, risky, compelled, and compelling. How can such a voice be called "disembodied," as it so often is? It (the flower, the voice) is not divine or transcendent, but sharply human, almost disintegrating while revealing itself under severe constraints. To speak of disembodiment entails a critical fiction in which "body" is bound to history, causality, biological and social identity. But considering the question of lyric "body" brings to mind Blake's lifelong battle with an empiricism antithetical to poetic vision. For him, the material "natural body" opposes the "spiritual body," the subtle body of the "human form divine" incarnate in the poem. Ostriker's observations about the likeness of H.D. to Blake represent a crucial insight with wide-ranging implications. H.D.'s poems have Blake's kind of bodied lyric voice.

H.D.'s early poetry has deliberate affiliation with a wide and diverse set of lyric predecessors and contemporaries, among which it makes its own fairly large claims for poetic presence through voice. Because lyric itself is indicted in de Man's terms – and certainly, according to his criteria, almost all its practitioners – it is not shameful to acknowledge that H.D.'s poetry too is so indicted. For purposes of interpretation, one may certainly question the terms of the indictment itself, and rather try to examine in particular H.D.'s project and achievement as a lyricist. This study may contribute to that effort in establishing the particularity of H.D.'s classical intertextuality. Her poetic engagement with classical materials has been discussed generally, or in terms of obvious predecessors like Sappho. However, until recently critics have dismissed the classical allusiveness of her poems as trivial or contrived, and the critical climate has not existed in which either her lyricism or her hellenism could be taken very seriously.

The very early poem "Sitalkas" (1913) points to the unacknowledged complexity of that lyric and hellenic project. Though often taken as an example of H.D.'s early imagism, "Sitalkas" has received very little positive comment.

> Thou art come at length
> more beautiful
> than any cool god
> in a chamber under
> Lycia's far coast,
> than any high god
> who touches us not
> here in the seeded grass,
> aye, than Argestes
> scattering the broken leaves.
> (*Collected Poems* 58)

No critic has attended sufficiently to the allusiveness of the poem, or asked what intended aesthetic effects might have determined that allusion, or indeed any of the other many technical choices it manifests.

Both C. K. Stead and Engel dismiss it as a failure with no more than two sentences of comment. Stead claims that H.D. relies for her chief effects on allusion to "assorted antiquities" (*Poetic* 104); and Engel asserts that H.D. here depends naively on the reader's sympathy with the classical (513–14). However, far from being blandly welcomed into the hellenic club, the reader of "Sitalkas" is stopped at the threshold with a riddle-like sigil. The title announces the strangeness and distance of hellenic space. Not only is the word phonetically difficult, but it is rare. The only occurrence noted in Liddell and Scott is in Pausanias (10.15.2), who records it as a cult title of Delphic Apollo, "protector of corn." Argestes too is a fairly uncommon Greek word in this usage, as the northwest wind, the "brightening" or "whitening" wind of autumn.[12] These names function both as sound and as cipher. Thus the title is a riddle, a kind of verbal "herm," a marker of boundaries. The poem undeniably presents a hermetic aspect, echoed in the hiddenness of the god "in a chamber under / Lycia's far coast" – referring to Delian Apollo's winter hibernation in Lycia, on the Asian coast.

Moreover, the syntactical, aural, and figural complexity of the poem is considerable: the ambiguity of "Thou" in the first line, unraveled only near the end, as well as the spatial/temporal/erotic ambiguity of "art come"; the temporal qualification "at length"; the parallel structure of the single sentence comprising the poem (more beautiful than . . . than . . . than); the intricate rhyming patterns of assonance and consonance (for example, e, a, and s in "here in the seeded grass, / aye, than Argestes"); the almost complete predominance of open vowels and diphthongs; the figural relation among Sitalkas, the "cool god . . . under / Lycia's far coast," the "high god / who touches us not," and Argestes; the placing of "us" within these divine vectors.

Considering the specific technical intricacy of the poem, one is surprised at Stead's judgment that the poem lacks concreteness, that here "we are inside the mind of one of two people. . . . the musical equivalent for a state of mind into which only two substantial facts are permitted to enter" (Poetic 104). The charge would seem again to be disembodiment, and even solipsism, the refusal of "facts." But the poem rather suggests the opposite. Here we are within a bodied desiring voice, preferring nearness to detachment, mortal immediacy to cool godlike repose.

The classical allusions in the poem – to the distant, withdrawn Apollo of winter (the "cool god" and "high god") and to the northern Hyperborean wind – establish the immortal parameters within which the mortal intimacy of the "we" is enacted. With many of the same tonalities as Keats's "To Autumn" – its sonority, its contemplative quality at once (malgré de Man) celebratory and elegiac – "Sitalkas" situates itself at this processual threshold. Unlike the gods, the "thou" of the poem exists in time, has "[be]come at length," through time, more beautiful, just as the mortal seasons come at length to this fullness ("here in the seeded grass") at the point of passing away (the wind "scattering the broken leaves"). Sitalkas, the Apollo who guards this liminal moment of autumn and harvest, is thus not a trivial and clichéd dependency from the classical, but the right sigil for a complex discursive event.

The discussion of H.D.'s lyric poetry in this chapter largely follows emphases apparent within an actual catalogue of classical subtexts discernible in Collected

Poems, 1912–1944 (given in the Appendix). It also, as in previous chapters, draws from commentary in H.D.'s narratives, which may be understood in part as retrospective analysis of her hellenism, and, more centrally, from commentary in her "Notes on Euripides, Pausanius, and Greek Lyric Poets," where separate essays are devoted to Euripides, Sappho, Theocritus, Meleager and the Greek Anthology, and Anacreon. With the exception of Anacreon, these emphases accurately reflect the predominant Greek subtexts in her poetry. To them one would need to add Homer, and, among Latin writers, Ovid and Catullus, and poetry of Renaissance neoclassicism. H.D.'s emphases in the essays on lyric poetry also represent very clearly, and perhaps deliberately, the literary hellenism that she shared with her husband Richard Aldington, who himself translated Sappho and commented on Theocritus, and who in the Poets' Translation Series translated all of the poems of Anyte, Meleager, and Anacreon, as well as Renaissance Latin poetry.

A mapping of H.D.'s literary appropriations reveals a few surprising emphases. At the same time it gives greater substance and complexity to critically acknowledged interchanges with writers like Sappho and Theocritus. Some poems, like "Sea Heroes," and "Thetis" (in *Hymen*), are much more specifically intertextual than has been recognized. Moreover, this exploration of H.D.'s allusiveness has also revealed historical contexts to poems thought only vaguely hellenic.

In each of the following sections, I have attempted to treat not only specific exchange, but a more general intertextuality – the way in which each author becomes the basis for formal or aesthetic exploration and defines a certain imaginative ground with its own predominant voice or voices.

"Perfected Subtle Breath of Metre": *Euripidean Choros*

Euripides was one of H.D.'s most important classical predecessors, and, along with Sappho and Theocritus, he shaped her conception of the Greek lyric. In particular, he taught her a mode of dramatic visualization and a complex lyric voice, which she exploited boldly in her early poetry. In her introductory essay on the dramatist in "Notes on Euripides," H.D. mentions before all else his greatness as a lyric poet, comparing the "psycho-physical intensity" of his choral odes to the poems of Sappho: "Is it not possible that the later censure that precluded so many of the most exquisite stanzas of Sappho, in like manner forbade these?" (1–2). H.D.'s pairing of Euripides with Sappho as an officially censored poet suggests her idea of him as a radical writer, experimenting in his lyric choruses, like Sappho in her monodies, with the limits of erotic speech. As a lyricist, as well as a political skeptic in wartime and as an Eleusinian "mystic," Euripides clearly served as a double for H.D. in her conception of her role as poet. To estimate the nature of her intimacy with him, one must see how she reimagines his choruses in her translations and how the distinctive character of the Euripidean chorus informs her as a lyric poet.

Through the influence of such figures as Walter Pater, Robert Browning, and the classicist Gilbert Murray, Euripides was popular among intellectuals in the late nineteenth and early twentieth centuries (Jenkyns 106–10). Moreover, because his choruses are often more detachable from their dramatic contexts than those of other dramatists – H.D. herself calls them "inset choruses" – they were often translated and performed as single pieces. Thus it is not unusual that H.D. should very early have established acquaintance with his plays and taken for granted the idea of the choruses as extended lyrics. However, the Greek chorus had still another importance for early modernists. Within the longer iambic line of the Greek play, it employs the short line, the traditional meters, the spare and nuanced language of lyric poetry. The Greek chorus became for Ezra Pound and his circle a model for the new classical purgation of poetic diction and – because of its varying meters and line lengths – for the new *vers libre* (*Literary Essays* 93).

H.D.'s fascination with Euripidean choruses dates from the beginnings of her career. Her interest may have been initiated in 1906 during her early association with Pound, then a student at the University of Pennsylvania, when he performed in the chorus of a Greek-language production of *Iphigeneia in Tauris*. But in any case they were an important presence in H.D.'s initial romance with Richard Aldington in 1912.[13] During the early years of her marriage, between 1913 and 1916, H.D.'s translation of Euripides' choruses was simultaneous with her first experimentation as a lyric poet. Indeed, publication of her *Choruses from the Iphigeneia* precedes by almost a year that of her first volume of poems, *Sea Garden*.[14] Between 1912 and the publication of *Collected Poems* in 1925, H.D. had been engaged to one degree or another with seven or eight Euripidean plays.[15] This preoccupation is indicated in H.D.'s story "Hipparchia" in *Palimpsest*, corresponding to events of H.D.'s life between 1916 and 1918. There the young poet Hipparchia is "dazed, drugged and drunk with snatches of Euripidean choros, with the new Alexandrians. This was the perfected ecstasy where body having trained its perceptions, finds itself the tool of sheer intoxicating intellect. She was dazed and in a state of drugged intellectual sensuality" (77).

This last remark about a "perfected ecstasy" that is both intellectual and sensual echoes Pound's famous definition of the image as "an intellectual and emotional complex in an instant of time" (*Literary Essays* 4); or his description of troubadour ascetic mysticism, where "the ecstasy is not a whirl or a madness of the senses, but a glow arising from the exact nature of the perception" (*Spirit of Romance* 91). Indeed, as many have remarked, H.D. in her translations presents Euripides as an imagist.[16] His choruses become for her a kind of image-theater of *phanopoeia*, words used "to throw a visual image on to the reader's imagination" (Pound, *ABC of Reading* 37). H.D.'s adaptation of Euripides in these terms is not without basis in the texts themselves. As Hugh Parry notes in his study of the lyrics of Greek tragedy, the choral odes of Euripides in comparison with those of Aeschylus and Sophocles possess distinct qualities: they are "imagistic rather than symbolic," and the "Euripidean lyric image is typically both picturesque and lucid" (61). Shirley Barlow emphasizes Euripides' preference for image rather than for metaphor or moral disquisition; his choral odes, she says, establish a consistent "visual idiom" (18, 20). Between Euripides' texts and H.D.'s translations one finds indeed a genuine exchange – Euripides giving H.D. clues to certain powerful rhetorical modes, and H.D. emphasizing Euripidean visual clarity and erotic intensity through an imagist style of translation.

To understand the nature of this exchange, one must look specifically at H.D.'s activity as a translator, which she articulates in a passage from *Bid Me to Live*:

> She brooded over each word, as if to hatch it. Then she tried to forget each word, for "translations" enough existed and she was no scholar. She did not want to "know" Greek in that sense. She was like one blind, reading the texture of incised letters, rejoicing like one blind who knows an inner light, a reality that the outer eye cannot grasp. . . .
>
> Anyone can translate the meaning of the word. She wanted the shape, the feel of it, the character of it, as if it had been freshly minted. (163)

This passage, of course, suggests an occult conception of the process of translation: the phrase "inner light" gives a fairly obvious clue. Many critics have commented on the distinctive visionary poetics articulated here, on H.D.'s effort to "make it new" in the act of translation. So much is this modernist originality emphasized that John Walsh in his edition of H.D.'s translation of the *Ion* retitles the work, changing H.D.'s title, *Euripides' Ion*, to *Ion: A Play After Euripides*. This is a significant alteration. Walsh in his afterword calls H.D.'s version of the *Ion* a "verse drama" like her *Hippolytus Temporizes*; referring to the *Ion*, he marks off in quotation marks the word "translation" as inadequate to define H.D.'s efforts (120). But though theorists of translation may debate nuanced positions between the poles of close paraphrase and linguistic incommensurability, it is clear that H.D. at least imagined herself as a translator of Euripides. Besides a brief passage from Homer's *Odyssey*, Euripides' texts were the only ones that H.D. ever called translations.[17]

Insisting upon the necessity for the modern translator of Greek to "make it new," D. S. Carne-Ross describes H.D.'s efforts very much in the way that she does. About her translation of the *Ion*, he remarks that though one may finally judge it a failure, "it's a failure that's worth a good many successes. One sees her, in the translation itself and in the rather mannered prose notes . . . really grappling with the problems a Greek play presents: . . . working her way to the reality of gesture and emotion behind the stiff, splendid words. . . . H.D. took her play to pieces, broke it down to a pre-verbal level and then set about reconstituting it in her own terms" (8). H.D. would be happy with Carne-Ross's recognition of the "sheer, hard brain-work" (*Notes on Thought and Vision* 26) entailed in the task (grappling, working, taking to pieces, etc.), as well as with his suggestion of intuitive clairvoyance and verbal regression. In these last suggestions of subconscious or superconscious effort, he echoes her own description of the process as interiorization (brooding, hatching), verbal disintegration (forgetting the words), and blind rereading of the submerged texture.

H.D.'s early *Choruses from the Iphigeneia* are the main focus of observations by Carne-Ross, and his comments allow us entrance into H.D.'s method as translator and as interpreter. Looking back at twentieth-century efforts of translation, Carne-Ross notes:

> In the field of Greek translation, however, the most interesting work was done not by Pound but by H.D., most successfully in her fragmentary sketches from the *Iphigeneia in Aulis*. . . . Here, to my mind, she suggested certain elements in the Greek lyric better than they have ever been suggested before or since. She leaves out an enormous amount. She is not interested in the syntax, in the elaborate weave of the Greek lyric; and she shows little dramatic feeling. She is hardly concerned with the "sense," it is the picture – the "image" – that she is after, and that is what she presents, a sequence of images as fresh and unexpected as though they had just been disinterred from the sands of Egypt. (7)

Carne-Ross here suggests – Douglas Bush notwithstanding – that H.D. is indeed faithful to the spirit of the Greek lyric, through she disregards much in the focused effort of reimagining. To get a better sense of the basis for his high estimate, we might consider passages from H.D.'s *Iphigeneia in Aulis* in comparison with the Greek text. The first chorus of the *Iphigeneia* suggests H.D.'s mode of "breaking down" and "reconstituting" its language. It also manifests a keen awareness of Euripides' themes and stylistic distinction. H.D. in her translation is in serious interplay with Euripides, grasping the effects he intends, learning from them, and heightening them with her own distinctive style. His "visual idiom" is honored and extended, as is his erotically compelled choral "I."

The following represents the barest literal translation of the first twenty lines of the first chorus (164–84), followed by H.D.'s version of the same lines:

> I came to the sandy seashore of Aulis by the sea, pushing through the rushing strait of Euripos, forsaking my city Chalkis, nursed by the seaside waters of renowned Arethusa, that I might see the army of the noble Achaeans and the ship-speeding oars of the heroes [*hemitheon*, half-gods], whom, our husbands tell us, with a thousand [pines = oars =] ships golden Menelaus and well-born Agamemnon have sent toward Troy to bring back Helen, whom Paris the herdsman took from reedy Eurotas, a gift of

Aphrodite, when at the pure-water springs Kupris held a contest, a beauty contest, with Hera and with Pallas.

> I crossed sand-hills.
> I stand among the sea-drift before Aulis.
> I crossed Euripos' strait —
> Foam hissed after my boat.
>
> I left Chalkis,
> My city and the rock-ledges.
> Arethusa twists among the boulders,
> Increases — cuts into the surf.
>
> I come to see the battle-line
> And the ships rowed here
> By these spirits —
> The Greeks are but half-man.
>
> Golden Menelaus
> And Agamemnon of proud birth
> Direct the thousand ships.
> They have cut pine-trees
> For their oars.
> They have gathered the ships for one purpose:
> Helen shall return.
>
> There are clumps of marsh-reed
> And spear-grass about the strait.
> Paris the herdsman passed through them
> When he took Helen — Aphrodite's gift.
>
> For he had judged the goddess
> More beautiful than Hera
> Pallas was no longer radiant
> As the three stood
> Among the fresh-shallows of the strait.
>
> (*Collected Poems* 71–2)

Carne-Ross is more liberal than many classicists in his insistence that the real translator of Greek, whose effort is indeed a poetic re-creation as well as an interpretation, needs to be given generous allowances by critics, because to "follow the curve of his original faithfully" may necessitate a "great deal of local distortion, of amplification and even excision" (6). In this opening passage, H.D. has boldly followed this tactic of "local distortion," with the object of giving the translation immediacy.

H.D. has broken the single utterance into thirteen short sentences. She replicates the short lines of the Greek and attempts to render their consonantal abruptness and rapid tempo.[18] The latter is achieved by incantatory repetition of the initial "I" in short sentences, as well as by the repetition of cadence patterns suggesting chant (I cróssed sánd-hills . . . . I léft Chálkis. . . . And the shíps rówed here). H.D. here emphasizes the immediacy of the present moment. As T. S. Eliot noted, she has changed participles to indicatives ("Classics" 102); and she has altered the aorist tense of the original to an interplay between past and present (I crossed, I stand, I crossed, I left, I come, etc.).

Moreover, she has significantly modified the sense of some lines. At times this is done to emphasize some aspect of the text. "I came to the sandy seashore of Aulis by the sea" becomes "I crossed sand-hills. / I stand among the sea-drift before Aulis." H.D. here suggests the excited and compelled action of the "I"; she also presents sharp visual images not in the original (sea-hills, sea-drifts); and she captures with "among the sea-drift before Aulis" a spatial sense of the preposition *amphi* and also a certain redundancy in the original two lines – "seashore" (*paraktian*), "sea-sand" (*psamathon*), and "by the sea" (*enalias*). Such metamorphosis goes on persistently. The next lines in H.D.'s version – "I crossed Euripos' strait – / Foam hissed after my boat" – convey a sense of rushing water in the narrow passage as well as the rushing action of the "I," in the sibilance of *Euripos, strait,* and *hissed* and in the added tactile image of the boat's wake.

There are also, as Carne-Ross predicts, significant amplifications. H.D.'s images of Chalkis with "rock-ledges" and of Arethusa ("It twists among the boulders, / Increases – cuts into the surf") invent a landscape in detail where none exists in the Greek. The latter in particular represents one of H.D.'s recurring liminal fascinations – the image of a river or spring as it meets the sea. The phrase in Greek referring to Arethusa, *agchialon hudaton*, "by seaside waters," refers to this peculiarity of the spring. In another instance, lines in the fourth stanza of H.D.'s version improvise with the roots of the word *elatais*, or "ship"; *elate* means literally pine tree, and by extension oar, and thus by extension ship. H.D. plays out this embedded sense with the declaration "They have cut pine-trees / For their oars," suggesting a primitive, Homeric aspect of war preparation.[19]

One of the clearest amplifications and distortions occurs in the lines referring to the judgment of Paris. Here H.D. once again elaborates a landscape where the text gives none, rendering the simple "reedy Eurotas" with a visual scene: "There are clumps of marsh-reed / And spear-grass about the strait. / Paris the herdsman passed through them." She then places the goddesses in this landscape, "Among the fresh-shallows of the strait." One should note that H.D. in this visual image has deliberately superimposed three different watery locations – Aulis by Euripos's strait, associated with the spring Arethusa; the Laconian river Eurotas, whence Helen was stolen (H.D. omits the name, given in the Greek text); and Asian Mount Ida, where by another freshwater spring the judgment of Paris was held. H.D. manipulates the locations here not, as Bush suggests, out of "an excessive fondness for unity of place" (498 n36). Rather, the blurring of locations serves to make this crucial mythical occurrence a part of the immediate landscape and the accessible past of the chorus and audience.

Indeed, there is some justification in the text for this spatial and temporal blurring. Euripides in a few condensed lines sketches past events back through a chain of consequences – the arrayed army present because of Helen, who is absent because of Paris, who acted because of the gift of Aphrodite, who won in a contest among goddesses. Euripides' lines represent a kind of excavation of origins, from the potent (and erotically driven) Greek army to the first divine instigations of *eros* and *eris*. The goddess Eris, at the root of the Trojan saga, is certainly recalled to Euripides' audience in the repetition in line 183: *Hera Palladi t' erin erin*. H.D. indeed emphasizes the roots of strife in elaborating the visual scene of the contest, figuring the ominous humiliation of two of the three goddesses standing in the shallow water before Paris, their bodies "no longer radiant" next to the beauty of Kupris.

H.D. thus takes from Euripides and returns through her translation a heightened sense of the visual scene, as well as the thematic underthought of the language. The same reciprocity exists in her adoption of poetic voice, the choral "I." We have discussed the choral voice of H.D.'s poetry in other contexts, but here one can see its close connection with Euripides as well as its complexity and subtlety as a lyric device.

The speech of the choral "I" in Greek tragedy presents a paradox: it is at once one and many, a single identity with a single complex of emotion and thought, and at the same time a multiple entity, projecting a kind of experience by consensus. This polyvalence can be easily naturalized in critical commentary, dissolved in discussions of dramatic function and convention – the chorus as citizen, as "collective conscience," and so on. However, Euripides more than Aeschylus or Sophocles exploits the complexity of the choral voice, which must in his dramatic songs be experienced lyrically both as "I" and "we."

In the first chorus of the *Iphigeneia*, the collective "I" at times reflects a disconcerting intimacy and subjectivity. She speaks of blushing, "reddening in my fresh budding cheeks in my shame" (H.D.: "Shame, scarlet, fresh-opened – a flower, / Strikes across my face"). She speaks of the vision of ships in clearly sensual terms, "Oh that I might fill up [or sate] my woman's eyes with the sight, a pleasure honey-sweet." At the same time, however, this intimate and overtly female voice is also heroic in its longing and epic in its view. The "I" of the first choral ode has been moved by a kind of reckless daring – braving the rushing straits, trespassing the *temenos* of Artemis – in order "to see the battle-line," the amassed ships and warriors. She projects throughout this very long initial ode a state of erotic beholding. Forms of the Greek verb *eido* and other references to vision and to eyes are used twelve times in the first chorus. Fascinated by legends, she is the heroic witness of the apparently noble beauty coming into shape at the onset of war – finally to be undermined, though in a way climaxed, by the sacrifice of Iphigeneia. Alert both to the panorama and to specific images and emblems, she gives a lyric version of Homer's catalogue of ships in the *Iliad*, recalling to the audience the larger heroic context within which the pettiness of the warriors and the courage of the young girl Iphigeneia are to be measured.[20]

H.D. emphasizes fully the complexity of this voice, both the immediacy of the "I" and the epic implications of the implied "we." But further, H.D.'s interpretation at times projects an ominous undertone to this erotic witnessing. In the opening lines, the incantatory repetition of the declarative "I" suggests the wash of desire and vision: "I have longed for this. / I have seen Ajax. / I have known Protesilaos . . . // I have seen Palamed." *Longing, seeing,* and *knowing* thus exist simultaneously. Coming suddenly from watching the warriors to the place of the amassed ships, the "I" as H.D. interprets her has a moment of painful and ambiguous epiphany:

> If a god should stand here
> He could not speak
> At the sight of ships
> Circled with ships.
>
> This beauty is too much
> For any woman.
> It is burnt across my eyes.
> (*Collected Poems* 73–4)

H.D. here improvises upon the original four lines. The powerful image of "ships / Circled with ships" is not present there; and, more remarkably, the last phrase, "It [beauty] is burnt across my eyes," replaces the image of honey-sweet satiation (233–4) noted earlier. H.D.'s modification here, however, retains the link between speech, vision, and desire.

So, indeed, does her powerful rendering of the last lines of the first ode. Translated literally, they read something like this: "Such a fleet I saw there, that hearing at home of the army called together, I keep [this image] in mind, unforgetting" (299–302). H.D. translates:

> I have heard –
> I myself have seen the floating ships
> And nothing will ever be the same –
> The shouts,
> The harrowing voices within the house.

> I stand apart with an army:
> My mind is graven with ships.
>
> (*Collected Poems* 76)

In H.D.'s amplification the image of the ships represents not a future patriotic memory, as in the original, but a point of no return and a graven mark on the mind. Just as in the earlier emphasis ("I have known Protesilaos"), this vision approaches clairvoyance, a seeing *through* the name or the image. It signals Cassandra-like foreknowledge, perhaps even of Agamemnon's fatal homecoming: "The shouts, / The harrowing voices within the house." H.D.'s interpretation here, as above in the image of vision burning across or slashing the eyes, emphasizes the ominousness of the arrayed mass – something not really given in the naive consciousness of Euripides' "I." H.D.'s erotic visionary, compulsively drawn toward the brilliance of the heroic, is prophetic in her awareness. Her vision sets her apart; it lacerates and burns.

What, then, is the importance of the Euripidean choral "I" to H.D.? In this play the choral voice, with its emotional immediacy and religious and epic scope, its simultaneously microcosmic and macrocosmic dimension, makes explicit the kind of supplement or oversound that poets attempt to bring into being through voice. The roots of the choral "I" are in the divine hymn and in the epinician ode praising heroes and victors. In Greek poetry Sappho and Pindar perhaps more than any others achieve this enlarged sense of presence within a deliberate poetic fiction of divine service, wherein every image and thought, however intimate, relates to the life of the god.

The polyvalence of the choral "I," taking on dimension within the context of a supreme fiction, is perhaps the most important lesson H.D. learned from Euripides. I would suggest indeed that the choruses from the *Iphigeneia* initiate H.D. into a more deliberate heroic sense of her role as lyric poet within a hellenic fiction. The choral "I" here raises the stakes, so to speak, in presenting a passionate overview of the Greek world and of the pivotal saga of Troy. It mediates between heroic myth and brutal wartime history, between divine mystery and human betrayal. The choral "I" of *Iphigeneia* represents the heroic and political dimension of H.D.'s early self-conception.

After the publication of these choruses in November 1915, H.D. begins for the first time to explore the possibilities of a choral poetry, in hymnal poems such as "The Helmsman," "Cliff Temple," "The Shrine," "Sea Gods," "The God," and "Adonis"; and in epinician poems praising victors and heroes, such as "The Contest," "Loss," "Prisoners," and "The Tribute." I would suggest that even later poems usually taken as presenting a personal or autobiographical "I" – for example, "Circe," "Eurydice," and "Pygmalion" – can be understood not simply as static classical masks, but as Euripidean monodies. Euripides was known for these "arias" – passages of lyric meter sung by a single speaker, such as those of

Iphigeneia as she laments and then accepts her death (*Collected Poems* 81–2). H.D. indeed has in mind such a dramatic context in the title "Ariadne / (*From a Lost Play*)." In her introductory essay on Euripides, H.D. begins by regretting the unfortunate fact of his "lost plays"; and this poem, like other monodies, represents perhaps one of those lost "love-lyrics" from Euripides' "great Love drama" ("Euripides" 1). One may see the "I" of these poems as quasi-choral, an "I" within a lost or fragmentary fiction. H.D. could not sustain the authority lent her through the Euripidean voice. Nevertheless, the powerful "I" of *Iphigeneia* resurfaces in the choral and bardic voice of *Trilogy*. Euripides is by far the most likely poetic predecessor in H.D.'s adoption of this mercurial and expansive voice.

"Little, but All Roses": Fragments of Sappho

Among the classical poets acknowledged in H.D.'s writing, Sappho has received more attention than any other. This is understandable; H.D. names Sappho in the title or subtitle of six poems, and her two early essays on Sappho have been readily available in published form.[21] Such evidence has led critics to consider H.D.'s relation to Sappho in several ways: within a lesbian literary context shared by male and female writers in the late nineteenth and early twentieth centuries; in relation to Bryher, her new companion at the time she wrote her essay on Sappho in California in 1920; and within a modernist poetics in which her adoption of hellenic masks serves as a revisionary strategy. Many of these critics rightly define Lesbian Sappho as one of H.D.'s principal hellenic fictions.[22]

However, this literary affiliation is still more extensive and complex than has been estimated. One problem is that critics have directed attention almost exclusively to H.D.'s "fragment" poems, whereas her textual play with Sappho, as the listing in the Appendix shows, goes far beyond these few explicit namings. They represent only one aspect of Sapphic intertextuality, and indeed a limited one, situated as they are within long-standing male-identified lyric conventions. One must acknowledge but go beyond the fragment poems in defining the nature of H.D.'s fiction of Sappho as precursor and erotic guide. Further, in considering Sappho's place in H.D.'s writing, one confronts as well puzzling questions of textuality: H.D.'s self-sanction against translating Sappho and her almost complete silence about the revolution in scholarship of Sappho taking place between 1909 and 1925, during which time the number of extant lines of Sappho's poems more than doubled.

As to the first of these self-censorships, critics often quote the poet Hipparchia in *Palimpsest*: "[I]t was desecration to translate [Sappho]"; "she had struggled to recapture Sappho and had finally given up the attempt as savouring of sacrilege. Hipparchia had given up the Mitylenean" (72, 84). In assuming this stance, H.D. very probably takes her measure from A. C. Swinburne, who, in remarks quoted in the introduction to the much-revered Wharton edition of Sappho, says:

I have wished, . . . that I might be in time competent to translate into a baser and later language the divine words [of Sappho]. . . . To translate the two odes and the remaining fragments of Sappho is the one impossible task, . . . Where Catullus failed, I could not hope to succeed; I tried instead to reproduce in a diluted and dilated form the spirit of a poem which could not be reproduced in the body. (Quoted in *Sappho*, ed. and trans. Wharton 34–5).

In light of her awe for Swinburne, one imagines that for H.D. Sappho in literary terms is many times awesome, not only a divine star but a constellation or galaxy of stars: where Catullus and Swinburne (and Shelley, Byron, and Rossetti) have failed, H.D. could not hope to succeed. One should note, indeed, how scrupulously H.D. avoids engagement with Sappho as a translator. She quotes Wharton's prose translations as headings in her fragment poems, and in her 1920 essay on Sappho she also occasionally quotes Wharton, or more often gives deliberately bare prose renderings of fragments. But at no point does she approach Sappho with the self-assured poetic intention with which she approaches Anyte, Moero, Nossis, Antipater of Sidon, Euripides, Ovid, and even *the* poet, Homer.

The other aspect of H.D.'s reticence – her silence about the new texts of Sappho – is also remarkable. An important Egyptian manuscript – the so-called Berlin Parchment – was first published in 1902 and in a German edition in 1907. Beginning in 1909 J. M. Edmonds published restorations and English translations of these fragments in the *Classical Review*. Other Egyptian manuscripts – the Oxyrhynchus papyri – were published by the Egyptian Exploration Society, and volumes containing Sapphic fragments appeared in 1914, 1922, and 1925. These too were almost immediately made available in restored versions and translations by Edmonds, in articles appearing in several classical journals.[23] These new texts were published in volume 1 of Edmonds's *Lyra Graeca* (Loeb) in 1922 and in a revised edition of 1928, as well as in an intermediary edition by Edgar Lobel in 1925.

Some of the longer new fragments give firm evidence of Sappho's legendary quality, arguably equaling in stature the only two lengthy poems available up to 1902 – the complete prayer to Aphrodite (Lobel and Page [LP] 1) and the almost complete love poem preserved in Longinus (LP 31: "He is like a god to me, the man who sits beside you"). Among the most notable Berlin fragments are two intimate love poems to female companions (LP 94 and 96), which more than any previous texts make clear the dimensions of the homoerotic life within Sappho's *thiasos*. The longest of the Oxyrhynchus fragments include a prayer to Kupris and the Nereids (LP 5), an encomium on love (LP 16), a prayer to Hera (LP 17), and a poem recounting the marriage of Hector and Andromache (LP 44). Among these one of the most important in terms of H.D.'s concerns is fragment 16, wherein Sappho argues for the excellence of erotic life against the traditional *arete* of the heroic life.

As Hugh Kenner has pointed out, literary people in prewar London were excited by the earliest of these new discoveries, the Berlin fragments (54–75). Unquestionably H.D. knew of them, and of the later fragments as well. She speaks in her 1920 essay of scholars "searching to find a precious inch of palimpsest among the funereal glories of the sand-strewn Pharaohs" (69).[24] Indeed, H.D. was instrumental in circulating these new fragments within her literary circle. In the first months of H.D.'s relationship with Richard Aldington, he studied the new fragments in transcriptions made for him by H.D. from back issues of the *Classical Review*, because Aldington in 1912 was too young to use the library of the British Museum.[25] He shared a translation of one of these fragments (LP 96) with Pound in late 1912, and Pound tried unsuccessfully to help him place it in *Poetry*. Aldington's translation, according to Kenner, led Pound to examine the published fragments as well, which resonate in his poetry, both early and late (54–9). Aldington's Sapphic translation was finally published in the *New Freewoman* in 1913, on the same page and immediately preceding H.D.'s poem "Sitalkas."[26] The same fragment also appears in Edward Storer's prose rendering in the Poets' Translation Series (1915), which H.D. helped Aldington to manage. In a later critical encounter, in 1925, H.D. reviewed an edition of Sappho by Edwin Marion Cox, who refers to recent scholarship in his introduction and annotated bibliography and includes one of the new Oxyrhynchus fragments (LP 16) in his edition (74–8).

Certainly not ignorant of this scholarly excitement, then, H.D. nevertheless alludes neither directly nor obliquely to fragments outside of Wharton's edition in any of her writing. Though in her 1920 essay she cites or alludes to more than fifty distinct fragments,[27] none of them are from the body of new fragments. There is one qualified exception to this general silence. In 1927, a phrase possibly from an Oxyrhynchus fragment appears as a subtitle to a poem – "Choros Sequence / from *Morpheus* / '*Dream – dark-winged*'"[28] – though here H.D. does not acknowledge Sappho, as she does in the other fragment poems. These lacunae in H.D.'s attention to Sappho are noteworthy, not only because of the quality of the new fragments, but because they so brilliantly verify themes of vital importance to H.D. – female homoeroticism (LP 94, 95, 96) and the antiepical stance of the lyric (LP 16).

How can one explain this reluctance to engage the new Sappho? In part it seems to come from H.D.'s habitual defensiveness with regard to professional scholarship and in part from a reluctance to surrender "our much-maligned and meagre poetess" ("Winter Roses" 596) – the one mediated, as in Wharton, by romantic poets. One can find a clue to H.D.'s stance in her review of Cox's edition. H.D. here engages in her recurrent animus against gentlemen-scholars, defending Wharton against Cox's charges of being out-of-date. When Cox speaks of his edition as an attempt to "bring the subject up to date," he is chiefly referring to the revised canon of poems, the "considerable quantity of new material [that] has come to light in the fragmentary papyri found in the delta of the Nile" (7). But H.D. takes him rather to be referring to the compendium of translations included in Wharton. Specifically, she is disturbed that Cox replaces translations by Swinburne or Rossetti with his own: "For myself I am superstitious. I feel that in the gallery or galaxy of translations of Sappho that particular translation of Swinburne is forever and ever wedded to that particular fragment" ("Winter Roses" 596).

One must take seriously H.D.'s claim to "superstition"; her relation to Sappho would seem indeed to be implicated in an irrational and ominous sense of taboo. Why else would an ambitious poet-translator and committed hellenic revolutionary to whom Sappho is a pivotal figure deliberately refuse a direct textual encounter, insisting rather on literary mediation and on a limited and thoroughly naturalized body of fragments? Unlike her male predecessors and peers, and indeed unlike female predecessors such as Michael Field and René Vivien,[29] H.D. chooses to abstain completely from public intercourse with the textual body of the Mitylenean.

H.D.'s literary relation to Sappho, then, would seem to possess this intricate dynamic: she overtly embraces Sappho as a precursor in the fragment poems and the essays, but at the same time avoids her as a translator and scholar; and all the while, as seems clear from the catalogue in the Appendix, she works out a covert textual exchange in her own terms. This assertion may seem excessively subtle. However, critics have come to similar conclusions about H.D.'s circuitous appropriation of male figures in her life, such as Lawrence, Pound, and Freud. Further, this stance toward Sappho reflects to some extent the hesitations of other modern women writers who discover the "liabilities of such a collaboration" (Gubar 47). But a crucial aspect of this puzzle lies in Sappho's centrality within fictions of maternal desire in H.D.'s writing. The fear of sacrilege surrounding the sacred text of Sappho may imply for H.D. that her words are not only untranslatable, but "unspeakable," in the sense that Deborah Kelly Kloepfer has amplified, associated with a "maternally connoted homoeroticism" (122). They are *ta arreta*, things interdicted, like the Eleusinian mysteries; and indeed Sappho, at least in some of H.D.'s writing, seems fairly clearly implicated in an Eleusinian territory.

Within H.D.'s intricate Sapphic intertextuality, one may distinguish between an overt and a covert interplay, the former evident in the fragment poems, the latter in some of the other early lyrics, especially the poems of "Hymen." Because the fragment poems have received substantial comment, I treat them here only briefly and somewhat generally, in an attempt to define their place within H.D.'s fictions of Sappho.

A quotation of a Sapphic fragment in the Wharton translation appears as the title or subtitle of six poems. Five name the number from Wharton, who follows the edition of Theodor Bergk (113, 36, 40, 41, and 68); and one, "Calliope," gives a fragment as a subtitle without a number. A seventh of these fragment poems – "Choros Sequence / from *Morpheus*" – quotes a fragment as a subtitle without appending Sappho's name. H.D.'s textual relation to Sappho in these poems is more complex than critics have granted. What precisely does it signify to entitle a poem, for instance, "Fragment 113 / *'Neither honey nor bee for me'* – Sappho"? The title insists on textuality – Sappho represented as a textual fragment, within a numbered sequence of fragments, within a specific edition (Bergk) and a specific translation (Wharton). But at the same time the poem flamboyantly denies or resists that specific textuality in a free extrapolation, in which the original phrase is often repeated, altered, played out, quizzed, and turned, to the point that its frail simple sense, much less its contextualized sense, is effectively dissolved. In "Fragment 113," the phrase "Neither honey nor bee for me" becomes a digressive, extenuated series of voluptuous denials of voluptuousness, leading to a rhetorical turn in affirming the dialectical opposite, a hard, skeletal asceticism.

The many-times-removed text of Sappho has indeed a spectral presence here. Where, how, and what is "Sappho" in these poems? The cited fragment, I would suggest, is not as important as the gesture of citation. The purpose clearly is not interpretation or representation, but rather invocation. "Sappho" stands as a sign announcing a certain conscribed and determined musing on states of passion. Each of these seven poems, regardless of the dramatic situation framing it, explores rhetorically a particular erotic crux or impasse. Erotic tension – or a kind of debate within the laws of love – is what all the poems have in common: tension or debate between sensual and ascetic possession and rapture ("Fragment 113"); between "song's gift" or "love's gift," vocation or sexual passion ("Fragment Thirty-six"); between spirit and flesh ("Calliope"); between love as sweet and as bitter ("Fragment Forty"); between the rancor of jealousy and the love of love ("Fragment Forty-one"); between desire for a betraying lover's presence and desire for death ("Fragment Sixty-eight"); and between Dionysian heat and oblivion and Apollonian cold and clarity ("Choros Sequence / from *Morpheus*"). Though certainly this summary does not communicate the complexity of the poems, it nevertheless makes clear that each of them turns rhetorically on the device of antithesis and that each engages a version of the oppositions central to H.D.'s fictions of divine mania.

"Sappho" in these poems is a marker, signaling a certain kind of imaginative engagement, even a certain literary *topos*. Longinus in his essay on the sublime praises above all Sappho's ability to express the oppositions and contradictions within erotic madness (*erotika mania*). Her poems express "not one single emotion but a concourse of emotions" (trans. Campbell 1:81) – the *concordia discors* that is the stock-in-trade of subsequent lyricists. Longinus then cites, and thus preserves, an example, "He is like a god to me, the man who sits beside you" (LP 31), a poem describing in detail the phenomenon of erotic seizure, likening it to the physical experience of dying. In part because of the preservation of this poem and commentary, Sappho has been traditionally seen as *the* consummate poet of eros, specifically, of erotic crisis.

By the time that H.D. engages this literary fiction, Sappho carries the cumulative weight of Western love theology, prominently the iconography of troubadour passion. Swinburne calls her "Love's priestess, mad with pain and joy of song, / Song's priestess, mad with joy and pain of love" ("On the Cliffs" 3:317). The aesthetic/decadent glamour of Sappho as a literary sign thus links religion, love, song, madness, pain, and joy. In late-nineteenth-century commentaries it was common to associate Sappho with the troubadours, as one who like them knows the dominion of Love or "overmastering emotion" (Symonds 1:293). In an extended comparison of Sappho as lyricist with the Provençal poets, J. M. Mackail says, "The Love whom she saw . . . 'descending from heaven clad in purple vesture,' is akin to the intellectual and spiritual love of Plato and of Dante" (*Lectures* 107). Like Dante she represents an openness to "Love terrible with banners." H.D. and her generation, inheriting the emphases of aesthetic hellenism, certainly knew of these associations: Pound in his early *The Spirit of Romance* finds Sappho in Arnaut Daniel and Dante (93, 122). She clearly possesses an iconic role in what H.D. and Pound, along with late-nineteenth-century hellenists, considered the main line of lyric development from the Greeks through the early Renaissance.

H.D. herself acknowledges this allegorical status of the figure: "Sappho has become for us a name, an abstraction as well as a pseudonym for poignant human feeling" ("The Wise Sappho" 67). The "Sappho" of the fragment poems, I would suggest, is this verbal icon, abstraction, "pseudonym," or metonym – a mark of magical glamour. She is in Swinburne's phrase "Our Lady of all men's loves" ("On the Cliffs" 3:322), and like the Lady of the troubadours, as Pound claims, she functions as a mantra focusing the creative energies of the poet.

Critics have insightfully read some of H.D.'s fragment poems as bold modernist "refabrications of Sappho" (DuPlessis, *Career* 23). However, one must at the same time grant their conventionality. H.D. here deliberately announces her participation in well-established traditions – the troubadour lyric performing the mesmerisms of erotic fixation and playing out the debate about love's laws, and the romantic tradition of "dilutions and dilations" upon Sappho, carried for her through the medium of Wharton's edition. Further, though critics have read the fragment poems as revealing H.D.'s female-centeredness – her adoption of a lesbian identity (DuPlessis, *Career* 24) or her quest for artistic identity within oppressive "female socialization" (Gubar 56) – they are as clearly implicated within a male-identified erotic discourse. That some of these poems "mark desire as heterosexual" is not as surprising as Gubar suggests (56–7), if indeed "Sappho" in these poems stands as a signifier not primarily within the context of lesbian desire but within a fiction of high romance, "romantic thralldom," in DuPlessis's phrase. This is Byron's "burning Sappho," celebrated in a continuous line of male poetic appropriations from Catullus and Ovid through Baudelaire and Swinburne.

Another kind of Sapphic intertextuality takes place in some of the early lyrics of H.D. – not the name/abstraction of Sappho, but traces of her images and tonalities unobtrusively marking individual lyrics. In arriving at the list of references to Sappho given in the Appendix, I was first led by Robert Babcock, who found embedded in the early poem "Pursuit" a clear allusion to Bergk/Wharton 93 (LP 105). Indeed, one can find this kind of covert interplay consistently in H.D.'s first two lyric volumes. H.D. absorbed Wharton's Sappho (both Greek and English texts) at a "pre-verbal level," as D. S. Carne-Ross says about her work with Euripides. Such an intimate acquaintance is indicated in the density of citation of the 1920 essay, clearly written with Wharton in hand.

Though some of the allusions noted in the Appendix may seem far-fetched, they may seem less so when taken not simply in isolation but as part of a pervasive and continuous textual interplay with Sappho as given through Wharton. As Babcock has shown, one finds the "wild hyacinth" of Bergk 94 (LP 105) in "Pursuit," mediated for H.D. through the Rossetti translation given in Wharton. One finds in "Pear Tree" ("you have mounted, . . . higher than my arms' reach") a fainter trace of Bergk 37 (LP 52): "I do not think to touch the sky with my two arms" (trans. Wharton). H.D.'s "Moonrise," suggesting a collective attendance upon a goddess at the moment of moonrise, echoes several fragments in Sappho describing such ceremonies, particularly Bergk 53 (LP 154): "The moon rose full, and the women stood as though around an altar" (trans. Wharton). One can find in "Orion Dead" a more significant echo of Bergk 29 (LP 138), and an even more complex intertextuality is suggested in "Storm" and "Night." Finally, almost all of the lyric songs of "Hymen" are in conversation with Sappho and with poets immediately following her in an epithalamic tradition. Because these early lyric poems, as well as the 1920 essay, indicate a concrete engagement with the fragments and with the discernible poet and poetics behind them, they allow us to see H.D. in the role of interpreter. One finds, indeed, that she discerns clearly some aspects of Sappho's lyric fiction: the candor and intimacy of the lyric voice, an insistence upon the vulnerable and delicate, the career – erotic trajectory – of women and flowers.

"Orion Dead" (*Collected Poems* 56–7) may seem an odd poem to read in a Sapphic context, because it ostensibly concerns Artemis, not Sappho's Aphrodite, and a male and not a female lover. But as we have seen, the Artemisian *thiasos* is H.D.'s preferred image of female erotic bonds, and the Artemisian lover/ beloved is androgynous. The poem does capture something of the intimacy in

Sappho's many addresses to loved ones, usually women who are now lost to her, available only in memory and in poetry. The refrain of the poem ("So arise and face me") echoes Bergk 29: "Stand face to face, friend . . . and unveil the grace in thine eyes" (trans. Wharton). What these lines have in common is the desire for the intimate, gracious gaze, the distinctively Aphroditic candor of "face to face." In H.D.'s poem that gaze is irrevocably lost, and the poem – originally called "Incantation" – gains its power by playing out the impossibility of language to revoke the irrevocable. It is about the impotence of the gesture of speech, which only in its brokenness can signal the power of the grief compelling it. Just as in Sappho's poetry, that grief concerns not simply a lost lover, but a lost companionship or friendship that once informed everything. The cornel wood – blazing, uplifting, yet at the same time deeply rooted – functions as the external correlative in the poem for that living affection.

Two other early poems from *Sea Garden* show another kind of intertextual relation to Sappho. In "Night" and "Storm" a Sapphic fragment serves almost as the absent referent of a riddle. "Night" (*Collected Poems* 33) ends with an apostrophe to night, which throughout the poem is personified as the cause of the progressive, relentless, and almost mechanical disintegration of the flower; the poem concludes: "O night, / you take the petals / of the roses in your hand, / but leave the stark core / of the rose / to perish on the branch." This sense of an irrevocable sequence ending with isolation and vulnerability finds a gloss in Sappho: "The moon has set, and the Pleiades; it is midnight, the time is going by, and I sleep alone" (Bergk 52; LP 168B). The fragment links night and time within larger processions of moon and stars, leading to the fact of loneliness, which is at the same time a tacit recognition of the subject's participation in those passages. H.D.'s poem is likewise about natural processions, about time, or whatever other force of necessity leaves one alone and mortally exposed.

"Storm" (*Collected Poems* 36), like many of H.D.'s early poems, works like a riddle, in presenting an image or images that clearly point beyond themselves and at the same time withholding the name of the referent. This riddling is similar to what Jeanne Kammer, following Philip Wheelwright, has identified as diaphor, which "produces new meaning by the juxtaposition alone of two (or more) images, each term concrete, their joining unexplained" (157). I would suggest that the "meaning" produced by the images of "Storm," the unnamed referent, deliberately relates to Sappho's well-known fragment: "Now Eros shakes my soul, a wind on the mountains falling on the oaks" (Bergk 42, LP 47; trans. Wharton). In her 1920 essay on Sappho, H.D. paraphrases this fragment: "High in the mountains, the wind may break the trees, as love the lover" ("The Wise Sappho" 59). "Storm" begins with an apostrophic address to this "you" who breaks the trees:

You crash over the trees,
you crack the live branch –
the branch is white,
the green crushed,
each leaf is rent like split wood.

You burden the trees
with black drops,
you swirl and crash –
you have broken off a weighted leaf
in the wind,
it is hurled out,
whirls up and sinks,
a green stone.

If one reads the diaphoric significance of this poem as erotic possession, it reveals a remarkable complexity and density of comprehension. This is the daimonic eros of the Orphics, very like Sappho's serpent-like, bittersweet, violent-seizing one, with all his power to break and crush, weight with blackness, elevate ecstatically, and transform. In light of this powerful verbal performance of a Sapphic fragment, H.D.'s later self-conscious evocation of romantic Sappho in "Fragment Forty / Love . . . bitter-sweet" seems relatively pallid and unconvincing. In the fragment poem these same qualities of eros and this same mysterious process of destruction and transformation are presented as rhetorical and abstract: "to sing love, / love must first shatter us" (Collected Poems 175). In "Storm," however, this mysterious change is performed in language.

By far the most serious of all H.D.'s engagements with Sappho's poetry is her masque "Hymen," the title poem of her second volume of lyrics. H.D. here writes within a long and revered tradition of the epithalamion, of which she was fully aware. I have elsewhere discussed at length H.D.'s adaptation of this tradition ("Scarlet" 90–9). Here I will focus on the specifically Sapphic nature of H.D.'s intertextuality. The clear orientation of "Hymen," as DuPlessis has noted (Career 29), is toward a female experience of life passages: "[T]he lyrics of ["Hymen"] form a carefully mapped ritual of passage, for and by a community of women, through female life-stages in which love is holy" (59). In this emphasis H.D. draws from Sappho very directly. Moreover, in "Hymen" the moments of female erotic life are signified in a sequence of flower-gifts. In this emphasis too H.D. shares a primarily Sapphic orientation.

Eva Stehle Stigers defines the distinctiveness of Sappho's lyric fiction by contrasting pivotal images of desire in her poetry with those of male poets with whom she is often associated, for instance, Achilochus, Anacreon, and Catullus. Stigers takes Catullus 62, a verbal contest between male suitors and female virgins, as a polemical criticism of Sappho's romantic portrayal of the virginal world. To Catullus, virginity defined apart from male penetration and from the social needs of procreation is sterile and narcissistic. His epithalamion celebrates the triumph of these elemental needs over the autonomy of the virgin. But in contrast, the fragments of Sappho imply a fiction of female relations in the *thiasos* that has a fullness in itself, apart from the male. That fullness is symbolized in Sappho's poetry continuously by the "flower image, with its implications of delicate, vulnerable beauty" (92). Thomas McEvilley affirms this aesthetic and mythical sense of the Sapphic flower image, finding that the maiden/flower represents "that brief moment when the beautiful shines out brilliantly and assumes, for all its perishability, the stature of an eternal condition in the spirit if not in the body" (269). The flower in Sappho is thus a kind of metonym of divine, especially Aphroditic, presence.

H.D. at the end of her essay on Sappho also arrives at a focus on the fiction of the *thiasos*, within which the ephemeral and ordinary gestures of young women assume the status of immortal epiphanies: "She constructed from the simple gesture of a half-grown awkward girl, a being, a companion, an equal. . . . She constructed . . . the whole, the perfection, the undying spirit of goddess, muse or sacred being from the simple grace of some tall, half-developed girl" (65). Recent critics confirm this insight about divine epiphany in Sappho. The manifestations of Aphrodite are latent and subjective, occurring at any moment of erotic *aphrodite*, which charmed state is indeed brought about through the incantation of the poem.[30] Thus the young girl, seen through the eyes of poet or lover, *is* for a moment the goddess. H.D. concludes her essay with a catalogue of the fictional *thiasos* – the lovers Atthis and Andromeda, a mother and a child name Cleis, Mnasidika, Gyrinno, Eranna, Gorgo, the young Timas, "lying with lily wreath and funeral torch." After this catalogue of women's names, H.D. returns to Meleager's comment on Sappho in the proem to his *Garland*: "Little – not little – but all, all roses!" (65–7). In this verbal association she affirms the link between girls, flowers, and poems.

Though only the barest fragments of Sappho's epithalamia survive, there is no reason to imagine that they are not in some way continuous with a primary focus on the woman's subjective experience of desire rather than on the male's privileged urgency and the social needs his rupture satisfies. Such, at least, is the interpretation of the epithalamion in "Hymen." In H.D.'s poem the bridegroom never appears, and he is mentioned only once. Instead Love appears, intimating obliquely the bride's entrance into the bridal chamber where her love waits. It is the *bride's* passion of which the choruses speak – "All the heat . . . Of desire / Is caught in her eyes as fire / In the dark center leaf / Of the white Syrian iris" (*Collected Poems* 106). Rather than the male and social elements, the poem concerns the interiorized Sapphic *thiasos*. The ceremony shows a procession of small groups of young girls, each group coming before the purple curtain (of memory, of dream) with distinct music, distinct voice, and each group (except one, which bears the coverings for the bridal bed) bringing gifts of flowers – "Gladiolus tall with dignity," the first pale gold petals of the crocus, the evanescent winter rose, the lapis-blue hyacinth, white lily and iris, the blossoming laurel, the purple cyclamen. The poem is concerned primarily with the subtle moments within the life of the maiden, and the coming of eros is one among many of those moments.

In H.D.'s "Hymen" Sappho provides not only the general concept of the epithalamion, but significant subtexts for individual songs. Attention to this Sapphic intertextuality might illumine what critics have taken to be an ambiguous tonality to the whole, which comes, I believe, from the different senses of "marriage" operative in the poem: as a traditional heterosexual union; as the homoerotic union within a *thiasos*; and as the *hieros gamos* of the mysteries, that is, the Eleusinian descent of the bride into the bridal chamber. Of these three senses, the most obvious one – traditional marriage – is the least important.

To speak of marriage in the context of Sappho's *thiasos* is of course metaphorical, but such an association, as McEvilley has argued, has a clear basis in the surviving poems. The love poems and other fragments, like the epithalamia, associate the young women with flowers and with a sacred context: "A typical scene in Sappho is of girls (never women) plaiting garlands for a rite that is never explained. What is dwelt on is their beauty as they do so and a certain unspecific sadness which this beauty evokes." McEvilley then argues that the rite in which Sappho's girls participate is finally the poetic process itself, "the rite in which the flowerlike beauty of girls is celebrated in an inner garden where such perishable stuff is transmuted into those timeless flowers, poems" (269).

Two of the first songs in "Hymen" allude to Sapphic fragments about the child (*pais*) or young girl (*parthenos*), emphasizing the primacy of bonds within the *thiasos* and the kind of imaginative rite that McEvilley describes. "Where the first crocus buds unfold" (103), in the image of "very little girls" gathering golden flowers, may have two Sapphic fragments as subtexts: Bergk 121 (LP 122): "A maiden [*pais*: child] full tender plucking flowers" (trans. Wharton); and Bergk 85 (LP 132): "I have a fair daughter [*pais*] with a form like a golden flower, Cleïs the beloved, above whom I [prize] nor all Lydia nor lovely [Lesbos]" (trans. Wharton). Both of these fragments capture the association of the child and flower at the moment of greatest tenderness and freshness, and the goldenness suggests its immortality. H.D. in her 1920 essay comments on the latter fragment, pointing out the legend that Cleis was the name both of Sappho's mother and of her daughter (66). Thus the association of the tender child and golden flower is linked in H.D.'s imagination to the bonds between mother and daughter.

In the third song, "Never more will the wind" (*Collected Poems* 103–4), one finds an unmistakable allusion to Sappho, Bergk 109 (LP 114), a lament over lost virginity: "A: Maidenhood, maidenhood, whither art thou gone away from me?

/ B: Never again will I come to thee, never again" (trans. Wharton). H.D.'s poem, spoken by older children bearing winter roses, reads:

> Never more will the wind
> Cherish you again,
> Never more will the rain.
>
> Never more
> Shall we find you bright
> In the snow and wind.
>
> The snow is melted,
> The snow is gone,
> And you are flown:
> Like a bird out of our hand,
> Like a light out of our heart,
> You are gone.

The intertextual play with Sappho here is very similar to that in "Storm": it re-performs the Sapphic text, playing out its distinct tonality by means of concrete images and musical effects. What Engel glibly dismisses as H.D.'s "tired neo-Elizabethan repetitions" (513) are in fact attempts to re-create the echoing quality of the original: "Parthenia, parthenia, poi me lipois' apoiche / Ouketi exzo pros se, ouketi exzo." H.D.'s poem is an intricate fabric of melodic repetition of phrase and sound, capturing the delicacy of *parthenia* in interwoven images of rain, wind, snow, and bird; capturing the suddenness and irrevocability of the loss in repetition of "Never more" (*ouketi exzo*) and "you are flown . . . you are gone." The poignancy of the longing is heightened by H.D.'s retaining the second-person address of the original, and that longing clearly, in both poems, is understood in the context of the bonds of the *thiasos* (a bird out of *our* hand, . . . a light out of *our* heart).

These poems as well as others in "Hymen" emphasize the collective dimension of erotic life; yet the ritual moves gradually to single out the bride and her desire. Clearly some ominousness and darkness begin to surface as the songs move toward the event of the bridal chamber. "From citron-bower be her bed" suggests unmistakably the homology between bridal bed and coffin, thus the traditional homology between virginal initiation and death. The visceral quality of the consummation is suggested in the last two poems. In a song sung by purple-clad Eros before the dark curtains of the masque, the event of deflowering is imagined metaphorically in the image of a bee entering not unpainfully the "purple flower lips." The last song, "Where love is king," sung by a group of young boys before the bridal door, suggests an overpowering presence that paralyzes action and silences speech.

How is one to interpret these dark undertones? They have been read in a sinister light, as representing in some way H.D.'s failed marriage to Aldington. Alicia Ostriker points to the "counter–truth" of the poem: "that a polarized active–passive, plunderer–prey pattern in sexuality makes the 'object' of love faceless, voiceless, blank" (21). Susan Gubar speaks of the poem as "a somber meditation on the predatory pattern of heterosexuality" (55). Though a biographical dimension of heterosexual union is hard to avoid, it undoubtedly coexists with, is even subsumed by, a religious meaning that indeed preoccupied H.D. throughout her career as part of her self-definition as a poet.

At this point one must recall the third sense of marriage being worked in the poem, the sacred marriage of the mysteries, that is simultaneously, in H.D.'s Orphic sense of these things, a union with one's daimon. The Sapphic context of the last poem makes clear this daimonic and divine significance. In "Where love is king," the chorus claims that "[o]ur limbs are numb / Before [Love's] fiery need; . . . Before his fiery lips / Our lips are mute and dumb" (110). This language echoes at least two famous fragments of Sappho likening the coming of Eros to terror and death: Bergk 40 (LP 130), "Now Love masters my limbs and shakes me, fatal creature, bitter-sweet" (trans. Wharton); and Bergk 2 (LP 31), "For when I see thee but a little, I have no utterance left, my tongue is broken down, . . . with my eyes I have no sight, my ears ring, sweat pours down, and a trembling seizes all my body" (trans. Wharton). H.D. knows very well this sense of daimonic eros, not only through Sappho but through Plato and Dante. The coming of Eros in "Hymen," as in Sappho's *phanetai moi*, brings the terror and devastation of a divine epiphany. Further, "I have gone down into the bridal chamber" is one of the slogans of the Eleusinian initiate, and in the Eleusinian rite, as in the conclusion to "Hymen," the torches are extinguished before the congregation at the point of the enactment of the marriage in darkness (J. E. Harrison, *Prolegomena* 563, 569).

The Sapphic intertextuality of "Hymen," then, points on the one hand to a sense of female identification serving, as in Sappho, as an antidote for conventional heterosexual expectations. Dedicating the volume *Hymen* to her newborn daughter, Perdita, and to her young companion, Bryher, H.D. in "Hymen," like Sappho, affirms the continuity between mother and daughter and at the same time celebrates the homoerotic bonds that have sustained her.[31] On the other hand, the ominous undertone of the poem, concerned with death, pain, terror, and paralysis, refers at least in part to the religious context of the mysteries. In one of her books in the Beinecke Library at Yale (Farnell 1:208) H.D. underlined the phrase "sacred nuptial rite" and wrote in the margin "Hymen Cornwall 1918," and on the same page she underlined *hieros gamos* and wrote in the margin "Corfu." Her fictional account of the summer of 1918 in *Asphodel* suggests that H.D. firmly imagined at this juncture (and perhaps at Corfu in 1920) some marriage with a god – like that of Cassandra, with whom Hermione compares herself in *Asphodel*, or of Evadne and Kreousa, raped by Apollo/Helios.

Whether Sappho serves H.D. as an enthralling Muse, or as a sacred and forbidden textual space, or as an intimate ground, her presence in H.D.'s poetry is fundamental, coincident with the ambivalences of a desiring female body and with a complex fiction of divine mania.

"Adequately Alexandrian": Theocritus and the Greek Anthology

We have elsewhere considered the centrality of Alexandria in H.D.'s fiction of Greece, signifying for her the locus of permanent displacement from Athens and Sparta, the lost islands and the lost gods; scribal recovery in library and museum and transmission of texts; visionary renewal through clairvoyant reading of Greek letters. As we have seen, Alexandria also suggests for H.D. a range of sometimes liminal erotic valences. This section specifies some of the lyric potentialities of Alexandria in terms of textual exchanges in H.D.'s poetry.

The two central sites of literary Alexandria in H.D.'s writing – Theocritus and the Greek Anthology[32] – were well established in the late nineteenth century. A look through popular literary publications at the turn of the century – like the American Thomas B. Mosher's pirated editions or his journal *Bibelot*, which H.D., Pound, and Aldington all knew – suggests that this literary emphasis is almost coterminous with hellenic aestheticism, equal to the fascination with Sappho and Renaissance hellenism.[33] If one tries to find the reasons for the popularity of this hellenistic writing, one must consider pragmatic matters, such as the availability of texts and translations, or the selections of authors used in textbooks in English public schools.[34] The last two decades of the century saw a tremendous increase in the publication of Greek writers, both editions and translations. Members of H.D.'s generation grew up not only with Wharton's Sappho but with Andrew Lang's *Theocritus, Bion, and Moschus* and with J. W. Mackail's *Select Epigrams from the Greek Anthology*, all of which served to propagate further interest. In addition, the ubiquitous Victorian habit of selective hellenic analogies, detailed in Frank Turner's *The Greek Heritage in Victorian Britain*, comes into play. Clearly Theocritus and the Anthology answered needs of an age that likewise considered itself Alexandrian, in both negative and positive connotations of that term.

H.D. read and knew well two of the foremost resident poets of early Alexandria. The divine hymns of Callimachus appear to have entered into her poetry both consciously and unconsciously. However, more important is Theocritus, who in H.D.'s repeated claim was the earliest of her hellenic models. In representing an aspect of H.D.'s fiction of Greece, Theocritus defines a serene and ample luxury belonging to what one might call a "Hesperidean" landscape. With his imagined settings in Sicily and southern Italy, Theocritus was associated in the late nineteenth century with such a distant realm of golden light.

H.D.'s large textual exchange with the Greek Anthology in both poetry and prose has long been recognized by critics, who have given attention to some of the earliest of her adaptations of epigrams – "Hermes of the Ways," "Orchard," "Epigram / (After the Greek)" – as well as later references to poets like Meleager, Nossis, and Moero. Rather than elaborate this commentary, it seems important here to consider more theoretical questions: the technical possibilities for modernist experiment afforded by the hellenistic epigram, and the fiction of the anthology itself as it shaped H.D.'s conception of her lyric project.

Theocritus

Though H.D. mentions Theocritus often in her prose writing and though she devotes an essay to him in her "Notes on Euripides, Pausanius, and Greek Lyric Poets," only two explicit traces of his writing can be found in her lyric poetry. "Simaetha," from *Hymen*, is taken from Idyll 2; and "The Shepherd," which H.D. claimed was written to Frances Gregg in a "Bion and Moschus mood" (*End to Torment* 36), has affinity with Idylls 11 and 20. Other possible references to Theocritus listed in the Appendix are more conjectural, though unquestionably H.D. drew on Idyll 18 in her revision of the epithalamic tradition in "Hymen." What follows here is an attempt to sketch the fiction of Theocritus within which H.D. wrote, though it is indicated in her writing only in an oblique and fragmentary way. Several poems not traceable directly to Theocritus appear nevertheless to share in this fiction.

Richard Jenkyns has pointed to the prominence of Theocritus in the late nineteenth century, linked for him to an idyllic homoeroticism fostered by Oxford figures like J. A. Symonds and Walter Pater (290–2). But the significance of this figure seems more complex than this. In terms of literary dissemination, it would appear that Theocritus comes to the late Victorians trailing clouds of Wordsworth, who in his posthumously published *Prelude* (1850) equates his poetic project of rustic and natural celebration with that of the ancient idyllist (11.424–70). This emphasis is quite in opposition to the highly artificial Renaissance pastoral tradition, in which the imitative Virgil was preferred to his Greek predecessor. Theocritus in the nineteenth century comes to represent specifically the landscape of romantic pastoral, coincident with reveries of childhood and with the active imagination. In Tennyson, whose poetry is filled with Theocritean echoes,[35] this landscape has been further interiorized, so that in "The Lotus-Eaters," for instance, it represents a territory of dreamlike sensuous fulfillment, the sublime unreal. Theocritus in Tennyson takes on the decidedly liminal erotic character that so attracted the late Victorians, the kind of trancelike *locus amoenus*.

Further, Theocritus's emergence at this time seems to come in part from the general fascination in romantic hellenism with the landscape of Italy, beginning indeed with Winckelmann's migration there from Germany. Upon Virgilian authority, Italy is known as "Hesperia," and its identification with the mythical Land of the Setting Sun is much elaborated in romantic hellenism. Shelley suggests this equivalence in his "Lines Written among the Euganean Hills," a favorite poem among Aesthetes (Aldington, *Aesthetes* 29). And Vernon Lee, in a prose piece in Aldington's anthology of the Aesthetes (137–40), amplifies the association of the blue and dreamlike hills near Venice with the "Orchard of the Hesperides" (139).

However, as Aldington himself suggests in his introduction to this anthology, generations of British travelers to Italy – surely including himself and H.D. in 1912–13 – were shaped by reading the Tauchnitz edition of Symonds's *Sketches in Italy* (*Aesthetes* 22), which details the lush landscapes of southern Italy. Generations of literati were even more fundamentally shaped by Symonds's *Studies of the Greek Poets*, first appearing in 1873 and then in 1876. This critical survey of Greek literature surely encouraged if it did not partially determine the literary emphases of Victorian hellenism.

In his essay on Theocritus, Symonds takes the landscape of the south as an essential determinate in understanding the poet, and he details its character and nuances at great length:

> It is on the shores of the Mediterranean – at Sorrento, at Amalfi, or near Palermo, . . . that we ought to study Theocritus, and learn the secret of his charm. Few of us pass middle age without visiting one or other of these sacred spots, which seem to be the garden of perpetual spring. Like the lines of the Sicilian idyllist, they inspire an inevitable and indescribable [*pothos*], . . . touching our sense of beauty with a subtle power, and soothing our spirits with the majesty of classical repose. (2:248)

The imagined landscapes of Theocritus, made vivid in southern Italy, seem the "garden of perpetual spring," the "bright garden of the age of gold" (2:250). In this golden garden, Symonds gives special attention to the effects of light:

> Light and colour are the glory of these mountains. Valleys divide their flanks, seaming with shadow-belts and bands of green the broad hill-side, while lower down the olives spread a hoary greyness and soft robe of silver mist, the skirts of which are kissed by tideless waves. (2:248)

This play of light and shadow, the discriminations of shades of green-gray and white, define a Theocritean configuration of images. Trees, too, are crucial in "idyllic scenery," the tall pine and the oak as well as the olive. Near Sorrento, for instance, "there are two gigantic pines so placed that, lying on the grass beneath them, one looks on Capri rising from the sea, Baiae, and all the bay of Naples" (2:250). This brightly illuminated landscape surrounding Vesuvius becomes an analogue for the Sicilian landscape around Aetna, in which some of Theocritus's idylls take place, and indeed an analogue for the "sunny brightness" of imagined Hellas.

This reverie of Theocritean landscape comes closer to H.D. when reenacted by Aldington in his essay "Theocritus in Capri," which is clearly an elegy for his early romance with H.D. in the spring of 1913, played out among the typical haunts of travelers in Italy. Aldington locates this reverie "[u]nder the whispering pine on the scarped and flower-scented side of Monte Salaro, . . . with Paestum far away on the one hand, Baiae on the other, and light foam about the islands of the Sirens" (*Literary Studies* 242). For *jeune hellenistes* this was a landscape animated with the presences of gods, particularly "our lord of Delos, who is sun and song"; and it was "by Theocritus we learned to see them" (243). This romantic élan is carried in a catalogue of flowers with Theocritean allusion:

> There were wild pear-trees in blossom, the green-silver olive gardens, the bees murmuring in the ivy and fern as once by the cave of Amaryllis, rock-cistus and asphodel, white violets or stars of Bethlehem (whichever were Leukoïa), from which the shepherds wove their flower-crowns. In the damp recesses of the rocks were scented wild narcissus and sometimes little cyclamen flowers. There were purple anemones, the flower perhaps which sprang from the blood of Adonis. (244)

Thus, in the late-nineteenth-century imagination of Theocritus inherited by H.D., the poet is associated with a landscape characterized by its fertility, its play of light and color within wide horizons, its hellenic amplitude and serenity, figured in the abundance of mythically charged flowers, and, above all, its rich sensuousness.

The typical *locus amoenus* in Theocritus's idylls confirms this emphasis:

> Here be oak trees, and here the galingale, and sweetly here hum the bees about the hives. There are two wells of chill water, and on the tree the birds are warbling, and the shadow is beyond compare with that where thou liest, and from on high the pine tree pelts us with her cones. (Idyll 5, trans. Lang)

> There we reclined on deep beds of fragrant lentisk, lowly strown, and rejoicing we lay in new stript leaves of the vine. And high above our heads waved many a poplar, many an elm tree, while close at hand the sacred water from the nymphs' own cave welled forth with murmurs musical. . . . All breathed the scent of the opulent summer. (Idyll 7, trans. Lang)

Tall pine and oak, poplars and elm, humming bees, cool water, and quiet rest on beds of loam under deep shade, especially during the heat of noontide: this *now* of the opulent summer or spring is the recurrent locus of the idylls.

This, too, is the landscape suggested in H.D.'s essay on Theocritus in "Notes on Euripides, Pausanius, and Greek Lyric Poets." H.D. imagines Theocritean landscape in terms of its black soil, "decadent" because covered with rich layers of decaying foliage, and both literally and metaphorically volcanic, associated with powerful hidden emotion. For H.D. the hellenism of Theocritus is in contrast to the crystalline light of Athenian clarity:

> This is the world of Theocritus, as different from that of Euripides as black earth from limpid water, water surface that reflects images of Olympians, pure spirits, as if the sun threw colour and fire, . . . there is colour everywhere, there is *light* in one city.
> But there is shadow elsewhere.

Theocritus represents "shadow," images "designed not to draw us toward the sky and its enchantments but to bring us close to wholesome, passionate things of earth." In his idylls "[t]here are spaces of blackness, warm and soft and restful; blackness which spreads soft cushions where we may tread, blackness of dream, witchcraft" ("Curled Thyme" 1–2). His is a "soft, yet full and ripe music, under great [windswept] pine trees, [beside full breakers,] a tone lower, no shrill Dionysiac ecstatic flute-note, but reeds, rich and quiet"[36] (4–5).

Within H.D.'s hellenic fiction, then, Theocritus does not represent the abstract category of pastoral otherness – for instance, the alternative world of the "sea-garden" with its Athenian stringencies and asceticism.[37] Rather he carries a very specific imagistic configuration – a quiet Vesuvian sensuousness, a shelter from insistences of spirit. The Theocritean in H.D. is focused not upon spiritual ecstasies but upon "passionate things of earth." Nor is it attached – as with Symonds and Aldington – to *pothos* or nostalgia, but rather to the fullness of the present moment. Such a Theocritean locus is suggested in "Sitalkas," for instance, wherein the lyric "I" rejects the high and cool detachment of the gods in favor of the immediate now of "seeded grass" and "broken leaves." "White World," perhaps more clearly than any other poem, suggests the amplitude and sensuousness of the Theocritean locus, "purple with rose-bays, . . . dark islands in a sea / of grey-green olive or wild white-olive, / cut with the sudden cypress shafts"; the blossoming citron and laurel; "the wind-breath / at the hot noon-hour"; "the bee's soft belly." The flora and the color views here echo unmistakably passages from Symonds and Aldington, and the last two images of noontide and bees are established literary markers for Theocritus.

In terms of H.D.'s biomythology, the Theocritean landscape is clearly associated with her early idyllic days with Aldington in southern Italy. In *Paint It Today*, Midget is translating Theocritus with her English companion, Basil (Aldington), and they discuss the translation of *leukoion*, white violet, that appears in the idylls (29). Ezra Pound, accompanying H.D. and Aldington in 1913 in Italy, writes cattily to Dorothy Shakespear: "The Theocritan Idyll is, I think still at Anacapri" (*Pound and Shakespear* 211). But another, postlapsarian side to this

Theocritean bond with Aldington is suggested in "Simaetha," in which a betrayed woman tries by witchcraft to charm her lost lover and to put a curse on her rival.

However, it is also clear that in H.D.'s biographical typology, Aldington is an interloper in Theocritean territory, which largely for her carries a homoerotic connotation. H.D. became intimate with Aldington during the time of her painful estrangement from Frances Gregg. She met him in late 1911, very soon after Gregg left H.D. to return home with her mother (October 1911), and her intimacy with him intensified during her stay in Paris beginning in May 1912, immediately after she received a letter from Gregg abruptly announcing her marriage and inviting H.D. to share in a strange ménage à quatre (April 1912). H.D. and Aldington continued their romance in Italy in the winter of 1912 and the spring of 1913, marrying in October 1913.[38]

H.D. records on two occasions that her early poetry, written for Frances Gregg, was modeled after Theocritus and that she read to Gregg Andrew Lang's translation, given to her by Pound ("Autobiographical Notes" [1]; *End to Torment* 36). The autobiographical narrative of these years, *Hermione*, alludes as well to this early writing (149), and the Pound character in *Asphodel* remarks that Fayne Rabb and Hermione are "like a vision of Theocritus" (52). "The Shepherd," found in H.D.'s papers at Yale but not published until 1983, represents, according to H.D.'s remarks in *End to Torment*, some of this Theocritean poetry for Gregg. It appears to allude chiefly to Idyll 11, wherein the Cyclops pleads his love to the nymph Galatea, recalling the time that he first went with her to pick hyacinths upon the hills. Gregg in H.D.'s narratives is associated with another Galatea as well as with the hyacinth. Moreover, H.D.'s Paris diary of spring and summer of 1912 preserves a partial draft of a poem that is apparently a translation or adaptation of Idyll 13, the story of Heracles and his lover, Hylas (verso of p. 40). Drowned when river nymphs pull him into the depths of the water, Hylas is fiercely mourned by Heracles, who temporarily abandons the journey of the Argo in order to search hopelessly for him. This idyll, a *topos* within late-nineteenth-century hellenism, in part because of its powerful testimony to homoerotic bonds, would seem for H.D. at this painful juncture a form of mourning for a lost companionship, similar in many respects to the later "Orion Dead."

In a last homoerotic association, H.D.'s essay on Theocritus in "Notes on Euripides, Pausanius, and Greek Lyric Poets" was written in 1920 in California, when H.D. was in the company of her new companion, Bryher. In pencil revisions to the carbon typescript of this essay, H.D. has deleted allusions to the coast of California,[39] obscuring an obvious parallel between Carmel and the southern Italian coast around Capri. As Diana Collecott has suggested, H.D. and Bryher shared the fantasy of California, the land of the golden West, as a kind of Hesperides ("Images" 323).

If indeed one may associate Theocritus in H.D.'s writing with a Hesperidean landscape, then a group of three poems published in 1921 under the title "Hesperides" – "Fragment Thirty-six," "Song," and "At Baia" – deserve further note. How may one imagine these three poems simultaneously within the fantasy of Hesperides? "Fragment Thirty-Six" (*Collected Poems* 165–8) suspends the reader within a debate considering the indirection of song versus the directness of bodily possession. "Song" (*Collected Poems* 133), which echoes a passage from Callimachus's hymn to Apollo, recalls the association between golden light and passionate eroticism; its imagery of the "white honey-comb" and of flowers "thick on the black limbs / of an Illyrian apple bough" is distinctly Theocritean in its sensuousness. "At Baia" (*Collected Poems* 128) alludes specifically to the Theocritean landscape of southern Italy (the bay of Baiae is one of the locations in the fantasies of Symonds and Aldington). The eroticism implied here is all the more powerful for having been deferred, "the blue veins / of your throat unkissed," and for being imagined in terms of a hypothetical dream of a gift of white orchids. The order of the three poems in "Hesperides" is probably also significant, because H.D. was by no means casual in her arrangement of poems.[40] One might imagine them as an erotic sequence: the first hovering on the brink of "awakening" the lover, the second suggesting the passionate engagement, the third the aftermath, registered not so much somatically as psychically.

It may be too facile to suggest that for H.D. the Theocritean or the Hesperidean is a complex figure for liminalities of many kinds: suspensions in memory between Capri and California, in eroticism between male and female, in affect between violent longing and peace, in awareness between golden illumination and Aphroditic sensuousness. In any case, the Theocritean landscape figures in H.D.'s writing as one of the alternatives to an austere Athenian hellenism governed by Artemis, Athene, and daimonic Helios. In the Theocritean mode the sun is not imperious and estranging but tactile and opulent, "as gold / as the half-ripe grain" ("Song"). In this configuration the light is muted, the eroticism not sublimated but bodily, and the ecstasies confined within subtleties of human relationships.

The Greek Anthology

Of the more than twenty distinct epigrams from the Greek Anthology referred to in H.D.'s writing, both poetry and narrative, twelve may loosely be called translations. A list of these epigrams in order of their publication reveals some unremarked features of H.D.'s intertextual exchange with the Anthology:

January 1913	"Hermes of the Ways" (Anyte and Anon.)
January 1913	"Orchard" (Zonas)
January 1913	"Epigram / (*After the Greek*)" (Anon.)

February 1914	"Hermonax" (Antipater of Sidon and Philodemus)
1922	"Heliodora" (Meleager)
1922	"Lais" (Plato)
1923	"Nossis" (Nossis and Meleager's proem) in *Heliodora*
1925	"Antipater of Sidon" ("Where, Corinth"); later in *Palimpsest*
1926	An epigram of Moero in *Palimpsest*
1926	An epigram of Antipater of Sidon ("I cast my lot") in *Palimpsest*
1928	An epigram of Posidippus in *Hedylus*
1928	An epigram of Asclepiades (Sikeledes) in *Hedylus*

This listing indicates that H.D.'s engagement with the Anthology is divided into two distinct periods. The earlier period is during 1913, the first year of her career ("Hermonax" would also have been composed in 1913).[41] The later period is throughout the twenties, in the aftermath of the war and the breakup of her marriage. These two periods of engagement with the Anthology are sharply distinct, representing different themes and different fictions. The division here is analogous to what we have already seen within H.D.'s Sapphic intertextuality. The first is concrete and active in its engagement with the Greek text; the second is nominal, concerned not so much with the text as with the gesture of citation. The first is dedicatory, ascetic, ritualistic, choral; the second is almost entirely amatory, with some memorial epigrams focusing on loss. The first is lyric; the second is narrative (i.e., in all of the epigrams of the twenties, the translation is an italicized "inset" within a dramatic or narrative discourse).

These two periods of H.D.'s engagement with the Anthology correspond to divisions within her career that have increasingly been noted by critics, most fully by Susan Friedman: the "early H.D.," with her stringent aesthetic disciplines; and the post-1916 H.D., beginning to re-create or rewrite a fiction of herself. That transitional self-fiction of the twenties, if the Sapphic fragment poems and the later contextualized epigrams are a reliable indication, is a decidedly erotic and romantic one, though still haunted by the old athenian daimons. This later fictional H.D., like Hedylus, has "a set Dionysiac mask . . . grown uncanny" (104).

Of the considerable comment generated by H.D.'s early imagist poetry, represented in the four 1913 poems listed above, very little has been said in any detail about the relation of the poems to the Greek epigrams at their origin. Brendan Jackson makes the argument that H.D. in these poems is *not* an imagist because she does not obey Pound's rules of concision, but rather dilates and expands on the original. But then these poems precede Pound's dictates on imagism, and H.D. never claimed to be following such rules. Robert Babcock ("Verses" 208–12) gives an excellent, detailed reading of the least known of these Anthology poems, "Epigram / *(After the Greek),*" though he accepts Jackson's argument that concision in translation of the original is the single criterion for judging the success of the poems.

The issue to be considered here is not H.D.'s obedience to critical definitions established by others, but rather her actual practice in intertextual engagement with the Greek text, which has its own distinct character and integrity. In this regard one should note that Mackail's *Select Epigrams from the Greek Anthology* is H.D.'s bible for the Greek text and the translation of poems within the Greek Anthology.[42] H.D.'s epithets for Sappho and for Theocritus in her essays – "little, but all roses," and "Curled Thyme" – come from Mackail's translations of epigrams, as do many of the epigrams quoted in the essays and in narratives, such as Simonides' epigram on the Spartan dead at Thermopylae.[43] In H.D.'s engagement with the Greek Anthology, Mackail's texts stand in the same intermediary role as Wharton's Sappho.

In the three dedicatory poems, "Hermes of the Ways," "Orchard," and "Hermonax," H.D. engages the Greek texts in very much the way that she does in the opening chorus of Euripides' *Iphigeneia in Aulis*. She plays on original images – sometimes from more than one epigram – to create a visual, dimensional, tactile space. Concision of translation is certainly not the point – rather it is cosmogony. The physical location of the herm implied in an epigram by Anyte – "I, Hermes, stand here by the windy cross-ways nigh the grey sea-shore" (trans. Mackail) – becomes in "Hermes of the Ways" the sensory, whirling, vectored space of part I (west, east, front) and the more static but differentiated space of part II (stream *below* ground, poplar-shaded hill *above*, sea foaming *around*). Moreover, in each of these three poems she shifts voice and perspective to the choral "I," the one who enters the created precinct and makes an offering. Finally, in each case the poems are reflexive: the offering or sacrifice to the god is the poem itself, which reflects the god in its harsh liminality ("Hermes of the Ways") or its broken, unlovely fertility ("Orchard") or its sea strangeness ("Hermonax").

"Hermonax," seen in relation to its model poem in the Greek Anthology, may illumine H.D.'s approach to the epigram. Here is Mackail's translation of the epigram by Antipater of Sidon, entitled by him "To Palaemon and Ino" (*Palatine Anthology* 6.223), followed by H.D.'s poem.

This broken fragment of a sea-wandering scolopendra, lying on the sandy shore, twice four fathom long, all befouled with froth, much torn under the sea-washed rock, Hermonax chanced upon when he was hauling a draught of fishes out of the sea as he plied his fisher's craft; and having found it, he hung it up to the boy Palaemon and Ino, giving the sea-marvel to the sea-deities.

> Gods of the sea;
> Ino,

leaving warm meads
for the green, grey-green fastnesses
of the great deeps;
and Palemon,
bright seeker of sea-shaft,
hear me.

Let all whom the sea loves
come to its altar front,
and I
who can offer no other sacrifice to thee
bring this.

Broken by great waves,
the wavelets flung it here,
this sea-gliding creature,
this strange creature like a weed,
covered with salt foam,
torn from the hillocks of rock.

I, Hermonax,
caster of nets,
risking chance,
plying the sea craft,
came on it.

Thus to sea god
gift of sea wrack;
I, Hermonax, offer it
to thee, Ino,
and to Palemon.
(*Collected Poems* 57–8)

The close correspondences with Antipater's epigram appear in the last three verse paragraphs, while the first two – not suggesting this epigram but perhaps borrowing from another[44] – establish a ritual space in relation to a lyric "I." The supplication is first to all sea gods, then to Ino and Palemon. H.D. alludes here to the mythical context of Ino's metamorphosis from mortal woman to the sea goddess Leucothea, her displacement from human "warm meads" to "green, grey-green fastnesses / of the great deeps." The alliteration of gutturals along with the assonance of *e* and *ea* suggest this double descent – into water, into inhuman form.

The offering or "sacrifice" to the gods is "this": ostensibly the found sea creature, but effectively the verbal gesture itself that creates it, the poem itself as "gift of sea wrack." This "strange creature like a weed, / covered with salt foam," broken and torn, is very like the sea flowers of *Sea Garden*, a metonym for the broken, fragmentary, imagist poem. "I, Hermonax," the phrase asserting identity, is twice given: the "I" of the adventurous seeker is like the visionary poet-gatherer, "caster of nets, / risking chance, / plying the sea craft."

H.D. attempts in "Hermonax" and these other early transformations of Greek texts a defamiliarization or estrangement of lyric expectations. One of the chief advantages of these dedicatory epigrams of the Greek Anthology for her purposes is precisely their distance from the overdetermined lyric speech of the late nineteenth century: their strangeness – strange gods, customs, creatures; their ordinariness, littleness, unloveliness, under the auspices of "Tycho the little god of small things."[45] What is also important is the absence of the naturalizing context of exfoliated forms like ode or elegy. These dedications are contextless but distinct gestures of speech within estranged landscapes.

The Greek Anthology in H.D.'s early writing carries the spiritual implications of the Alexandrian project; it is a gathering of flowers/poems that in their re-creation have the subversive power of making the old gods live again. In her early textual engagement with the Greek Anthology, she participates in the hermetic project described by Hipparchia in *Palimpsest*, "a correlation of gods, temples, flowers, poets" that reanimates the imagined cosmos of the islands (71). Carrying this spiritual urgency, the idea of the "anthology" becomes central to H.D.'s early poetic efforts. *Sea Garden* is such a gathering of poems-as-flowers, and H.D., with Aldington in the Poets' Translation Series and with other imagists in collections of imagist verse, worked steadily within this hellenic fiction. For H.D. at least, the effort signified in the imagist anthologies had its own kind of vengeance, since her poetry was thereinafter persistently linked to the "little, but all roses" of modern anthologies. The Greek Anthology preserved poets and poems from oblivion, but in the modern anthology one sees the corollary motive of epitome more clearly – the determination of some to extinction.

This hellenic fiction of the Greek Anthology did not endure the war and the collapse of the Alexandrian enterprise of the early poetic brotherhood in London. Another emphasis is apparent in the translations of epigrams after the war. H.D.'s later interest is almost entirely in amatory traditions, increasingly those of a group of male love poets from the Greek Anthology: Meleager; Anacreon, a poet of the sixth century B.C. known through the pseudo-Anacreontics appended to the *Palatine Anthology*; and the group of poets from hellenistic Samos – Asclepiades, Posidippus, and Hedylus – that H.D. treats in her second published novel, *Hedylus* (1928). Strangely, however, none of these poets, except Meleager in two poems, enters H.D.'s lyric poetry. H.D. has with them little of the imaginative affinity she shares with Sappho, Euripides, or Theocritus. The quality of their very male-oriented eroticism seems far distant from hers. One wonders at the prominence she gives them, as two of the four subjects in her essays on Greek lyric poets (Meleager and Anacreon) and as chief figures in a historical narrative (the Samian poets). They seem to represent another aspect of her hellenic fiction, a memorial tribute to the hellenic enthusiasm she shared with Aldington and moreover an allusion to a broader classical tradition that these poets, especially Anacreon, influenced.

If the early fiction of the Greek Anthology exists within the Alexandrian recovery of the lost gods and the lost islands, the later fiction is doubly exiled, exercised in the absence not only of Hellas but of a shared belief in Hellas. The Greek essays of "Notes on Euripides, Pausanius, and Greek Lyric Poets," begun in 1920, in large part have Aldington as an imaginary audience: they express the shared universe of their hellenism. In separate essays H.D. treats two poets that Aldington had recently translated in the Poets' Translation Series – Anacreon (1919) and Meleager (1920). The other subjects of H.D.'s essays on lyric poets, Theocritus and Sappho, also belong to this early shared project. The poems of the early twenties, such as "Heliodora" and "Nossis," are, as Caroline Zilboorg has indicated, tributes to a past intimacy with Aldington, each of them situated within the dramatic context of the collaborative making of Meleager's *Garland* ("Influence" 28–9). The later narrative exploration of the poets of Samos follows another emphasis in the Poets' Translation Series – translation of Asclepiades and Posidippus by Edward Storer. In other words, H.D. in the twenties is trying to work old ground, to understand old fictions reflectively in light of their loss.

Thus she arrives in her 1924 essay on Meleager and in *Hedylus* at a sublimated fiction of the Greek Anthology, indeed the one most common since the Renaissance – that it is the source of a continuum of constantly imitated love poetry, prominently Anacreon, Asclepiades, and Meleager, passing into the mainstream of poetic discourse. In this sense one can understand the importance for H.D. of the hellenistic Samian poets, renewing the older Anacreonic tradition in Alexandria, which renewal has consequence in Meleager's *Garland* and thus in the pagan rebirth of the Renaissance. This is the classical tradition of the neo-Latin poets translated by Aldington in 1915 and the tradition of the cavalier poets Ben Jonson and Robert Herrick, whose poetry H.D. in late life claimed to have been fundamental to her craft. This refined and sophisticated love poetry, in the repeated phrases of her essay on Anacreon, represents "nonchalance" and "indifference" to the great old gods of the hellenic world ("A Poet in the Wilderness" 1, 4). The only narrative in H.D.'s madrigal series published in her lifetime – *Bid Me to Live* – takes its title and the name of its central figure, Julia, from poems in Herrick's Anacreonic *Hesperides*. This collection of poetry is a figure in the novel for the old hellenic dream now shattered, as well as for the courtly erotic traditions in which Julia, the male figures of the story, and the narrator are all caught.

This later extension of the fiction of the Greek Anthology, coincident with H.D.'s exploration of romantic erotic postures in her lyric poetry, is as ephemeral a hellenic guise as the innocent early enthusiasm. H.D. in the late twenties begins to understand its limitations, both poetic and personal, as she moves gradually away from Hellas into its prehistories.

"His Wine-Dark Sea": Homer and the Heroic

Another predominant emphasis in the classical intertextuality of H.D.'s poetry has been little considered: reference to Homer and to the heroic. The Appendix lists eleven fairly unambiguous allusions to Homer, most to the *Odyssey* but a few to the *Iliad* as well; and with rare directness H.D. translated the opening hundred lines of the *Odyssey*.[46] The specificity of these references to Homer indicates that H.D. had a good acquaintance with both his epics in her early years.[47] Moreover, another fifteen or so poems concern a heroic figure or athlete or evoke the classical context of heroism. H.D. may be read as antiheroic, antimilitary, or antiepic; as we have emphasized throughout this study, her choices as a writer are informed by a steady resistance to the destructiveness of war. Nevertheless, much evidence in the poetry challenges or qualifies an antiheroic interpretation of H.D.'s writing.

One must acknowledge the complexity of H.D.'s engagement with the classical hero, with the panorama of war, and with heroic norms – an engagement informed by the same ambivalences characterizing other aspects of her hellenism. References to the Homeric and heroic in H.D. point to sometimes overlapping fictions: a conception of vocation and discipline; an imagination of erotic fraternity; an elegiac remembrance of the dead, who carry the significance of a repeatedly destroyed world; and a romantic/erotic fiction, in which the fatal hero is central.

The early H.D. is in many ways a warrior-poet, like the Argive Telesila: "*In Argos – that statue of her; / at her feet the scroll of her / love poetry, in her hand a helmet*" ("Telesila," *Collected Poems* 184). One recalls that H.D. takes the armed Athene, with visored steel helmet, as the goddess of her craft, her "glamour of will" ("Prayer," *Collected Poems* 141). The last lines of H.D.'s translation from the *Odyssey* suggest the centrality of Pallas within her imagination of poetic making:

> *She spoke*
> *and about her feet*
> *clasped bright sandals,*
> *gold-wrought, imperishable,*
> *which lift her above sea,*
> *across the land stretch,*
> *wind-like,*
> *like the wind breath.*
> (*Collected Poems* 98)

This figuration of Athene in terms of imperishable gold and swift, windlike flight over sea and land corresponds closely to the poetic project that the early H.D. envisioned when she recorded this passage from A.E. (George Russell) in one of her Greek texts of Euripides: "We should wish rather [?] for our thoughts a directness such as belongs to the messengers of the Gods, swift, beautiful flashing presences but in purposes never understood."[48] The transcendent, armored Pallas is a daimon of poetic constraint and discipline, which alone can garner the godlike power of words.

H.D. clearly imagines her vocation as poet in heroic terms, and though the shape of the conception changes over the years, it remains large in scope. From her earliest years as a poet, H.D. puts the goddess Nike near the center of her Greek pantheon – the female goddess of the Victory of Samothrace in the Louvre, which H.D. first saw in 1911. In literary terms, "victory" is the golden moment of the athlete in Pindar's odes, of the warriors at Marathon and Thermopylae memorialized by Simonides, of Homer's Odysseus and Achilles. In all of these instances, of course, the poem makes memory possible, and thus the poem as agent is to some extent synonymous with Nike: the power of the pen makes the power of the sword imaginable, as H.D suggests in *The Walls Do Not Fall*, the first poem of her *Trilogy*.

This Nike dimension of H.D.'s hellenism is associated with a Dorian/Spartan emphasis and thus with a fiction of homoerotic bonds. H.D. began reading Pindar in the spring of 1916, and thereafter "Pindaric" poems in praise of athletes punctuate her poetry.[49] The athlete, as we have seen, stands within H.D.'s Dorian hellenism as an image of the unity of beauty and strength, associated with the artistic perfection of the androgynous statue. Moreover, Simonides' epitaphs for the heroic dead, reiterated in H.D.'s writing, refer to the absolute demands of her own heroic calling as a poet: "O passer-by, tell the Lacedaemonians that we lie here obeying their orders" ("People of Sparta" 419; *Hermione* 221; trans. Mackail). After her betrayal by Fayne Rabb, Hermione evokes a heroic conception of artistic calling, made more desperate now that a comrade is lost. She here conflates the athlete with the hero Pheidippides, the runner at Marathon: "Run and run and run Hermione. Runners wait at each station to carry on the message. . . . You know running and running and running that the messenger will take (lampadephoros) your message in its fervour . . . run, run, Hermione. Tell the Lacedaemonians . . ." (220–1). The Lacedaemonian "orders" are simultaneously military battle orders, poetic orders, and absolute demands within a fiction of heroic hellenism, in which the light is kept alive in a succession of "torchbearers" or guardians. These "orders" are the Delphic "laws of song, laws of being, laws of hospitality" by which the poets Hipparchia and Ray Bart in *Palimpsest* are compelled: "The salt of heroic metres had in no way lost savour" (150). The heroic meters reverberate in the "[f]eet, feet, feet, feet" of soldiers marching to war (140 and passim), the sound that haunts Ray Bart, bringing back the memory of the death of her child, linked with the death of the young men going to war. This amplification from the autobiographical narratives suggests the complex interplay in H.D.'s writing of heroism, comradeship, poetic calling, and the catastrophes of war.

After H.D. meets Bryher in 1918, this young boyish adventurer – who liked the poem "Loss" "because it has battle in it" – becomes implicated in H.D.'s Dorian hellenism.[50] In late 1918 Bryher inspires H.D. to turn to Homer's *Odyssey*, a textual engagement issuing in "Sea Heroes," which takes its catalogue of names from those of Phaiakian seamen in book 8, and in her translation of book 1.[51] In many of H.D.'s poems written in tribute to Bryher, the image of a hellenic heroism that can turn the tide surfaces repeatedly, in the "line of heroes" standing against chaos ("Sea Heroes"), in the defenders at Marathon and Thermopylae ("I Said"), in the defenders of Athens against the Persians ("Let Zeus Record"). The images of both athlete and warrior, as we have seen, are imagined within the fiction of male fraternity and homoeroticism, standing at once for a desired equality with men and for a female homoerotic bond.

For H.D., Nike takes on increasingly psychological valences, connected even in *Tribute to Freud* with the saving wisdom of Athene. Nevertheless, this key concept never loses its relation to a whole complex of heroic associations – which are indeed indicated more than ever in this memoir. By the time H.D. comes to Freud in the thirties, the image of Nike forms part of the configuration of a lifelong war phobia. But as is suggested above in the link between "feet, feet, feet" and the Spartan orders of poetry, this extreme resistance to war itself is only one aspect of the picture. In H.D.'s progressive mythologizing of her own experience, Beauty, War, and Love are bound inextricably together in the creation and destruction of selves.[52]

The Homeric panorama of war and ships that initiates the choruses from Euripides' *Iphigeneia in Aulis* is repeatedly evoked in H.D.'s poetry, always attached with an elegiac remembrance of the dead. One finds it in "Tribute," with its image of the beauty of the young who are sacrificed: "And this we will say for remembrance, / speak this with their names" ("The Tribute," *Collected Poems* 66). The catalogue of nautical names in "Sea Heroes," likewise, is simultaneously a mourning for a lost hellenic world and for the immediate "line of heroes" that have withstood chaos: "greater even than the sea, / they live beyond wrack and death of cities, / and each god-like name spoken / is as a shrine in a godless place" (*Collected Poems* 129). In H.D.'s meditations on war, the dead are always present, signaling a more than personal trauma and grief. Friedman points out that the title of H.D.'s autobiographical novel of the war years – *Asphodel*, originally entitled *Fields of Asphodel* – refers to Odysseus's journey to the underworld, wherein the dead heroes are gathered in fields of asphodel.[53] Thus the personal activity of memory, crossing the threshold of the painful past, is bound to an imagination of a larger chthonic journey.

However, the image of Telesila standing with helmet and scroll of love poetry brings to mind another dominant glamour associated with the heroic in H.D.'s poetry: the conventional erotic fascination with the virile or dark male, explored in images of adoration ("The Contest," "Loss," "Prisoners," "Red Roses for Bronze"), of abandonment and abasement ("At Ithaca," "Cuckoo's Song," "Circe"), of anger and bitterness ("Calypso," "At Croton," "Ariadne"). These poems have led critics to emphasize H.D.'s antiheroic stance, her awareness of the violence and duplicity associated with traditional heroes like Odysseus and Theseus, and, by extension, her conception of the masculine hierarchy of power signified in the "Command" of the war.[54] Though such a bitter analysis of male prerogatives is undoubtedly present in these poems, the female lover is just as clearly complicit in the dynamics of desire. To assess the full complexity of this romantic configuration of the heroic, one must remember the figure of Achilles appearing throughout H.D.'s career, from *Iphigeneia in Aulis*, to the two Thetis poems of the twenties (1920, 1923) and the meditation in "Myrtle Bough" (1927), to *Helen in Egypt*. Achilles is from the beginning an image of the fatal hero at his most complex: the hero as brilliant light, but as dark Hades as well, initiator to the underworld; sacrificer and sacrificed, wounding and wounded, lover and son.

This brief summary of H.D.'s relation to Homer can only suggest the complexity of a lifelong engagement, ending in *Helen in Egypt* (written 1952–55) and "Winter Love" (*Hermetic Definition*, 1958). Within this continuing conversation is a poem from midcareer, "A Dead Priestess Speaks." In trying to understand this powerful but puzzling poem, one may turn, as many have, to biographical explanations – reading it as H.D.'s response to analysis with Freud or to Lawrence's *The Man Who Died*.[55] But here it seems important to note the centrality in the poem of Homer and the epic tradition he represents – an engagement whose terms are by no means entirely negative. In regard to Homer and the heroic this poem in many ways anticipates the later *Helen in Egypt*.

"A Dead Priestess Speaks" (*Collected Poems* 369–77) is set in Miletus, a location with complex significance – political, religious, and poetic. It was a powerful Ionian colony on the coast of Asia Minor, known for its economic ambitions, manifest in large-scale colonization, and also for its persistent self-interested involvement in wars. The poem alludes to this highly politicized climate of colonization (Arton's son's "dictatorship / in a far city") and successive wars ("the new archon spoke of a new war"). Miletus is also the site of a famous temple to Apollo Oulios, the god of health and healing, and Delia's gifts of pharmacy may be associated with this god, never named in the text. In a last coincidence, Miletus is the birthplace of Arctinus, supposedly a pupil of Homer who wrote portions of the Greek epic cycle. This ghost of the epic poet at Miletus may give a context for the persistence of Delia's concern to resist an epic definition of her poetic role: "I never made a song that told of war" (376). But Delia's relation to Homer in the poem is not as clear as it might seem.

Though Delia as healer, poet, and priestess finds herself increasingly in the role of public service, she repeatedly places herself outside an epic tradition of heroic praise. She is asked to submit for a contest "an epitaph / to a dead soldier." Delia declines this task — but not out of rebellion or disdain:

> for I looked over the sea-wall
> to the further sea —
> dark, dark and purple;
>
> no one could write, after his *wine-dark sea*,
> an epitaph of glory and of spears; (372)

Delia does not here condemn Homer's epic vision but rather acknowledges its definitive, even appalling, power. H.D. in later comments on this poem emphasizes the phrase "no one could write," speaking of her inability as a poet to cope with "her problem, the world problem" — war (*H.D. by Delia Alton* 211, 209). But in terms of the poem itself, how is Homer's epithet for the sea an epitaph for the dead? His *wine-dark sea* carries the suggestion both of blood and of the darkness underlying the war tragedy — the chthonic realm of Hades.

Like H.D.'s later Helen, Delia is wholly misunderstood by her fellows, who find in her an image they wish to see, in this case, a positive rather than a negative falsification. All the while, Delia has a secret life enacted at night, in wanderings in the forest. That life grows more intense with the return of war, when Delia begins to wander blindly in the forest seeking some kind of oblivion, returning only at dawn — like a witch, a courtesan — oblivious to all around her. But the more her possession increases, the more she is mistakenly esteemed and honored. At her death none realize that "I was never pure nor wise nor good," but rather outside these categories altogether:

> [T]hey did not see the reach of purple-wing
> that lifted me out of the little room,
> they did not see drift of the purple-fire
> that turned the spring-fire
> into winter gloom;
>
> they could not see that Spirit
> in the day,
> that turned the day to ashes,
> though the sun
> shone straight into the window. (375)

This Spirit, who veils all life and light with the pallor of death, is a dark bridegroom, who says: "late, / I waited too long for you, Delia, / I will devour

you, / love you into flame, // O late / my love, / my bride, / Delia of Miletus"
(376–7).

Of course, one may invoke many biographical equivalents for this figure,
whom H.D. later identifies as a version of the "Eternal Lover" (*H.D. by Delia
Alton* 217). I would suggest an immediate textual connection between Delia's
dark lover and Homer. The poet who "never made a song that told of war" is
nevertheless wedded in some way to the poet of war. She looks out over *his* sea,
"dark, dark and purple"; she is increasingly overcome by a "purple-fire" that
overshadows life and light, particularly in the context of "new war"; increasingly
surrounded by "the reach of purple-wing." The dark bridegroom, one may say,
is one of the dead, is Hades from the underworld, master of the chthonic world
of dreams. He is all the dead, those whose epitaphs she may not write, but who
somehow inhabit her in her wanderings on the margins of ordinary life. He is the
ghost of Homer, the poet of the warrior, of death and the underworld. In any
case, undoubtedly the bridegroom here is connected with war, death, and poetry,
like the "master-lyrist" of the contemporaneous poem "Sigil XVII," who is also
connected with the dark sea.[56] One finds this same configuration of images later
in H.D.'s Helen, who, also a *femme noir*, waits in Egypt, the realm of the dead
and of dreams, for Achilles to come; but his coming summons all the dead of the
war who inhabit her, the thousand ships coming "with great wings unfurled"
over "his *wine-dark sea*."

This reflection upon the place of Homer in "A Dead Priestess Speaks" is
speculative. Nevertheless, it captures something of the complexity surrounding
the hero and the heroic. It suggests the ambivalence running throughout H.D.'s
writing: a poet in resistance to epic vision and the destruction of war, who
nevertheless imagines vocation in heroic terms and whose vocation necessitates a
working of chthonic ground, a sailing of wine-dark seas.

Chapter Six

Euripides: Dream Time and Dream Work

In 1949, H.D. turned to the task of rereading and reassessing her separate writings, and her criticism is recorded in *H.D. by Delia Alton*. H.D. – or "Delia Alton," the author of this work of criticism – attempts to discern patterns and directions in the writing as they trace out an overall story or legend. These suggest a "labyrinth," and "[i]t does not stay, with all its meanderings, on one plane and time goes slowly, goes swiftly; our dream-time is relative but we have yet no formula for this relativity." Nevertheless, she says, "I am trying to pin down my map, to plot the course of my journey" (220). At this late point in her career, having accumulated an enormous body of writing, H.D. appears to mean by this master plot or journey through the labyrinth a timeless and recurring "mystery" or "romance" in which her writing and life participate. This critical H.D. is somewhat baffled by the early "crystalline" H.D. and by hellenic figures like Hedylus, Hippolytus, and Ion. In puzzling out the fiery matrix of these crystalline projections, H.D./Delia arrives at an important distinction: "I have said that it would be difficult for a critic to assess the matrix – difficult for myself to assess it. But it is not so difficult if we visualize or imagine the two streams of consciousness, running along together (the time-element and the dream or ideal element) but in separate channels" (221).

If the "time-element" represents generally the rootedness of H.D.'s writing in history, the "dream or ideal element" is manifest in fictions with a mythical, atemporal context. Susan Friedman has most fully explored this antithesis in opposing the "lyric" H.D. with the "narrative" writer, finding a "double discourse" running throughout her writing, manifest in "twin" texts functioning in necessary relation to each other. More generally, critics approach the hellenism of H.D.'s writing as a sublimation, evasion, or repression of traumatic events, as opposed to the historical confrontation found in narratives and memoirs or in *Trilogy*.[1]

However, if one takes seriously H.D.'s deeply ingrained hermeticism, it is not sufficient to say that in her writing "real" life events are converted into "unreal" myths, as though the empirical had unquestionable precedence in experience, because it is also true, in hermetic terms, that the eternal has precedence, as a generative seed that unfolds in the events of one's life, according to necessities only dimly intelligible. Indeed, a necessity of increasing urgency to H.D. – though present implicitly from the beginning – is the necessity to *understand* necessities, daimonic compulsions that shaped her life and writing, "my own intense, dynamic interest," she says in *Tribute to Freud*, "in the unfolding of the unconscious or the subconscious pattern" (6). This is the hermetic task of self-illumination, of finding the great world in the small. Even in her earliest, most un-self-conscious writing, such as "Hermes of the Ways," one finds an instinctive positioning of the lyric "I" within a reflective space, though determined by compelling paths.

Of all the figures within H.D.'s hellenic star map, Euripides has by far the largest role – precisely that of carrying the "dream or ideal element" as H.D. describes it here. Far more than in isolated lyric poems, H.D.'s long interchanges with Euripides allow one to discern that constant and persistent hermetic effort of comprehending necessities, including the necessity of the *opus* itself. The tensions in the lyric – between asceticism and sensuality, enactment and allegory, effacement or inflation of the lyric "I" – all may be dramatized as well as contemplated in the "dream-time" provided by Euripidean intertexts. Moreover, these are clearly parallel with and implicated in the autobiographical explorations of recurrent personal patterns.

H.D.'s engagement with Euripides falls roughly into four periods. The first comes before and during World War I (1912–19), when H.D. begins to explore the Euripidean chorus as a form, translates "choruses" from *Iphigeneia in Aulis* (1915) and *Hippolytus* (1919), and makes some effort at translating from the *Ion*, perhaps throughout the whole period between 1915 and 1920. A second period of activity occurs during the early twenties (1920–5), when H.D. continues her engagement with the *Hippolytus* in lyric poems, concluding in the drama *Hippolytus Temporizes* (1927).[2] During this same period, in conjunction with writing four essays on Euripides for "Notes on Euripides, Pausanius, and Greek Lyric Poets," H.D. reads many of Euripides' plays and works at translations of the *Helen*, the *Ion*, and the *Bacchae*, publishing choral songs from the latter two, as well as from the *Hecuba*.[3] A third period occurs immediately before and after H.D.'s analysis with Freud in 1933 and 1934. During the period between 1932 and 1935, H.D. works extensively with the texts of the *Electra* and the *Orestes*, a labor issuing in *Electra–Orestes*, partially published in 1932 and 1934, and (after Freud) in "Orestes Theme" (1937). She also completes a translation of the *Ion* (published 1937) and possibly attempts again a translation of the *Helen*.[4] A final period of activity comes in the early fifties, when H.D. returns to the matter of

Troy in conjunction with the composition of *Helen in Egypt*, rereading five Trojan plays of Euripides in Leconte de Lisle's translation. Thus this late poem is more deeply implicated in a Euripidean exchange than anyone has yet acknowledged.[5] Even after completing this poem, H.D. contemplates translating Euripides again, and she rereads her old Euripides essays as late as 1958 in light of new critical discoveries.[6]

The extent of H.D.'s conversation with Euripides suggested in this summary is remarkable. No modernist poet shows a greater literary exchange with an ancient writer. Its consistency and persistence from the beginning to the end indeed give one a way to "plot the course of [her] journey," to discern at least some aspects of the ambitious trajectory of her career. That trajectory, despite the labyrinthine paths by which it is achieved – through aestheticism, archaeology, hermeticism, and psychoanalysis, through lyric, narrative, and essay – is mythically defined by figures and images from Euripides. By the time one comes to *Helen in Egypt*, which brings into play the germinal images and themes of Euripidean texts from a lifetime of study, one can turn again to see the steadiness of focus from the beginning, the gradual alchemy worked upon initial material, extrapolating its spiritual and erotic implications. Euripides is the architectonic poet of H.D.'s hellenism.

In her early introductory essay on Euripides, H.D. isolates three significant aspects of his writing that clearly mirror her own concerns. She sees him as a "modern" poet, skeptical of war and patriotic slogans; as a lyricist, "a white rose, lyric, feminine" (*Notes on Thought and Vision* 32); and as a "mystic," parallel to Christ in the scope and depth of his spiritual exploration ("Euripides" 1–3, 5). In other portions of this study we have considered the first two of these pointers. This chapter, which treats explicitly the intertextual engagements with Euripides apart from the lyrics, concerns itself largely with the "mystical" Euripides.

H.D.'s early use of the term "mystical" is undoubtedly vague, carrying the implications of Pater's and Wilde's aestheticism. Nevertheless, there is continuity between this early orientation to the mystical and her late sense of The Mystery. In terms of the specific Euripidean plays that most engaged H.D., the "mystical" certainly pertains to the Eleusinian mysteries, a pattern of virginal initiation and maternal grief, issuing in a sacred marriage and spiritual illumination. The Eleusinian configuration may be said to constitute the "matrix" of many of Euripides' plays. Precisely this matrix, I would suggest, draws H.D.'s persistent attention, which she comes to acknowledge late in her career, after completing *Helen in Egypt*. As we have seen, the many plays of Euripides that concerned H.D. over the years – twelve altogether – almost all have a maternal figure at or near the center of attention, and around that figure are played out patterns of desire, loss, grieving, rage, and remorse. Indeed, in the specific plays of Euripides that H.D. translated and adapted, a virginal figure or figures – Iphigeneia, Hippolytus/Phaedra, Ion/Kreousa, Helen – enact a Persephonean descent.

Thus very late in her life H.D. was excited by the critical commentary of Henri Grégoire, which suggested structural connections among the very plays that had preoccupied her, the *Helen*, the other *Iphigeneia* (in Tauris), and the *Ion*. H.D. calls these the "lost oracle plays" and relates them to an "Elusinian [*sic*] cycle" in which she imagines her whole poetic effort. They are Eleusinian in that they concern the recovery of one who has been lost – and particularly the recovery of a figure of divine authority, an "oracle"; and clearly she sees her work, like the Helen of her *Helen in Egypt*, in relation to these mysteries of recurrent losing and finding and losing again. She says about this Euripidean pattern interpreted by Grégoire, "[W]ill it be given me to serve again this other temple, cycle or circle?" ("Compassionate Friendship" 71).

H.D.'s major exchanges with Euripides over the course of a lifetime are sites of enactment as well as of analysis and contemplation, allowing her a way to reflect imaginatively upon erotic and spiritual trajectories to which she was committed. Euripides provides H.D. with participation in "dream-time," the kind of countertime of liminal passage, and participation as well in dream images reflecting her own complexes. But he also increasingly provides her with sites of "dreamwork" – using this term metaphorically and not precisely in its Freudian sense – the labor of querying and puzzling over dream signs within a therapeutic context. Euripidean textual engagements constitute for H.D., I would suggest, something analogous to the "writing cure" that Friedman sees as the motive of her autobiographical narratives. Friedman proposes that the narratives of the twenties serve for H.D. as efforts "to free herself from repetition by remembering through her writing" (*Penelope's Web* 96). It is certainly true, as Friedman argues, that narrative allows some form of remembrance that the hellenic lyrical mode cannot allow: H.D. in her working of Euripidean texts is repetitious and redundant, to some extent fixed on recurring figures, removed from actual memory. While its removal into the sublimity of myth makes this psychological work less fruitful than that of the narratives – sometimes, perhaps, even obstructive – nevertheless, I would claim, the Euripidean exchange represents an important auxiliary in a lifetime of psychological reflection. In his complex role Euripides for H.D. is parallel to Freud as a figure of healer and guide – skeptic, scientist, wise man, visionary – as H.D. indeed comes to acknowledge in 1935 in her commentary on the *Ion*.

Diane Chisholm in her study of H.D.'s "Freudian Poetics" rightly connects H.D.'s early activity of translation with her later engagement in Freudian "translation," the deciphering of dream and symbol: "But in the course of her career, her art of translation changes from being something like interpretation, involving the transfer of significance between historical or national languages, to a heuristic device of self-discovery, involving the decoding of the 'hieroglyph of the unconscious'" (12; *Tribute to Freud* 93). I would suggest that H.D.'s Greek translation – specifically her translation and adaptation of Euripides – is never merely "a transfer of significance between . . . languages," that it is rather from the begin-ning, to one degree or another, engaged in the effort of "self-discovery." In particular, H.D.'s Euripidean engagements indicate her work at deciphering a parental bind – the adoration of and resistance to father and mother – as well as a related erotic/homoerotic bind.

Each of H.D.'s major textual exchanges with Euripides represent distinct moments within her increasing awareness of her own psychological necessities, of the nature of her hellenic fiction, of the complexities of textual exchange itself. The following sections attempt to define the character of each of those different moments, manifest in distinct poetic modes and kinds of exchange with Euripidean texts.

Initiations: Choruses and Essays (1915–1924)

In her essay on Euripides' *Helen*, H.D. comes to a point of self-consciousness, aware suddenly of the vividness of her presentation of the opening scenes of the play. She suspects that she has been "carried away too much by my own imagination . . . intoxicated a little" by a reading of the Greek words. This imaginative participation and release is an important aspect of H.D.'s engagement with Euripides. "These words are to me portals, gates," she says; the poet, mystic, or child "[sees] *through* the words" (8–9). As we have seen, this hermetic effort, an attempt to interiorize the text and to follow an inner light in rendering it, guided H.D. as translator. As Adalaide Morris has shown, the concept of "pro-jection" functions in H.D.'s writing from early to late in manifold meanings – poetic, psychological, cinematic, alchemical. H.D.'s early engagements with Euripides' plays represent projection in many of these senses, a form of active imagination explored verbally.

Moreover, Euripides' "dream-world," clairvoyantly interpreted by the poet, apparently shaped the woman's hellenic dreaming. For instance, the famous incident of the "writing on the wall" at Corfu in 1920, a waking dream described in *Tribute to Freud* (44–56), represents an oneiric intertextuality with Euripides. This episode, a crux within her later Freudian analysis, "set the aims, announced the means, and disclosed the dimensions of her great work, . . . and it seemed to guarantee her gift as seer and prophet" (Morris, "Projection" 273). However, for all its later Freudian significance, this vision – of soldier/brother, "mystical chalice," tripod, Nike, and sun disk – is also fairly obviously the aftermath of an intense identification, during the preceding years of trauma, with the figures of Euripides' *Ion*. The vision is certainly intertextual with the meditation written concurrently with the Corfu episode, "Helios and Athene," which projects the triad of Helios/Delphi, Athene/Athens, and Demeter/Eleusis. Both the vision and the meditation unquestionably reflect the configuration of the *Ion*, which is set in Delphi and predicated on Helios, Athene, the visionary tripod of the

Pythian priestess, and, implicitly, the Eleusinian mysteries. The matter of the play has become intersubjective, as though it were a dream of her own. It *is* effectively a dream of her own. One does dream according to one's dream master, and an early Euripidean dreaming is later rewritten as Freudian dreaming.

The early "choruses" from the *Iphigeneia in Aulis* and the *Hippolytus* may be seen in this same light – not simply as literary exchanges, but as important psychological sites, defining or clarifying constructs so clearly that, like the *Ion*, they become architectonic in H.D.'s discourse. These early translations enact, without interpreting, a psychological territory overcrossed and complicit with Euripides. However, though H.D. becomes increasingly conscious of the import of her engagement with Euripides, she is not capable in her early years of interpreting this Euripidean dream matter. After the intensity of her early hellenic writing and the collapse of a shared hellenic enterprise, H.D. in the twenties attempts to approach in essay form some plays of Euripides of most importance to her – the *Helen*, the *Ion*, and the *Bacchae*. However, these efforts to speak discursively enact, to various degrees, as much a retreat from as a confrontation of the intersubjective matter of the plays.

Choruses

H.D.'s earliest two "choruses" from plays of Euripides really represent a composite literary form of her own, a model for later experiments. In effect, these are lyric sequences or "long poems" with integral effect. They are carefully selected and edited, suggesting that H.D.'s purpose here is not simply a translation of choral odes. She omits lines from the passages she translates, not, as T. S. Eliot said, because they are too hard for her, but because she is crafting a single lyric piece with its own interpretative emphases, within which philosophical musings are inappropriate.[7] The selection from the play in each of these "choruses" is similarly deliberate. Critics have universally assumed that H.D. arbitrarily combines choruses with selected passages from the dramas, but this is not the case. H.D.'s selection represents a choice to give major *lyric* interludes from the plays – that is, passages in lyric meters rather than in normal dramatic meter (iambic trimeter). Each set consists of the choral odes (sometimes abbreviated), along with other portions of the play in lyric meters, such as the hymn at the opening of the *Hippolytus*, the processional at the conclusion of the *Iphigeneia*, Iphigeneia's lyric monody or lament over her death, the dialogue in lyric meters between Phaedra and her nurse. Thus H.D.'s term for these selections – "choruses," that is, distinct passages in lyric, nonstictic meters – is not entirely a misnomer. In H.D.'s two "choruses" only one passage – Hippolytus's opening prayer to Artemis – is not originally in lyric meters, but even this follows immediately a choral hymn to Artemis in lyric meter, and H.D. rightly takes it as a continuation of the ceremonial hymn.

In presenting these lyric sequences, H.D. establishes the dimension of the play that most concerns her: an affective intensity, rendered in visual images and mythic allusion, which in a subliminal way figures the action of the drama. Such, according to Ruth Padel, is the character of Euripides' famous "escape odes": to create "mythological and pictorial associations that lead to a lyric vision of the appropriate action, and [reassemble] motifs of the play in a new mode, as a dream regroups the thoughts and events of the waking day" (241). H.D.'s sequences attempt to configure this "lyric vision," the play as signified in a kind of dream mode. As a form, the lyric sequence does not have the closure or resolution belonging to the plot itself, nor can it communicate clearly the ironies of the play, which depend to a large extent on structure. Rather, the sequence, which asks to be read palimpsestically rather than linearly, carries the erotic or affective significance of the drama, with all its contradictions and indeterminacies. For this very reason, it is a site of complex erotic signification for H.D.

If one reads *Choruses from the Iphigeneia in Aulis* as an integral lyric sequence, it represents a complex enactment, indicating something of the conflicting erotic necessities at play at an early moment in H.D.'s career. It establishes the vertical or heroic axis of H.D.'s hellenism, and at the same time it undercuts it, though ambivalently. One begins with the epic overview of the choral "I," focusing on the beauty of the warriors and armament, the pleasure of the men's games among themselves. The initial cosmos is unitary, whole, as is suggested by H.D.'s added, interpretative images of the circle – "Circles of horses," "ships / Circled with ships," the semicircular "great arc" of the panorama (*Collected Poems* 72, 73, 76). This opening patriotism, however, is qualified in the third ode when the chorus imagines the coming of these very ships to the straits of Simois and the inevitable bloody destruction of Troy: "And Pergamos, / City of the Phrygians, / Ancient Troy / Will be given up to its fate" (78). This passage, which H.D. published in *Selected Poems* (1957) as a separate lyric ("And Pergamos" 21–2), renders a starkly elegiac sense of the loss and waste brought by war.

At the axial center of this cosmos is the "great light" (80) of Hellas, Achilles, with whom is associated the reiterated myth of the origin of the war: the marriage of his parents, Peleus and Thetis, the exclusion of Eris from the feast, the consequent judgment of Paris among three goddesses, the abduction of Helen, the revenge of the Atreidae. Achilles is also the promised bridegroom of Iphigeneia, replaced, however, by the bridegroom Hades. Thus, as divine son, warrior, ominous mate, Achilles defines in a sense the vertical axis linking death and divinity.

However, on this very pole turns the disillusionment of the choral "I," who in the fourth ode compares the divine hymeneal festival at the marriage of Peleus and Thetis with the rituals of sacrifice to be enacted in place of Iphigeneia's marriage. In contrast to the "great light" of Achilles is the "scattered light" of Iphigeneia's hair, about to be bound for sacrifice. Thus the women who initially share in the grandeur of the heroic panorama now "ask this – where truth is, / Of what use is valour and is worth?" (80). The lyric sequence establishes the dynamics of wartime eros, founded upon the pleasure of male games and, more importantly, upon scapegoating, a concealment of political motives under a rhetoric of justice. Though Helen is the chief verbal target of this obsessive scapegoating, Iphigeneia comes to take her place in literal sacrifice, revealing the baseness of the military illusion.

Though H.D.'s lyric sequence indicates the ambivalences of heroic hellenism, suggesting the brutality of its patriarchal hierarchies, it finally confirms rather than denies the authority of father/king/priest. One may claim that H.D. as poet is detached from such a significance, merely translating Euripides and thus replicating *his* vision. However, such a claim is not entirely justified. Euripides himself presents the dynamics of power in the play with unrelenting skepticism and irony. It is unclear, however, how much H.D's translation reflects such irony. Moreover, H.D. does not in fact merely translate Euripides: she manipulates some lines of the text in ways that suggest her complicity with a patriarchal closure, her identification with Iphigeneia's final confirmation of Hellas and Nike, even when it means self-immolation and violence.

The drama of Euripides' Iphigeneia is played out between father and mother: Agamemnon, the weak, vainglorious, and betraying father, and the dignified, strong figure of Clytemnestra, who accompanies her daughter to prepare her for marriage. In part V of H.D.'s sequence, Iphigeneia, at the point of recognizing her father's intention to kill her, laments her fate. This monody begins with the daughter's recognition of symbiosis with the mother in suffering: "Ah, mother, mother, / The same terror is cast on us both" (81). However, the movement of Iphigeneia in the play is toward identification with the father and rejection of the mother's pathos. H.D. reinforces the sense of such a shift. Later in this same monody H.D. has omitted lines 1312–14, given here in a fairly literal translation: "But he that begot me, ah mother, my mother, he has gone and left me forsaken" (trans. Hadas). Moreover, she has altered lines 1317–18: "I am slain, I perish, foully slaughtered by a godless father" (trans. Hadas). In place of these lines, H.D.'s translation at this point reads: "O I am miserable: / You cherished me, my mother, / But even you desert me. / I am sent to an empty place" (82). These alterations seem too pointed to be simply errors; the text is not obscure. H.D. in this lyric sequence has censored any reference to the father's desertion and perfidy; instead she has Iphigeneia accuse her mother.

These changes seem to be related to Iphigeneia's final choice to accept her own sacrifice, in which gesture she elects to abandon her mother and surrender to the demand not only of Agamemnon but of Hellas. In choosing sacrifice willingly, instead of suffering it under compulsion, Iphigeneia becomes herself the greatest image of the heroic in the play. She comes indeed to stand for the accumulated sense of retributive justice and glory assigned to the cause as a whole: "I come – I free Hellas. / My father, as priest awaits me / At the right altar step. // Hail me now. / I destroy Phrygia and all Troy" (83). Agamemnon finally is not the perfidious father, but "priest" – a title not indicated in the Greek text. He is, in the concluding words of the chorus, a hero "encircled / By Greek spear-shafts" (84), once more part of a unitary cosmos. Iphigeneia serves that heroic purpose. She names herself, and the chorus names her, *heleptolis*, "destroyer of cities" (lines 1475, 1511), as Helen is famously named in Aeschylus's *Agamemnon*.

In this lyric sequence, Iphigeneia's willing self-immolation is an ambivalently charged gesture that in some sense defines the early hellenic self-conception of H.D. She is heroically dedicated to Nike; she serves the pure and absolute Artemis, "rejoicer in blood-sacrifice" (84). Indeed, the image of immolation pervades H.D.'s early hellenic writing – ubiquitous references to Hyacinth, Niobe, Adonis, Daphne, Cassandra, Persephone, and Orion – and it seems necessary to try to understand its sobering implications.

The theme of sacrifice in H.D.'s writing is not primarily associated with victimization, as Janice Robinson suggests in her reading of the choruses from the *Iphigeneia*.[8] Rather, it seems repeatedly to refer to vocation, "the terror / and cold splendour of song / and its bleak sacrifice" ("The Islands," *Collected Poems* 127). In her essay on Pausanias, H.D. recalls the words of the Greek scholar Wilamowitz-Moellendorff: "Ghosts to speak must have sacrifice, . . . and we must give them the blood of our hearts" ("Pausanius" 6). Such a sacrifice is suggested in the enactment within H.D.'s initial choruses from the *Iphigeneia*: "For I come to do sacrifice, . . . To honour the queen, if she permit, / The great one, with my death" (83). In the initial gesture of Pound's *Cantos*, Odysseus offers sacrificial "blood for the ghosts" so that they might gather and speak, enacting the poet's invocation to the dead who might speak through him. H.D.'s gesture enacted through Iphigeneia in this initial volume is similar, though here the blood, sacrifice, and death do not belong to surrogate victims.

H.D. in her writing reiterates the necessity of immolation, always linking it with terror. In her essay on Sparta H.D. reflects on the violence of Spartan male rituals, specifically the Hyacinthia: "But beyond Athens, . . . beyond the consciousness, beyond the intellect, is the terror of the unexpressed, the fear that rages, tearing us like the young men each other, inchoate, undefined, or the beauty unexpressed and dying to be worshipped dead" ("People of Sparta" 418–19). The last puzzling phrase suggests that expression is itself linked to death. Perhaps writing is death, the writer "dying" – longing – "to be worshipped dead." In H.D.'s favorite image of Hyacinth, immolation seems associated with terrifying unconsciousness or frenzy, but also with expression (the "lettered" hyacinth) and immortality.

There is undoubtedly something disturbing in the idea of this necessary immolation. The vocation of the early H.D., like that of Iphigeneia, seems implicated in death, in being killed and killing, as though to create were to be destroyed and to destroy. This is a difficult nexus. One may read it in the context of the creation of the impersonal, inhuman "H.D.," which entails the killing of Hilda Doolittle, the "extinction of personality" that Eliot refers to in his credo of modernist classicism. This reading is consistent with the evidence of internal tyrannies of father/scientist/intellect suffered by the practicing poet: Hilda, slain by the father, brings H.D. into being. Moreover, H.D. only gradually works through the implications of this murder as it is inextricably tied to the fiction of Hellas itself, a violence and imperialism that is the shadow side of its immortal light. In her early years she seems more or less caught in the glamour of its great mission, which seems necessarily to involve destruction, as in "Toward the Piraeus": "*Slay with your eyes, Greek, / . . . the host, / puny, passionless, weak*" (*Collected Poems* 175).

In another light, as Friedman suggests in her reading of H.D.'s narratives, the creation of the author also entails killing the mother, the "angel in the house," in Virginia Woolf's phrase, who binds her to conventional definitions of the feminine (*Penelope's Web* 24). In the case of H.D./Iphigeneia, this distancing from the mother is simultaneously an alliance with the father/brother, signified in Helios, Artemis, and Athene. But of course in these psychological territories, the murderer and the murdered are the same.

Moreover, because H.D. understands poetic vocation in religious terms, these inner enactments have for her a religious or mystical dimension as well, which cannot entirely be resolved into psychological categories. "What is this note of death?" H.D. comments in her early essay on the *Ion*, in reference to a speech of Ion: "It seems from the bright exultation of the boy's voice to refer to some knowledge, . . . guessed at or actually experienced in the mysteries of the inner worship [of Helios]" ("Opening Scenes" 141). At some level the theme of sacrifice in H.D. always refers to this dimension of religious self-extinction in the context of enlightenment. She increasingly identifies not simply with the aesthetic Christ, lover of beauty, but with the wounded and sacrificed Christ of her Moravian heritage. As we shall see, the acceptance of the wounded sun/son has religious as well as psychological significance.

If the *Iphigeneia* sequence points to a paternal plot, the daughter's sacrifice to the father's will and her abandonment of the mother, the *Hippolytus* choruses suggest a maternal plot, the son's immolation through the device of the mother. The one figures a heroic axis of H.D.'s hellenism, the other an erotic axis. Though we will consider H.D.'s amplification of Hippolytus's story further in the following section, here we might emphasize the complexity of the erotic fable as suggested in this lyric sequence.

The opposition in both plot and choruses of *Hippolytus* between Artemis and Aphrodite is suited to an allegorical reading of H.D.'s early poetry, with its tensions between asceticism and sensuality, and of H.D.'s biography, with its tensions between (Artemisian) homosexual and (Aphroditic) heterosexual love, and with H.D.'s various falls during the war years into erotic triangulation, betrayals, and jealousies. However, H.D.'s Euripidean sequence complicates such easy dichotomies. Chiefly, one must account for what appears to be H.D.'s intimate association of this erotic plot with the Eleusinian mysteries, an interpretation that anticipates by fifteen years some of the insights of her Freudian analysis.

As a lyric enactment, the sequence from *Hippolytus* clearly presents Hippolytus and Phaedra as two aspects of a single necessity, both under the auspices of Eros, who fuels the Eleusinian process as it is broadly understood here, and of a female deity carrying the potency of Eleusis. We have an initial glimpse of Hippolytus in part I, pure Orphic *parthenos*, offering heavenly Artemis flowers from an uncut meadow. But this image is immediately juxtaposed in part II with images of the impure female body, the seemingly mortal disease of Phaedra. Part III, giving the dialogue between Phaedra and her nurse, suggests a woman bound within a painful and tormented body – "bruised, bones and flesh" – an erotic torment that is doubly or triply impure, not only viscerally sexual, but adulterous and incestuous as well.

Both of these erotic vectors define H.D.'s early hellenism, and both are cast, in H.D.'s interpretation, in the context of a larger mystery. All of the remaining choral odes concern bondage to all-powerful Eros and Aphrodite (IV), concluding in Phaedra's noose (V), in Hippolytus's exile from his virginal landscape of sea and shore (VI), and in the final hymn to Kupris (VII). However one may find equivalents in the *Hippolytus* sequence for tensions within H.D.'s life and poetry, it suggests a broader view, tied to the sense of a necessary initiation and process within desire.

In this Eleusinian context, one may read the opening of the choruses, the address to Artemis as "Daemon initiate," a translation of the Greek title *potnia semnotata* (line 61). H.D. renders the phrase in this curious way perhaps because *semnos* is a word especially associated with the Korai of the Eleusinian mysteries and because H.D. here reflects the direct and oblique allusions to Eleusis in the play.[9] When one attempts to assess the significance of the choruses from the *Hippolytus* within H.D.'s early hellenism, this daemon initiate (initiated? initiating?) is a key.

It appears at the beginning to be Artemis, the goddess of Hippolytus's ascetic purity, of Iphigeneia's self-immolation. But H.D. chooses to conclude the sequence with the fifth choral ode rather than with a subsequent lyric lament by Hippolytus, which would shift the terminal focus of the sequence to the father. She thus chooses to conclude with Aphrodite, who is the actual initiator of both Phaedra and Hippolytus: "[Y]ou alone, Kupris, / creator of all life, / reign absolute" (*Collected Poems* 93). H.D. grants Kupris as much as does Euripides in the phrase "reign absolute," but she adds the epithet "creator of all life," strongly suggesting her interpretation of the goddess's place in the initiation announced in the first words of the sequence. All desire is under the auspices of this Eleusinian figure, goddess of initiates.

H.D.'s early Euripidean engagements in these choruses suggest erotic dynamics that Friedman has delineated in her discussion of H.D.'s Freudian analysis, in which her paternal and maternal transference with Freud allowed the emergence of very old configurations, the specters of the Agamemnon-like father and of the mother in whom all erotic exchanges, heterosexual and homosexual, are implicated. For the early H.D., affiliation with either father or mother, while necessary and generative, also signals immolation, woundedness, and death. H.D.'s imaginative process of working through these binds – which Friedman has so carefully examined in H.D.'s narratives – is slow and painful. But that process involves, I would suggest, the attempt at a Euripidean self-analysis.

Essays

H.D.'s essays on Euripides' *Helen, Ion,* and *Bacchae* in "Notes on Euripides, Pausanius, and Greek Lyric Poets" represent her earliest attempt to analyze Euripidean dreaming. Two of these plays to some extent rehearse the dilemmas of the early choruses – the *Helen* returning to the *Iphigeneia* (a virginal figure defined in relation to father and mother, to a dark bridegroom, to the Greeks at war), and the *Ion* returning to the *Hippolytus* (a male virgin defined in relation to an impure mother). But they also introduce other crucial psychological locations, Egypt and Delphi, and play out hellenic themes that have unnerving and traumatic associations for H.D. – "Helen" in relation to nostalgic longing, Apollo/Helios in relation to H.D.'s self-immolation during the war years, Kreousa in relation to her traumatic childbearing and general sense of betrayal. In her essays on these two plays H.D. engages in an imaginative free play; however, a censorious critical voice within the discourse works to curtail that exploration.

The *Helen* and the *Ion* are such crucial psychological sites that H.D. repeatedly initiates, abandons, and reengages her efforts with them. The *Bacchae* is apparently of less personal importance. She begins translating the *Ion* in 1917, working on it throughout World War I, returning to it between 1920 and 1924 in this essay, and again in 1935. With regard to the *Helen*, textual allusions in "Leda" indicate that H.D. was reading the play as early as 1919, and one of her most important lyrics, "Helen" (published in January 1923), comes from later reading. She wrote her essay probably sometime between 1920 and the end of 1923, and she returned to the play again in 1935, 1952, and perhaps later as well. Evidence of H.D.'s specific textual engagement with the *Bacchae* does not appear in her lyric poetry; and her essay is relatively late, written during or after 1924.[10]

In these essays on Euripides H.D. seems to imagine herself in the role of a mediator rather than a critical interpreter, helping her reader to imagine the hellenic cosmos accessible through the ciphers of the ancient Greek words: "[W]e also need poets and mystics and children to re-discover this Hellenic world, to see *through* the words" ("Helen in Egypt" 9). However successful one may judge this effort, H.D. does illumine the imaginative territory she cohabits with Euripides.

Though one might approach these essays from many vantages, here I consider their importance within the maternal plot suggested in the early choruses and increasingly elaborated, as Friedman has shown, in the narratives of the twenties. From this vantage, the essay on the *Helen* is by far the most significant, that on the *Ion* less so, that on the *Bacchae* still less. Ironically, the plays themselves, in the importance each gives to the figure of the mother, would suggest the reverse order. However, the more a maternal matter is foregrounded in the play, the more the writer exerts rhetorical control to distance herself and the reader from imaginal engagement. The essay on the *Helen* is rhetorically the most open, playful, semipermeable, the most daring in its attempt to imagine a maternal territory, though mother figures (Leda, Cybele) are only tangentially present. The *Ion*, which contains the potent, Eleusinian figure of Kreousa, is approached with much greater detachment, as though the writer were giving a critical guide to Greek theater. The essay on the *Bacchae* is a highly controlled, relentlessly linear paraphrase of the drama with interspersed translations, while the play itself from beginning to end concerns maternal ground, the Great Mother, hysteria, matermania. Only at one point in this essay does the writer indulge in fantasy, in visualizing the scene of the maenads on Mt. Citheron, nursing animals at their breasts and surrounded by flowing fluids. But in her fantasy here she takes refuge in Pre-Raphaelite, Botticelli-like pastoral images, blatantly distanced from the visceral matter of the passage ("The Bacchae" 13–18). The rhetorical guardedness of the essay on the *Bacchae* makes it difficult to read as other than a kind of interpretive paraphrase. Thus my remarks here chiefly concern the other two essays.

In another context I have already suggested the rhetorical peculiarity of the essay on the *Helen* – the way in which the writer plays out a dialogue with a censor who would curtail the extravagance of her imagination. But before that censor begins to take hold at the midpoint of the essay, H.D. probes the imaginal locus of Helen in provocative and prescient terms, foreseeing the later reconciled landscape of Egypt in *Helen in Egypt*, governed by Isis/Thetis.

One may read this essay as a complex meditation on maternal nostalgia surrounding the figure of Helen. Many Helens are here overlaid: Helen Doolittle of H.D.'s childhood; the Helen of Poe's poem, alluded to in "Egypt / (To E. A. Poe)," who is associated with the desire for home/Greece; the Helen of Sparta, an H.D.-like Artemisian ascetic caught in nostalgia for her hellenic homeland, remembering her mother, Leda. Moreover, if this essay was written after February 1923, as is quite possible, it may have been animated by H.D.'s trip to Egypt with her mother, Helen Doolittle, and Bryher. "Egypt" here is thus a complex locus of maternal displacement as well as symbiosis.

The plot of the play as a whole, as we have seen, suggests such an Eleusinian matrix. But the initial visualization of waters gives a more specific rendering of an imaginal territory. The writer asks the reader to imagine the setting of the play on a sea shelf:

> I do not hear music but a blending of waters (one) the sea at very low tide almost at rest, yet breaking in small back-drawn waves, waves that seem, if you can understand how exactly I imagine it, to break backwards, those waves at very low-tide that run out swiftly, spend their strength in that, and creep tentatively back.
>
> The tide is very low. But there is this slight rush of water. That is the first sound, perhaps grasped first because most familiar. The other sound (two) is a steady rush, and silver. It is away to the right. And I know what it is; though I do not see the river, I can visualize the sand-shelf it cuts over and the edge of that fresh moving tide, where it lies clear across the white sand it has scooped out and the backs of the shells it has washed so clean of salt.
>
> There are two sounds of waters. The sea at lowest tide and the Nile flowing over the sand. ("Helen in Egypt" 1)

This exercise in disciplined imagination seems intimate, as though the "I" were actively present on the scene and in the process of unraveling the subliminal signals of sound. At this moment, the tide is breaking backward, while fresh water rushes to the sea, making a path of cleaned shells. There are two simultaneous "tides," two rushings, the receding oceanic rhythm as a backdrop, the "fresh moving tide" of a silver river (though it *is* hard to imagine the muddy Nile as silver).

As I have suggested elsewhere, this liminal landscape "[w]here the slow river / meets the tide" ("Leda," *Collected Poems* 120), where sweet water overcrosses salt, seems especially associated by H.D. with the story of Helen. It suggests something of the complex eroticism that she assigns the figures of Leda and Helen. The visualization itself is erotically charged, the rhythm of the tide and the rush of river suggesting an erotic animation of the female body. But the opening description brings to mind other significances as well. The image of the sea breaking backward would appear to be an important aspect of H.D.'s imagination of Egypt, which seems here associated with the dead and the underworld (the "temple-tomb of Proteus," 2) and with erotic regression and memory. Helen in her first speech recalls her mother, Leda, and the essayist invents her affection for her dead guardian, King Proteus, who reminds her of her Spartan foster father, Tyndareus (5). The chorus of captive girls, in the midst of the Egyptian desert, sing in longing for their Greek home, remembering their childhood (14–15). They articulate most clearly the many-faceted nostalgia at work in the essay as a whole.

The image of the clear stream flowing into the sea is also a romantic/hermetic figure of the activity of imagination itself, the lesser mind joining the *nous*, as in the famous opening of Shelley's "Mont Blanc." The Greek text itself is a "great water" that fascinates by its play of surfaces (3); the old myths retold are like "a great sea and the roaring of its tides" (4); the words give access from our small "restricted minds" to "a free, large, clear, vibrant, limitless realm; sky and sea and distant islands" (9); the clairvoyant reader is a sailor on that vast sea (9–10). Implicitly, of course, we sail backward on this imaginative sea, to a finally inaccessible original world, through a lost language to a lost sea – lost stories, lost mother, lost islands, lost homeland.

This opening image of two waters, then, serves to clarify a maternal eroticism, nostalgia, and poetics. In this interpretation Helen is removed from a male-oriented sexuality; she resides not within a seminal but within an ovian economy, hatched from an egg (3). As Friedman has explicated, H.D.'s narrative efforts throughout the twenties concern an exploration of the psychological and aesthetic implications of this territory, and this meditation on the *Helen* is consistent with those efforts.

So too is her essay on the *Ion*, exploring a figure that looks back to the pure Hippolytus of the chorus sequence and forward to Hedylus of her 1928 novel. That later narrative replicates the two figures of the *Ion* of central concern to the early H.D.: the Helios-possessed rhapsodist and the shadowed Athenian mother.

H.D.'s essay purports to give the reader a kind of entrée into the play, explaining how we are to get past the conventions of Greek theater and into its vivid drama. "Life was to merge with art," she explains, and the prologue was a kind of bridge between the two ("Opening Scenes" 134). But H.D. herself, like the Athenian citizen whom she describes, makes that merger only when she comes to the figure of Ion in the first scene. Before that point, she is a glib literary guide; then, life merges with art, H.D./writer with Ion/rhapsodist. The essay focuses chiefly on Ion's lengthy lyric monody in the opening of the play and the choral ode that follows it. But unwillingly, the writer of the essay admits, she becomes distracted, drawn from her exclusive identification with Ion by the entrance of Queen Kreousa. Paradoxically H.D.'s fantasy of Kreousa is the most exciting part of the essay. Though H.D. allows only a glimpse of her, she is clearly the obscured matrix forcing itself into the light.

Ion, like Iphigeneia, is caught between father and mother, and H.D.'s interpretation of this dilemma suggests the same pattern of immolation and suffering already noted. The young boy of the opening monody represents the quintessence of the early H.D.: servant of Helios/Apollo, rhapsodist, associated with purity and holiness; he is "a young priest and a young poet" rapt in the golden light of Delphic Apollo. His rhapsody is sung in honor of king/priest/father:

> never weariness can touch
> a servant of such rapture servant,
> Helios is father-spirit:
> hail, Helios, my pledge of life,
> father, father, . . .
> Paion,
> O Paion,
> king,
> priest (140)

In this rapture, the essayist says, "[w]e close our eyes . . . to escape this vision, the boy caught, struggling, a white bird in a great wind, a flower, exposed to the sun" (*Ion* 139). This sense of unbearable exposure before the demands of the daimon – specifically here the service to father Helios – precisely defines the sense of immolation we have noted earlier. The alliance of Ion and of the essayist – who repeats three times the word "father" given in the Greek text – is unquestionably with this immolating power.

However, when Kreousa, Ion's unknown mother, enters, this paternal alliance becomes complicated. As H.D. notes, Kreousa and Ion immediately sense "a strange rapport between them" (147). Kreousa swerves attention away from the father, into a Demetrian ground. She wears Demeter's blues:

> All of his queens are beautiful and there are others of Euripides' women that are robed in blue. Thetis especially I see, as she appears in the last scene of the *Andromeda* [*Andromache*]. . . . But Kreousa, queen of Athens, wears the blue of stones, lapis blue, the blue of the fire in the earth, a blue that seems to symbolize not only her pride and her power but also her passion and her loss. (148)

On this note the essay ends, presenting the figure who compellingly draws Ion away from vertical ecstasy and into erotic and passionate complexity. The last sentence only suggests the power and darkness of Kreousa's rage at father/king/ Helios, which is, like that of Demeter, the rage of a mother over a lost child.

The configuration of the *Ion* in a sense completes the residual rage of the *Iphigeneia* at the betrayal and abandonment of the mother. It also replicates the *Hippolytus* as H.D. interprets it in her choruses, in that it presents both the male virgin and the powerful maternal figure in whose mysteries he must be initiated. H.D.'s *Hippolytus Temporizes* (1927), which we will consider next, represents the earliest extended extrapolation of these early patterns.

Thresholds: Hippolytus Temporizes *(1927)*

Hippolytus Temporizes represents a pivotal moment within H.D.'s engagement with Euripides. More than in any previous poem, translation, or essay, H.D. here seems deliberate in her use of Euripidean interplay as a means of reflection, self-awareness – even perhaps self-parody – and therapy. As a sustained lyric poem, *Hippolytus Temporizes* represents a considerable achievement, an accomplished polyphony of the several lyric modes of *Collected Poems* (1925) discussed in the last chapter. However, its significance can be measured only in the context of H.D.'s persistent hellenic figuration. The general inaccessibility of the play to critics until recently[11] may indeed come from its complex referentiality, from the fact that it serves as an extrapolation of those hellenic constructs and iconographies as well as a commentary on them. Here I attempt to situate *Hippolytus Temporizes* within the larger Euripidean conversation explored in this chapter.

Seen in this light, the play presents again, but clearly and definitively, the valences of earlier Euripidean translations and essays. However, at the same time it establishes a deliberate confusion between two erotic domains, which resolves itself finally in Hippolytus's incestuous desire for his absent mother, Hippolyta. The play concludes with a sustained apotheosis of Hippolytus as the Loved-of-Love; of a syncretic, undifferentiated goddess outside the confines of the Greek world; and of a consummate father/healer/enlightener – self-transcended Helios – who takes Love as his lord. With regard to H.D.'s self-analysis, the play begins with a certain clarity, suggesting the writer's awareness of excessive postures within her hellenic constructs, but ends in another ecstatic mystification, with higher stakes than ever.

In contrast to H.D.'s previous Euripidean writing, *Hippolytus Temporizes* is remarkably clear in demarcating and estimating the figures of the male rhapsodist and the female hetaera that have so preoccupied her. Hippolytus and Phaedra represent another version of a pervasive dichotomy in H.D.'s early hellenism, the tension between the domains of father (spiritual, ascetic, clear) and mother (bodily, erotic, obscure) that would appear to be part of the attraction in her exploration of the *Iphigeneia* and the *Ion*, as well as the *Helen*. H.D. explores the same kind of tension within the chief figures of her hellenic narratives, "Hipparchia" (1926) and *Hedylus* (1928), which form a kind of Greek trilogy with *Hippolytus Temporizes* (1927). Moreover, we have suggested analogous tensions in the lyricism of *Collected Poems* (1925), an opposition between Dorian and Ionian poetics: the difference between the poets of *Sea Garden* and of *Hymen*, between the severe and textual poet of "Storm" and "Hermonax" and the self-consciously romantic poet of the Sapphic fragment poems and "Nossis."

Hippolytus Temporizes represents these two postures with an eye to the obsessiveness of each, with an analytical estimate of excess and distortion. Both Hippolytus and Phaedra are absolutizers. Each claims divinity, Hippolytus suggesting equality with Artemis, Phaedra effecting an impersonation of both Artemis and Aphrodite. Hippolytus's intent to capture Artemis, to "catch the sea / within a song" (41), has hubris about it and an ecstasy bound to fall: "[W]hat is song for, . . . if it cannot imprison all the sea, . . . if it cannot drown out / our human terror?" (41). The desire to imprison the sea comes of course from a terror *of* the sea, of the obliteration of identity: "crystallization" of self intuits the enemy in the inchoate and indistinct, in visceral feeling. But of course song cannot drown out terror, and this the writer of the play well knows from her own experience of the war and its aftermath. Phaedra also gives divine status to her personal desire, iconizing her own body, as does the "early H.D." in some of her romantic postures: "[C]an no one greet / my south! . . . *red, wild pomegranate mouth?*" Phaedra claims indeed to be Artemis, when she sends the Cyprian boy with a message to Hippolytus (63), while during her night with Hippolytus she imagines herself as a manifestation of Aphrodite (79).

Hippolytus represents a "Greek" exclusivity, a "tyranny of spirit," according to Phaedra, that insists on differentiation and discrimination: "Must we encounter / with each separate flower, / some god, some goddess" (49). This is exactly the pride of Hipparchia in *Palimpsest*, of Hedylus in *Hedylus*, both of them rhapsodists infatuated with Helios. Phaedra, on the other hand, represents an equally willful and reductive insistence upon the rapture of passion, with its "merging" and dissolution of self. She too is close to H.D.'s self-figuration as hetaera–poet (in Hipparchia and Hedyle).

In analyzing the limitations of two postures essential to her self-conception as a hellenic poet, H.D. appears to be attempting to move beyond her early hellenism. But just as she is doing in her narratives of the same period, she is circling old ground to arrive at a resolution or healing of desperate psychic tensions. In *Hippolytus Temporizes* she aims at a resolution in suggesting the confusion and complexity of desire, which cannot be exercised in exclusive terms, and in pointing to some underlying unity within all desire. However, her solution at this point can only be a mystical and transcendent one.

The eroticism of the play is multivalent. The many relationships, both mortal and divine, are all triangular. Artemis loves Hippolytus as he reflects her mortal lover, Hippolyta, but perhaps also as he reflects her brother, Helios, in his purity and vision. Helios loves Hippolytus as he reflects his mortal lover, Hyacinthus, but also as he reflects his sister, Artemis. Hippolytus loves Artemis as she reflects his mother, Hippolyta, but his love of Hippolyta's "cold steel" and his adoration of the phallic white plinth of Artemis suggests male homoeroticism, reiterated in his love for Helios. One might even say, especially drawing upon the Phaedra poems of *Hymen*, that Phaedra's love is also triangulated. In "She Contrasts with Herself Hippolyta" (*Collected Poems* 136–8), Phaedra projects herself imaginally into the body of Hippolyta at the moment of conception, when she becomes aware of the child in her womb. Likewise in "She Rebukes Hippolyta" (*Collected Poems* 138–40), Phaedra is seized by a clairvoyant vision of the virginal Hippolyta and of her "chaste" eroticism. In other words, through Hippolytus Phaedra longs for Hippolyta, the maternal/virginal woman's body.

This general obliquity, doubling, and mirroring within eroticism – which suggests the homoeroticism and incest of Dorian hellenism – takes place within the more obvious parameters of a contrast between Artemis and Aphrodite. H.D., like Euripides, presents a tension between the two goddesses and at the same time obscures the distinction between them (Gregory, "Virginity" 142–6). In addition to the polarity between their two followers Hippolytus and Phaedra, a network of images in *Hippolytus Temporizes* reiterates the difference between the two goddesses. Artemis is associated with Greece, with wilderness, daylight, cold, white flower, with a silver headband. Aphrodite is associated with Crete, with civilization, night, heat, citron, rose, myrrh and myrtle, with purple clothes and headband, and with goldenness – though at moments she assumes some signs of Artemis as well. At the same time H.D., like Euripides, shows that both goddesses are identified with similar elements of nature – with birds, with fresh life (dew, flowers, and delicate fragrances), with luminosity or radiance, and, most importantly, with the salt sea and the shore.[12] Indeed, the precise drama of this long poem is the confusion of these divine domains in the consciousness of Hippolytus and Phaedra. The writer deliberately emphasizes this confusion through the agency of the Cyprian boy, who, as in a Shakespearean comedy, naively mistranslates signs of the two goddesses, imagining them both as his own Cyprian deity. Hippolytus and Phaedra move through their exclusive desires into the liminal territory of a female presence (prehellenic, undifferentiated) suggested by the ancient island Cyprus and the Cyprian boy/Eros who brings them together. That presence is figured, too, in the absent mother Hippolyta, who in her erotically charged virginity stands at the boundary between the two realms. Present in all desire, the play suggests, is "the trace / of one / long since forgotten" (34).

As we have indicated in earlier discussion, this "ruse of the triangle," according to Anne Carson, "irradiat[es] the absence whose presence is demanded by eros." The poem of triangular desire is "about the lover's mind in the act of constructing desire for itself." It bespeaks the liminal, hermetic character of desire (Carson 16). The liminal, triangulated eroticism of the proem "Hippolytus Temporizes" gives a clue to the whole play (Gregory, "Virginity" 146–9). There Hippolytus is caught between explicit worship of distant and cold Artemis and remembrance of an Aphroditic erotic body. In the play, the absent presence within this eroticism is his mother, Hippolyta. Phaedra seems to recognize this in asking Hippolytus after their night of lovemaking to pray for her – not to Artemis, or to Aphrodite, but to "the first," to Hippolyta, his mother (84–5). And clearly, in Hippolytus's desire, Artemis, with whom he believes he has made love, figures for his mother (29). Hippolyta's presence is suggested also by the fact that both Phaedra and Hippolytus in their intimacy have seemed both the child and the mother to each other (80, 135).

This "she" as the occluded object of desire comes to be associated in the play with the original goddess of Cyprus, the figure that H.D. elaborates as well in "Songs from Cyprus":

> All flowers are hers
> who rules the immeasurate seas,
> in Cyprus, purple and white lilies tall;
> how were it other?
> there is no escape
> from her who nurtures,
> who imperils all.
> (*Collected Poems* 281)

With this goddess, spirit (white) and bodily passion (purple and red), as well as nurturance, are not differentiated and opposed. She resembles most closely the prehellenic figure of Jane Ellen Harrison's *Prolegomena*, existing before the differentiation of goddesses in Olympian religion and surviving most fully, according to Harrison, in Aphrodite or Venus Geneatrix (314–15).

Hippolytus Temporizes represents the first of many subsequent explorations of this fundamental "matri-sexuality" (DuPlessis, *Career* 114). Such an erotic confusion is intolerable in terms of a hellenic cosmos, with its patricentrality, its structural oppositions, and its discriminations of functions. Both Artemis and Aphrodite are retributive, protecting violations of their limited domains; the transgression of boundaries means destruction for both Phaedra and Hippolytus. Thus, too, the uncovering of the Cyprian goddess clearly strains the limits of H.D.'s imagined Hellas itself. To address this hellenic crisis, Helios enters in the last act of the play, to stand as a herm at the boundary of that known world and to point beyond it.

Under the auspices of Helios, the last act represents a mammoth effort of transcendence on the writer's part. The separate self-destructive desires of Hippolytus and of Phaedra have come together for a moment through the absent intercession of Hippolyta in their union, and Hippolytus dies imagining having been transported to Cyprus, the "elsewhere" of his erotic longing (135). However, the suffering of Phaedra and Hippolytus is not mitigated or healed within this Greek context, but rather transcended within the Greater Mysteries of Love, affiliated with the Cyprian goddess. In Hippolytus's dying presence the gods themselves admit their mortal contamination through eros: "None, none is pure, / and none, none, is alone" (123). But Love as it is described in the latter part of the play ("His soul is beautiful / in Love's great name" [114]) suggests less the Greek than the troubadour sense of the "Lord of Love," just as the wounded hands and side recall *the* Passion. In this syncretism H.D. clearly points beyond the Greek world to a larger continuum of mysteries. Finally, the very god of transcendence transcends himself; Helios, as the chief deity of H.D.'s hellenic cosmos, dissolves into an arch-mage, within a continuum of light and healing.

The last scene of the play represents the farthest limits of H.D.'s Greek spirituality. One can't get any purer than this – a discourse between the whitest, most immaculate of divinities, Helios/Apollo and Artemis. This is a scene of judgment, wherein H.D. (through the figure of Hippolytus) attempts to see her own early vocation in terms of some kind of ultimate measure, only to find the measure itself insufficient and in need of transformation. The divine names representing spiritual boundaries – Artemis, Helios – must be left behind, or enter again into hidden namelessness. Helios/Asclepios decides finally to resurrect Hippolytus. And in his paean to Paeon itself, his invocation of Invocation, Helios transcends himself – straining beyond the confines of his names or even his godhead: "Come, / Paeon, / Paeon, / Power, / myself but beyond shape / of god or man, / come then Myself / abstraction, mystic fire" (130).

The Greek world remains, at the end, static and contained, Artemis repeating the identical prayer with which she began the play. But H.D. has, in a sense, left it – or has striven to leave. The play opens in a vivid way the territory of maternal eroticism, though at the same time it climaxes with the most extravagant of paeans to that immolating paternal authority of the earlier writing. The entire third act of *Hippolytus Temporizes* represents a strained, apostrophic incantation to her visionary guides, a calling of Calling itself, suggesting a certain desperation, perhaps an intuition of exhausted resources, a sense of the arc of the career going awry. The poet of *Hippolytus Temporizes* cannot yet envision the territory beyond Greek boundaries; Helios is a nimbus of "mystic fire" obliterating any actual discrimination. The poet is still apparently mesmerized by a fantasy of aesthetic transfiguration. But she has envisioned with some clarity her own "death" as a poet, the death of the hellenic rhapsodist as well as of the rapturous hetaira. Indeed, *Hippolytus Temporizes* is a requiem for what must be left behind.

Mourning the Mother: Electra–Orestes (1932–1934)

H.D. published two portions of a lyric sequence called *Electra–Orestes* in the early thirties: "Electra–Orestes – Choros Sequence" (1932) and "Elegy and Choros / From *Electra–Orestes*" (1934). The version published by Louis Martz from a typescript in the Beinecke (*Collected Poems* 378–88) contains these two published portions, but in addition a previously unpublished dialogue between Electra and Orestes constituting roughly the last third of the poem (384–8). It is unclear whether the version of *Electra–Orestes* as we now have it in Martz's edition represents a single composition written around 1932 or rather a composite piece written over a longer period, the concluding dialogue possibly postdating H.D.'s last sessions with Freud in late 1934.

In any case, this poetic sequence returns to the familial territory explored in earlier Euripidean engagements – the relation of the child (daughter/son) to the father and mother. But, as the word "Elegy" in the second published segment indicates, it suggests as well the necessity of "mourning," which, in Dianne Chisholm's argument, constitutes a significant discovery within H.D.'s analysis with Freud (121–2). The poem represents a partial Euripidean diagnostic of H.D.'s creative impasse at this transitional point in her career.

The Euripidean dramas of prominence in H.D.'s early writing mirror the central ambivalences that critics have explored in her narratives, in particular an ambivalence toward the mother, tied to dilemmas of a woman's vocation as writer. *Iphigeneia in Aulis*, *Ion*, and *Hippolytus* all show a central figure existing within a vertical spiritual orientation – an alliance with the father or with the Olympian twins, Apollo and Artemis. That alliance is finally predicated on a rejection of the mother: Iphigeneia chooses father/king/priest, accusing her mother of betrayal; Ion likewise adores father/king/priest in the god Helios, and indeed unknowingly attempts matricide; Hippolytus adores the heavenly and inviolate Artemis, detesting the erotic draw of his stepmother, Phaedra. At the same time, however, H.D. recognizes in her essays on the *Helen*, the *Ion*, and the *Bacchae* that Euripidean figures are implicated in an Eleusinian pattern, predicated on the bond between mother and child. *Hippolytus Temporizes*, like the narratives of the twenties, attempts to dramatize and to work through this persistent duality of desire, concluding on the one hand with the hypostasis of a figure of the Great Mother, the Cyprian goddess, in whom all desires are contained, and on the other with a final extravagant crystallization of the vertical Olympians, Artemis and Apollo/Helios.

Very early in her narrative explorations of the twenties, the figures of Orestes and Electra – and the pivotal gesture of matricide – come to represent this bind associated with maternal desire. In *Paint It Today*, as Midget meets her mother's resistance to her desire to stay in London rather than to return home, she has a moment of matricidal rage:

> How did Orestes feel when he held the knife ready to slay his mother? What did Orestes see? What did Orestes think? . . .
>
> "Your mother has betrayed your father," spoke the present to Orestes. "Your mother, your mother, your mother," the present said to Midget, "has betrayed, or would betray, through the clutch and the tyranny of the emotion, your father, the mind in you, the jewel the king your father gave you as your birthright. Look," said the present, "and choose. Here is a knife, slay your mother. She has betrayed or would betray that gift." (42–3)

The father is allied with the mind, with the creative gift, the mother, with betrayal of the father/gift. Orestes the son is allied with the father against the mother; Electra the daughter is allied with the dead father against the mother, though able to act only *through* the brother. The sister, unlike the brother,

Deborah Kelly Kloepfer points out, "does not slay the mother; she waits." Thus in this myth, according to Kloepfer, "the myth out of which H.D. operates, partially, for years . . . to be the daughter means to be sacrificed [like Iphigeneia] or to sacrifice the mother or to be (impossible) the son" (51). On the other side of this picture of mimetic desire, however, is the incest motif that Kloepfer elsewhere treats: the desire of the child for the mother, and the desire between brother and sister.

In her examination of what she calls the "maternal quest plot" in H.D.'s fiction, Friedman concludes her commentary on the narratives of the twenties and thirties with *Nights* (written in 1930). This novel, she indicates, dramatizes most extremely a "psychic split" in H.D.'s self-figuration "between masculine mind and female body." It concludes with the detached and emotionless speech of the narrator, John Helforth, framing and contextualizing the narrative of Natalia, who has recorded her own story leading to her suicide. At the conclusion, "the male fragment of the author's split psyche is the survivor," but the "female voice is left behind, silent, or silenced through death" (*Penelope's Web* 278). *Electra–Orestes*, written during the same period as *Nights*, also examines this tragic dichotomy, in the context of H.D.'s recurring familial paradigm.

Though this "choros sequence" is a lyric and not a dramatic meditation, it clearly bears an intertextual relation to Euripides. H.D.'s poem echoes lines from the *Electra* and the *Orestes* and takes from these plays the configuration of the sister and brother in relation to the mother and father and to Apollo/Helios. Euripides' treatment of this story borrows from both Aeschylus's *Libation Bearers* and Sophocles' *Electra*. But Euripides is distinct from them in ways quite significant to H.D. In both the *Electra* and the *Orestes* Euripides emphasizes the love between brother and sister: "O Sister, I found you so late, and so soon / I lose you, robbed of your healing love" (*Electra* 1308–10, trans. Vermeule). In H.D.'s poem Orestes says: "It is too late. I have found you too late. You can't be a lover to me" (385), and he confuses her with the Pythian priestess of his austere dedication to Apollo. More important, Euripides is unique in presenting the matricide as a terrible, finally unjustifiable mistake, dictated by paternal authorities.

In Euripides' plays, both Electra and Orestes after the murder are immediately filled with remorse and incredulity at what they have done. Electra says, "Weep greatly for me, my brother, I am guilty. / A girl flaming in hurt I marched against / the mother who bore me" (*Electra* 1183–5, trans. Vermeule). They both are grief-stricken at the sight of the crimson-stained robe covering Clytemnestra's body, and this image of blood brings recollection of what hate has destroyed. "Behold!" Electra says, "I wrap her close in the robe, / the one I loved and could not love" (*Electra* 1230–2, trans. Vermeule). The *Orestes* dramatizes the psychological effect of the murder. Whereas Electra can fully realize the emotions brought into play, Orestes suffers the murder of the mother as a debasing madness, the aftermath of a kind of suicide. Speaking to Helen about Orestes' collapse, Electra says that "he killed himself when he killed her" (*Orestes* 91, trans. Arrowsmith).

In the aftermath of the murder, both brother and sister recognize the compulsions that have driven them to this deed, for Electra an obsession with her dead father, for Orestes with Apollo. Ultimately, everyone in the play seems to place the blame on Apollo: "Apollo killed us both, / . . . / when our father's ghost cried out / against our mother, *blood, blood!*" (*Orestes* 191–3, trans. Arrowsmith). At the end of the *Electra*, the god Castor names the "brutal song of Apollo" as the cause of this suffering (1302, trans. Vermeule). These recognitions of daughter and son are possible only in the aftermath of their murder of the mother, which brings to awareness the excess of their hate, as well as the desire for Clytemnestra that it has concealed.

H.D.'s *Electra–Orestes* echoes these Euripidean emphases – the power of hate concealing love, the wounded body of the mother, the tyranny of the dead and of the song of Apollo, the murder as self-killing, the bond between sister and brother. Like Euripides' plays, it centrally concerns a repercussive recognition in the aftermath of death. However, H.D.'s lyric exploration further emphasizes the interiority of the event of the mother's death, as a complex of psychic compulsions and affective suffering.

In *H.D. by Delia Alton* (1949), H.D. comments on the poems of the mid-thirties, those in the proposed collection, *A Dead Priestess Speaks*, in light of her subsequent discovery, with Freud, that "there is in life, as in death, resurrection" (210). In this context, H.D. remarks that the *Electra–Orestes* "has a vivid integrity, with its motive or leit-motif, 'to love, one must slay,' and its answering refrain, 'to love one must be slain.'" Its "costume, colour and rhythm" are "striking and authentic" (212–13). That authenticity and integrity in H.D.'s lyric rendering of Electra and Orestes comes from the achievement of an "elegy" for the lost mother. However, like the poems of the later *Trilogy*, this elegy concerns not simply biographical projections, but rather the paradoxes of the psyche itself – its growth, death, and transformation. These are the terms, at least, in which Electra – the dominant figure in the sequence – attempts to sort through a tangle of emotion and remembrance.

The first lines of the poem, as H.D. herself indicated, have an arresting and disturbing vividness, one indeed that is difficult to approach. Electra speaks, apparently already in retrospect, of Clytemnestra's death:

> To love, one must slay,
> how could I stay?
> to love, one must be slain,
> then, how could I remain,
> waiting, watching in the cold,

> while the rain
> fell,
> and I thought of rhododendron
> fold on fold,
> the rose and purple and dark-rose
> of her garments, (*Collected Poems* 378)

The opening axioms state paradoxical necessities that come into being at the moment that one loves. This ominous act of love, however, is not ordinary or familial desire, which imposes no such radical dicta, which indeed attempts to naturalize and nullify such urgencies. To whom or what, then, is this love directed? Not, apparently, the mother, since this love has caused in fact the inability to wait any longer in abeyance before her charm. It appears rather to be a love of the "soul" itself coming into awareness. The next lines suggest that necessities of action and passion (slaying and being slain) come about because of the soul's gradual growth. Though the mother's way is "toward an open temple," the daughter's is "toward a closed portico." And those enclosed walls of the soul must fall:

> [N]o one knows
> what I myself did not,
> how the soul grows,
> how it wakes
> and breaks
> walls,
> how, within the closed walled stone,
> it throws
> rays and buds and leaf-rays
> and knows
> it will die
> if the stones lie much longer
> across the lintel and between the shafts
> of the epistyle, (378)

The soul in waiting, desiring an inaccessible life and expansiveness represented in the mother, "thrives on hate." This hatred, coming in part from the urgencies of psychic life and the fear of death-in-life, finally becomes a motive of action, necessitating radical change. Thus one may read the opening paradox: to love this growing soul one must venture a gesture that destroys, that shatters walls; one cannot "stay" or "remain" in suspension and in hatred, but must change, and that change entails a complex death.

To slay in this sense opens up the possibility of remembrance and knowledge. The genuinely elegiac passages given to Electra and Orestes, as in Euripides' plays, reveal the magnitude of the loss: "[S]he does not move, / no light / can strike any more / from her sandal; / she will tread / no still hall, / running to answer her dead; / for her dead / will not call" (383). But they also suggest the way in which recollection knows, and magnifies, the object of its love. The image of the flower associated with Clytemnestra suggests disturbing paradoxes surrounding the event of her death: she is a "rhododendron-name," wearing "rose-of-Cos" perfume that troubles the child with longing. But that erotically charged flower is somehow inaccessible to specific knowledge until it is lost. Electra speaks:

> No one knows the colour of a flower
> till it is broken,
> no one knows the inner-inner petal of a rose
> till the purple
> is torn open;
> no one knew Clytemnestra:
> but –
> too late, . . .
> Electra. (381–2)

This knowledge, however, as it combines intimacy with irrevocable absence, is poignant and terrible.

For the male Orestes the mother-as-flower is more viscerally implicated. In his lines the purples and roses of the mother's beauty merge with the flower of the wound in her body:

> and her gown
> is so beautiful,
> soft, pleated, and wonderful,
> and her breasts under her gown
> are cold,
> for a flower has grown,
> murex-red
> on the red gown,
> where my insatiate sword
> went home. (384)

His violence is a form of intercourse, the intimacy of his child's awareness of the softness of the red robe overlaid with his wounding gesture bringing him "home."

This nexus of intimacy, desire, and violence in the transformation of the mother within the child's apprehension is presented not with sentimentality, but with awareness of violence, of painful contradictions, remorse, and guilt. Indeed, the aftermath of the violence is a recognition of self-violence. As Orestes says: "[W]hen I struck Clytemnestra, I struck myself. I cut right through myself, and

I am nothing but the cold metal, I am cold, the sword, I don't feel anything at all" (384). The poem, which unnervingly states the terms of necessity, leaves one with no sanguine resolution of the conflicts it enacts through the figures of sister and brother. However, the concluding dialogue between Electra and Orestes rather shrewdly analyzes the distortions that have led to an impasse requiring such radical remedies.

In this exchange H.D. performs an imaginary dialogue between two distinct necessities that have shaped her early writing and life, and she clearly indicts the excess and violence of gestures that have concluded in loveless frigidity and spiritual suicide. Electra claims that in his adoration of Helios, Orestes − like Hippolytus and Ion − has loved "an Image" and an imaginary authority, the "Pythian who was drunk-with-god like wine − ... Un-sexed, / inhuman, / doomed," a "travesty / of love." Moreover, Electra, Orestes claims, has been distorted as well in loving "love-for man / and love-for-woman" (387−8). Bound as witness to sexual triangulations of father/mother/lover, Electra's travesty of love appears to be an aggrandized heterosexual preoccupation, which couches a sublimated incestuous desire. The male fragment is dehumanized in abstraction and surreal fantasy, the female fragment in visceral mimetic or triangular desire. This analysis suggests with some accuracy the tensions within H.D.'s early writing and points in particular to the "split psyche" that Friedman discusses in relation to *Nights*.

Electra−Orestes concludes with a choral lament that suggests the point to which this Euripidean performance brings H.D.: a recognition of the loss of "*Clytemnestra / and home*," a sense of grief at having "*spent / life-blood / in hate*" (388). However, its "vital integrity" that H.D. later admires comes also from the sense that the poem records this moment as part of a necessary process of transformation. Chisholm analyzes the way that H.D. in her Freudian analysis was confronted by the necessity of moving from "melancholia" to "mourning," "from a frozen, incarcerated crying to a liberation of tears and, beyond that, to a revelation of what was originally lost − the gift" (122). *Electra−Orestes*, in its analysis of psychic need, of grief, paralysis, and self-immolation, foresees this necessity.

Etiology: Euripides' Ion *(1935, Published 1937)*

In her study of H.D.'s fiction, Friedman argues that the autobiographical narratives, beginning with the novels of the twenties, served H.D. therapeutically, as part of a "writing cure" that became more explicit after the "talking cure" of her analysis with Freud in 1933 and 1934.[13] This chapter has attempted to show how H.D.'s engagements with Euripides, spanning the whole of her career, likewise represent a kind of "writing cure." This therapy is certainly of a different kind than that of the narratives, which, as Friedman shows, can perform the splitting, doubling, and weaving of selves characteristic of the "talking cure" of psychoanalysis (83). The psychodrama performed in Euripidean texts is dream*like*, but not dream. It is psychological in a way – reflecting a quest to comprehend repetitive patterns – but without the immediate engagement with actual events and memories. As a sublimated performance – an acting through a "universal" script written by another – it may have limited efficacy in terms of personal healing or change. Nevertheless, it does allow H.D. some means of psychological exploration.

The benefits and limitations of this Euripidean writing cure are evident in H.D.'s *Euripides' Ion*. It was begun in the summer of 1934, a year after her first sessions with Freud (1 May to 12 June 1933), and completed in the summer and fall of 1935 after her final sessions with Freud (31 October to 2 December 1934). It would appear to be H.D.'s first sustained effort to follow Freud's advice, or to satisfy his reiterated expectation, that she resume writing.[14] H.D. clearly understood the writing of *Euripides' Ion* as "the Freud contribution,"[15] and when it was published in 1937, H.D. sent Freud a copy. But one may read "contribution" here as a euphemism; in a way Freud fathered this book. It is a divine child (Ion) of a sacred intercourse (Kreousa and Helios), a sign of (re)birth through a father-lover. But of course *Euripides' Ion* is also the "Euripides contribution," and the fact that H.D. in her important letters of this period takes this for granted bespeaks a generative affiliation long preceding that with Freud. *Euripides' Ion* may be seen as a double tribute to these two writers whom H.D. considered equal and similar "modern" fathers and masters of psychological life.

Coming at a pivotal moment in her career, *Euripides' Ion* reflects the considerable burden that H.D. wanted it to bear. H.D.'s letters to Bryher during the period of its composition, especially during August 1935, reflect her excitement and urgency.[16] "The attitude one takes at this time," she wrote to Bryher in the midst of her composition, "is all-important for the rest of ones [*sic*] life" (24 August 1935). H.D. imagined this undertaking as a rite of passage, a way of gaining orientation and clarity for the future. Writing in almost complete isolation in Switzerland in the summer of 1935, under the urgency of Freud's paternal expectations that she produce, under the threat of incursions of Nazi violence that might necessitate flight, H.D. exerted great pressure in this effort of translation and commentary: "I am really working – never so hard nor toward such a concentrated purpose" (27 August 1935).

In reassuming work on the *Ion* at this time, H.D. deliberately chose to return to materials associated with the most traumatic events of her life. Taking together her isolated comments on the dating of her writing, H.D. appears to have been engaged intermittently with the *Ion* throughout the whole of the war years, from 1915 through 1920.[17] As various sources suggest, especially her correspondence with Bryher during August 1935, H.D.'s labor on the *Ion* is associated not only with the hellenic comradeship of her marriage, but with its collapse in infidelities; with the war terror itself; with her second pregnancy and her meeting of Bryher in the summer of 1918; with the mystical/hallucinatory episodes of that summer, suggested in *Asphodel* and in *Hedylus* (a marriage to the sun, a bird sign indicating the divine origin of the child); with the Scilly Islands experiences in 1919; and with the vision at Corfu in 1920.[18] The dedication of *Euripides' Ion* – "For / B. Athens 1920 / P. Delphi 1932" – carries still other associations. This female configuration, linking the writer with her companion, Bryher, and her daughter, Perdita, is reinforced by her association of the play with a trip to Athens in 1922 (*Ion* 111), accompanied by Bryher and her mother. In the dedication, this Eleusinian circle is linked with the chief sites of her heroic hellenism, the two sites of the play itself, Athens and Delphi.

For H.D., Euripides' *Ion* signifies obliquely a large portion of the primary matter engaged in psychoanalysis, and her resumption of the task in the summers of 1934 and 1935 constitutes a deliberate and risky attempt to come to terms with the past, armed with post-Freudian insight. This project, in other words, does indeed suggest a "concentrated purpose." H.D. wanted very badly, and Freud wanted, a creative breakthrough, a sign of a successful analysis, a sign of victory. Apparently, for her, this writing achieved that goal, enabling her "to say to myself I am, I am, I AM a POET" (7 August 1935). Affirmation of this sign of her own victory, simultaneously a tribute to Freud, is perhaps the most encompassing of the agendas of *Euripides' Ion*. The paean at the end of the play thus seems inevitable: this *opus* is enacted under the aegis of Athene Nike.

Along with this conception goes another "concentrated purpose," consistent with the heroism implicit in H.D.'s hellenism from the beginning. In "Advent," H.D. records Freud's remark that "not only did I want to be a boy but I wanted to be a hero" (*Tribute to Freud* 120), and she imagines the task of *Euripides' Ion* in such a heroic light. H.D. is convinced that somehow her work will ameliorate the terror and destruction of the contemporary world: "My work is creative and reconstructive, war or no war, if I can get across the Greek spirit at its highest I am helping the world, and the future" (24 August 1935). This redemptive purpose is suggested repeatedly in *Euripides' Ion* in the way the commentator situates the drama in the context of the Persian Wars and the devastation of Athens. Furthermore, the text of *Euripides' Ion* shows evidence in another sense of her effort to "get across": not only to convey the Greek spirit, but to bridge the chasm separating present from past. On one level this heroism is an aggrandizement of H.D.'s strenuous efforts to close her own gaps in time. But in any case the effort of apology and cultural interpretation, the effort to make a dead world accessible to the living, imposes a burden of public authority on the commentator that she does not bear with great ease or success.

The other motives of *Euripides' Ion* are more specifically related to a long-standing textual engagement with Euripides. They too bear the mark of H.D.'s fragility at this time, her urgent desire for change, for a revelatory sign of wholeness. That desired wholeness or unity is in some sense the allegorical sign of the play. The word "ion," we are told in the "Translator's Note," "*may be translated by the Latin UNUS, meaning one, or first, and is also the Greek word for violet, the sacred flower of Athens*" (7). In this imagined etymology H.D. reads the sign of unity and origin, of the perfected, sacred beauty of Athens. In terms of numerology, which H.D. surely takes into account, the nineteen divisions of the play given in the translation signify one (19 = 10 = 1).

That desired wholeness requires some violence. At the beginning of her translating, H.D. tells Bryher of her feeling that "if I get this Ion done, it will break the back-bone of my H.D. repression" (14 August 1935). H.D.'s correspondence with Bryher during this period indicates that she did indeed experience the writing itself, the enactment of translation, as such a liberation from repression. With increasing exaltation she repeatedly insists in these letters that she is swimming in the unconscious, acting out in some way a union with Hellas/Helen, her mother.[19] At the same time that it allows this participatory awareness, her work with the play also enables a new clarity or synthesis; she indicates in a letter to Bryher that "it is good to get the pattern" (14 August 1935).

As a psychological enactment *Euripides' Ion* represents not so much a beginning as an ending, a closure. Here H.D. does successfully lay a ghost – the crystalline male virgin, along with his pure vertical worship of Artemis and Apollo/Helios. After this point in her writing, such a figure is no longer present as the object of stubborn fascination. Instead, another persistent focus of attention emerges with increasing force: the occluded mother, or an idealized "primal Mother" (Friedman, *Penelope's Web* 313). Apparently, then, H.D. is successful here in "breaking the back-bone" of that recalcitrant and fixed figure by undertaking an etiology, a study of its origins in the mother. This Euripidean enactment is important, then, in allowing H.D. to "get the pattern," to resolve an iconography in which are implicated many of the entanglements and traumas of her early career.

Euripides' Ion, then, represents a complex point of intersection within H.D.'s long hellenic engagement. Just as it seems compelled by distinct purposes, so it is composed of distinct voices, distinct imaginal selves. In its complex hybrid form, *Euripides' Ion* in some ways suggests the splitting of selves that Friedman has discussed in H.D.'s narratives. One finds the old lyric H.D., here an extravagant version of the early rhapsodist. There are as well the imagined selves of the characters, assumed by the writer in the liminal passage of the drama, chiefly the imagined Ion, the pure servant of Helios, and the imagined Kreousa, the betrayed mother. Besides these, one can differentiate three distinct imagined selves within the commentary, in some respects discordant.

There is the superior "expert" who is going to get this thing across to a modern audience. This commentator is something of an aesthete dilettante, aware of the "*various degrees of literacy*" within her audience (8). Attempting to bridge gaps in refinement, she condescends to belabor whatever bourgeois comparisons may be necessary, referring to opera, to the vulgarity of late theatergoers, or, like the narrator of "Hymen," to attic statuary and mannered choreography. This voice, which dominates at the beginning but recedes in importance, represents an effort at control and normalcy in approaching a dangerous territory. It is the voice of a John Helforth, persistently distancing itself from the power of the figures through a fastidious technical emphasis. If in Greek drama, as H.D. claims in her earlier essay on the *Ion*, "[l]ife was to merge with art" ("Opening Scenes" 134), then this initial voice undermines such intimate significance, insisting in its aestheticism on their separation. However, another voice within the commentary exerts a counterforce, working through a vigorous intellectual engagement and emotional identification with the figures of the drama. This is a less self-conscious reader/interpreter, attempting to comprehend Euripides' text, to imagine the characters, and to articulate the implicit interplay among them that indeed constitutes much of the power of the play. This voice, engaged in "getting the pattern," grows increasingly in authority and command after the first entrance of Kreousa, though at times cut across and arrested by Helforth's mannerism. A third voice is distinguishable as well – the voice of the heroic apologist, who sees this play, and her own gesture of rewriting it, as a multiple sign of victory.

In approaching this complex text, I would like to consider the interplay among some of these imagined selves: the lyricist, the reader/commentator, and the apologist. The following discussion focuses on the translation of the drama into lyric terms, the significance of the figures as the commentator reads them, and, finally, the Freudian apology rising finally to a point of apotheosis.

As critics have noted, H.D.'s translation of Euripides' *Ion* converts a drama into a lyric (Lattimore, "Lyricist" 160; Carne-Ross 8). It is as much like an extended "choros sequence" as the writer can make it. As in her early choruses, H.D. has here omitted the passages of the play having an ethical, sophistical, or political cast – such as Ion's debate with Xouthos foreseeing his political problems as a bastard son and Athene's closing prophecy about the descendants of Ion. These interludes, important for the Athenian dramatic context, distract from the religious and psychological elements that H.D. clearly sees as primary. The commentator's insistence in the beginning that *"Greek drama was religious in intention, directly allied to the temple ceremonies"* (9) gives license to these exclusions. The translated portions of the play are divided and subdivided into small segments of roughly lyric size. This deliberate fragmentation does away with any ordinary sense of dramatic coherence and effect, juxtaposition and irony. The weight of effect and unity rather falls on lyricality, and H.D. has translated here with a maximal lyric intensity.

This translation represents H.D. at her most apostrophic, suggesting the strain of an effort to evoke the redemptive sublimity of the Greek world. Ion's opening

speech is perhaps the most exaggerated instance of this persistent impulse.
A literal translation of the lines is approximated here, followed by H.D.'s
version:

> See the gleaming car of the sun! His brilliance streams over the earth;
> before his fire the stars flee from the sky into mysterious night. Parnassus'
> untrodden peaks, kindling into flame, receive for mortals the wheels of
> light. (trans. Hadas).

> O, my Lord
> O, my king of the chariot,
> O, four-steeds,
> O, bright wheel,
> O, fair crest
> of Parnassus you just touch:
> (O, frail stars,
> fall,
> fall back from his luminous onslaught:)
> O, my Lord,
> O, my king,
> O, bright Helios, (14–15)

Here the sense of the original text is almost wholly disintegrated into separate
elements, all offered up to the unitary O that gathers the aspiration into the realm
of the ineffable.

This lyricism carries over as well into some of the dialogues. The translator
here gives a boldly innovative interpretation of the stichomythia – the alternating
dialogue of single lines – as a "*broken, exclamatory or evocative vers libre*" (32). This
mode of presentation collapses discrete voices – and the sometimes ironic interplay between them – into an associational single voice. For instance, the first
dialogue between Kreousa and Ion, who are unknowingly mother and son,
suggests not simply an intellectual or pragmatic but an intuitive exchange:

Ion:	– are you alone?
Kreousa:	– with my husband –
Ion:	– what do you want?
Kreousa:	– we ask one thing –
Ion:	– wealth or children?
Kreousa:	– we are childless –
Ion:	– you are childless?
Kreousa:	– Phoibos knows it –
Ion:	O, my poor heart –
Kreousa:	– you, who are you?
Ion:	– the god's servant –

Kreousa:	– given or sold here?
Ion:	I am Loxias' –
Kreousa:	– child, your mother?
Ion:	I don't know her – (34)

The translator has severely abbreviated and simplified the dialogue as it exists in the Greek text. There it is given in the long lines of dramatic meter (iambic trimeter) and comprises a syntactically and rhetorically coherent exchange – a "sustained narrative," the translator calls it (32). H.D.'s modification underscores the crucial issues between Kreousa and Ion: origin, identity, kinship; the desire of one for a child, of the other for a mother. It suggests an uncanny sense of mutual recognition or mirroring, "the image of two people who understand each other so well they can almost read each other's minds" (Vanderwielen 71).[20]

The lyricality of H.D.'s translation of the *Ion* does not represent a new direction, but rather an extrapolation of old techniques, present in her earliest Euripidean choruses. But though ostensibly a translation, the text as a whole is closer to another old experimental form – the essay – than to the choruses. The commentator says at the beginning that *"the play may be read straight through with no reference, whatever, to [the translator's notes]"* (7). However, such a reading of the play alone, though strictly possible, is effectively impossible. *Euripides' Ion* requires reading as a composite text, with interplay between lyric and discursive personae.

One of these discursive personae is a sympathetic and intelligent reader of Euripides, aware of his themes and of the kinds of questions he raises, appreciative of the "underlying psycho-physical intensity" that his plays achieve ("Euripides" 1). This reader provides keys to understanding Euripides' *Ion* that go beyond H.D.'s previous attempts to engage this fable, in "Helios and Athene" and in her earlier essay on the play. "Helios and Athene" (*Collected Poems* 326–30) gives the abstract schema of powers configured in the *Ion*: Helios, Athene, and Demeter. But the real focus in this sketch or prose poem is on the interplay between Athene and Helios, Athens and Delphi. Athene emerges as the Androgyne par excellence, combining father and mother, Helios and Demeter. But the mother of Eleusis herself is least explored and least approachable. Likewise the commentator in the early essay on the *Ion* unwillingly turns attention from the Apollonian Ion with his ecstatic opening song to consider the dark Demetrian queen. It ends, as we have seen, with an image of Kreousa's lapis-blue cloak, symbolizing "not only her pride and her power but also her passion and her loss" ("Opening Scenes" 118). However, H.D. as translator/interpreter is now finally capable of approaching this figure within a broad grasp of the patterns and themes of the play, mirroring the personal patterns emerging in psychoanalysis.

The guiding question of this reader is suggested in the commentary to the prologue: "*[W]hat can this all signify?*" This reading of significance, and the assurance that it does indeed possess significance, takes place under the patronage of Hermes, the figure of the prologue. This writing is thus part of a hermetic *opus*. As "*the god of writing, of writers, of orators, of the spoken word*" (9), Hermes is carrying a script, the script of the play itself perhaps, the script of H.D.'s *Euripides' Ion* perhaps. For of course H.D. as writer inscribes the significance of this god of writing, assigns him this attribute. So he *is* her writing; he signifies her writing itself. Moreover, this reading of signs takes place in the theater of Delphi, in the context of inviolable "*Delphic integrity*," intellectual honor and power (20). However, this inviolable god of Delphi, the fable goes, violates others; his purity is essentially associated with violence; and his integrity, in human terms, is essentially duplicitous, "*double-edged*" or oblique.[21] However, the commentator says, the "*manuscript of the poet, Euripides*" is like the indestructible temple at Delphi (20) – thus this script, implicitly, renders the same kind of duplicitous and dangerous truth.

The fable of the *Ion* captured H.D. for so long a time in large part because of its central figures of virgin and mother, acting out a drama in the context of the deities that most fascinated her. But she was captured as well by the implicit themes this configuration invokes. The play is for one thing etiological: it enacts a founding – the founding of Hellas itself. It is concerned with origins and roots. For this reason it poses questions to H.D. that remain pending throughout the long course of a psychological, hermetic search, coming to a climax with Freud.

Moreover, as a kind of revision of Sophocles' *Oedipus*, it is about the severe, Apollonian quest to know oneself, the quest of both Kreousa and Ion. However, this quest leads not to psychic disaster but to grace, not to the collapse of identity in parricide and incest as in *Oedipus*, but to the discrimination of familial identities. In this mythical context – the *Ion* serving as a haunting, unrealized metafiction – H.D. attempted to come to terms with and resolve her own disasters, so many of which like the *Ion* entail loss of innocence, betrayals and self-betrayals, black bitterness. H.D.'s stubborn insistence on this play reflects her intuition of its scope as a spiritual fable. The *Ion*, Cedric Whitman says, most fully represents the long psychological and spiritual process that in his view Euripides attempts to explore in his late plays – a process concerned with innocence, its violation, and its recovery. This process is figured in Ion and Kreousa, the former, in Whitman's terms, innocent, the latter pure: "Innocence is what is necessarily lost by action, and purity is what must be found by suffering and knowledge." Purity in this sense is "a kind of spiritual wholeness, which comes upon a person when an experience, of grave and threatening dimensions, has been lived through in all its active and passive phases, and comprehended at last as the shape and token of one's being" (93).

The interpreter in *Euripides' Ion* comprehends the spiritual dimensions of this fable. She also clearly acknowledges in these figures an etiology of "H.D." The boy-priest Ion, in his worship of Helios, represents the early poet's fascination with "*chriselephantine [sic] beauty and flawless, detached, deified virginity*" (45). However, the central event of the play, as the interpreter renders it, is the emergence of Kreousa with her power of long-acquired integrity, coming both from uncompromising intellect and from rage and bitterness. This second figure is the woman-mother-as-poet, challenging the male-virgin-as-poet. The commentator admits her own resistance to the shattering of old categories: "*A woman is about to step out of stone, . . . A woman is about to break out of an abstraction and the effect is terrible. We wish she would go back to our pre-conceived notions of what classic characterization should be*" (30).

Euripides' Ion represents the first full-fledged recovery of what H.D. later names the matrix of the crystal: "For what is crystal or any gem but the concentrated essence of the rough matrix, or the energy, either of over-intense heat or over-intense cold that projects it?" (*H.D. by Delia Alton* 184). Kreousa – with "*the inhumanity of a meteor, sunk under the sea*" – is that matrix of heat and cold, that absolute matter, standing in complex relation to the crystal Ion. As matrix and crystal, Kreousa and Ion replicate or mirror each other: both are virginal, their virginal "*unity violated by this god [Helios], by inspiration*" (61); both in some sense belong to Helios, both Apollonian in their uncompromising intellectual quest. Moreover, both have Athene as a "spiritual mother": Athene is the foster mother of Kreousa's family, and Kreousa becomes the embodiment of Athene, the "Virgin Mother" (61); Athene is then figuratively Ion's mother, as is the wise Pythoness of Delphi.

However, alongside their purity and integrity, both have the chthonic blood of Erechtheus/Erecthonius, the earth-born semiserpent who is the grandfather of Kreousa. Indeed, the capacity of both for bitterness, anger, and venom forms one strain of their identity, and thus turns the plot toward its resolution in the revelation of kinship. Kreousa has a vial, entrusted by Athene to her family, containing drops of the Gorgon's blood that can both heal and destroy. This kinship with the bitter, venomous earth, also the source of life and healing, brings one close to the alchemical and mystical sense of the matrix. In "Helios and Athene," a gloss on the *Ion*, H.D. emphasizes the way in which the image of the serpent ties together Helios, Athene, and Demeter. She interprets in this context the message of all the mysteries: "Be wise as serpents" (*Collected Poems* 326).

A reader of H.D. might anticipate the inevitable emphasis here on Athene and Helios. However, the exploration through this play of a dark chthonic inheritance is more remarkable. Without Kreousa's Apollonian desire for knowledge, she would not be Kreousa and would not recover her child. But without Kreousa's rage and violence, she would not be Kreousa and would not find her child by attempting to kill him. The same dynamic applies to Ion, who also acts from these contradictory motives, conscious (Heliadic) and unconscious

(Erechtheid) compulsions, and also finds his mother through violence. This chthonic wisdom, associated with the workings of the unconscious, is above all what is acknowledged and affirmed by the commentator in *Euripides' Ion*. At the moment of her decision to kill Ion, the commentator remarks, Kreousa has not, as critics have claimed, become a savage. Rather, she has realized her magnitude as queen and foster child of Athene, who is intimate both with serpents and with violence: "*Kreousa, the queen, stands shoulder to shoulder with the sword-bearer of the Acropolis. She, too, holds a weapon; she, too, strikes infallibly at the enemy of her city. Kreousa, the queen, standing shoulder to shoulder with Pallas Athené, becomes Kreousa, the goddess. The price? Kreousa, the woman*" (73).

Kreousa's humanity – and Ion's humanity – can be restored only after their murderous drive has run its course, at which point they are revealed to each other by the double intervention of the Delphic priestess and Athene standing in for her brother, Helios. The death of the pure virgin Ion in the impurity of violence and the extinction of Kreousa within the bitter salt of rage are necessary before rebirth can take place. When H.D. in her letter to Bryher speaks of "break[ing] the back-bone of my H.D. repression," she is speaking within the violent imagination of Kreousa. The hatefulness of this gesture, the chthonic mother wishing to destroy its child, is forgotten or obliterated in the letters within an idealized amniotic language of swimming in the "un-c." But the play itself, and its interpreter, give authenticity and integrity to the necessity of anger and hate in a way that H.D. in her writing seldom does.

The third voice within the commentary, however, abstracts from this comprehension of the matrix into a larger synthesis, and finally into a celebration of the father, who subsumes the mother's attributes. In his letter of thanks to H.D. upon receiving a copy of *Euripides' Ion*, Freud praises the book for exactly the reason that H.D. would have wished her scientist-father to praise it: that in her commentary "you extol the victory of reason over passions" (*Tribute to Freud* 194). This voice of the apologist alludes to both Euripides and Freud in the concluding apotheosis of Mind in the image of Athene, who replaces Kreousa as the image of the mother, though herself motherless and born of the father alone. Though this apologist gives an Einsteinian spin on classical rationalism, she nevertheless sees it as a main hope for the redemption of the world in the context of war.

This overarching argument is initiated early in *Euripides' Ion* as the commentator situates Euripides and the *Ion* – as well as the present act of re-visioning – at a crucial turning point in world history, the moment of "modernity," when the sunrise is and is not a "miracle," is and is not a theophany:

> *At this moment, in the heart-beat of world-progress, in the mind of every well-informed Greek – . . . there was a pause (psychic, intellectual), such a phase as we are today experiencing; scientific discovery had just opened up world-vistas, at the*

same time the very zeal of practical knowledge, geometry, astronomy, geography, was forcing the high-strung intellect on a beat further beyond the intellect. As today, when time values and numerical values are shifting, due to the very excess of our logical deductions, so here. (14)

The implication of these remarks is that rational science, with its skepticism and pragmatism, goes so far that it goes round the bend into a recovery of mystery: "*Is Euripides ironical, or has his knife-edge mind seen round the edge, round the corner, as the greatest scientists and thinkers of today are doing? Has the circle turned, the serpent again bitten its own tail?*" (14). This argument is an essentially hermetic and romantic one, suggesting the continuity, rather than discontinuity, between rational enlightenment and occult illumination. Such an implication is indeed sealed in the allusion to the Uroboros, the alchemical, gnostic sign of final unity. As Adalaide Morris has proposed in her study of H.D.'s lifelong dialogue with scientific traditions, "As the twentieth century progressed through two world wars . . . H.D.'s desire to temper modern mechanical science with the old hermetic wisdom became more and more urgent" ("Mythopoeic" 201). But there is also the suggestion in the commentary of *Euripides' Ion* that H.D. sees the modern scientific view in Einsteinian terms, as a "shifting" of "time values and numerical values," just as in the liminality of drama time and space are warped, "*accordion-pleated, as it were*" (80).

In the context of H.D.'s persistent autobiographical concerns, this reflection on the place of scientific reason embraces her father-astronomer and many surrogate father-scientists, primarily Freud, as well as her own persistent fascination with "*knife-edge mind*," figured in Helios and Athene. The implicit reference to Freud in this discourse emerges immediately as the commentator refers to Euripides, at the time of his writing of the *Ion*, as one of the *gerontes*, old men exempt from military service: "*[D]oes this 'old man' throw his psyche back into the first lyrical intensities of youth?*" (14). This image of the *geron* is extended at a crucial moment when Kreousa enlists the aid of an unnamed, sympathetic old man, who, according to the commentator, symbolizes "*Time, the grandfather, as it were, of her own brain-birth*" (61). Thus this pause "*in the heart-beat of world progress*" noted by the commentator can be seen as an aggrandizement or projection of H.D.'s own Freudian pause, wherein a "*high-strung intellect*" was forced back upon itself and beyond itself. Euripides and Freud merge a figure of the old wise man, "the old Hermit" (*Tribute to Freud* 13), who "*throw[s] [the] psyche back*" into the intensities of childhood, who is the progenitor of a "*brain-birth*." In hermetic fashion, H.D. reads the great world in the small, or projects the small as the great. The macrocosm of the *Ion* is the image theater of her therapy with Freud. His is the hermetic script, his the hermeneutic, and his the Delphic shrine, the "*incontrovertible . . . two-edged honour*," the "*Delphic integrity*" that demands truth and self-knowledge (20).[22]

H.D.'s vision of her heroic role as poet shares in the kind of "reconstructive" effort in which she envisions Euripides and Freud. Euripides, H.D. emphasizes, is writing this play at the time that the Parthenon is under construction, after the devastation of the old temples by the Persians at the beginning of the century. Though she does not mention it explicitly, the specter of war reminds one that Euripides is also writing during the Peloponnesian Wars, which eventually so devastate Athenian integrity. Euripides' play is itself part of a reconstructive effort, as it in fact attempts to define the autochthonous identity of Athens and Attica and to give a kind of heroic myth of founding affirming the centrality of Athene and the Erechtheid house. So too Freud's grave philosophy – enacted in the context of a war-torn and psychically damaged world – is reconstructive. This Freudian context is surely implicit in the commentator's reference to the French archaeologists who rebuilt the Athenian treasury at Delphi. These are men "*of almost superhuman intuition, intellectual devotion and integrity*" who "*have managed to trace wide scattered fragments and re-build*" (20). Freud styled his own efforts archaeological, and H.D. in *Tribute to Freud* uses this same language in describing Freud's analytical method (14).

This heroic dimension of the commentary in *Euripides' Ion* is climaxed at the end of the work in the image of Athene:

> [T]his most beautiful abstraction of antiquity and of all time, pleas for the great force of the under-mind or the unconscious that so often, on the point of blazing upward into the glory of inspirational creative thought, flares, by a sudden law of compensation, down, making for tragedy, disharmony, disruption, disintegration, but in the end, O, in the end, if we have patience to wait, she says, if we have penetration and faith and the desire actually to follow all those hidden subterranean forces, how great is our reward. "You flee no enemy in me, but one friendly to you," says the shining intellect, standing full armed. (112)

Athene carries the paradoxical wisdom belonging to Euripides the *geron* and, implicitly, to the old hermit Freud: the wisdom of the serpent biting its tail. Athene too is close to the serpent and to the Gorgon, and her "*shining intellect, standing full armed*" can see one Perseus-like through the descent into serpentine meanderings, disintegration, and darkness. Athene appears to stand as well as a sign of H.D.'s own victory, a realization through Freud of the Nike figure of her long-standing fantasy, whom she discerned in the "writing on the wall" at Corfu in 1920. She is a sign both of the analyst and of the imagined wholeness and unity of the analysand.

This paean to Athene is clearly what Freud has in mind in noting in a letter of congratulation to H.D. the way that she "extol[s] the victory of reason over passion":

The human mind today pleads for all; nothing is misplaced that in the end may be illuminated by the inner fire of abstract understanding; hate, love, degradation, humiliation, all, all, may be examined, given due proportion and dismissed finally, in the light of the mind's vision. Today, again at a turning-point in the history of the world, the mind stands, to plead, to condone, to explain, to clarify, to illuminate. (113)

Like Shelley's Prometheus, the commentator projects the old hope of the rational enlightenment in the romantic guise of hellenic revival. It is offered as an implicit tribute to Freud, standing Athene-like within the chaos and irrationality of the world that surrounds him.

The heroic apologist, participating in this hellenic reconstructive activity, gives tribute to Athene by the offering of a story of a fugitive fleeing Athens during its destruction by the Persians, who returns to the Acropolis to view the lost temple to Athene and her burned olive tree and, in the midst of the ruins, sees a living, fresh shoot of olive branch. This story calls attention to the devastation of war that, though only barely mentioned in *Euripides' Ion*, is one of its most significant contexts. H.D. knew that Euripides was in Athens when the Persians destroyed the city; as a boy he fled with the other citizens down the Eleusinian highway.[23] The strange Athenian of H.D.'s story who rebelliously dares to confront the destruction of the lost city and to witness new life is a figure of Euripides himself. Just as this fugitive gives witness to the live olive branch of Athene's ruined temple, so Euripides through the *Ion* has preserved the spirit of Athens; and so H.D. – in the implicit context of impending war – has preserved through *Euripides' Ion* this same spirit – of Euripides, of Athens/Athene, of Hellas, of redemptive light.

Taken in all its textual complexity, *Euripides' Ion* suggests the way in which H.D.'s therapeutic engagement with Euripides serves simultaneously to advance and to arrest her psychological self-awareness. There is certainly evidence here of H.D.'s recognition and clarification of old patterns, as well as evidence of her keenness as a reader and interpreter, her attempt to do justice to aspects of the story that she had previously avoided. However, the heroic apologist suggests a false turn in the labyrinth. This imagined voice reflects a certain desperation and willfulness in the context of threatening uncertainties. H.D. writes in a letter to Bryher in August 1935 that she anticipated working at other Greek plays after completing the *Ion*, because "[t]he Greek will hold me to my centre, now whether here or in London. . . . and already I feel stabalized [*sic*] and balanced" (24 August 1935). She is counting on Athene Nike for center, balance, stability; but "*this most beautiful abstraction*" is not enough to hold her. Indeed, after *Euripides' Ion* H.D. appears to have abandoned fairly soon her orientation to the Greek world, and she did not resume it in any sustained way until 1952. Rather the project of memory in *The Gift*, begun four years later in London after the beginning of the war – memory not sublimated or fictionalized – represents something closer to the breakthrough and rebirth that H.D. desired and imagined with the writing of *Euripides' Ion*. It recovers not only "shining intellect" but heart and humanity as well.

Eidolon: Helen in Egypt *(1952–1955, Published 1961)*

Critics of H.D.'s *Helen in Egypt* have persistently read it in terms of the epic genre, because of its apparent revision of Homer and because of a desire to set it beside other modernist neoepics.[24] In this reading *Helen in Egypt* certainly appears as a kind of antiepic. Late in the poem, Helen recognizes that the things most important to her – "the million personal things, / things remembered, forgotten" – never "came into the story," because "it was epic, heroic" (289). This passage, situating a woman's intimate world against the public world of the male cult of war, may be taken as evidence that H.D. here, as Friedman claims, is writing a revisionary epic, reversing the cultural valuation implicit in the traditional epic. However, claims for the poem as epic, assuming Homer's *Iliad* as the "approximate source," as Rachel DuPlessis suggests (*Career* 111–12), must be qualified in light of its more proximate but little considered classical contexts.

In *Helen in Egypt* H.D. alludes both generally and specifically to the *Iliad* and the *Odyssey*.[25] However, she at no point mentions Homer, though she explicitly acknowledges other, post-Homeric classical writers – Stesichorus and Euripides. The initial headnote implies that Stesichorus originated the tale of Helen in Egypt and that it was later elaborated in Euripides' *Helen*. This information is not entirely accurate.[26] In fact Euripides' play is the sole extant source for the myth that H.D. here takes for granted,[27] and it constitutes the principal classical subtext of her poem. Indeed, the first lyric concludes with a key textual reference to the *Helen*: "Helen hated of all Greece" (2).[28] One should also note the obvious fact that H.D. gives her poem the same title by which she always refers to Euripides' *Helen* – *Helen in Egypt*.[29] The identity of titles cannot be coincidental to a writer obsessed with names and parallels. Euripides' "*later, little understood* Helen in Egypt" (1) – as the commentator calls it – also signifies in some sense H.D.'s own "late, little understood" poem.

The discursive and lyric voices of *Helen in Egypt* repeatedly make allusion not to epic narrative but to drama: "[W]ho set the scene? / who lured the players from home" (231). The commentator remarks about this lyric: "*There is a story, a song 'the harpers will sing forever.' It is a play, a drama – . . . The players have no choice in the matter of the already-written drama or script. . . . They would play their parts well*" (230). At one point in the first section of the poem, the commentator muses about Helen's process of recollection: "*She would re-create the whole of the tragic scene. Helen is the Greek drama. Again,* she herself is the writing" (91). Upon her image or name, within her memory, is inscribed the story of the fatal house of Atreus, itself at the origin of the definitive hellenic story – the "phantasmagoria of Troy," as Helen calls it (17). These pointed references to tragedy and drama indeed accurately reflect the important intertextual relation of H.D.'s *Helen in Egypt* with "the Greek drama" – specifically, the drama of Euripides. To emphasize the implicit claim here: she herself is Euripidean tragedy.

It would be fruitless to insist on generic distinctions in relation to *Helen in Egypt,* or indeed to any of H.D.'s writing. H.D. consistently eludes all such strategies beloved of critics. And I do not mean here to insist on exclusive categories. As this study has emphasized, H.D. read the *Iliad* and the *Odyssey* in her early years;[30] she imagined her role as poet and her poetic project in heroic terms. Undeniably Homer is a subtext for all of H.D.'s appropriations of the classical in working the matter of war   Homer is the subtext of classical writing itself, he is *the* Western poet of war, as Delia suggests in "A Dead Priestess Speaks" (*Collected Poems* 372). Nevertheless, throughout her career Greek drama appears more significant and accessible to H.D than Homeric epic, and she explicitly and implicitly invokes it in this last major poem. A recovery of this context is necessary in the effort to take seriously the considerable intellectual and literary exchanges within H.D.'s writing.

Why Greek drama? The "harpers" – a generic name in *Helen in Egypt* for writers of all kinds, for mythic dissemination in general – endlessly recount or rewrite the Homeric or para-Homeric myths. But in particular they form the basis of classical Greek drama, where they are chewed over repeatedly in versions that have determined the lines of their transmission. In fifth century B.C. Athenian drama, the mythic stories become enactments. In this performative context they become fertile ground for modern psychology. Freud explores the family drama in essentially tragic configurations, and, as H.D. was well aware, he is closer to Euripides than to any other ancient writer both in his skepticism and in his emphasis on eros and the irrational. So too for H.D. in *Helen in Egypt* the myths become enactments: *"There is a story. . . . It is a play, a drama."*

As we have seen, Euripidean tragedy in particular constitutes for H.D. an important intermediary in the dissemination of Greek myth. Periclean Athens adapts the ancient Homeric stories as part of a deliberate effort to construct an idealized Athenian identity in the context of military supremacy following its defeat of the Persians. Aeschylus and Sophocles are full participants in that self-idealizing city, promoting emulation of noble heroic paradigms and political pieties. Euripides, however, is distinct from them in his deliberate, systematic, self-conscious evasion or refusal of idealizations, a refusal that becomes more pointed and bitter as Athenian empire building runs amok during the Peloponnesian Wars. Among the plays most important to H.D., the *Trojan Women* was written in the immediate aftermath of the brutal Athenian massacre of the people of Melos, the *Helen* in the immediate aftermath of the disastrous Sicilian campaign, and the *Iphigeneia in Aulis* during Euripides' voluntary exile from Athens at the end of his life, soon before the fall of Athens to Sparta. Refusing the Athenian disposition to paradigms, Euripides steadily questions the old myths and the old heroic figures; more profoundly, he questions the illusion-worshiping activity of the political order and the illusion-making capacity of poetry itself. War increasingly becomes in Euripides' plays the context for the acting out of brutal and vicious illusions.[31] As Helene P. Foley has suggested, Euripides to some extent exposes the dynamics of what René Girard has called the "scapegoat mechanism," the nomination and sacrifice of a victim who may deflect political crisis (Foley 100). H.D., as we have seen, admired Euripides for precisely these reasons, and his plays are thoroughly implicated in her final meditation on the destructiveness of war.

H.D.'s knowledge of Euripides' plays was comprehensive, her engagement with them specific and detailed, and from time to time she even read secondary criticism of his work,[32] a concession she made for few other literary figures except Shakespeare. Thus it is insufficient in discussing the classical intertextuality of *Helen in Egypt* to demonstrate H.D.'s extensive recasting of Euripides' figure of Helen, but to assume that his *Helen* may be dismissed as representing the "phallocentric structures and figures of classical literature," which H.D. would seek to undo.[33] Such a reading indeed confirms H.D.'s initial claim that the *Helen* is "little understood," and it belies her own obvious, increasing respect for the play, which she could no more interpret in these terms than she could the equally phallocentric writing of Freud. *Helen in Egypt* is intricately engaged not only with this Euripidean play but with many others as well.

H.D. probably first knew Euripides' *Helen* around 1911, a little before her initial voyage to Europe with Frances Gregg, when she read *The Divine Fire* (1904) by May Sinclair, later her friend in London.[34] In that novel the central male figure, Keith Rickman, is reading and translating Euripides' *Helen*. His intensity in encountering the mysterious and potent Greek script prefigures that of H.D.'s hellenic figures: "*EΛENH* He saw it very black, with the edges a little wavering, a little blurred, as if it had been burnt by fire into the whiteness of the page. Below, the smaller type of a chorus reeled and shook through all its lines" (49–50). He is himself engaged in writing a play inspired by the *Helen*. Entitled *Helen in Leuce* (108), it takes as its epigraph a line from Euripides' play: "you, Helen, begotten the daughter of God" (1148). *Helen in Leuce*, like H.D.'s late poem, concerns the afterlife of the figure: Helen's marriage to Achilles on Leuce (Leuké) after his death and her deification (Sinclair 137–8).[35] This early acquaintance may explain why H.D. first turned her attention to the *Helen* and why she seems from her earliest years fascinated by the figure of Achilles, but it does not explain her recurrent attention to the play in subsequent decades. For many reasons, the *Helen*, like the *Ion*, constituted for H.D. a difficult nexus of significance, which she was very late in unraveling; and evidence clearly indicates that she considered her *Helen in Egypt* in the context of past efforts to come to terms with this play.[36]

Moreover, though the *Helen* is the major Euripidean subtext of *Helen in Egypt*, H.D. during its composition deliberately reread several of Euripides' Trojan plays – not only the *Helen*, but the *Andromache*, the *Trojan Women*, the *Iphigeneia in Aulis*, and the *Iphigeneia in Taurus*.[37] The poem also draws upon her earlier textual engagement with the *Hecuba*, the *Electra*, and the *Orestes*, and as well upon her late reading of a commentary on Euripides' plays by Henri Grégoire. *Helen in Egypt* constitutes a Euripidean refiguration of Greek mythology in light of Euripidean tragic themes.

H.D. in *Helen in Egypt* is unconcealed in pointing to an extensive Euripidean intertextuality. The names of all three of the main sections of the poem – "Pallinode," "Leuké / *L'isle blanche*," and "Eidolon" – are associated with H.D.'s Euripidean study.[38] *L'isle blanche* is an especially revealing marker, indicating as subtext not only Euripides' *Andromache* but the French translation of Leconte de Lisle in which she was reading it. Her notes on reading Euripides during the composition of *Helen in Egypt* (transcribed in Gregory, "Euripides") verify the way in which she extrapolates details of Greek mythology from his plays to establish her cosmology and primary drama. Here are details from Euripides' plays alluded to in *Helen in Egypt*: Helen seen in relation to Egypt (*Orestes*, *Helen*), to the Dioscuri (*Orestes*, *Helen*), to Achilles as an early suitor (*Helen*); Helen placed at the tomb temple of Proteus (*Helen*); Helen situated in triangular relation to Egypt, Troy, and Sparta (*Helen*); Helen seen as a parallel with Persephone (*Helen*); Helen deified as a goddess of mariners (*Orestes*, *Helen*); the vilification of Helen as a Hecatean witch with "evil philtres" (*Andromache*, also *Trojan Women*, *Iphigeneia in Aulis*, *Helen*); Achilles seen in relation to Thetis (*Rhesos*, *Iphigeneia in Aulis*, *Andromache*); the "brides" of Achilles-as-Hades, Iphigeneia and Polyxena (*Iphigeneia in Aulis*, *Iphigeneia in Taurus*, *Trojan Women*, *Hecuba*); the White Island, or Leuké, where Achilles goes after death (*Andromache*, *Iphigeneia in Tauris*); the figure of Thetis as a protean goddess of the sea (*Andromache*); the *eidolon* of Thetis at the masthead (*Iphigeneia in Aulis*) and as divine epiphany (*Andromache*); the story of the judgment of Paris (conjured in every Trojan play); the story of the casting out of Paris by Hecuba, and of his title "wolf-slayer" (*Iphigeneia in Aulis*); the family relations between Iphigeneia and Clytemnestra (*Iphigeneia in Aulis*) and among Iphigeneia, Electra, Plyades, Hermione, Neoptolemus, and Orestes (*Orestes*, *Electra*, *Andromache*, *Iphigeneia in Tauris*). Moreover, though some of the themes of H.D.'s poem belong generally to Greek drama (fatal marriage, Nemesis, and mythical recurrence), others are distinctly Euripidean: a ubiquitous emphasis on Aphrodite and daimonic Eros; the network of Eros and Eris, defined particularly in *Iphigeneia in Aulis*; the duplicity and obscurity of divine will, elaborated consistently in his plays; the incommensurability of name and thing, of image and truth, amplified specifically in the *Helen*.[39]

In claiming Euripidean tragedy as a subtext for *Helen in Egypt*, however, one should recall H.D.'s peculiar poetic slant, her primary emphasis on the "choros sequence" and her translation of Euripides' *Ion* into predominantly lyric rather than dramatic terms. *Helen in Egypt* may be understood as an extended and greatly amplified choros sequence, in H.D.'s distinct invention of that form. There are five lyric "monodists" in *Helen in Egypt*, Helen and her three lovers (Achilles, Paris, Theseus), as well as a choral voice, or "Choragus" (the Eidolon of Thetis). These mixed lyric voices effectively function like those in H.D.'s "choruses" of the *Iphigeneia in Aulis* and the *Hippolytus*. A Greek chorus often indeed works precisely as do the lyric sequences of *Helen in Egypt*: it evokes within an affective or erotic context a series of images from mythic stories that accrue significance as they overlap, blur, and amplify each other and that appear to point to a discernible pattern in the relation between mortal and immortal. So the voices of *Helen in Egypt* together give an associational dreamlike reflection on a large, composite drama, *"the whole of the tragic scene"* – specifically, the drama of war. At the same time, these distinct voices, as figures of dream, are aspects of an oneiric questor/questioner, puzzling over continuously generated *eidola* of self.

Thus H.D. extrapolates the choros sequence, but she also returns to the experiment of *Euripides' Ion*, the juxtaposition of lyric and discursive voices. The critical or analytical voice of *Helen in Egypt*, like that of *Euripides' Ion*, arises out of a need to mediate or contextualize lyric speech to an imagined audience.[40] This continued experiment in *Helen in Egypt* is on the whole more successful, the discursive voice less Athene-like and more Hermes-like, less agenda-ridden and more meditative. Critics have only recently begun to engage the complexity of the discursive voice of the poem, which, like those of the lyrics, continually queries, wonders, and extrapolates in its decipherment of signs. As Friedman indicates, the notes "do not provide authoritative readings of the lyrics, but rather, in their rhetoric of indeterminacy, emphasize the Penelopean endlessness of (re)interpretation and inscription" (*Penelope's Web* 358). At the same time, as Peter Middleton has suggested, the critical voice is much more inclined than the lyric personae to "truth-claim," to a realistic stance of resolution and clarification that the lyrics consistently disallow (359).

In *Helen in Egypt*, H.D. engages her classical master, just as she does her modern master, Freud,[41] in his most subtle philosophical mode, and in a way that allows her to adapt the figures of drama to a dream spectacle, an oneiric quest. Euripides has been consistently interpreted in reductive ways, following the biases of traditional classicism.[42] However, in recent decades critics have begun to acknowledge the complexity of his plays, in which he appears not as a propagandist for any point of view (rationalist, sophist, feminist, misogynist, pacifist), but rather as systematically resistant to all ideological stances. As Ann Norris

Michelini proposes, in his plays "[t]here is no point of rest; and no position, once established, is left unchallenged"; "[t]he balancing play of ideas puts a sign of irony on all ideas and denies most of all the possibility of reliance on the *logos* as a source of stability" (119, 121). However, as critics have always noted and attempted to explain in various ways, this skeptical habit exists somewhat discordantly with certain religious emphases, which become more evident in his late plays. The interpretation of these plays by Cedric Whitman in light of the process of virginal initiation is reinforced from another vantage by Foley's consideration of their preoccupation with ritual and sacrifice.

This attempt at a reading of *Helen in Egypt* in light of Euripides' plays presumes this sense of "the contradictions and ambiguities of signification" in his writing (Michelini 126), but also an apparently serious religious concern. Both of these elements seem equally important for H.D. The implications of Euripides' standard coda, coming at the end of five extant plays, including the *Helen*, may be taken as a significant context of H.D.'s poem. It is here given in H.D.'s translation:

> Many the shapes the gods take
> many and many the things they plan
> and the plans they break;
> what was to have been, was not;
> for God has invented a plot
> far different from any we could have dreampt [*sic*];
> behold,
> as in this event. ("The Bacchae" 29)

The coda articulates a principle of uncertainty – that what one takes to be certain is radically unstable – but at the same time a human phenomenology held together by minimal belief in divine purposes. It suggests a version of the Ovidian theme of metamorphosis, a central feature in *Helen in Egypt* signified in the figures of Proteus and Thetis, who represent the many-named, polymorphous divinities of this cosmos. Focusing on Euripides' *Helen* one can see the way in which H.D. in *Helen in Egypt* has taken up and played out the kind of epistemological questioning presented in Euripides, in the context of an Eleusinian pattern of losing and finding determined by the protean gods.

If indeed Euripides' *Helen* is the subtext of *Helen in Egypt*, how does H.D. here "translate" it? We have already noted some of her emphases in reading the play, suggested in her early essay. A dominant line of criticism has always dismissed Euripides' play, citing its escapist character and the triviality and insipidity of Helen as an idealization of the dutiful wife, very much as does Dianne Chisholm from another vantage.[43] But H.D., as we have seen, took very seriously the figure of Helen here, locating her within a maternal and erotic landscape and emphasizing her character as a virginal figure within an Eleusinian configuration – her location at the tomb of Proteus, the threat of her marriage to a dark bridegroom, the hope of her *nostos*, or homecoming, to Greece. The Euripidean Helen of H.D.'s early essay is one aspect of the later figure in *Helen in Egypt*: an Artemisian, Spartan, prelapsarian Helen.

H.D.'s later critical awareness of Euripides' *Helen* suggests a much more dense and complex conception of Helen, specifically situated in religious and political contexts. Essays by Grégoire, read by H.D. during the composition of *Helen in Egypt*,[44] establish a detailed structural parallel between the *Iphigeneia in Tauris* and the *Helen*, and H.D. includes the *Ion* within the framework of his argument. Here are her remarks in the late memoir "Compassionate Friendship":

> The strictly scholarly but almost clairvoyant findings of the translator of these plays, . . . leave me breathless. He classes them with the *Ion* which I have already done. Originally, I worked on Iphigenia choruses – but Aulis.
>
> I am living this Elusinian [*sic*] cycle – will it be given me to serve again this other temple, cycle or circle?
>
> I put aside my Euripides volumes and the notes that I have done, as for the *Helen* and the comparison of the Iphigenia and Helen, "l'identité presque absolu de la composition." Of the 20 plays, "les filles immortelles d'Euripide . . . deux jumelles." These twins are companions to the *Ion* that I worked on so many years. These all deal with a defamed or "lost" oracle, Helen herself being exiled to Egypt and the Helen theme degraded through the mock-mysteries of Alcibiades, before the ill-fated Sicilian expedition. . . . She is lost, to be found again. (71)

The detailed arguments of Grégoire need not concern us here, but rather the specific emphasis given by H.D.: that the Euripidean versions of the legends of Iphigeneia and Helen constitute a return to Greece of a lost or exiled goddess.[45] H.D. clearly (and rightly, in the context of the plays) reads this return in terms of an "Elusinian [*sic*] cycle," a Persephonean return to life (71). Why she emphasizes the lost "oracle" is not clear from reading Grégoire – perhaps because all three of these Euripidean plays are located at the site of a temple and involve the speech of an oracle. In particular, Grégoire gives a very compelling account of the role of Theonoë in the *Helen* as a regal and wise precursor of Socrates' Diotima, interpreting the divine *nous*. But in any case, H.D. clearly imagines her own recovery of Helen in *Helen in Egypt* as the recovery of a lost oracle. Also, finding that the Iphigeneia of her earliest hellenic engagement was a "twin" of the Helen of her late years affects the final shaping of *Helen in Egypt*. Grégoire's interpretations are traceable in the prose headings being written at this time (1955), and they may in part account for H.D.'s renewed interest in the latter stages of revision with the "sister motive" of the poem ("Compassionate Friendship" 140).

Later remarks by H.D. – comments on the typescript of her early essay on the *Helen* in "Notes on Euripides, Pausanius, and Greek Lyric Poets" – suggest her awareness of the political dimension of the play. H.D.'s marginal comments throughout the typescript conclude in a note dated 16 August 1958: "Re-reading *Helen*, some quarter century later, or more, gave me an entirely new idea of this enigmatic drama. This play, in the light of history, the ill-fated Sicilian expedition, is one of the most poignant & devout of the series of the 'lost oracle,' making a trilogy with *Ion* and *Iphigenia*" ("Helen in Egypt" 18). H.D here again refers to Grégoire's reading of the *Helen* in the political context of Athens. Grégoire finds in it a reflection of Euripides' "émotion angoissée" at the catastrophe of the Sicilian expedition, his analysis of the "psychose du sacrilège" of the last phases of the Peloponnesian Wars, and his final affirmation of a divine *nous* in the speech of the priestess Theonoë (5:12, 14, 45).

H.D.'s response to Grégoire reflects some of the lines of her interpretation present from the beginning – the location of Euripides in the context of the "mysteries" and of political dissent – and it also clearly suggests her conception of Helen in *Helen in Egypt*. Moreover, H.D. in *Helen in Egypt* engages other more intricate themes of the *Helen*. Charles Segal has pointed to sets of oppositions in the play that very much correspond to those in H.D.'s poem. Perhaps the most important of these is a persistent questioning in the *Helen* of the relation between name and "real" presence (*onoma* and *soma*), between word or story and thing (*logos* and *pragma*), between image and truth (*eidolon* and *saphes*) (Segal, "Two Worlds" 224). These oppositions cannot be easily resolved into a Platonic distinction between false and true, bad and good, lustful and ideal Helens, as Chisholm proposes, the bad Helen the one who follows her own desires, the good Helen the one who submits to patriarchal codes (177). As critics have remarked, the play rather suggests a radical instability in the effort to discern the "true." Helen in the beginning doubts whether the story of Leda's rape is true – thus calling into question one of the myths constituting her own identity. The play swarms with language play upon derivatives of *eido*, to see, or to appear to be, or to know; *eiko*, to have the likeness of; and *dokeo*, to think or imagine, to seem or appear. While Helen herself tells Menelaus to trust appearances – he who has in fact been doing just that in trusting the false image – and to believe that her form (*eidos*) is truly Helen, the apparent form of Helen (*eidolon*) is vanishing, disclosing the "real" truth as she goes. As William Arrowsmith has observed, the dramatic effect of the play's contrasts and reversals "is the sense of something unstated or unresolved at the very heart of things, an ellipsis or enigma in reality itself" (xi).

Regardless of the way one interprets these philosophical themes, it is easy to see in simplest terms how Euripides' presentation of Helen would strike H.D. forcibly, how he would seem to her not a censor but a liberator. "All Greece hates . . . God's daughter, born of love": H.D. in "Helen" translates literally the line spoken by Teucer to Helen early in the play (line 81). Teucer is speaking about an *eidolon* of Helen that he mistakes as the truth; "Helen" is the illusory object, the projection, of a violent male eros. This is precisely the point of H.D.'s early poem. The human disaster of illusory male desire is undeniably the import of the *Helen*, an emphasis confirmed later in the *Iphigeneia in Aulis* where Euripides portrays the erotic violence of the Greek warriors. In "fact," Euripides claims, the Greeks fought the war over an illusion, and the name or image for which they fought, and which they have cursed, is not a true one, but comes from their own "diseased eyes" (line 575). Which is the more "real" Helen, according to Euripides: the flesh-and-blood one in Egypt or the unreal male projection in Troy, the cause of thousands of real deaths, a real devastated city, real human suffering? Euripides leaves that question open (Arrowsmith xi). However much one may disapprove of the too-conventional portrayal of Helen in the play, it is obvious that H.D. comprehends and enters into its skeptical critical framework, which allows her genuinely radical reversals of perspective.

The condemnation of male erotic violence in the *Helen* is confirmed in another theme delineated in Segal's study: the consistent distinction between the male world of violence, glory, possession, and war, and the female world of love, affiliation, and pity ("Two Worlds" 232). The whole war is fought over possession, but possession is illusory. Twice in the play the same circumlocution is used, first by Helen and then by the phantom Helen: "[Paris] imagines (*dokei*) he possesses me in an empty imagination (*kenen dokesin*), possessing me not" (lines 35–36); "[the Greeks] imagining (*dokountes*) that Paris possessed Helen, possessing [her] not" (611). This mode of illusory possession is tied to the typical violence and vanity of all the male figures of the play. Neither Menelaus nor Theoklymenos, the real or the would-be husband, each exclusively concerned with his own glory, can imagine any other mode of social negotiation than brutal action. In contrast, Helen and the priestess Theonoë, the sister of Theoklymenos, choose gestures of affection and pity that forestall or mitigate violence. Undoubtedly Euripides intends this structural opposition between male and female worlds, reiterated in other Trojan plays.

Another theme of the *Helen* also relates to the kind of transference H.D. here makes: the confusion in the play between living and dead (Segal, "Two Worlds" 247). Those believed dead are alive (Menelaus), those believed alive are dead (Leda). Menelaus when he first sees Helen imagines her to be a Hecatean phantom, a specter or ghost. And in many ways she is. She dwells in the tomb of Proteus in a state of limbo; the reiterated Eleusinian allusions connect her with Persephone, snatched away to Hades; she awaits deliverance and rebirth. But in order for Helen to emerge again, she undergoes an ambiguous ritual, which, as Foley has pointed out, is at once a marriage rite to the Hades bridegroom and a funeral rite for Menelaus (88). After this pretended ritual descent into death, both she and Menelaus escape from Egypt, reborn with their "true" identities.

Finally, the *Helen* suggests a configuration of divinities much in keeping with that in *Helen in Egypt*. Generally, the question of divine purposes – and of the possibility of knowing them – is as much a difficulty in this play as in others by Euripides. The chorus articulates this difficulty in a much-quoted passage (lines 1137–43):

> What is god, what is not god, what lies in between
> man and god? Who on this earth, after searching,
> can claim to have been
> to the end of that question's tortuous lane?
> For every man has seen
> the plans of the gods lurching
> here and there and back again
> in unexpected and absurd
> vicissitudes. (trans. Mitchie and Leach)

The nature of the gods is hidden in the apparent chaos of incalculable happenings. After pondering the fact that the name of Zeus's own daughter has unjustly been made into anathema, the chorus concludes, "I cannot grasp what the truth is" (lines 148–9).

This sense of anguish at the impenetrability of the divine veil is, however, mitigated by the framing divinities of the play: Proteus, the king/father/god at whose tomb the action of the play takes place; and Theonoë, his daughter, an oracular priestess (*mantes*) of his temple. The former is clearly associated with the authority of the dead, the latter with the pure heavens (*aether*). Theonoë, as Grégoire, Whitman, and others have pointed out, is a remarkable religious figure, "quite without parallel among the characters of extant Greek drama" (Whitman 53). Her original name, Eido, meaning "to see" or "to know," and her name as priestess, Theonoë, meaning "the mind of god," both allude to her special closeness to the gods. Apparently it is given to her to decide the issue of Helen's fate, now being debated on Olympus by the gods themselves. But this high authority to interpret the divine *nous* comes not from her office as oracle, or even from daimonic inspiration, but from her own integrity. In articulating this pivotal decision, according to Whitman, "[t]here is a controlled, though slightly tremulous, heroism in her words" (57). She says, "By nature and by will I love piety, I love myself, and will not stain my father's honor" (998–1000). Her authority comes from self-knowledge and a love of self that is inseparable from love of the gods and of the dead. H.D., I would suggest, borrows this divine framework in *Helen in Egypt*, situating Helen between Zeus/Proteus and the complex figure of Thetis, who is at once a kind of daughter of Proteus, a mother to both Achilles and Helen, and an image of Helen herself, as Helen comes gradually to realize the nature of the divine within herself. Helen like Theonoë by the end of the poem finds an oracular authority coming from self-knowledge, simultaneously a knowledge of the gods.

This brief treatment of Euripides' *Helen* suggests some of the matters at work in H.D.'s long-delayed response to the play. Friedman in particular has explored in some detail the opposition in *Helen in Egypt* between male and female worlds, the former identified with war, the latter with love, just as in Euripides; and she has also delineated the complex way in which H.D. here figures Helen's psychic descent and rebirth, similar to the Persephonean theme of the play. However, perhaps the most encompassing of the Euripidean themes in *Helen in Egypt* is its philosophical questioning, the theme of the *eidolon*, as this is related to the mystery of the gods.

Helen in Egypt begins like Euripides' *Helen* with questions about the name or image, *onoma* or *eidolon*, of Helen "hated by all Greece." It questions whether figures of the drama are "ghosts" (Hadean *eidola*), and the "action" is in large part composed of the phenomena of *eidola* in memory, in vision, or in divine manifestation (Achilles at the end is an *eidolon*, as is Thetis as Choragus). Moreover, *Helen in Egypt* ends with a focus on the *eidolon*/doll/idol of Thetis treasured by Achilles as a child and later figured on the masthead of his ships. This image was first suggested to H.D. by Euripides' *Iphigeneia in Aulis*, in which an *eikon* of a Nereid is on each of the Myrmidon ships: "On the prow of each / A goddess sheds gold: / Sea-spirits are cut in tiers of gold" (*Collected Poems* 74). The *eidolon* of Thetis herself, manifest at the end of "Pallinode" and again at the end of the poem, comes from Euripides' *Andromache*, which begins with Andromache at the temple of Thetis, having taken sanctuary there as Helen takes refuge in Proteus's tomb, and which ends with the appearance of the goddess as deus ex machina. Euripides is thus implicated in the complex eidetic play of *Helen in Egypt*.

In H.D.'s poem, this theme of the *eidolon* – of the relation of illusion to reality, dreaming to waking – is explored within the context of the most "*enigmatic question*" in Helen's lyric musings: "[W]hich was the dream, / which was the veil of Cytheraea?" (36). This question, which Achilles first asks Helen after their union in Egypt, seizes Helen's reflection and imagination. Though the commentator in "Pallinode" repeatedly insists on resolving the issue, it nevertheless remains a question for the lyric Helen throughout the other two sections of the poem. She circles around it in more or less pertinent evasions, and comes back to it repeatedly. This recurring question constitutes one of the "spiral" structures in the poem – or, in Adalaide Morris's concept, one of the "strange attractors," forming a pattern within the nonlinear generation of images ("Mythopoeic" 212–16). The question indeed becomes more and more implicated in the image of the spiral and of the "veil," both belonging to the protean goddess Thetis/Isis.

The very meaning of Achilles' question is in doubt, as is its answer. "What does he mean by that?" Helen asks with some irritation. *"What does he mean? She does not know. We do not know"* (37), the commentator remarks. In simple terms, do the two questions represent an opposition or an identity: the dream *or* the veil; the dream, *that is to say*, the veil? This issue is never really resolved, but evaded. Effectively, the question seems to call for a distinction between imaginary and real happening, the dream or veil in contrast to something "actual," with "reality." The commentator in "Pallinode" insists on such a distinction, positing repeatedly that Egypt and Helen's meeting with Achilles constitute the "dream," but her insistences are coercive: *" 'One kiss in the night?' That is obviously, the dream. Helen could have told him that"* (41); *" 'Which was the dream?' Surely, 'the deathless spark of Helena's wakening [with Achilles]' "* (42); *"The Dream? The Veil? Obviously, Helen has walked through time into another dimension"* (107). "[O]bviously," "Surely," "Obviously," are not indicators of how one is to interpret the lyrics (where things are very far from obvious and sure), but signs of the discomfort of the commentator herself, engaged in her own kind of quest, very different from that of the lyric Helen. As Middleton remarks: "The prose is not a character but a discursive truth-claim. The prose comes with the certainties of objective reason and truth, certainties that are neither embodied nor located, . . . The prose asks questions of embodiment" (359). However, Helen is less concerned with certainties and embodiment, and *if* she arrives at these, she does so in a dimension altogether different from that of the commentator.

Discriminations are made throughout the poem indicating different difficult-to-define stages in Helen's self-consciousness, and critics have rightly seen these in a Freudian psychotherapeutic context, in terms of the suppression, recovery, and working through of traumatic memories. But, finally, the distinction insisted upon here between dream or veil and *something else* presumably more real cannot be maintained in the poem: all is imaginary, all is real, all is dream, all is waking. Nor does this indicate a glib dissolution of boundaries, but rather a psychological insight to which the lyric Helen is faithful: everything *is* imaginary and the imaginary *is* real. One notes the contradiction in the commentator's remarks above: that the *dream* is *Helen's wakening*. Later in the poem Theseus tries to articulate the confusion: "[I]t was all a dream until Achilles came; // and this Achilles? / in a dream, he woke you, / you were awake in a dream" (157). Then this waking dream is apparently broken or suspended when Helen is transported to Leuké: but she was brought here in a dream (116), and the island belongs to the protean Thetis (117), a mistress and geneatrix of *eidola*. Is she dreaming on Leuké? No, apparently she is remembering, reliving "actual" memories. But are memories "actual" or imaginary? Apparently imaginary. Helen says regarding her earlier life with Paris: "I remember a dream that was real" (110). In "Eidolon" she again wakes up into a waking dream when she returns to Egypt (220).

The rephrasing of his original question, given by Achilles near the end of the first part of the poem, moves Helen beyond the lesser (personal) mysteries to the Greater Mystery, which finally resolves itself into a manifestation of the divine *nous* in the goddess Thetis:

> how are Helen in Egypt
> and Helen upon the ramparts,
> together yet separate?
>
> how have the paths met?
> how have the circles crossed?
> how phrase or how frame the problem? (63)

Achilles, unable even to frame the question, asks Helen to request the answer from the oracle – very likely that same oracle at Proteus's tomb as in Euripides' play. But Helen refuses to do so – needing like Theonoë to be herself, finally, the oracle of her destiny, reading its pattern and participating in its mysteries.

The mystery of the dream/veil is the encompassing mystery of Aphrodite/Thetis/Isis, the one who has woven the pattern of eros that Helen discovers through her enactments and remembrances. The "veil" is the "cloud" of Achilles' legions that surrounds Helen at the moment he will kill her, the "child" of their union sent by Aphrodite, which is Eros (41): "[I]t was they, the veil / that concealed yet revealed, / that reconciled him to me" (44). Helen's musings throughout the poem constitute a kind of archaeology of this ultimate union with Achilles. Thus, when in Leuké she remembers her flight from Sparta with Paris, she acknowledges that desire itself *is* and *is within* the generative motion of the veil: "[G]oing forward, my will was the wind, // (or the will of Aphrodite / filled the sail, as the story told / of my first rebellion; // the sail, they said, / was the veil of Aphrodite)" (109–10). The veil of Aphrodite and the arrow of Eros come together in the moment of Achilles' death: as he watches Helen on the ramparts, enchanted by her scarf fluttering in the breeze, he is mortally wounded by Paris's arrow, which, Helen insists, was really Love's arrow. In "Leuké" Helen is again associated with the veil, and increasingly also with the spiral, the image of the mystery introduced by Thetis at the end of "Pallinode." His last glimpse of Helen in Troy, Paris remembers, was of her tearing veil as she turned "at the stair head" (123). Helen and Aphrodite are overlaid in Paris's remembrance of a poor "torn garment, rent veil" that both of them wear (134, 145). Finally, this recognition of human poverty and vulnerability as well as immortality as aspects of Helen's identity is resolved in the concluding image of Thetis in "Eidolon," not only a goddess of beauty and desire, but of ordinary things, "the million personal things, / things remembered, forgotten" (289).

Helen's entrance to the Greater Mystery at the end comes in a final decipherment of her first meeting with Achilles, in which his desire for and resistance to

Helen hides remembrance of his mother, Thetis. Thus Helen enters into imagination of Achilles as a child, treasuring a doll/idol of Thetis. His longing for this absent figure signified in the imago on the masthead of his ship explains his restlessness and rage, explains also his fascination with Helen, leading to his death. This protean goddess weaves all *eidola* and desires; all desire, in DuPlessis's phrase, is "matri-sexual" (*Career* 114): "I say there is only one image, / one picture, though the swords flash; / I say there is one treasure, // one desire, as the wheels turn" (243). The dream and the veil are one in the metamorphic recurrent epiphanies of the gods within erotic experience.

The veil is the weaving of Proteus/Amen and Thetis/Isis, and the oracular authority of Helen, like that of Theonoë, comes from grasping that pattern within a love that simultaneously honors the gods and her own integrity. Though Helen identifies her early image with that of the virginal and innocent Iphigeneia, she finally achieves the kind of paradoxical purity of Theonoë, a spiritual wholeness, as Whitman describes it, that is the aftermath of grave experience "lived through in all its active and passive phases, and comprehended at last as the shape and token of one's being" (93).

In its pivotal images and themes, *Helen in Egypt* represents many decades of an intimate intertextual engagement with Euripides' *Helen*. This "enigmatic play" is for H.D. densely packed: it implicates a maternal territory of desire, a psychic process of encounter with the *eidola* of the dead, the Eleusinian pattern of descent and rebirth, and the figure of Helen herself opening the questions of the relation between war and desire, Eris and Eros. Its epistemological questioning in the context of a recognition of divine mysteries opens for H.D. the complex querying and weaving of this, her "later, little understood *Helen in Egypt*."

Appendix

Classical Texts in H.D.'s
Collected Poems, 1912–1944

―――――――――

This appendix presents a catalogue of the literary subtexts in H.D.'s *Collected Poems, 1912–1944*, edited by Louis L. Martz. Martz's edition includes her *Collected Poems* (1925), *Red Roses for Bronze* (1931), *Trilogy* (1944–6), as well as uncollected and unpublished poetry. Reference to specific classical texts is most frequent in H.D.'s early poetry, in *Sea Garden* (1916), *Hymen* (1921), and *Heliodora and Other Poems* (1923). One can trace some precedent classical text or texts in almost 70 percent of the hundred titles in *Collected Poems*. However, such references become increasingly rare after 1925, though broad allusions to classical myth continue in *Red Roses for Bronze*.

The first listing ("Descriptive Catalogue") follows the sequence of poems in Martz's edition, and it is divided into his designated sections. Poems in each section are given by the title in Martz, with page reference to Martz's edition. A note then gives the text or texts that H.D.'s poem engages, both primary classical texts and intermediary texts, where these are discernible. The note also refers to associated writing by H.D. and her circle. When the literary source of a poem has been identified by another critic, the note so indicates.

Some of these literary references are very precise – a certain epigram, fragment, or idyll, a certain passage from a narrative, even a certain line from a play. Other references are more broad, or the attribution more speculative. In approaching H.D.'s texts, I have noted not only conscious and deliberate allusion to other texts, but more generalized and covert interplay, within a range of texts that H.D. was likely to have known. I have tried to locate as many such traces as possible, in part to establish a "star map" of H.D.'s textual constellations. In order to give this overview, I have at times mentioned in the "Descriptive Catalogue" auxiliary or corollary texts from H.D.'s hellenic narratives – such as epigraphs of Moero and Antipater of Sidon in *Palimpsest*.

In referring to Greek texts I have followed standard numbering, using current editions from the Loeb Classical Library, unless otherwise indicated. For H.D.'s translations of Euripides and Homer in *Collected Poems*, I have given, for each section of H.D.'s version, the corresponding line numbers in the Greek texts, according to the Loeb editions (ed. Way for Euripides, ed. Murray for Homer). Omitted and significantly altered lines are also noted. All references to fragments of Sappho give where possible the numbering of the edition of Bergk – a standard at the turn of the century that Wharton follows – as well as the numbering in Lobel and Page (LP), a current standard. In references to the Greek Anthology, the numbering corresponds to that of the Loeb edition (ed. Paton). Translations from Sappho, the Greek Anthology, and Theocritus are taken from the editions that H.D. knew best: Wharton, Mackail, and Lang, respectively.

The second part of this appendix ("Summary by Author") presents a listing of classical texts referred to in the descriptive catalogue, arranged alphabetically according to author. As a kind of index to the first list, it indicates the predominant literary emphases within H.D.'s early hellenism. Under each author's name are listed the poems of H.D. suggesting a classical reference, along with the specific text or texts referred to.

A DESCRIPTIVE CATALOGUE BY POEM

Sea Garden (1916)

"The Helmsman" (5–7): Possibly Plato's *Phaedrus* 247c–d (*Dialogues* 3:154), which speaks of reason as the "pilot" of the soul; identified by Bruzzi, "Hieroglyphs" 42. Bruzzi (41) also suggests Plato's *Symposium* 202d–e (*Dialogues* 1:534), in the discussion there of Eros as a "daimon."

"The Shrine / ('She watches over the sea')" (7–10): The subtitle is a reference to Anyte of Tegea, *Palatine Anthology* 9.144, entitled in Mackail "The Shrine by the Sea." See also the translation by Aldington in the Poets' Translation Series, *The Poems of Anyte* (1915) 5; and by Ezra Pound, *Lustra* (1916) 113.

"Pursuit" (11–12): Lines 11–15 ("But here / a wild-hyacinth stalk is snapped") are an allusion to a Sapphic fragment, Bergk 94 (LP 105). Identified by Babcock, "Pursuit." Babcock also discusses an intermediary source, a translation of this Sapphic fragment by D. G. Rossetti. He cites H.D.'s comments on Rossetti's version, in her review of an edition of Sappho by Edwin Marion Cox ("Winter Roses"). See also Edward Storer's translation of this fragment in the Poets' Translation Series, *Poems and Fragments of Sappho* (1915) 7.

"The Contest" (12–14): Bruzzi ("Hieroglyphs" 41–2) points to the myth of the charioteer in Plato's *Phaedrus* 246a–e (*Dialogues* 3:153), associating this image with the discussion of the Delphic Charioteer in *Notes on Thought and Vision* (24–6). See "Secret Name," in *Palimpsest* (177, 190), for an indication of H.D.'s thorough awareness of Plato's trope of the charioteer.

"The Wind Sleepers" (15): There are two possible anthropological sources for this poem. One is Edward Burnett Tylor's concept of "nature-souls" propitiated in primitive religion (391). H.D. read Tylor's *Anthropology* at Bryn Mawr (Wallace, "Athene's Owl" 110). The second is the description of "wind-daimones" in Jane Ellen Harrison's *Prolegomena* (179–83).

"Huntress" (23): A possible echo of *Hippolytus* 215–22, 228–31, where Phaedra seems to be in the throes of an Artemisian frenzy. See H.D.'s translation of these lines, *Collected Poems* 88; and Swinburne's *Atalanta in Calydon*, the first chorus ("When the hounds of spring are on winter's traces").

"The Cliff Temple" (26–8): Part III of this poem ("Shall I hurl myself from here, / shall I leap and be nearer you?") is a possible echo of Ovid's *Heroides* 15 173–220, where Sappho contemplates hurling herself from the Leucadian cliff; a translation of this famous poem is included in Wharton's edition of Sappho, from which H.D. often draws. See also *Palatine Anthology* 6.251, an epigram by Philippus to Apollo, "who holdest the sheer steep of Leucas" (trans. Mackail).

"Orchard" (28–9): Dioscoros Zonas, *Palatine Anthology* 6.22. Given as anonymous in Paton. Retallack (70–1) first identified this source. See translation by Bryher in "Nine Epigrams of Zonas."

"Acon" (31–2): From "Acon," by Giovanni Battista Amalteo, a Neo-Latin Italian poet of the sixteenth century. See Aldington's translation from this poem, entitled "Hyella," in *Images* 26. In a letter from Norman Holmes Pearson to Thomas Burnett Swann, dated 8 February 1960, Pearson reports H.D.'s remarks about this poem: "I think *Acon* was title of a poem in a *Renaissance* Latin anthology that Ezra gave me in the very early days. I think he suggested that I translate. It was beautiful and *easy* Latin."

"Night" (33): This poem, which personifies night as the cause of the progressive, relentless, and almost mechanical disintegration of the flower, ending with images of isolation and vulnerability, finds a gloss in a Sapphic fragment, Bergk 52 (LP 168B): "The moon has set, and the Pleiades; it is midnight, the time is going by, and I sleep alone" (trans. Wharton).

"Storm" (36): This poem may be considered an adaptation of a Sapphic fragment, Bergk 42 (LP 47): "Now Eros shakes my soul, a wind on the mountain falling on the oaks" (trans. Wharton).

"Sea Iris" (36–7): The reference to "murex-fishers" in the second part of the poem may be associated with a line from a poem by Robert Browning ("Popularity"), "Who fished the murex up?" The line serves as a subtitle to the second part of *Palimpsest* and appears in the narrative frequently (95, 157, and passim). Kloepfer (115) was the first to identify this quotation.

"Hermes of the Ways" (37–9): Anyte of Tegea, *Palatine Anthology* 9.314. Identified by Swann (85n). Babcock ("Verses" 205–6) suggests another anonymous epigram (10.12) that bears the title "Hermes of the Ways" in Mackail's edition. See also the translation of Anyte by Aldington in the Poets' Translation Series, *Anyte* 5.

"Pear Tree" (39): In lines 3 and 6 there is a possible echo of Sapphic fragment Bergk 37 (LP 52): "I do not think to touch the sky with my two arms" (trans. Wharton).

"Cities" (39–42): Though there are no specific classical references in this poem, Maurice Maeterlinck's *La vie des abeilles* is clearly a subtext; see especially chap. 3, "La fondation de la cité," describing the construction of a new hive in a desolate place after abandonment of the orderly old hive. Hermione in *Hermione* (61) mentions reading this book in French, which was brought to her by her fiancé George Lowndes (Pound).

The God (1913–1917)

"Adonis" (47–8): The classical contexts of this poem include Bion's "Lament for Adonis," Theocritus's Idylls 15 and 30 (attributed to Theocritus in Lang), and two fragments of Sappho, Bergk 62 and 63 (LP 140a and 168). H.D.'s focus on the leaves of winter may allude to Bion's poem, describing Adonis's death in the forest, his body lying on a bed of leaves. See Bryher's translation of *The Lament for Adonis* (1918). A source from another quarter might be *The Golden Bough* of Sir James George Frazer, who discusses Adonis prominently in terms of the natural cycles of life and death. The most influential portion of *The Golden Bough* for modern writers was *Adonis, Attis, Osiris*, first published in 1906 and appearing in 1914 in the twelve-volume third edition. The festivals of Adonis were in midsummer, at the change into the waning cycle of the seasons leading to winter. Swann (94–5) interprets Adonis here as a fertility god.

"Pygmalion" (48–50): The story of Pygmalion is told in Ovid's *Metamorphoses* 10.243–97. The Pygmalion theme was commonplace in the last half of the nineteenth century; although H.D. undoubtedly knew the story from Ovid, very few of her emphases correspond to his.

"Eurydice" (51–5): The story of Orpheus and Eurydice is told in Ovid's *Metamorphoses* 10.1–63. H.D.'s version, as many have remarked, constitutes a deliberate revision of her sources, in dramatizing the perspective of Eurydice at the moment of Orpheus's turning back to behold her, thus committing her again to the underworld.

"Moonrise" (56): The choral "we" singing in attendance upon a goddess associated with the moon suggests Sappho, Bergk 53 (LP 154): "The moon rose full, and the women stood as though around an altar" (trans. Wharton).

"Orion Dead" (56–7): There are many myths about the relation between Orion and Artemis, but H.D. seems to hold to a version similar to that in Hesiod, that Orion hunted in company with Artemis and Leto, until, after threatening to kill all the animals, he was killed by a scorpion sent by Earth (*Astronomy 4*, in *Hesiod*, Loeb ed.). See H.D.'s remarks in *Notes on Thought and Vision*: "But when there was a question of Artemis losing caste by her association with the too boorish giant, Orion, the giant was slain" (38). A specific literary subtext may be present in the line "So arise and face me" – Sapphic fragment Bergk 29 (LP 138), "Stand face to face, friend . . . and unveil the grace in thine eyes" (trans. Wharton).

"Hermonax" (57–8): Antipater of Sidon, *Palatine Anthology* 6.223. See also another epigram by Philodemus (6.349) that in Mackail bears the title "To the Gods of the Sea and Weather" and refers also to Palemon and Ino as Melicerta and Leucothea, as well as to other sea gods. The beginning of H.D.'s poem seems to allude to this epigram in that it invokes all sea gods and hints at the myth of the metamorphosis of Ino and Melicerta into sea deities: "Ino, / leaving warm meads / for the green, grey-green fastnesses / of the great deeps." This epigram by Philodemus also refers to Leucothea as *glauke*, gray-green, as in H.D.'s lines.

"Sitalkas" (58): This poem layers allusions to Apollo in little-known aspects. In a letter to Swann (8 February 1960), Pearson reports H.D.'s remarks about this poem: "I thought *Sitalkas* was an autumn sun-god but I can't find a reference. I do find Argestes – (vent) qui blanchit le ciel (de nuages)." The only reference to Sitalkas that I have been able to locate is in Pausanias (10.15.2), who mentions a statue to Apollo Sitalkas [protector of corn] at Delphi (identified by Swann 83). The phrase "any cool god / in a chamber under / Lycia's far coast" refers to the myth that Delian Apollo in the winter months retired to his temple at Patara in Lycia (on the Asian coast); Lycia was called *hiberna* because of Apollo's winter retreat there. The poem also, more obliquely, alludes to Delphian Apollo's winter withdrawal to the far north, among the Hyperboreans. *Argestes*, originally an epithet of Zephyros, by the fourth century B.C. (e.g., in Aristotle and Theophrastus) was known as the northwest wind, coming especially in the autumn (see Theophrastus, *Concerning Weather Signs* 35–7). It is a fresh, cleansing wind that brightens or whitens the sky. In this poem, which gives a Delphic title of Apollo and alludes to the Lycian "cool god," Argestes becomes yet another sign of an autumn, Hyperborean Apollo. A passage in *Asphodel* throws light on this poem; Hermione, speaking of Vérène, the fiancée of Walter Dowell [Rummell], says, "The wind had ruffled her petal, the lordly king-wind had stooped from the North, had swept down from the cold irradiance of glaciers to embrace her" (99).

Translations (1915–1920)

"From the *Iphigeneia in Aulis* of Euripides" (71–84):
- I. Chorus: 164–302
- II. Chorus: 573–97 (543–72 omitted)
- III. Chorus: 751–800
- IV. Chorus: 1036–97
- V. Iphigeneia: 1279–1335
    - 1311–12: given to Chorus
    - 1313–14: omitted
    - 1315–19: significant alteration
- VI. Dialogue Iphigeneia and Chorus: 1467–1531

"From the *Hippolytus* of Euripides" (85–93)
- I. Chorus: 61–9
    - Hippolytus: 70–87 (79–81, 85–7 omitted)
- II. Chorus: 121–60 (161–75 omitted)
- III. Phaedra and Nurse: 198–231
- IV. Chorus: 525–64
- V. Chorus: 732–75
- VI. Chorus: 1120–50 (1102–19 omitted)
- VII. Chorus: 1267–82

"*Odyssey*" (93–8): 1.1–98

Hymen (1921)

"They Said" (101): The last lines of the poem (violets glowing "gold and purple and red / where her feet tread") allude to the myth of Persephone, by way of a tale of Nathaniel Hawthorne, "The Pomegranate Seeds," in *Tanglewood Tales*, a collection that H.D. read as a child (Swann 10).

"Hymen" (101–10): The songs of this masque allude to a long classical epithalamic tradition, including many fragments of Sappho, Idyll 18 of Theocritus (Helen's nuptial), and Odes 61 and 62 of Catullus.

One may find in the first song, "From the closed garden," a possible reference to several epithalamic fragments of Sappho praising the bride and bridegroom (Bergk 103, 105; LP 117, 116) and mentioning the "cry of Hymen" (Bergk 91, 107; LP 111), and to another fragment (Bergk 133, not in LP) that urges the bride to go to the marriage bed "honouring Hera of the silver throne, goddess of marriage" (trans. Wharton).

The second song, "Where the first crocus buds unfold," giving the image of "very little girls" gathering golden flowers, may have two Sapphic fragments as subtexts: Bergk 121 (LP 122): "A maiden [*pais*: child] full tender plucking flowers" (trans. Wharton); and Bergk 85 (LP 132): "I have a fair daughter [*pais*] with a form like a golden flower, Cleïs the beloved" (trans. Wharton).

In the third song, "Never more will the wind," one finds a specific allusion to Sappho, Bergk 109 (LP 114), a lament over lost virginity: "Never again will I come to thee, never again" (trans. Wharton).

In the fourth song, "Between the hollows / Of the little hills," there is possible reference to two Sapphic fragments. In its reference to scattered hyacinths, it may refer to Bergk 94 (LP 105). The address to the bride as "Lady, our love, our dear, / Our bride most fair" suggests Bergk 93 (LP 108): "O fair, O lovely" (trans. Wharton). The same phrase in Greek (*o kale, o chariessa*) is used in Theocritus, Idyll 18.38; moreover, there is here specific allusion to Theocritus, Idyll 18.1–6, the song of twelve Spartan maidens bearing hyacinths.

The fifth song, "But of her / Who can say if she is fair?" gathers images from epithalamia of Sappho, Theocritus, and Catullus. The images of the bride's "blanched face" and of "desire . . . caught in her eyes" echoes Sapphic fragment Bergk 100 (LP 112): "And a soft [paleness] is spread over the lovely face"; "and thine eyes . . . honeyed, and love is spread over thy fair face" (trans. Wharton). Theocritus may be imitating the same image from Sappho in his epithalamion to Helen, "within whose eyes dwell all the Loves" (Idyll 18.37, trans. Lang). This song, "But of her," also appears to suggest many lines of Catullus 61. One may compare, for instance, his lines 6–10 – "put on the marriage veil, hither, hither merrily come, wearing on thy snow-white foot the yellow shoe" (trans. Cornish) – with H.D.'s lines: "We fastened the veil, / And over the white foot / Drew on the painted shoe."

I find no specific literary allusion in the sixth song, "Along the yellow sand."

The seventh song, "From citron-bower be her bed," again echoes Sappho's fragments on the loss of virginity, Bergk 102 and 108 (LP 107 and 114); Wharton's translation of *parthenia* in these fragments as "maidenhood," as echoed in the last lines of H.D.'s poem "for losing of her maidenhood," particularly suggests H.D.'s reading of Wharton's Sappho.

Another Sapphic fragment is echoed in the headnote to the eighth song, "The crimson cover of her bed." In Bergk 64 (LP 54), Eros is described as "[c]oming from heaven wearing a purple mantle" (trans. Wharton), as here the figure of winged Hymen/Eros is elaborately purple.

Finally, in the last song, "Where love is king," the claim that before Love "[o]ur limbs are numb. . . . Our lips are mute and dumb" echoes at least two famous fragments of Sappho likening the coming of Eros to terror and death:

Bergk 40 (LP 130), "Now Love masters my limbs and shakes me, fatal creature, bitter-sweet" (trans. Wharton); and Bergk 2 (LP 31), "For when I see thee but a little, I have no utterance left, my tongue is broken down, . . . with my eyes I have no sight, my ears ring, sweat pours down, and a trembling seizes all my body" (trans. Wharton).

Besides these literary allusions, the headnotes to the poems of the masque allude to well-known Greek religious festivals, which H.D. may have known through various sources, including Pausanias, essays of Pater and Symonds, and Farnell's *Cults of the Greek States*. Some of the festivals clearly echoed in "Hymen" include a ritual at Elis in honor of Hera; the Brauronian ritual of initiation, for very young girls (five to ten years old), in honor of Artemis as bear-goddess; the Cheilidonia, a Rhodian spring festival centering upon a procession of children singing a "swallow song"; the Hyacinthia, in honor of Apollo, involving young boys and girls in puberty; the Daphnephoria, involving a chorus of maidens and a young boy carrying laurel in honor of Apollo in his aspect as sun god; and the Panathenaic festival in honor of Athene, involving young marriageable women carrying the woven veil of the temple goddess. There are also references to popular Greek artifacts, known to H.D. through visits to European museums: a chryselephantine statue, medallions, a temple frieze (Elgin marbles), and Tanagra statuettes.

"Demeter" (111–15): The statue speaking here is probably the Demeter of Cnidus, in the British Museum. It is discussed in Pater's essay on Demeter and Persephone (*Greek Studies* 150–2).

"Simaetha" (115–16): Theocritus, Idyll 2. Identified by Swann 60.

"Thetis" (116–18): Ovid, *Metamorphoses* 11.229–37. The first two parts of this poem (the only ones ever published by H.D. herself) follow very closely the passage in Ovid. Gregory, "Ovid," examines H.D.'s complex intertextual play with Ovid in this poem.

"Circe" (118–20): Homer, *Odyssey* 10.210–19, the description of Circe's palace surrounded by enchanted beasts.

"Leda" (120–1): This poem recalls images from Euripides' *Helen* and H.D.'s commentary on this play in her "Notes on Euripides, Pausanius, and Greek Lyric Poets." The place where "the slow river / meets the tide" is the setting of the play as H.D. imagines it; it begins with Helen's story of the ravishment of Leda. Moreover, a configuration of images from the first choral ode (179–90) is clearly echoed here. In this ode the women speak of washing purple robes in the river, beneath the blaze of the golden sun, a confirmation of images suggested in the poem, "the deep purple / of the dying heat . . . the level ray of sun-beam . . . flecked with richer gold."

"Hippolytus Temporizes" (121–2): Euripides, *Hippolytus*, particularly Hippolytus's opening prayer to Artemis (70–87), and also his vision of Artemis as he is dying (1391–3). See also H.D.'s translation of the former lines, in *Collected Poems* 85. Also, the conception of Hippolytus's erotic confusion owes much to Pater's version of the story in "Hippolytus Veiled" (*Greek Studies* 157–94).

"Cuckoo Song" (122–4): The reference to Calypso and specifically to burning cedar wood suggests Homer, *Odyssey* 5.59–62.

"The Islands" (124–7): The catalogue of islands recalls the catalogue of ships in Homer, *Iliad* 2.494–760.

"At Baia" (128): This poem possibly alludes to a well-known comment by Horace (*Epistles* 1.1.83) about the Roman resort of Baiae near Naples: "Nothing on earth . . . like the exquisite Bay of Baiae for light" (trans. Passage). However, the notoriety of Baiae as a place of sensuality and excess may also be implicit in H.D.'s poem, and in this regard she may echo Propertius 1.11. In Propertius's elegy Baiae is a place of seductions and betrayals where vows are forgotten, where "all love's advances give cause for fear": these are shores which "to many a loving pair shall . . . bring severance" (trans. Butler). H.D.'s "At Baia" apparently points to a rejection of such sensual dangers in favor of a more subtle "perilousness."

"Sea Heroes" (129–30): The catalogue of heroes here – lines 7–26 of H.D.'s poem – takes its names from those of the Phaiakian sailors in Homer, *Odyssey* 8.111–19. All of the names in H.D.'s poem come from the passage in Homer, though with some mistakes (or modifications) in transliteration. H.D. may have chosen this passage because all the names have nautical significance. Amphialos means "sea-girt," Okyalos "swift-sea," Anabesineos "embarking ship," Klytoneos "ship-builder," and so on. H.D. plays on the nautical names in a complex way, but not apparently in an effort at literal translation. Some of the epithets in her poem correspond at least obliquely to the literal meaning of the names in Homer: Akroneos as "helm-of-boat" (top-ship); Nauteus as "sea-man"; Agchialos as "sea-girt" (near-the-sea); Elatreus as "oar-shaft" (rower); Eurualos as "broad sea-wrack" (wide-sea); Ooos [Thoon] as "swift" (swift). H.D. here, as in "The Islands," also alludes to the catalogue of ships and heroes in Homer's *Iliad* 2.

"Fragment 113 / 'Neither honey nor the bee for me' – Sappho" (131–2): The numbering (following Bergk) and the translation in the subtitle are from Wharton. The fragment is LP 146.

"Evadne" (132): Pindar, Olympian Odes 6.29–35. Identified by Swann (66).

"Song" (133): There would appear to be an oblique reference to Callimachus, "Hymn to Apollo" (*Hymns* 2.32–41). Callimachus elaborates Apollo's goldenness and the fragrance of his hair.

"Why Have You Sought?" (133–4): The reference in the last lines to Achilles suggests a specific but ambiguous context: "Love, why have you sought the horde / of spearsmen, why the tent / Achilles pitched beside the river-ford?" An obvious source is the *Iliad*, where Achilles' tents are indeed closest to the river Xanthos. But Eros is not generally associated with Achilles the warrior. Also the poem mentions "Greece" and "Grecian porticoes," not Troy. The lines may allude obliquely to *Iphigeneia in Aulis*, where the tents of the Greeks are pitched by the strait of Euripos; if this is so, then the love that comes to Achilles here is for Iphigeneia, whom he finally desires to marry. The context of the poem, however, focusing on Eros's intimacy with his mother Aphrodite in heaven, suggests as well Achilles' relation to his immortal mother Thetis.

"White World" (134–5): This poem may refer obliquely to Callimachus, *Hymns* 6.118–23, the hymn to Demeter, as translated by Pater: "As the four white horses draw her sacred basket, so will the great goddess bring us a *white* spring, a *white* summer" (*Greek Studies* 127; emphasis in Pater). This possible Demetrian connotation of the poem is reinforced by an echo of Lawrence's *Aaron's Rod* (1922) pointed out by Gary Burnett ("Two Allusions" 32–3). Burnett quotes a passage describing the belief of Aaron's wife Lottie in her cosmic maternal role, which was "the substantial and professed belief of the whole white world" (169). "The Whole White World," the first phrase of the poem, is the title of H.D.'s poem first appearing in *Hymen* (1921). Burnett suggests that Lawrence is here responding to H.D., rather than H.D. to Lawrence. In Chapter Five I discuss this poem in terms of the typical landscape of Theocritus.

"Phaedra" (135–6): The original source is Euripides' *Hippolytus*, choruses from which H.D. had translated immediately before writing this poem and the other two in this sequence. However, the conception of Phaedra comes from Swinburne's "Phaedra" (1:27–33) and Pater's "Hippolytus Veiled," *Greek Studies* 157–94.

"She Contrasts with Herself Hippolyta" (136–8): See the note to "Phaedra." Hippolytus's mother is unnamed in Euripides and named Antiope in Pater, but the Amazon queen Hippolyta appears in Shakespeare's *A Midsummer Night's Dream*, in Walter Savage Landor's "Theseus and Hippolyta," and Swinburne's "Phaedra." Another specific reference to Swinburne's "Phaedra" is present in the image of the sword in connection with the conception of Hippolytus. Swinburne's lines read: "Hippolyta, / That had the spear to father, . . . Even she did bear thee, thinking of a sword" (1:29). The reference to Pater is also very specific, as H.D.'s Phaedra imagines Hippolyta's sensing her child in the womb. Pater says, "In the wild Amazon's soul, to her surprise, and at first against her will, the maternal sense had quickened from the moment of his conception" (*Greek Studies* 169–70).

"She Rebukes Hippolyta" (138–40): For the images of Hippolyta in the abandon of the chase, see the passages from *Hippolytus* noted for "Huntress."

"Egypt / (To E. A. Poe)" (140–1): The last stanza – referring to "wisdom's glance, / the grey eyes following / in the mid-most desert – / great shaft of rose" – alludes to the last choral ode of Euripides' *Helen* (1451–1511). There, as Menelaus and Helen escape, the chorus of Greek women enslaved in Egypt imagines a flock of birds flying over the Nile delta, where life springs out of the desert, homeward to Greece, to the temples of Pallas and Phoebus. H.D. in the unpublished "Notes on Euripides" describes the Egyptian land of Euripides' *Helen* as an intense rose color, and she emphasizes throughout the brilliance and severity of the Egyptian desert. Though Poe is evoked in the subtitle, the text or texts alluded to are difficult to trace; see his lyrics "Dream-Land," "The Sleeper," and "A Dream within a Dream" – all suggesting a narcotic experience of the kind that H.D. relates in "Egypt." See also the peculiar story "Silence: A Fable," set in Libya or Egypt. There may also be an oblique allusion to one of H.D.'s favorite poems, "To Helen," in the general movement of "Egypt" from desperation to a homecoming or rebirth, associated with Greece.

"Prayer" (141–2): The description of the work of armor suggests the images of Hephaestus's craft in the *Iliad* 18.478–608. See also Pater's description of the bases of Greek art in metal hammerwork, describing the shield of Achilles in particular (*Greek Studies* 207–8, 211–12).

"Helios" (142–3): In speaking of Helios's power to "break with a light touch / mayhap the steel set to protect," H.D. alludes to the *Iliad* 16.786–804, where Apollo strips Patrokles of armor.

Heliodora (1924)

"Lais" (149–50): Plato, *Palatine Anthology* 6.1. H.D. quotes this poem in *Notes on Thought and Vision* (32–3) and in *Hedylus* (12 and passim). H.D. also frequently quotes another epigram of Plato (*Palatine Anthology* 7.670) in Shelley's translation (epigraph to "Adonais"): "Thou wert the morning star among the living, / Ere thy fair light had fled; – / Now, having died, thou art as Hesperus, giving / New spendour to the dead" (Shelley 720; *Paint It Today* 12 and passim; "The Wise Sappho," in *Notes on Thought and Vision* 68).

"Heliodora" (151–4): Meleager, *Palatine Anthology* 5.144, 147. Paton's translation of the fragments appears to be a subtext in H.D.'s poem; identified by Davis 153–5. See the translation of these fragments by Richard Aldington in the Poets' Translation Series, *The Poems of Meleager of Gadara* (1920) 8, 9.

"Helen" (154–5): Euripides, *Helen* 81. In H.D.'s edition of Euripides' plays translated by Theodore Buckley, she underlined this line of *Helen* (translated by Buckley [201], "for all Greece hates the daughter of Jove"); and on the back covers of this volume she wrote what is apparently the first draft of "Helen"; see Friedman, "Serendipity," for a transcription of this draft.

"Nossis" (155–7): This poem is cast as a dialogue with Meleager as he is in the process of assembling his anthology. It includes translations from Meleager's proem to the *Garland* (*Palatine Anthology* 4.1.1–10) and from Nossis, *Palatine Anthology* 5.170. Identified by Davis 150–51. Aldington translates Meleager's proem in his translation of Meleager's poems (*Meleager* 5–6). Moero is mentioned in the Proem along with Nossis and Sappho as part of Meleager's *Garland*. Hipparchia in *Palimpsest* (71 and passim) is translating Moero's epigram, "You rest upon a golden bed, / in Aphrodite's golden house," *Palatine Anthology* 6.119.

"Thetis" (159–63): This poem alludes to the epiphany of Thetis in Euripides' *Andromache* 1249–62. In that passage Thetis speaks of making Peleus immortal as a sea god and of seeing Achilles after his death, on the White Island in the Euxine Sea. In H.D.'s poem, Thetis speaks of putting away Peleus and seeking her son's footprint on the white beach.

"At Ithaca" (163–4): This poem is based on the image from the *Odyssey* of Penelope's weaving and unweaving a robe (supposedly a shroud for Laertes), putting off her suitors while waiting for Odysseus to return; see *Odyssey* 2.104–9.

"Fragment Thirty-six / *I know not what to do: / my mind is divided* – Sappho" (165–8): The numbering (following Bergk) and the translation of the fragment in the subtitle are from Wharton. This fragment is LP 51.

"Cassandra / *O Hymen king*" (169–71): The phrase in the subtitle is from Euripides' *Trojan Women* 307–14. The poem alludes to Cassandra's ironic hymn to Hymen when learning of her bondage to Agamemnon and foreseeing her fate as an agent of retribution. In Euripides' play Hymen and Phoebus Apollo are ironically conflated, as they are here, in H.D.'s poem.

"Epigrams" (172): Lines from the second of these epigrams ("Love has no charm / when Love is swept to earth . . . [Love is a] god up-darting, / winged for passionate flight") may refer to Plato, *Phaedrus* 246a–e (*Dialogues* 3:153), where, in the context of a discussion of Eros, Socrates speaks of the soul in the image of a chariot with a mortal and an immortal horse: the immortal steed of the chariot is winged and soars high, but the mortal has shed its wings and descends into an earthly body. See "Secret Name," in *Palimpsest* (177, 190), for an indication of H.D.'s thorough awareness of Plato's trope.

"Fragment Forty / *Love . . . bitter-sweet* – Sappho" (173–5): The numbering (following Bergk) and the translation of the fragment in the subtitle are from Wharton. This fragment is LP 130. The poem, in elaborating the "fire / spilt from Hesperus," alludes to fragments of Sappho; see Bergk 95 and 133 (LP 104).

"Toward the Piraeus" (175–9): The reference in the title to the Piraeus, the large harbor outside of Athens, seems in the poem to have a military significance. The route to the Piraeus was heavily defended with walls and towers during the Peloponnesian Wars, and the Athenian fleet was moored there. Thus the title would give a specific context to the militant hellenism of the opening of the poem and its language of warriors and weapons.

"At Eleusis" (179–80): The conception of the Eleusinian ritual in this poem, I have suggested in Chapter Four, indicates an Orphic reading, such as that in Harrison's *Prolegomena*.

"Fragment Forty-one / . . . *thou flittest to Andromeda* – Sappho" (181–4): The numbering (following Bergk) and the translation of the fragment in the subtitle are from Wharton. This fragment is LP 131.

"Telesila" (184–7): The epigraph is paraphrased from Pausanias 2.20.8. Identified by Swann (66).

"Fragment Sixty-eight / . . . *even in the house of Hades* – Sappho" (187–9): The numbering (following Bergk) and the translation of the fragment in the subtitle are from Wharton. This fragment is LP 55.

"Charioteer" (190–7): H.D. informed Swann in a letter in 1960 that this poem "was inspired by the Louvre replica of the [Charioteer at Delphi]" and that the "epigraph to her poem, which would seem to indicate the inspiration of an ancient author, is her own invention" (Swann 98n). In H.D.'s epigraph, the statue is described (in Baedekeresque manner) as though in its place at the museum at Delphi, which H.D. had not at this time visited. However, the location of the statue given in the epigraph – "*mid-way in the hall of laurels . . . between the Siphnians' offering and the famous tripod of Naxos*" – does not correspond with the location of artifacts given in the Baedeker guide (fourth edition, 1909) that H.D. possessed at this time. With regard to the Charioteer at Delphi, see also "The Contest" (12–14) and *Notes on Thought and Vision* (24–6).

With regard to other subtexts, Althaia is the name of the famous Aetolian queen, mother of Meleager, who is the slayer of the Calydonian Boar (see Swinburne's *Atalanta at Calydon*); in an ambiguous passage she seems to be imagined here as the mother of the (female?) speaker and her brother, who might then be Meleager.

The names of the horses in this poem come from Pausanias or from Farnell's *Cults of the Greek States*, both of which H.D. was reading at the time of the composition of the poem in spring 1920. (A draft of the poem survives written on stationery from a hotel in Mullion Cove, Cornwall, the same used in correspondence from May 1920.) Alea is an Arcadian cult title of Athene as goddess of light and air (Pausanias 8.4.8); Elaphia, an Elean cult title of Artemis as deer-goddess (Pausanias 6.22.10–11); Daphnaia, a Laconian cult title of Artemis as tree-goddess (Pausanias 3.24.8–9); and Orea, a cult title of Demeter as mountain-mother (Farnell 3:32). These titles all represent the Peloponnese (Arcadia, Elis, Laconia), with its wild natural landscape, although the mythical Althaia is not Peloponnesian. All of these cult titles are listed in the index in volume 5 of Farnell.

"The Look-out" (197–201): Lynceus was one of the sailors on the *Argo*, known, according to Apollonius of Rhodes, for his keenness of vision (*Argonautica* 1.151–5); he has the legendary reputation here and elsewhere for supernatural powers of sight. The heroic voyage of the *Argo* and the heroic endurance of the seer would appear to be the contexts of the poem, since Lynceus is here imagined as the helmsman of a ship. Swann identifies Lynceus as one of the Argonauts (104).

"*From the Masque* / Hyacinth" (201–6): Allusion to the Hyacinth story in H.D.'s writing is ubiquitous, as indeed it is in classical myth. Prominent versions of the story for H.D. are Ovid's *Metamorphoses* 10.162–219 and Pater, "Apollo in Picardy" (*Miscellaneous Studies* 142–71). In this poem there appears to be no specific literary reference. The title "From the Masque" may suggest a Renaissance-style obliquity or allegory in the mythical play within this poem.

"*The Bird-Choros of / Ion*" (206–8): Euripides' *Ion* 154–83. An earlier version of this chorus and translations of other portions of the play appear in H.D.'s essay on the *Ion* in "Notes on Euripides, Pausanius, and Greek Lyric Poets," published as an appendix to the Black Swan edition of H.D.'s *Ion* 134–48; it of course appears as well in her translation of the whole play (20–3).

Red Roses for Bronze (1931)

"Red Roses for Bronze" (211–15): The speaker of this poem is identifiable as the Athenian sculptor Phidias, who resided in voluntary exile at Olympia in Elis after successful completion in Athens of the Parthenon and the gigantic statue of Athene within it. In Olympia he worked on an even greater statue of Zeus. Pausanias (5.15.1) noted the workshop or studio of Phidias near the sacred grove (the Altis) surrounding the temple of Zeus at Olympia (the Olympieum); it is still today pointed out to tourists. Pausanias also mentions Phidias's young athlete-lover, Pantarces, and one of the athletic sculptures Pausanias records at Olympia – a young man tying a fillet around his head – was thought to be an image of this boy (6.10.6, 5.11.3). In H.D.'s poem the sculptor, erotically and aesthetically drawn to a young athlete, invites him to his "studio / near the Olympieum" (Phidias's workshop), to finish the work he has begun, "the tall god standing / where the race is run" (the enormous statue of Olympian Zeus, possibly). Phidias's statue of Zeus was chryselephantine, though he also worked in marble and bronze; H.D.'s sculptor works in bronze.

"If You Will Let Me Sing" (222): The story of Apollo and Daphne is told in Ovid's *Metamorphoses* 1.452–567; of Apollo and Hyacinth in 10.162–219.

"Choros Translations / from *The Bacchae*" (223–31):
   I. Chorus: 68–87 (64–7, 88–104 omitted)
  II. Chorus: 105–19 (120–34 omitted)
 III. Chorus: 135–65
 IV. Chorus: Strophe: 862–81
             Antistrophe: 882–901
             Epode: 902–11
  V. Chorus: Strophe: 977–96 (antistrophe and epode, 997–1023, omitted)
 VI. Agave: 1381–7

Versions of these choruses appear in H.D.'s essay on the *Bacchae* in "Notes on Euripides, Pausanius, and Greek Lyric Poets." A French translation of the *Bacchae* by Mario Meunier (*Les bacchantes* [Paris: Payot, 1923]) provided the basis for translations of the choruses in the essay and here in *Red Roses for Bronze*. In her copy of Meunier's book (at Yale), H.D. notes on the half-title page the correspondence between pages of his text and of *Red Roses*.

"Sea-Choros / from *Hecuba*" (237–41): Euripides, *Hecuba* 444–83. This chorus is being translated by Hipparchia in *Palimpsest* (73 and passim).

"Wine Bowl" (241–3): This poem recollects Theocritus, Idyll 1.29–56, in the extended image of the elaborately crafted wine bowl that opens the idyll.

"Trance" (244–5): Though classical names of a king and his bride – Enydicus and Lycidoë – are given here, I have been unable to locate a specific textual reference.

"Myrtle Bough / *'I'll wreathe my sword in a myrtle-bough'* – Harmodius and Aristogiton" (245–52): The poem is an elaboration of the "Harmodius Song," a famous Athenian drinking song by Callistratus (Campbell 5: frag. 895). Identified by Swann (102).

"Choros Sequence / from *Morpheus* / *'Dream – dark-winged'*" (253–70): The title and the images in the poem certainly recall the description of the kingdom of Somnia and of the god Morpheus in Ovid's *Metamorphoses* 11.592–652. The subtitle is possibly from a Sapphic fragment (LP 63) first published in 1922, and later in a 1925 edition of Sappho by Edgar Lobel (pp. 28–9).

"Halcyon / *'Bird – loved of sea-men'*" (270–7): Out of many references to the halcyon in Greek poetry, I have not been able to locate the exact quotation in the subtitle. However, see Theocritus, Idyll 7.57–60: "The halcyons will lull the waves, and lull the deep, . . . the halcyons that are dearest to the green-haired mermaids [Nereids]" (trans. Lang). The poem itself, in the description of the young girl addressed by the speaker as a graceless child, with "only those small, small hands, / funny little gestures . . . a figure under-small" – suggests allusion to Sapphic fragment Bergk 34 (LP 49): "A slight and ill-favored child thou didst seem to me" (trans. Wharton). This possible allusion to Sappho was first suggested by Swann (34).

"Songs from Cyprus" (277–81): Cyprus is the traditional birthplace of Aphrodite, who would appear to be the goddess alluded to in the poem, figured as the Great Mother. In part 4 of this series ("Where is the nightingale") there may be a reference to a choral ode in *Helen* 1107–16, to which H.D. refers in her essay on the play in "Notes on Euripides." These are H.D.'s remarks on that chorus: "It is to a bird, they call; . . . to a small familiar loving spirit, one whose voice calls them home, back to the woods, veiling the elements and fire and strength of the earth, the kind woods, tender as a lover's arms after the fire and the elemental power of love is scattered" (14–15).

"Calliope / '*And thou thyself, Calliope*' – Sappho" (286–8): Bergk 82 (LP 124). The translation here is Wharton's.

"All Mountains / '*Give me all mountains*' – Hymn to Artemis" (288–90): Callimachus, *Hymns* 3.18. Identified by Swann (31).

Uncollected and Unpublished Poems (1912–1944)

"Epigram / (*After the Greek*)" (309): Anonymous epigram on Claudia Homonoea, Mackail 165, not in Loeb. Identified by Babcock in "Verses" (208).

"Amaranth" (310–15): Martz, who in his edition publishes this and the next two poems for the first time, points out that portions of this poem appear in *Heliodora* under the title "Fragment Forty-one / . . . *thou flittest to Andromeda* – Sappho." He observes that "Amaranth" was originally written with that Sapphic fragment in mind, since it mentions Andromeda and Atthis (xv–xvi).

"Eros" (315–19): Martz points out (xvii) that portions of this poem were published in *Heliodora* under the title "Fragment Forty / *Love . . . bitter-sweet* / Sappho." It is unclear whether "Eros" was originally written with that Sapphic fragment in mind, though it does mention "love . . . bitter and sweet" (317).

"Envy" (319–21): Martz points out (xviii) that portions of this poem were published in *Heliodora* under the title "Fragment Sixty-eight / . . . *even in the house of Hades* / Sappho." There is no evidence from "Envy" that H.D. originally had the Sapphic fragment in mind.

"I Said / (1919)" (322–5): The association in the first stanza between honey, violets, and Mt. Hymettus is ancient. The long-famous bees and honey of Hymettus are mentioned by Pausanias (1.32.1). The epithet "violet-crowned" with regard to Athens comes from a well-known Pindaric fragment (76, Loeb). The story of the battle of Marathon is told by Herodotus in the *Persian Wars* 6.102ff. Here and elsewhere H.D. apparently conflates the Battle of Marathon with the Battle of Thermopylae. See *Hermione* 220–1, in which Pheidippides (the famous runner at Marathon) is mentioned in connection with Simonides' epitaph on the Spartan dead at Thermopylae: "O passer-by, tell the Lacedemonians that we lie here obeying their orders" (*Palatine Anthology* 7.249, trans. Mackail). Herodotus tells the story of Thermopylae in the *Persian Wars* 7.228ff., where he also quotes this epigram of Simonides and two others. H.D. in her poem alludes explicitly to one of these epigrams, when the speaker mentions that at Marathon a thousand soldiers routed a million; Simonides writes about Thermopylae: "Four thousand from Peloponnesus once fought here with three million" (*Palatine Anthology* 7.248).

"Helios and Athene" (326–30): Part I makes allusion to Euripides' *Ion*, as well as to the Phidian statue of Athene in the Parthenon. Part II draws from Pater's essays on Greek statuary, "The Marbles of Aegina" and "The Age of Athletic Prizemen" (*Greek Studies* 266–319).

"Ariadne / (*From a Lost Play*)" (330–5): There are no recorded "lost plays" of Aeschylus, Sophocles, or Euripides with this title, though fragments remain of a *Theseus* by Euripides, which tells the story of Theseus and Ariadne in Crete. According to Gilbert Murray it concludes with an epiphany of Athene "warning Theseus that Ariadne shall not be his, but must be left on the island of Naxos to become the bride of Dionysus" (*Euripides and His Age* 352). The specific context of the poem is unclear – whether Ariadne speaks of her abandonment by the Athenian Theseus, a warrior representing "the manifold armies," or by the chthonic god Dionysos, "the ghost / rising at nightfall." In Ovid's *Heroides* (10) and *Fasti* (3.459–516) Ariadne bewails her abandonment first by Theseus and then by Dionysos (see also *Metamorphoses* 8.169–82 and Catullus 64.52–75). Theseus and Dionysos seem to be conflated in H.D.'s poem. The reference in part 2 to a woman and her child "set afloat to drift" and a "chest / flung on the water" seems to refer not to Ariadne but to another "divine bride," Danaë, and her son, Perseus; see Simonides's famous "lullaby" of Danaë for Perseus (Campbell 3: fragment 543); see also Hawthorne's "The Gorgon's Head," in *A Wonder Book for Girls and Boys*, which H.D. read as a child (Swann 10). The unusual focus in part 2 on Athene may have to do with the presence of Athene in the Theseus story (e.g., in her epiphany in Euripides' lost play) and with the fact that the Ariadne legend is part of the founding story of Athens and has memorials in the city's sacred precincts (see Pausanias 1.3.1, 1.20.3, 1.22.4–5).

"The Shepherd" (335–6): In *End to Torment* H.D. says, "I read [to Frances Gregg] Andrew Lang's translation of Theocritus that Ezra had brought me. I wrote a poem to Frances in a Bion and Moschus mood" (36). She then quotes the refrain of this poem, "O hyacinth of the swamp-lands, / Blue lily of the marshes." Though the poem does not correspond closely to any specific lines from Theocritus, Bion, or Moschus, it most closely echoes Theocritus's Idyll 11, wherein the homely Cyclops sings a song to the shepherdess Galatea, who has mocked him. This identification also seems likely, since elsewhere in H.D.'s writing Frances Gregg is associated with another Galatea, of the Pygmalion story (*Asphodel* 67–8). The reference to the lover as a city girl suggests Idyll 20.

"At Croton" (336–7): Why Croton? This city on the eastern coast of Italy was a Greek colony that, according to Strabo (6.1.12), excelled at warfare and athletics. It had many winners in the Olympic games, including the famous wrestler Milo, until its numbers were decimated in war. The city, unlike Baiae, had little importance in Roman times. The poem, suggesting an erotic encounter, would appear to refer to this aggressive masculine tradition of Croton, in speaking of a lover's clasping "the wrist with steel" and of "this light game / of take and break and yield." The situation of the speaker in the poem would seem similar to that of Hipparchia in *Palimpsest*, subjected to a military lover.

"Antipater of Sidon" (337–8): Epigram from *Palatine Anthology* 9.151. Hipparchia, in the story "Hipparchia" in *Palimpsest*, is translating this poem (5 and passim) as well as another epigram by Antipater (*Palatine Anthology* 7.413) to the Cynic philosopher Hipparchia, wife of Crates: "I cast my lot with cynics, not / with women seated at the distaff" (see *Palimpsest* 8 and passim).

"Psyche / '*Love drove her to Hell*'" (339–40): I have not been able to locate the exact quotation in the title. Because the translation of "Hell" for Avernus is uncommon, it might be a paraphrase of the well-known Renaissance translation of Apuleius's *The Golden Ass* by William Adlington (Loeb). Cf. 6.17: "[Psyche] was compelled to go upon her own feet to the gulf and furies of Hell." In any case, the poem alludes to the story of Amor and Psyche in Apuleius, books 4–6.

"A Dead Priestess Speaks" (369–77): Why Delia of Miletus? Miletus was historically a powerful Ionian colony on the coast of Asia Minor. It is known for its economic ambitions, manifest in large-scale colonization, and also for its persistent self-interested involvement in wars – with its neighbors, with the Persian rulers, and with its fellow Greeks. It appears to have been prone to political intrigue and was condemned by the Delphic oracle for its treachery (Herodotus 6.19). The poem alludes to this highly politicized climate of successive wars.

Miletus was also the birthplace of Arctinus, supposedly a pupil of Homer who wrote portions of the Greek epic cycle. Delia alludes to Homer's famous epithet "wine-dark sea," but she deliberately places herself outside this epic tradition: "I never made a song that told of war" (376).

Near Miletus – at Branchidai or Didyma – was a famous double temple to Apollo and Zeus, and an oracle of Apollo. The name of Delia, as well as Delia's gifts of healing, may be associated with Delian Apollo; according to Strabo, Apollo Oulios, the god of health and healing, was worshiped both at Delos and at Miletus (14.1.5–7). In the associations of Miletus with the wise physician and with the god of healing, H.D. may have had a memory of Theocritus; the poet's friend Nicias, who is mentioned in several idylls, was a physician of Miletus. See for instance Idyll 28.19–21, where the poet speaks of Nicias as "a wise physician, who has learned all the spells that ward off sore maladies" and who dwells "in glad Miletus with the Ionian people" (trans. Lang). See also the epigram by Theocritus in the *Palatine Anthology* (6.337): "Even to Miletus came the son of the Healer to succour the physician of diseases Nicias" (trans. Mackail). Though the deity whom Delia serves is likely to be Apollo or Zeus, epigrams in Mackail refer to Miletean Aphrodite and Artemis as well.

"*From Electra–Orestes*" (378–88): The characters of Electra and Orestes, and specific passages in the poem, are taken from Euripides' *Electra* (1177–1232) and *Orestes* (280–316, 1018–55).

"Calypso" (388–96): This poem gives a prehistory and alternative perspective of the Calypso episode told in book 5 of Homer's *Odyssey*.

"In Our Town" (396–400): A headnote indicates that the monologue of Menexeus is set "before the Egilian breakwaters." There is an island between Crete and Cythera named Aegilia, though it seems never to have had much importance. The details of the poem would rather suggest the island Aegina as the local context of the poem. Aegina, located in the Saronic Gulf between Attica and Argolis, had early connections with Crete and Mycenae; it was eventually settled by Dorians and was especially affiliated with Sparta. Aegina was well known in the sixth and fifth centuries B.C. for its naval and commercial strength, and also for its excellence in sculpture. Because of its propensity to take the wrong side in wars (siding with the Persians against the Greeks, then with Athens against Sparta), it was repeatedly punished and decimated and its citizens deported, until finally it sank into inconsequence. It also contained a famous temple to Aphaea, a version of the Cretan goddess Britomaris, as well as a temple to Apollo. The poem suggests the moral weakness of the successively conquered islanders and the prominence of commercial materialism. The merchant Menexeus refers to his father as a sculptor-architect who still follows the Dorian orders of architecture (the "Doric kymation") and to a sister-poet who sings by the Lion Gate (alluding to the Mycenaean gate dedicated to the ancient goddess). Perhaps the poem takes place in the first part of the fourth century, during the time of Theban hegemony, since Menexeus's sister is unwillingly married to a Theban patrician. H.D. in her early years certainly assimilated Pater's essay "The Marbles of Aegina" (*Greek Studies*), which sculpture Pater takes as representative of the Dorian (as opposed to the Ionian) strain within hellenism; this emphasis would seem to be echoed in the Dorian tradition of sculpture still practiced by Menexeus's father. Pater also emphasizes that this Dorian art is firmly within the religion of Apollo, and this emphasis fits the character of the poet-sister as Pythian priestess. On her hellenic cruise in 1932, H.D. made a visit to Aegina that powerfully affected her and that she rendered in a short story, "Aegina" (1932).

"Delphi" (401–6): There would seem to be no specific subtext in H.D.'s treatment here of the Delphic oracle.

"Dodona" (406–11): There would seem to be no specific subtext in H.D.'s treatment here of the oracle to Zeus at Dodona.

"Dancer" (440–50): The name Rhodocleia appearing in part 6 of this poem evokes a line from an epigram by Rufinus in the *Palatine Anthology* (5.74): "I send thee, Rhodocleia, this garland . . ." (trans. Mackail). It is quoted repeatedly in one of H.D.'s narratives of her early London years (*Asphodel* 71, 87, 104, 108).

"The Master" (451–61): A reference in part 1 to Miletus puts this poem in contextual relation to "A Dead Priestess Speaks," where Delia is a priestess of Miletus in service possibly to Apollo-Healer and Zeus. The note for that poem suggests the associations of Miletus with Asclepios and the wise physician – associations pertinent when this poem is read as a tribute to Freud. For the reference to Rhodocleia in part 13, see the note to "The Dancer."

"Orestes Theme" (466–8): See the note for "*From Electra–Orestes.*"

"Ancient Wisdom Speaks / *For April 14, 1943*" (482–4): Though no explicit allusion is apparent, the "cloak of blue" belonging to the "she" of the poem is one of the marks of Demeter, emphasized in Pater's essay on Demeter and Persephone and echoed repeatedly in H.D.'s writing (Hedyle, Kreousa, and Thetis all wear blue). Blue is, of course, also the color of the Virgin Mary's veil.

A SUMMARY BY AUTHOR

Amalteo, Giovanni Battista (Neo-Latin)

"Acon": "Acon"

Anonymous

"Epigram / (*After the Greek*)": Mackail 165, not in Loeb
"Hermes of the Ways": *Palatine Anthology* 10.12

Antipater of Sidon

"Antipater of Sidon" ["Where, Corinth, charm incarnate, are your shrines?"]:
  Palatine Anthology 9.151
"Hermonax": *Palatine Anthology* 6.223
"I cast my lot with cynics" [*Palimpsest*]: *Palatine Anthology* 7.413

Anyte of Tegea

"Hermes of the Ways": *Palatine Anthology* 9.314
"The Shrine / ('She watches over the sea')": *Palatine Anthology* 9.144

Apollonius of Rhodes

"The Look-out": *Argonautica* 1.151–5

Apuleius

"Psyche / '*Love drove her to Hell*'": *The Golden Ass* (trans. Adlington) 6.17; the
  story of Amor and Psyche is told in books 4–6.

Asclepiades (Sikeledes)

In *Hedylus, Palatine Anthology* 12.163

Bion

"Adonis": "The Lament for Adonis"

Callimachus

"All Mountains / '*Give me all mountains*' – Hymn to Artemis": *Hymns* 3.18
"Song" ["You are as gold / as the half-ripe grain"]: Hymn to Apollo, *Hymns*
  2.32–41
"White World": Hymn to Demeter, *Hymns* 6.118–23

Callistratus

"Myrtle Bough / '*I'll wreathe my sword in a myrtle bough*' – Harmodius and
  Aristogiton": Campbell 5: fragment 895

Catullus

"Ariadne / *(From a Lost Play)*": *Poems* 64.52–75
"Hymen" ["But of her"]: *Poems* 61.6–10

Euripides

"Ariadne / *(From a Lost Play)*": *Theseus*, a lost play
"*The Bird-Choros of / Ion*": lines 154–83
"Cassandra / O Hymen king": *Trojan Women* 307–14
"Choros Translations from *The Bacchae*": For line numbers, see descriptive list
"Egypt / (To E. A. Poe)": *Helen* 1451–1511
"*From Electra–Orestes*": *Electra* 1177–1232; *Orestes* 280–316, 1018–55
"From the *Hippolytus* of Euripides": For line numbers, see descriptive list
"From the *Iphigeneia in Aulis* of Euripides": For line numbers, see descriptive list
"Helen": *Helen* 81
"Helios and Athene": *Ion*, general reference
"Hippolytus Temporizes": *Hippolytus* 70–87, 1391–3
"Huntress": *Hippolytus* 215–22, 228–31
"Leda": *Helen* 179–90
"Orestes Theme": *Electra* 1177–1232; *Orestes* 280–316, 1018–55
"Phaedra": *Hippolytus*, general reference
"Sea-Choros" from *Hecuba*: lines 444–83
"She Contrasts with Herself Hippolyta": *Hippolytus*, general reference
"She Rebukes Hippolyta": *Hippolytus* 215–22, 228–31
"Songs from Cyprus" ["Where is the nightingale?"]: *Helen* 1107–16
"Thetis" [*Heliodora*]: *Andromache* 1249–62
"Why Have You Sought?": *Iphigeneia in Aulis*, general reference

Herodotus

"I Said": *Persian Wars* 6.102ff., 7.223ff.

Homer

"At Ithaca": *Odyssey* 2.104–9
"Calypso": *Odyssey* 5
"Circe": *Odyssey* 10.210–19
"Cuckoo's Song": *Odyssey* 5.59–62
"A Dead Priestess Speaks": general reference
"Helios": *Iliad* 16.786–804
"The Islands": *Iliad* 2.494–760
"*Odyssey*": translation of 1.1–98

"Prayer": *Iliad* 18.478–608
"Sea Heroes": *Odyssey* 8.111–19; *Iliad* 2.494–760
"Why Have You Sought?": *Iliad*, general reference

Horace

"At Baia": *Epistles* 1.1.83

Meleager of Gadara

"Heliodora": *Palatine Anthology* 5.144, 147
"Nossis": *Palatine Anthology* 4.1.1–10

Moero

"Nossis": Moero is mentioned; see *Palimpsest* (71 and passim) for a translation of Moero's epigram, "You rest upon a golden bed, / in Aphrodite's golden house"; *Palatine Anthology* 6.119.

Nossis

"Nossis": *Palatine Anthology* 5.170

Ovid

"Ariadne / (*From a Lost Play*)": *Heroides* 10; *Fasti* 3.459–516; *Metamorphoses* 8.169–82
"Choros Sequence / from *Morpheus* / '*Dream – dark-winged*'": *Metamorphoses* 11.592–652
"The Cliff Temple": *Heroides* 15.173–220
"Eurydice": *Metamorphoses* 10.1–63
"*From the Masque* / Hyacinth": *Metamorphoses* 10.162–219
"If You Will Let Me Sing": *Metamorphoses* 1.452–567; 10.162–219
"Pygmalion": *Metamorphoses* 10.243–97
"Thetis" [*Hymen*]: *Metamorphoses* 11.229–37

Pausanias

"Ariadne / (*From a lost play*)": *Description of Greece* 1.3.1, 1.20.3, 1.22.4–5
"Charioteer": *Description of Greece* 8.4.8, 6.22.10–11, 3.24.8–9
"I Said": *Description of Greece* 1.32.1
"Red Roses for Bronze": *Description of Greece* 5.15.1,, 6.10.6, 5.11.3

"Sitalkas": *Description of Greece* 10.15.2
"Telesila": *Description of Greece* 2.20.8

Philippus

"The Cliff Temple": *Palatine Anthology* 6.251

Philodemus

"Hermonax": *Palatine Anthology* 6.349

Pindar

"Evadne": *Olympian Odes* 6.29–35
"I Said": fragment 76 (Loeb)

Plato

"The Contest": *Phaedrus* 246a–e (*Dialogues* 3:153)
"Epigrams": *Phaedrus* 246a–e (*Dialogues* 3:153)
"The Helmsman": *Phaedrus* 247c–d (*Dialogues* 3:154); *Symposium* 202d–e (*Dialogues* 1:534)
"Lais": *Palatine Anthology* 6.1
"Thou wert the morning star among the living" [in *Paint It Today, Notes on Thought and Vision*]: *Palatine Anthology* 7.670

Posidippus

In *Hedylus, Palatine Anthology* 12.45

Propertius

"At Baia": *Elegies* 1.11

Rufinus

"The Dancer": *Palatine Anthology* 5.74
"The Master": *Palatine Anthology* 5.74

Sappho (H.D.'s numbering of fragments refers to Wharton/Bergk)

"Adonis": Bergk 62 and 63 (LP 140a and 168)
"Calliope / 'And thou thyself, Calliope' – Sappho": Bergk 82 (LP 124)
"Choros Sequence / from *Morpheus* / 'Dream – dark winged'": LP 63 (Lobel 28–9)

"Cliff Temple": No reference to Sappho's poems, but to the common legend of Sappho's Leucadian leap. See this title under Ovid.

"Fragment 113 / *'Neither honey nor bee for me'* – Sappho": LP 146

"Fragment Forty / *Love . . . bitter-sweet* – Sappho" [entitled "Eros" in an earlier version]: LP 130; also Bergk 95 and 133 (LP 104)

"Fragment Forty-one / *. . . thou flittest to Andromeda* – Sappho" [entitled "Amaranth" in an earlier version]: LP 131

"Fragment Sixty-eight / *. . . even in the house of Hades* – Sappho" [entitled "Envy" in an earlier version]: LP 55

"Fragment Thirty-six / *I know not what to do: / my mind is divided* – Sappho": LP 51

"Halcyon / *'Bird – loved of sea-men'*": Bergk 34 (LP 49)

"Hymen" ["From the closed garden"]: Bergk 103, 105 (LP 117, 116); Bergk 91, 107 (LP 111); Bergk 133 (not in LP)

"Hymen" ["Where the first crocus buds unfold"]: Bergk 121 (LP 122); Bergk 85 (LP 132)

"Hymen" ["Never more will the wind"]: Bergk 109 (LP 114)

"Hymen" ["Between the hollows"]: Bergk 94 (LP 105); Bergk 93 (LP 108)

"Hymen" ["But of her"]: Bergk 100 (LP 112)

"Hymen" ["From citron-bower"]: Bergk 102, 108 (LP 107, 114)

"Hymen" [headnote to "The crimson cover"]: Bergk 64 (LP 54)

"Hymen" ["Where love is king"]: Bergk 40 (LP 130); Bergk 2 (LP 31)

"Moonrise": Bergk 53 (LP 154)

"Night": Bergk 52 (LP 168B)

"Orion Dead": Bergk 29 (LP 138)

"Pear Tree": Bergk 37 (LP 52)

"Pursuit": Bergk 94 (LP 105)

"Storm": Bergk 42 (LP 47)

Sikeledes

See Asclepiades

Simonides

"Ariadne / *(From a lost play)*": Campbell 3: fragment 543

"I Said": *Palatine Anthology* 7.248 (Thermopylae), 7.249 (Marathon)

Telesila

"Telesila" (from Pausanias's description of her statue in Argos)

Theocritus

"Adonis": Idylls 15 and 30 [attributed to Theocritus in Lang]
"A Dead Priestess Speaks": Idyll 28.19–21; *Palatine Anthology* 6.337
"Halcyon / '*Bird – loved of sea-men*'": Idyll 7.57–60
"Hymen" ["Between the hollows"]: Idyll 18.1–6, 18.38
"Hymen" ["But of her"]: Idyll 18.37
"The Shepherd": Idyll 11, 20
"Simaetha": Idyll 2
"White World": general reference
"Wine Bowl": Idyll 1.29–56

Theophrastus

"Sitalkas": *Concerning Weather Signs* 35–7

Dioscoros Zonas

"Orchard": *Palatine Anthology* 6.22

Notes

Introduction

1. The most notable of recent readings taking this critical approach is that of Walker: "Women and Time: H.D. and the Greek Persona," in *Masks* 105–34.
2. In these conclusions I am indebted to Friedman's *Penelope's Web*, which studies the narratives in detail, giving particular attention to H.D.'s continual manipulation and staging of different identities.
3. The phrase comes from the discussion of modernism in volume 1 of Gilbert and Gubar, *No Man's Land*.

1. Modern Classicism and the Theater of War

1. See "Poetics" 56–8. My discussion here is greatly indebted to this essay by Burnett on H.D.'s review of Yeats's *Responsibilities*, first published in 1988. Burnett dates the review between 1916 and 1918 (56–7).
2. For discussions of the relation of aesthetic to political positions among modernist poets, see Perl 256–82; J. R. Harrison 25–33; Craig 2–25; Stead, *Modernist Movement* 194–235.
3. For a discussion of Nietzsche's early reputation in England, see Thatcher. On his influence among early modernists, see in particular chap. 5 ("Nietzsche and the Literary Mind") and chap. 6.
4. This remark was made in Eliot's *Syllabus of a Course of Six Lectures on Modern French Literature* (Oxford 1916), republished in Schuchard, "Extension", see 165.
5. For Pound's promotion of H.D. as imagist, see his letter to Harriet Monroe, October 1912 (*Letters* 11); and his quotation of "Oread" in his manifesto on the "Vortex" in *Blast* 1 (June 1914): 154. For his perception of H.D.'s desertion of craft, see his letter to Margaret Anderson, August 1917 (*Letters* 114).
6. See Pound's letter to William Carlos Williams, 11 September 1920 (*Letters* 157); and see Eliot's letter to Aldington concerning H.D.'s second volume of poems, *Hymen*, 17 November 1921 (*Letters* 488).
7. See in particular the discussions of Engel and Jackson.

8. Riddel interprets elements of H.D.'s classicism as desperate attempts to redeem her deficient, phallus-less female state (448). Kenner likewise finds H.D.'s classical discipline as a poet simply one instance of "a series of self-destructions" characterizing her life (175–6).

9. Levenson's chapter on *The Waste Land* (165–212) gives an account of Eliot's "shift from provocation to consolidation," concluding in an articulation of classicism.

10. In the discussion of the debate between romanticism and classicism, I am greatly indebted to Perl, not only for his specific discussion of the controversy (58–62) but for the clarity afforded by his critical construct. I have also benefited from discussions by Brombert; Baker 247–50; Meisel, *Modern* 1–10; and Ross 65–9. I am indebted as well to Laity's discussion of H.D. in relation to romanticism and decadence, considered in early modernism as the "feminine" predecessors to be overcome ("Swinburne").

11. For a discussion of this dynamic of modernist historical interpretation see Perl (chap. 1); and Meisel, *Modern* (Introduction).

12. Eliot had immediate tutelage from Babbitt at Harvard and a close affiliation with Pound during his earliest years in London; for his knowledge of these men and of Hulme in the first stages of his career, see Schuchard, "Eliot and Hulme."

13. See Brombert on Eliot's designation of "heresies" and his critical pretensions to spiritual authority.

14. For examples of Bush's epithet of "masculine," see 88 (regarding Keats), 210 (regarding Tennyson), and 232 (regarding Ralegh). For examples of the epithet of "feminine" or "effeminate," see 88 (regarding Keats), 231 (regarding Landor), and 344 (regarding Swinburne).

15. On the equivalence between women writers and romantics in twentieth-century literature see Gilbert and Gubar, *No Man's Land* 154. See also Laity, "Swinburne," for a discussion of H.D. in these terms (465).

16. See Nietzsche, *Birth of Tragedy* 69–71. See also Perl's discussion of Nietzsche's classical model, especially 229, 118–19.

17. Newspaper reports of the war theater at Gallipoli generally referred to the Homeric as well as the Turkish names of the sites. One of the early reports in the London *Times* of the assault on Gallipoli (30 April 1915) has the headline "Battle on Trojan Plain" and describes the fight "in the Troad" from the "summit of Tenedos" (11, col. 4).

18. S.v. "*Agamemnon*, H.M.S," *Oxford Companion to Ships and the Sea*. I am indebted to Roessel's remarks for opening this avenue of approach.

19. Eliot in "Mr. Murray and Euripides" remarks with oblique condescension: "We do not reproach him for preferring, apparently, Euripides to Aeschylus. But if he does . . ." (*Selected Essays* 49). In his review of H.D.'s choruses, Pound's aversion to Euripides is more pronounced: "not that I am convinced one can approach the Greek drama via Euripides . . ."; "But if, via Homer and Aeschylus [not Euripides] one have contracted an interest in the Atreidae . . ." ("H.D.'s Choruses" 16).

20. Correspondence between Pound and Eliot in December 1921 and January 1922 seems to indicate that Eliot sent Pound some of his work on the *Agamemnon*, to which Pound responded (Eliot, *Letters* 499, 504, 505, 508). For a discussion of this exchange, see Pound, *Guide to Kulchur* 92–3; and Reid xi.

21. Pound's admiration of Aeschylus was not unequivocal; he solidly preferred Homer and thought that the Greek dramatists "decline from Homer." But his remark in this

regard that "[e]ven Aeschylus is rhetorical" signifies his predominance in Pound's estimation over the other dramatists (*Literary Essays* 27). His most positive remarks regarding Aeschylus appear in *Guide to Kulchur*. "If one greek play can claim pre-eminence over the best dozen others . . . that play wd. be the *Agamemnon*" (92). This last remark was made even after Pound had already become actively engaged in translating Sophocles.

22. The eschatology of the *Oresteia* remained vivid for Eliot – his *Murder in the Cathedral* having the place of the *Agamemnon* (see Reid xi), his *Cocktail Party* having the position of the *Eumenides*. Pound's embrace of the imagined future was eventually, after the fall of Mussolini, much more tenuous. Reid suggests that Pound turned to Sophocles because he could no longer entertain the "recuperative energies" implied in the conclusion to the Aeschylean trilogy (xiii).

23. Swann suggests Aeschylus as the source of several of H.D.'s poems that clearly refer to Euripides' plays, for instance "Cassandra" and the "Orestes" sequence (59, 62). H.D. very rarely mentions Aeschylus or Sophocles, and when she does, it is often with implicit resistance. See, for example, her remarks about Aeschylus in "From Megara to Corinth" 1; and about Sophocles, in *Hedylus* 20. To my knowledge she never alludes to an Aeschylean or Sophoclean play as a mythological source, but almost solely, among the Greek dramatists, to Euripides.

24. Citations for announcements in the *Egoist* in conjunction with the Poets' Translation Series are given here. *Rhesos* announced 2.8 (2 August 1915): 131; and 2.9 (1 September 1915): 148. *Iphigeneia in Aulis* announced 2.10 (1 October 1915): 163; and published in part in 2.11 (1 November 1915): 171–2 and simultaneously published as a pamphlet. *Ion* announced 3.1 (1 January 1916): 15. The dating of the pamphlet publication of *Iphigeneia* is contested. Boughn in his bibliography of H.D. gives it as 1916, but the pamphlet itself bears no date. H.D. was finished with the choruses by early October (letter to Amy Lowell, 7 October 1915), and the an-nouncement of the series in October 1915 indicates that the *Iphigeneia* translations would be ready in November, published simultaneously with their appearance in the *Egoist*, according to the advertisement for the series. The translations of the *Ion* did not appear because the planned second series of translations was suspended, only to continue in 1919.

25. Mackail published the very favorable anonymous review in the *Times Literary Supple-ment* in 1916 (4 May 1916: 210). Boughn in his bibliography does not list authorship of this review, but in letters Aldington and H.D. mention Mackail as the author, and they are likely to have had reliable knowledge. See, for instance, Aldington's letter to Charles C. Bubb (quoted Boughn 4). Bubb, who printed a limited American edition of *Choruses* for the Clerk's Press, Cleveland, Ohio, says in a printer's note following the text: "[The translation] has been highly praised in England, especially by Professor J. W. Mackail, himself of recognized ability" (Boughn 4).

26. Euripidean plays from which H.D. translates or to which she alludes repeatedly are, in addition to the four already mentioned, *Hecuba, Andromache, Trojan Women, Helen, Bacchae, Electra, Orestes,* and *Iphigeneia in Tauris*.

27. This information comes from the London *Times* for the months of May through August 1915.

28. H.D. mentions Brooke's death in a letter to Amy Lowell, dated 27 April 1915. Several obituaries to Gaudier-Brzeska appeared in the *Egoist*.

29. Letter from Aldington to Lowell, 11 June 1915. This letter is in the Houghton Library, Harvard University.

30. One gains some indication of the importance for H.D. of this lament for Troy in the chorus of the *Iphigeneia* by her inclusion of it as a separate poem, "And Pergamos," in *Selected Poems* (1957).

31. For an articulation in postmodern criticism of the political complicity of modernism, see, for example, Eagleton 102–61; and Robbins 237–9. Nietzsche, in his "self-criticism" of *The Birth of Tragedy*, scorns the idea of "metaphysical comfort" voiced in that work, countering it with Zarathustra's call to laughter (26–7). The widespread deconstructionist criticism of the "nostalgia" and "essentialism" of modernism takes its clues from Derrida's essay, "Structure, Sign and Play in the Discourse of the Human Sciences."

32. Stauth and Turner in various essays, particularly in *Nietzsche's Dance*, present an analysis of modern and postmodern figures in the context of a "nostalgic paradigm" in sociological theory. They define that paradigm (29–32) and to some degree or another treat Nietzsche, Marx, Freud, Weber, Heidegger, Adorno, and Foucault in these terms.

33. For a concise formulation of Girard's theory of mimetic desire, see Golsan 1–27.

34. See Ross on the question of "subjectivity" in modern criticism; the Preface poses the question of subjectivity, explored as the major argument of the book. See Levenson on the various attempts in early modernism to address the ambiguities of "consciousness" as a ground of artistic truth; chapter 2 poses the problem, explored throughout the book.

35. For an excellent discussion of the medical and philosophical history of the word "nostalgia," see Starobinski; Rosen gives a specifically medical history. For the word history, see the *OED*, 2d ed. (1989), s.v. "nostalgia."

36. "For the first time the nostalgia of the vast Roman and classic world took possession of her" (297); "The terror, the agony, the nostalgia of the heathen past was a constant torture to her mediumistic soul" (315). Lawrence wrote *The Lost Girl* soon after leaving England in 1919, and it was published in 1920. He had an intimate friendship with H.D. between 1915 and 1918, sharing poetry, exchanging letters, even living in the Aldingtons' flat in London at one point.

37. No clear evidence exists that H.D. had seen Bush's commentary, published in the United States in 1937. However, H.D. and Bryher were in New York in December of 1937, where H.D. first met Pearson, and it is hard to believe that Bush's criticism did not come into discussion. I am indebted to Collecott for pointing out the synchronicity of H.D.'s letter and Bush's remarks ("Memory and Desire" 66). Quotations from H.D.'s letter to Pearson in the subsequent discussion will refer to the original version of the letter published in *Agenda* rather than to the version edited by Pearson for the *Oxford Anthology*; see Collecott, "Memory and Desire," for a discussion of Pearson's emendations.

38. For important refutations of Bush's charges against H.D.'s poetry, see Greenwood, Swann 9–12, Collecott, "Memory and Desire", and Friedman, *Penelope's Web* 60–1.

39. Aldington in several poems published during the war expresses this kind of disillusionment. He wrote in a 1916 poem, "The Days Pass": "All the solitudes of grey hills, / All betwixt sea and sea, / Useless!" (*Egoist* 3.11 [November 1916]: 169). Also see the fictional dialogue in H.D.'s *Palimpsest* 135.

40. For dating, see H.D.'s letter to Pearson 71; and Benét 75.

2. The Survival of the Classics

1. Ong (207–8) discusses Latin education in Western history as a male puberty rite, deliberately separated from female contamination. Homans gives an analysis of the problematic status of women within literary transmission, in the context of nineteenth-century writing. Her analysis of the ambivalence of "bearing the Word" is relevant to classical transmission and to H.D.'s conception of her own role within transmission (29–33). For a discussion of the difficulties of women in male institutions of classicism, see Skinner.

2. See F. M. Turner (187–263) for a discussion of the debate on the merits of Athens as a political model for liberals and conservatives. For elaboration of the Spartan political model in English politics, see Rawson chap. 20. Jenkyns 87–111 treats the Victorian conception of the merits of the Greek tragedians. See Turner 369–446 and Jenkyns 227–63 for a discussion of the various uses to which Plato was put in the Victorian period.

3. McKnight proposes that the aims of hermetic spirituality, espoused so ardently in the Renaissance by Pico and other humanist magicians, have contributed to the character of modernity as surely as the more obvious models of empirical materialism. The "sacralization of the world" through its visionary participation in human consciousness, McKnight proposes, is the gnostic double of the scientific aim of "secularization"; see 25–49. On the dissemination of hermeticism in the seventeenth and eighteenth centuries, see Yates, *Rosicrucian*, who traces the prominence of Rosicrucian ideas in the phase between the Renaissance and the scientific revolution and later Enlightenment, indicating "the *historic* channels through which the phase was distributed" (xiii). See also Viatte, who treats exhaustively the influence of many occult sects and spiritualist doctrines on French revolutionary sentiment and on romanticism.

4. On Freemasonry in the eighteenth century as a "link in the hermetic chain," see Tuveson 170–9; see also Bernal 161–77 on Rosicrucianism and Freemasonry in the seventeenth and eighteenth centuries.

5. Critics have long acknowledged the hermetic and Neoplatonic concerns of individual writers within romanticism and, like Tuveson and McKnight, have pointed to the fundamentally gnostic cosmology of romanticism more generally. Also, there are many fine studies of romantic hellenism: Stern and Larrabee treat hellenism in English romanticism, and F. M. Turner and Jenkyns treat the Victorian period. However, to my knowledge, no one has elaborated the specific connection between romantic hellenism and visionary hermetic traditions.

6. See Desonay for a comprehensive study of romantic hellenism in the Parnassian movement. See also Knight 153–80.

7. See Perl 17–33 for a discussion of the prominence of the model of crisis and dissociation in modern formulations of literary history.

8. See Pound's *Spirit of Romance* 90, 101. For a good summary of Pound's interpretation of the heretics of Provence destroyed in the Albigensian Crusade and the Inquisition, see Makin 217–55.

9. The first of these was a series of essays entitled "Elizabethan Classicists," running in five consecutive issues of the *Egoist*, from September 1917 through January 1918. A second series of essays, the first three entitled "Early Translators of Homer" and the last three "Hellenist Series," appeared in six consecutive issues from August 1918 through March–April 1919.

10. See Bernal chaps. 7 and 8 on the "Hellenomania" in German thought after Winckelmann.
11. Pound reports on Hulme's use of these terms in a lecture before the Quest Society in early 1914; see "The New Sculpture" 67. See also Levenson 94–102 on Hulme's late anticlassical stance. Gaudier-Brzeska in 1914 echoes Hulme's language in his discussion of the history of the vortex in relation to modern cubism (in Pound, *Guide to Kulchur* 63–8).
12. See Pound's 1931 essay "Terra Italica" for his famous statements concerning the survival of pagan cults (*Selected Prose* 54–60). Also see Makin 240–50 and Surette for a discussion of the "Eleusinian" myth in Pound's writing.
13. Duncan clearly notes the relation of Pound to the hellenistic inheritance of Alexandria. See "Two Chapters" 82; and "Part II, Chapter 5" [*Stony Brook*] 340.
14. See for instance Stedman's discussion of Tennyson in relation to Theocritus (205–8); and Lang xli.
15. For a discussion of Alexandrian decadence as a universal attitude, represented in Cavafy's poetry, see Golffing.
16. Cavafy made his first appearance in English letters through a short review by Forster, "The Poetry of C. F. Cavafy," *Athenaeum* 23 April 1919; it was reprinted four years later in *Pharos and Pharillon*.
17. In pointing to the specific aesthetic norms of Callimachus in relation to imagism, I am indebted to a conversation with Robert Babcock, spring 1990.
18. For a concise discussion of the history of Alexandria in connection with the poetry of Cavafy, see Pinchin 3–33.
19. Anacreon wrote in the sixth century B.C., but he is accessible only through hellenistic imitations in the Greek Anthology.
20. H.D. follows Pater (the opening of *Plato and Platonism*) in situating Plato in Athens's decadence. Ray Bart in *Palimpsest* muses: "Modern life Plato said (circa 500 B.C. [*sic*]) was like that. All Athens in its dying splendour.... All Athens in its brilliant decadence" (168–9).
21. See DuPlessis, *Career* 20–3 for an excellent, though brief, discussion of the importance of Meleager in H.D.'s work.
22. H.D. seems to have accepted the obvious Egyptian dimension of Greece's history suppressed in the Aryan model, and shows some awareness of the importance of the Semitic in this context. Throughout her essay on Meleager in "Notes on Euripides," H.D. emphasizes his Jewishness as part of his distinct gift (1, 4). But a more ambivalent response to the Semitic is indicated in her discussion of him in *Notes on Thought and Vision* (33–7), where she imagines his chagrin at his "ill-omened begetting," from "a Jew father, a Greek mother" (the actual parentage was the reverse of this) and his frustration with "the Hebrew script he would die to forget – the tongue he would die to forget – but that in dying he would forget that other – gold – light of gold [Greek]" (33). In this last emphasis H.D. seems to confirm the Aryan model so deeply entrenched in the popular imagination of Greece at the turn of the century.
23. H.D. refers to *Salammbô* in *Asphodel* 15. She mentions *Aphrodité* on several occasions; see *Asphodel* 53, 54. She alludes indirectly to *Thaïs* in her essay on Meleager in "Notes on Euripides" 1. She notes her early reading of Bulwer-Lytton in a letter to Swann (10).
24. S.v. "texts, transmission of," and "canons," in the *Oxford Companion to Classical Literature*; s.v. "epitome," in the *Oxford English Dictionary*. The latter word was

suggested by a remark in Wright, *Girdle*, in his opening discussion of the transmission of the text of the Greek Anthology: "[B]y the rule that holds almost universally in ancient literature, the epitome displaced the complete book" (vii).

25. S.v. "classic" in the *Oxford Companion to Classical Literature*.

26. See Wright, *Poets* 77–98, for a discussion of ancient women poets that was of great importance to H.D. For an extensive treatment of Greek and Roman women poets, commentators, and philosophers, see Snyder.

27. S.v. "texts, transmission of ancient," in the *Oxford Companion to Classical Literature*.

28. For a discussion of the exclusive male rituals of classicism, see Skinner 183–4; and on classical education as a male puberty rite, see Ong. On women's negotiation of the male territory of the "classics," see Fowler.

29. For discussions of H.D.'s education at Friends' Central School in Philadelphia and at Bryn Mawr, see Wallace, "Friends' Central" and "Athene's Owl."

30. Accounts of H.D.'s first publication in *Poetry* suggest that Pound not only edited the poems but was preoccupied with "entitling" not only H.D. but the poems themselves. See *End to Torment* 18. Since Pound himself sent the poems to Harriet Monroe, and since she herself frequently had much to do with the manner of presentation in *Poetry*, it is very likely that these entitlings are not entirely H.D.'s gestures. Babcock, in "Verses" 203, proposes that the title of the selection was made by Monroe, to avoid the suggestion that the poems were translations.

31. On Woolf's ambivalent attitude to Greek, see Fowler 346–8.

32. Note also Eliot's conception of intellectual lineage in his 1920 essay on Murray, referring to him as the "friend and inspirer of Miss Jane Harrison" (*Selected Essays* 49).

33. On the details of the enterprise of the Poets' Translation Series, see Zilboorg, "Joint Venture."

34. I discuss this aspect of H.D.'s Sapphic intertextuality in Chapter Five.

35. H.D frequently quotes from this book in her essay on Meleager in "Notes on Euripides"; and it is likely that in her conception of the political setting and aesthetic relations of *Hedylus* she used Wright's description, in a chapter on Asclepiades, of the literary life of Samos in the third century B.C. (10–15). Moreover, H.D. seems to have borrowed details from Wright's chapter on Antipater of Sidon, as well as from the chapter on Meleager, in imagining the action of "Hipparchia" in *Palimpsest*.

36. Wright's emphasis upon this Semitic/Egyptian/Greek becomes more remarkable in light of the dominant Aryan model of Greek civilization, persuasively argued by Bernal. However, when H.D. mentions Meleager's parentage in *Notes on Thought and Vision* (33), she reverses it, giving him a Jewish father and a Greek mother. Thus she still claims matrilineality, though her hellenizing of the mother is a significant mistake.

37. For a discussion of Douris of Samos and his literary circle, see Wright, *Poets* 9–10; for a description of the library of Lucullus, see Plutarch, *Lives*, "Lucullus" 42.1–4.

38. See Kloepfer on *Palimpsest* (chap. 6). See also the discussion of the "maternal quest plot" in "Hipparchia" in Friedman, *Penelope's Web* 244–52.

39. The dates ascribed to Meleager vary from scholar to scholar, but I use Wright's dating here, in *Poets* 121.

40. Regarding Hipparchia, Marius recalls: "Lucullus had explained his romantic finding of her on some curious expedition with some young relative who was shot dead on the outworks of their temporary encampment (even then Lucullus's envoys were making their first tentative essays toward the Mithradateans)" (8–9). Lucius Licinius Lucullus was one of the generals in charge of the continued war against Mithridates in the

eastern Mediterranean, which began in 74 B.C. See Plutarch, *Lives*, "Lucullus"; s.v. "Mithridatic War," *Dictionary of Wars*.

41. This lineage, continually recalled by Hipparchia, seems externally confirmed by Julia Augusta's knowledge of it (91).

42. Hipparchia was presumably an acquaintance of Philip of Macedon himself, and Crates reputedly entertained Philip's son, Alexander. Hipparchia's brother (also a follower of Crates) was once a pupil of the Athenian Theophrastus, the disciple of Aristotle. These details are given in Diogenes Laertius 6.88, 94, 96–8.

43. Swann (123) notes this discrepancy, but without suggesting an explanation.

44. Hipparchia says, "We all agreed [Philip, her mother, and Hipparchia] that Great Wisdom herself had perished finally, when after Macedon's swollen policy, the Romans had attacked us. I think Hipparchia's grey coarse linen was in mourning for our Corinth which . . . we belonged to" (13–14).

45. H.D. read Roman and Greek history in high school, at Friends' Central (Wallace, "Friends' Central" 19), and she studied Livy in Latin studies at Bryn Mawr (Wallace, "Athene's Owl" 108).

46. H.D. used Diogenes Laertius (ca. A.D. 220), *Lives of Eminent Philosophers*, for details from the lives of Crates, Hipparchia, and Theophrastus. Diogenes quotes the epigram on Hipparchia from Antipater of Sidon. H.D. also certainly refers to Plutarch (ca. A.D. 100), *Lives*, for details from the life of Lucullus. Appian of Alexandria (ca. A.D. 150), *Roman History*, is a likely source for the historical context of the Mithridatic Wars and, in particular, his story of the siege of Athens by Rome (86 B.C.) in book 12. Pausanias (ca. A.D. 160), *Description of Greece*, book 7, gives a very moving description of the destruction of Corinth by Rome (146 B.C.), and he gives details of the Macedonian conquest throughout. Arrian (ca. A.D. 140), *Anabasis Alexandri*, describes the destruction of Thebes by Alexander (336 B.C.), book 1.6–10.

47. For references to Hyacinth, see *Palimpsest* 11–12, 13, 81; for references to the Niobids, see 29–30, 56, 70.

48. See Laity, "Romantic Landscapes" 116–22 for a discussion of the sexual ambivalence of the Hyacinth figure in H.D.'s poetry.

49. The phrase "lettered hyacinth" is used in Lang's translation of Idyll 10 (57).

50. W. A. Wigram, the canon of Malta, and William Inge, dean of St. Paul's Cathedral, were on this cruise; Wigram and perhaps Inge presented lectures to the elite passengers. H.D.'s participation in this cruise will be discussed in Chapter Four.

51. This typescript is bound with miscellaneous poems and with "Responsibilities." It is numbered 39–64.

52. A notebook in the Beinecke entitled "Carmel Highlands – 1920" contains drafts of all but one of the essays on Pausanias and a draft of the essay on Sappho; Bryher's autobiographical novel, *West*, mentions that the H.D. character (Helga) reads Pausanias in California (66). The essays on Anacreon and Theocritus allude to the landscape of California. The exact dating of the other essays cannot be ascertained, but they would appear to be from the early twenties. A chorus from *Ion* was published in *Heliodora* (1923), and a chorus from *Bacchae* in *The Imagist Anthology* (1930) and in *Red Roses for Bronze* (1931). A review of an edition of Sappho, finally comprising part of the group, was published in 1925.

53. Correspondence between H.D. and Marianne Moore and Amy Lowell in 1921 and 1922 indicates that H.D. was trying to place individual essays as well as a collection of essays; see H.D. to Moore, 17 January 1921, in which she mentions an essay that

she is sending for consideration in *Dial*; H.D. to Lowell, 6 October 1922, in which she mentions a collection of essays rejected by Holt that she will send to her; and a letter from Moore to H.D., 18 November 1922, in which she indicates that she has forwarded a copy of the essays to Lowell. See also a letter from H.D. to Louis Untermeyer, dated 9 January 1923, asking him to check on her manuscript of essays in Lowell's possession. Letters to Moore are in the Rosenbach Museum, Philadelphia; the letter to Lowell in Houghton Library, Harvard University; the letter to Untermeyer in the Lilly Library, Indiana University. One of the essays comprising this collection was finally published in 1924.

54. Remarks about artificiality and coldness of tone may come from Murray, *Euripides and His Age* (1913) 144–6, though he is not unsympathetic to the play. More likely, H.D. here refers to A. W. Verrall, *Four Plays of Euripides* (1905) 43–133, who is acutely critical of the play on technical grounds.

3. *Pagan Mysteries*

1. In a chapter on Pater in *Yeats*, Bloom argues for Pater's influence on subsequent writers like Yeats and Stevens (23–37). Meisel, *Absent*, makes an extended and persuasive argument for Pater's influence on Virginia Woolf. See also Monsman, *Walter Pater*, chap. 6 ("Pater and the Modern Temper"), and the general argument of McGrath, who treats Pater's influence on Yeats (passim), Eliot (129–35 and passim), Stevens (passim), Joyce (231–81), and other modern writers in passing.

2. The introductory note to *Choruses from the Iphigeneia in Aulis* (1915) alludes disparagingly to outmoded Victorian translators (e.g., Gilbert Murray): "[A] rhymed, languidly Swinburnian verse form is an insult and a barbarism" (1). However, this note is not signed, and there is no evidence that H.D. wrote it; the style and diction suggest Aldington, the series editor, and not H.D., who elsewhere has only positive things to say about Swinburne. In her autobiographical narratives, she associates Poe and Swinburne with her first stirrings as a poet (*Hermione* 72–3, 123–5; *Paint It Today* 52–5).

3. H.D. indicates her early extensive awareness of his writing, and her great respect for it, in a late, retrospective letter to Norman Holmes Pearson (8 May 1947): "Actually I couldn't concentrate during those horrible years [of World War II], though I started in 1940 to review Walter Pater, I just got so far – it wasn't that he didn't come up to my expectations or that he had not worn well, as it were, it was simply TOO BEAUTIFUL, one could not turn aside from the desert of one's predestined journey, into that oasis; that was all." My thanks go to Donna Hollenberg for calling my attention to this letter.

4. In a letter to Swann (Swann 10), H.D. indicates that Pater was a major early influence. She mentions Pater by name frequently in her autobiographical narratives; oblique allusions to Paterian *topoi* are even more frequent, since his writing was widely disseminated. For instance, Pater introduced Botticelli to the English and intensified interest in the artists treated in *The Renaissance*. Some of Pater's images are so endlessly reinvoked as to become commonplaces – particularly his treatment of major paintings of Botticelli and Leonardo (Bullen 279–80). The following represents a catalogue of direct and oblique allusions to Pater. H.D.'s unpublished 1912 Paris diary (recording chiefly visits to the Louvre): 21 (reference to Pater by name). *Asphodel*: 20 and 118 (quotation from Pater's description of the Mona Lisa); 21 and

136 (allusion to Pater's discussion of Aphrodite in *Greek Studies*); 52 (quotation from the "Conclusion" to *The Renaissance*); 55 (Pound character discussing Luca della Robbia, Leonardo da Vinci, Botticelli – central figures in *The Renaissance*); 96 (Pater mentioned by name); 155 (reference to Apollyon, Apollo's name in "Apollo in Picardy"). *Paint It Today*: frequent quotation (22 passim) of the *Pervigilium Veneris*, a central text in Pater's *Marius. Palimpsest*: 103 (references to Botticelli with influence of Pater's discussion); 128 (reference to Primavera and also to Pico della Mirandola, with echoes of Pater's essay in *The Renaissance*); 168–9 (reference to Plato's Athens in its decadence, echoing the emphasis in the opening of *Plato and Platonism*). *Bid Me to Live*: 17 (allusion to Pater's essay on Leonardo in *The Renaissance*). *Hermione*: 61 (reference to Lang's translation of *Aucassin and Nicolette*, made popular by Pater's essay in *The Renaissance*); 98 (allusion to the Primavera and possibly to the Uffizi Medusa of Leonardo, discussed in *The Renaissance*). *Notes on Thought and Vision*: passim, the discussion of Leonardo da Vinci in the occult language used by Pater in *The Renaissance*. Also Aldington in letters to H.D. mentions Pater familiarly as a shared knowledge; see letter of 10 July 1918 (*Early Years* 103), in which Aldington speaks of "Pater's detachment"; and letter of 13 June, 1918 (69), in which Aldington mentions Pater's "Imaginary Portraits." Moreover, in her early poetry and prose one can see the presence of Pater in H.D.'s fascination with Apollo and Hyacinth – the myth that is retold in "Apollo in Picardy" and mentioned frequently in Pater. Pater is clearly present as well in "Hymen," in the description of various kinds of classical artifacts, following the Ionian/Dorian emphasis in "The Beginnings of Greek Sculpture," in *Greek Studies*; and in "Demeter," referring to the statue of the Demeter of Cnidus, described by Pater in *Greek Studies*.

5. These writers in the tradition of romantic hellenism are all mentioned in the course of *The Renaissance*. The final essay on Winckelmann mentions Hegel and speaks extensively of Goethe; Heine's idea of the "gods in exile" forms the basis of the essay on Pico della Mirandola and is mentioned elsewhere in Pater's work (see J. S. Harrison).

6. Pater mentions Müller's thought in *Plato and Platonism* (199–200); and, as Monsman has pointed out, Pater's interpretation of Greek culture is clearly derived from his ideas (*Portraits* 7–9). For a succinct summary by Pater of the "Aryan" model of Greek cultural development, see *Plato and Platonism* 220–8; and *Greek Studies* 224–32. For Bernal on Müller as one of the chief architects of the Aryan model, see 308–16.

7. Conlon treats allusions to French writers in Pater in chronological order of his writing; thus references to these writers are scattered throughout. For Pater's relation to Baudelaire, see Monsman, *Autobiography*, chap. 5.

8. Knight's study concerns the poetics of the flower in nineteenth-century French poetry, and in that context he finds the association of mysticism with hellenism, particularly beginning with the Parnassians and continuing among the symbolists. With regard to esoteric traditions and hellenist flowers, see 18–25, 43–7, 137–53.

9. See C. Ryan for a discussion of Blavatsky's presence in Paris and London in the last two decades of the century (chaps. 12, 16, and 17).

10. Wind elaborates the Renaissance language of the pagan mysteries in detail; for crucial elements of his argument see 1–25, 191–217.

11. In *Miranda Masters*, a fictional account of Cournos's early career in England, Miranda clearly represents H.D.: "'I want to see the old gods back!' said Miranda in nervous,

quavering tones, as if it were a personal matter, a matter of life or death. 'They are not dead. They are but in hiding, waiting to emerge when their time comes!'" (6).

12. Studies of Renaissance hermeticism began appearing in the late fifties; see Yates, *Bruno* ix.

13. The relation of hermeticism to the scientific enlightenment is the theme of Yates's *Bruno* as well as *Rosicrucian*. See also McKnight, who links the secularization characteristic of modernity to the "sacralization" of the world in hermetic gnosticism; his argument regarding the origins of modernity in Renaissance gnosticism is given in chap. 2.

14. Dowling accounts for the veiled rhetoric of *The Renaissance* in terms of an Oxonian educational agenda, emphasizing the need for cultural revitalization through a recovery of Platonic eros (*Hellenism* 92–9).

15. For a discussion of the Victorian icon of the languishing and neurotic woman, see Dijkstra, chaps. 2 and 3.

16. For a recent discussion of Pater within a philosophical tradition of empiricism, see J. Ryan 25–37.

17. H.D. suggests such a judgment by Pound, or perhaps her own self-judgment, in *Hermione* (63), when Hermione wants George to orient her by his definitions, such as naming her a "neuropathic dendrophil" or saying "God, you must give up this sort of putrid megalomania, get out of this place." On Freud's indications of H.D.'s megalomania, see *Tribute to Freud* (51).

18. On the enterprise of the Poets' Translation Series, see Zilboorg, "Joint Venture." See also the advertisements for the series in the *Egoist*, beginning in August 1915, in which its declared purpose is to bring ancient poetry to life from the death it has suffered at the hands of scholars.

19. For an extensive discussion of Pater's influence on modernist concern for the discipline of craft, summed up in Pater's term *ascesis*, see McGrath, chap. 11.

20. Throughout this discussion of Pater's use of *ascesis* and *crystal*, I am indebted to chap. 2 of Meisel, *Absent*.

21. See, for instance, Homer, *Odyssey* 13.288–9, where Athene appears to Odysseus in "the shape of a woman / both beautiful and tall, and well versed in glorious handiworks" (trans. Lattimore).

22. Pater's essay "Hippolytus Veiled" (*Greek Studies* 157–94) undoubtedly influenced H.D.'s interest in this figure, as I will later argue. With regard to the *Ion*, see *Marius*, where Pater speaks of Marius's *ascesis* in assuming "the sacerdotal function hereditary in his family," comparing it to that of "the young Ion in the beautiful opening of the play of Euripides, who every morning sweeps the temple floor with such a fund of cheerfulness in his service" (25). H.D.'s essay on the *Ion* in "Notes on Euripides" likewise treats the opening of the play.

23. H.D. begins working on translations from the *Hippolytus* and the *Ion* during World War I. She continues her reflection on both during her crucial 1920 trip to Greece, when she writes "Hippolytus Temporizes" and "Helios and Athene," which alludes to the *Ion*; and shortly after this time (1920–4) she writes a prose commentary on the *Ion*. She completes the play *Hippolytus Temporizes* in 1927, and she returns to the *Ion* after her analysis with Freud, publishing a complete translation in 1937.

24. In her book on H.D.'s fiction, *Penelope's Web*, Friedman points to H.D.'s own ironic distance from what she herself called "the early H.D." (62–8), associated by critics with marble and crystal (50–4).

25. See DeJean chap. 3 for an intricate treatment of the scholarly commentary concerning Sappho, from which the argument here is drawn. The German scholars that DeJean treats with regard to male love are Friedrich Gottlieb Welcher, M. H. E. Meier, K. O. Müller, Paul Brandt, and Ulrich von Wilamowitz-Moellendorff (207–20).

26. On the contrast between Dorian and Ionian, see Müller 2:1–7. On a summary of Müller's historical argument, see Bernal 308–16; on its racial underpinnings, see Bernal 31–3.

27. See Rawson 142–3 for an elaboration of this Spartan political model; chap. 20 deals with its presence in English politics.

28. This kind of equivocation, according to Cartledge, is intended in Oscar Wilde's Dorian Gray, where the name "Dorian" alludes ironically to the "law and order" of Spartan asceticism and subversively to the Spartan institution of pederasty.

29. Edward Carpenter, for instance, writes a eulogy to Müller's Dorian Sparta in the pages of the New Freewoman in 1913 ("The Status of Women in Early Greek Times").

30. Cronin finds the Neoplatonic distinction between white light as the One and color as the Many operative in one form or another throughout the eighteenth and nineteenth centuries, in such diverse figures as Newton, Goethe, Coleridge, and Shelley (22–9).

31. On the traditional equation of bisexuality with asexuality see Delcourt 52–3; on hermaphroditism and primordial unity, see 67–84; on hermaphroditism and the *opus* of alchemy, see 80–2.

32. Busst studies the figure of the androgyne in the late nineteenth century in relation to its hermeticist and spiritualist sources; on its pervasiveness, see 4–6.

33. See Friedman, *Psyche* 193–4, for a discussion of the importance of *Seraphità*; see also Bruzzi, "Hieroglyphs." H.D. was given this novel by Pound during their early friendship in Pennsylvania; see *End to Torment* 11, 19, 23, and passim.

34. The French text reads: "Tout, dans cette figure marmoréenne, exprimait la force et le repos" (21).

35. Another possible source of the name Althea is the main female character in Swinburne's *Atalanta in Calydon*; however, Lee's Althea, a young androgynous woman, seems to have more in common with H.D.'s character than does the vengeful maternal queen in Swinburne's play.

36. Laconia is the territory in the Peloponnese of which Lacedaemon, or Sparta, is the capital.

37. In "Winckelmann" (*Renaissance* 237), in the essay on Demeter and Persephone (*Greek Studies* 110), and in "Hippolytus Veiled" (*Greek Studies* 192), Hyacinth is mentioned as one of many figures of the dying youth, part of the "mournful mysteries" of Greek religion (*Renaissance* 237). In an essay on Greek sculpture (*Greek Studies* 248–9), the story of Hyacinth's death is told more elaborately; and in his late essay "Lacedaemon" (*Plato and Platonism* 228–30), Pater describes with some detail the Dorian festival of the Hyacinthia. Finally, in the last published work of his life, "Apollo in Picardy," Pater gives another version of the myth of Hyacinth in one of his stories of the "gods in exile."

38. There have been several acute readings of this story as Pater's attempt to analyze his own experience of "the frustrated and destructive career of desire within a male homosocial community akin to the Oxford that he knew intimately" (Dellamora 186). Dowling regards the story in very much the same way, though interpreting

differently its implications with regard to the effects of homoeroticism (*Hellenism* 138–40). See also Monsman, *Autobiography* 155–9.

39. Laity in "Romantic Landscapes" analyzes "Hyacinth," discussing the way in which this myth encodes for H.D. both her lesbian relationships and some ideal figure within heterosexual relationships (116–22). Friedman notes that the Hyacinth story refers to H.D.'s relationship with Bryher (*Penelope's Web* 256).

40. See letters from H.D. to Bryher, 5 September 1920 and 9 September 1920; for reference to Ellis as Hyacinth, see Silverstein, "Acronyms."

41. I follow throughout the text H.D.'s spelling of this name in her translation of the *Ion*.

42. On Kreousa, see *Euripides' Ion* 29 and "The Opening Scenes of Ion" 146–8; on Hedyle, see *Hedylus* 21–2; on Thetis, see "Thetis," in *Heliodora* (*Collected Poems* 160). On Hippolyta, see *Collected Poems* 136–7.

43. Friedman treats this Artemisian figure at length in relation to lesbian desire; see in particular her discussion of *Paint It Today* (*Penelope's Web* 190–211). See also Laity, "Lesbian Romanticism" xxi–vi.

44. See Friedman, "Hilda Doolittle" 131; Faderman in her anthology of lesbian literature includes "At Baia" (505–6).

45. Freud 110 quotes this remark of Pater in his argument for Leonardo's fixation on his mother's image: "Pater's confident assertion that we can see, from childhood, a face like Mona Lisa's defining itself on the fabric of his dreams, seems convincing and deserves to be taken literally. . . . [W]e begin to suspect the possibility that it was his mother who possessed the mysterious smile" (111).

46. The phrase belongs to DuPlessis, *Career* 44; see also 104, 114–16. Perhaps most prominently, see Kloepfer's whole study, which specifically focuses on the absence/presence of the mother in the writing of H.D. and Jean Rhys. Friedman, in *Penelope's Web*, explores in *Hermione* "a multilayered matrix of maternal and homoerotic desire" (135).

47. Ostriker remarks about the difference between *Sea Garden* and *Hymen*: "But the imagery changes, becoming less white, chaste and sculptural, richer, more deliquescent and glowing, more full of fire, darkness, gold, deep reds and purples, spilled wine" (18). See also Gregory, "Scarlet."

48. Eliot, *Letters* 488. See also the letter from Aldington to H.D., dated 2 January 1919, in regard to the poem "Hymen" (*Early Years* 179–80).

49. Letter to John Cournos, 4 July 192–.

50. In a letter to Bryher, dated 14 February 1919, H.D. tells of having just sent off "Hymen" to Harriet Monroe of *Poetry*: "I am really excited now as to what Harriet will write me – a lecture, I know, on my Asiatic abandon!"

51. See DuPlessis, *Career* 23–6; Gregory, "Rose" 137–9.

52. This is fragment 58 in Campbell 2:435; it is quoted with this translation in Jane Ellen Harrison, *Prolegomena* 638.

4. Anthropology and the Return of the Gods

1. For a summary of romantic mythography, see Ackerman, *Myth*, especially chaps. 3 and 6. For a view of the Victorian conception of mythology in particular, see Kissane, Burstein, Payne, and F. M. Turner (chap. 3).

2. In her copy of Farnell's *Cults of the Greek States*, received as a gift from Bryher in

1919, H.D.'s underlinings and marginal annotations from multiple readings suggest the psychological and spiritual importance of the gods. In a chapter on Ge, H.D. notes a sentence about "two different periods and processes of Delphic *mantike*," and beside it she writes "Father / Mother"; in a chapter on Apollo, "the god 'who led the way'" is underlined, "U.S.A. 1912 / Greece 1920 / etc." written in the margin; in another chapter on Apollo, "the hair falling in a thick mass" is underlined, "G.D. [Gilbert Doolittle] / E.P. [Ezra Pound] / 1884 / 1885" written in the margin. The first example is in 3.9; the second in 4.150; the third in 4.330. H.D.'s copy of Farnell is in the Beinecke Rare Book and Manuscript Library, Yale University.

3. On the importance of Ellis in the dissemination of Nietzsche's thought, see Thatcher chap. 4. A series of three essays by Ellis published in the *Savoy* in 1896 had considerable impact among intellectuals. On the significance of Orage, see Thatcher chap. 7.

4. Vickery's study describes the literary significance of Frazer in detail; see especially chap. 5. See also the collection of essays edited by Robert Fraser, *Sir James Frazer and the Literary Imagination*, among which are considerations of Frazer's influence upon Yeats, Synge, Conrad, Eliot, Lawrence, and others.

5. On these aspects of Harrison's life see Ackerman, *Myth* 67–87; and Stewart.

6. In a late address, Duncan indicates that "H.D. was ignorant of Jane Harrison in the early years" ("H.D.'s Challenge" 29). His remarks are notable because they are perhaps – though not certainly – based on knowledge gained in his conversations with H.D. In his correspondence with her, Duncan asked H.D. if she had ever met Harrison; she replied that she had not (Duncan, *Admiration* 43, 46). If the anthropological books in her library are any indication, she seems to have had a predilection for respectable scholars affiliated with Frazer rather than for affiliates of Harrison, whose reputation among classicists was far from secure. Among the early books of anthropology in H.D.'s library (published before 1925), most adopt a Frazerian model. In *Cults of the Greek States* (1896–1909) and *Greek Hero Cults and Ideas of Immortality* (1921) Farnell applies Frazerian concepts throughout; and he was a chief adversary of Harrison and her group (Ackerman, *Myth* 95–7). Other studies of ancient civilizations in H.D.'s library also take Tylor and Frazer as models: S. Langdon, *Tammuz and Ishtar: A Monograph upon Babylonian Religion and Theology* (1914); John Cuthbert Lawson, *Modern Greek Folklore and Ancient Greek Religion: A Study in Survivals* (1910); and William Perry, *The Origin of Magic and Religion* (1923). The books by Farnell and Perry are located in the Beinecke Rare Book and Manuscript Library, Yale University. The books by Langdon and Lawson are located in the Bryher Library in East Hampton, New York; see Smyers 21.

7. The twelve-volume third edition of *The Golden Bough* was published between 1911 and 1915. Ackerman, *Myth* chap. 7, discusses the writing of the ritualists during 1912–14 as the "years of achievement," which saw the publication of Harrison's *Themis* (1912), containing an essay by Gilbert Murray, "Excursus on the Ritual Forms Preserved in Greek Tragedy," and her *Ancient Art and Ritual* (1913); Cornford's *From Religion to Philosophy* (1912) and *The Origins of Attic Comedy* (1914); Murray's *Four Stages of Greek Religion* (1912), *Euripides and His Age* (1913), and his essay "Hamlet and Orestes" (1914); and A. B. Cook's *Zeus* (1914) (Ackerman, *Myth* 118–19). Payne (185) discusses a broader range of writing between 1909 and 1914 that proposed theories about ritual drama. Among these are William Ridgeway's *The Origins of Tragedy with Special Reference to the Greek Tragedians* (1910) and *The Dramas and*

Dramatic Dances of the Non-European Races in Special Reference to Greek Tragedy (1914) and Farnell's *The Cults of the Greek States* (1896–1914). The latter two writers present their theories in animadversion to the ritualists.

8. A series of essays appeared in the *New Freewoman* in 1913 entitled "The Eclipse of Woman" and written by F.R.A.I. In one of these he/she recommends *Prolegomena* as "one of the most instructive and fascinating [works] ever written on the subject of religious origins, and one which [unlike Frazer's study] vindicates the part played by woman in the evolution [of religion]" (69). See also the review in the *Egoist* of *Ancient Art and Ritual* by Huntley Carter.

9. Harrison's *Ancient Art and Ritual* begins with a description of an Athenian theatergoer and describes the Athenian drama in its religious function (10–15). Harrison's thesis is that ritual may be understood as a "bridge" between life and art (205–7). In an early essay on Euripides' *Ion* and in the commentary on her translation of the play, H.D. also begins with the Athenian playgoer and speaks of the religious function of the play ("The Opening Scenes of Ion" 134–6; *Euripides' Ion* 8). Moreover, she echoes Harrison's emphasis in a slightly different context, speaking of the dramatic prologue as a bridge between life and art: "Life was to merge with art. But it was to merge, to be bridged gradually. The long prologue was this bridge" ("Opening Scenes" 134). These emphases may have come from Murray's *Euripides and His Age* (1913), which shares seamlessly Harrison's ideas about Greek theater (see chaps. 8 and 9).

10. H.D. indicates in Swann (10) that she read Murray's prose (rather than translations) in her early career, but she almost certainly consulted his translations too, if only for their excellent notes. The publications of Murray to which H.D. refers would have included his widely read history of Greek literature (1897) and several very popular studies propounding models of Greek religion conceived in affiliation with Harrison: his introduction to *Euripides* (1902), translations with notes of the *Hippolytus* and the *Bacchae*; *Four Stages of Greek Religion* (1912); and *Euripides and His Age* (1913), in the Home University Library series. The last book and *Five Stages of Greek Religion* (1925) are in H.D.'s library at Yale. H.D. wrote a notice of *Five Stages* when it appeared in 1925 in *Adelphi*. In a letter to Havelock Ellis, dated 29 March 1932, H.D. asks Ellis for an introduction to Murray: "I do so very much admire Prof. M. and would like one day to meet him."

11. On his indebtedness to Harrison, see Murray's *Euripides* vii; *Euripides and His Age* 63; *Four Stages* 6–7 and passim. Murray states that the first chapter of *Four Stages* is a summary of Harrison, and the second an outgrowth of her studies. The first chapter, on primitive Greek religion, summarizes material in *Prolegomena* and *Themis*. Clear traces of H.D.'s reading of Murray's book on Euripides are apparent in her early essays on Euripides as well as in her final commentary on the *Ion*. For instance, in "Euripides" (7) H.D. alludes to the background given in chapter 2 of Murray's book, and she generally borrows Murray's overall interpretation of Euripides' plays in light of the Athenian experience of successive wars. She speaks of Euripides' having "lived through almost a modern great-war period" (2). Her general sense of Greek drama, with emphasis on the prologue and the chorus, may well have come from chapters 8 and 9 of Murray's book. In H.D.'s commentary on the *Ion*, she emphasizes the Persian invasion of Athens and the flight of the Athenians, alluding perhaps to Murray's account (36–7) of Euripides' childhood experience of fleeing the city.

12. In its first publication, "Orchard" was entitled "Priapus, Keeper-of-Orchards"; it is taken from an epigram to Priapus by Dioscoros Zonas in the *Palatine Anthology* 6.22.

All the more notable for this explicitness is H.D.'s omission of Priapus's name from *Sea Garden*.

13. In the index of cult titles in Farnell (vol. 5), all of the titles here are indicated, except "Zeus Melios." "Melios" is not a Greek word and not a cult title. Nor is "Melas" a title in any cult, but it may be the word H.D. had in mind. "Zeus in the black earth" would probably refer to the title "Chthonios."

14. Bachofen sees the earliest, most primitive stage of matriarchy as associated with Aphrodite, but he is moralistic and censorious in his treatment of the barbaric rule of the hetaera (92–5). Farnell in his chapters on Aphrodite delineates a range of her aspects as manifest in cult, but he emphasizes throughout her alienness to the true Aryan hellenes (2:618–69). On the avoidance of Aphrodite by specialists on Greek myth and religion, see Friedrich 1–3.

15. Postcard dated 15 April 1932.

16. In a letter to Havelock Ellis dated 10 May 1932, H.D. refers to the presence on the trip of Dean Inge and "Alington" (possibly Reverend C. A. Alington). Wigram in his 1947 travel guide to Greece acknowledges his work with the "Hellenic Travellers' Club," which makes Greece "accessible to tourists who can appreciate her marvels" (5).

17. In her notes H.D. records under "Eleusis" the lecturer's remarks about the influence at Eleusis of the cult of Isis and Osiris, mediated through Orphism, and about Orpheus as a historical reformer of Dionysian religion (cf. *Prolegomena* chap. 9). He then apparently presented Harrison's distinctions regarding Greek ritual practice. H.D.'s notes read: "*1*. Olympian – *I give that you may give* business transaction. *2. I give that you may keep away* – grave of hero etc. *3*. Orphism & Dionysius – new idea – mysticism . . . the *union* of being – *communion & union* – gloriously drunk – out of touch with earth: touch with heaven." This summary derives from *Prolegomena*, chaps. 1 and 9. Compare, for example, the passage from Harrison (7): "The formula of that [older] religion was not *do ut des* 'I give that you may give,' but *do ut abeas* 'I give that you may go, and keep away.'" In his 1947 travel guide to Greece, Wigram credits Harrison's *Prolegomena* and *Themis* as chief sources of his presentation of Greek religion (11). His treatment of Eleusis in this book (chap. 4) corresponds closely to the lines suggested in H.D.'s notes.

18. See Harrison, *Religion* 52–3. Foucart, a contemporary of Harrison, bases his interpretation of Eleusinian mysteries heavily on the influence of the Isis–Osiris cults; see 437–47.

19. Neither Farnell nor Foucart, the major commentators on the mysteries at the time of *Prolegomena*, suggests such emphases. Cf. Farnell 3:126–98; Foucart 106–13, 457–97.

20. On the Orphic mysteries, see Harrison, *Prolegomena* chap. 10.

21. Murray in *Euripides and His Age*, published after *Ancient Art* in the same year (1913), gives "a re-statement [from Harrison's *Themis*] of the orthodox view of the origins of tragedy" in Dionysian ritual (61–83). In his last two chapters on Euripidean art, Murray borrows often from Harrison (see 220); his treatment of the chorus literally echoes her language in *Ancient Art*: "And lastly is the Chorus, at once the strangest and the most beautiful of all these ancient and remote conventions. If we can understand the Chorus we have got to the very heart of Greek tragedy" (226).

22. See Rosenthal and Gall for a comprehensive study of the poetic sequence in modern poetry; they give brief notice to *Sea Garden* (477–8).

5. H.D. and the Classical Lyric

1. The most comprehensive treatment of H.D.'s poetry is that of Burnett. His book, *H.D. Between Image and Epic*, discusses chronologically all of the poetry after *Sea Garden*, concluding with a consideration of "A Dead Priestess Speaks"; a separate essay on *Sea Garden*, "Identity," completes his attempt at a comprehensive assessment of the early career. Recent studies of the lyric poetry include Gregory, "Rose" and "Scarlet," essays that read *Sea Garden* and *Hymen* as integrative volumes; Moody, who reads the early poems in terms of initiation into "the elemental process of life" (86); Bruzzi, "Fiery Moment" and "Hieroglyph," both focusing on the hermetic character of the early poetry; Laity, "Romantic Landscapes," emphasizing late-romantic *topoi* of the sublime and of the garden; and Alfrey, exploring the "intersubjective" character of the poems of *Sea Garden*. An essay by Boughn ("Sounding") treats the aural dimension of some of the earliest poems. Discussions of H.D.'s literary appropriation of Sappho include Gubar (53–9); DuPlessis, (*Career* chap. 1) who also discusses Meleager at length; and Gregory, "Rose."

2. Engel and Jackson take their titles from Pound's remarks about H.D.'s flaws, and Rainey uses as an epigraph the statement by Eliot voicing prim "dislike" of the "carnality" in the poems of *Hymen* (99).

3. For my assessment of the theory of the lyric in the context of postmodern thought I am generally indebted to New's *The Regenerate Lyric* and to several essays in *Lyric Poetry: Beyond New Criticism*, edited by Hošek and Parker, particularly essays by Culler and Arac. For a Bakhtinian reading of the romantic lyric, see the essay by Rajan in this collection. On the predominance of narrative in postmodern theory, see Culler, "Lyric" 41–2, and New 8.

4. See de Man's "The Rhetoric of Temporality," in *Blindness and Insight* (1969); "Lyric and Modernity," in *Interpretation: Theory and Practice*, ed. Charles S. Singleton (1971); "The Intentional Structure of the Romantic Image" (1970) and "Anthropomorphism and Trope in the Lyric" (1984), in *The Rhetoric of Romanticism* (1984).

5. In the preparation of *Selected Poems*, Pearson and Horace Gregory made a preliminary list, to which H.D. responded and adapted. My grateful acknowledgment goes to Donna Hollenberg for this information culled from the H.D.–Pearson correspondence. *Selected Poems* contains a dedication to H.D.'s grandchildren, an intimate gesture suggesting her personal responsibility for the selection. Several poems in the volume appearing under different titles elsewhere ("Pallas") or as segments of longer poems or sequences (such as a portion of a chorus from *Iphigeneia* entitled here "And Pergamos") are almost certainly H.D.'s preferences.

6. Martz clearly implies (viii) that H.D.'s failure to collect or to publish the longer poems is a gesture of self-limitation: "H.D. herself contributed to her delimitation and neglect by not publishing, or not collecting" the sequences showing her real powers.

7. These are Martz's emphases in his introduction to *Collected Poems* and to *Selected Poems*; see also DuPlessis's comments on the poems of 1917 and on Sappho (*Career* 15, 23–6); and Laity on the "sexual politics" of *Sea Garden* and "Hyacinth" ("Romantic Landscapes" 116–22).

8. See, for example, the discussion in Gilbert and Gubar, *Madwoman* 582–6. Two extended treatments of the self-limiting postures of female poets are those of Walker: *Nightingale's Burden* treats major women poets of the nineteenth century within what

Walker calls the "nightingale" tradition, and her concluding chapter suggests the continuity of this tradition in twentieth-century women poets; *Masks* considers in detail the nightingale tradition in some twentieth-century women poets: Lowell, Teasdale, Wylie, Millay, H.D., and Bogan.

9. See Gregory, "Rose" 129–32, for a discussion of the problem of the Poetess in modern and contemporary treatments of women poets. See Roethke 134.

10. Friedman, *Penelope's Web* 58, notes the passive verbs as a sign of vulnerability.

11. DuPlessis, *Career* 12–13, notes this consistent address: "In *Sea Garden* . . . an erotic plot is essayed, in which 'I' occurs in awed breathless yearning for an elusive 'you.' "

12. For "Sitalkas" as an epithet of Apollo at Delphi, Pausanias is undoubtedly the source of H.D.'s allusion. Argestes, originally an epithet of Zephyros (Hesiod, *Theogony* 379, 870), by the fourth century B.C. was known as the northwest wind, coming especially in the autumn. Aristotle mentions Argestes in his treatise on winds, and Theophrastus in his treatise on weather signs; rare instances of its use in the Greek Anthology are given in Liddell and Scott's unabridged Greek lexicon.

13. In her 1912 Paris diary (59) H.D. mentions that Aldington is "deep in Greek Choruses," very likely those of Euripides.

14. *Choruses from the Iphigeneia* was published in November 1915, *Sea Garden* in September 1916. A presentation inscription to Aldington by H.D. in a copy of *Sea Garden* in the Beinecke reads: "For 3–9–16." This is probably the date of publication.

15. These plays were *Rhesos*, *Iphigeneia in Aulis*, *Ion*, *Hippolytus* (these four in conjunction with the Poets' Translation Series); *Helen*, *Trojan Women*, and *Andromache* (indicated in allusions within poetry and prose), and possibly the *Bacchae*.

16. See Lattimore, "Lyricist" 160; Bush 498; Carne-Ross 7.

17. The title of H.D.'s first group of poems published in *Poetry* – "Verses, Translations, and Reflections from 'The Anthology' " – was probably not assigned by herself but by Pound or Harriet Monroe (see Babcock, "Verses" 203). An early poem was called "Epigram / (*After the Greek*)," and it is very close to an original in the *Palatine Anthology*.

18. In terms of sound, the first chorus seems relatively rough compared with other more songlike choral odes, dominated by plosives like *p*, *k*, *t*, *ph*, *th*. Though it is impossible to compare quantitative with accentual meter – and free verse at that – one can say at least that both the original and the translated lines have rapid tempo. The meter of the Greek, as analyzed by one commentator on the play, is logodaeic, "which, speaking musically, is in triple time" (England, ed., *Iphigenia at Aulis of Euripides* 155).

19. One is reminded of Odysseus's preparation of a raft in book 5 of the *Odyssey*, beginning with cutting trees. Frazer in *The Golden Bough* speaks of primitive rites associated with the slaying of trees.

20. Arrowsmith in his foreword to the translation of *Iphigeneia* by Dimock makes this argument, suggesting that Euripides evokes the Homeric context as a measure for the nobility of the figures in the play.

21. A review of the edition of Sappho by Edwin Marion Cox was published in 1925 in the *Saturday Review of Literature*; "The Wise Sappho," from "Notes on Euripides, Pausanius, and Greek Lyric Poets," was published in 1982 with *Notes on Thought and Vision*.

22. Gubar 53–9 discusses H.D.'s "fragment" poems in the context of turn-of-the-century and early-modernist uses of the fiction of Sappho, such as Michael Field, Virginia Woolf, René Vivien, and Amy Lowell; DuPlessis, *Career* 23–6, speaks of these poems

within a general discussion of H.D.'s hellenism and her modernist revisionary poetics; Collecott, "Images," more broadly explores the imaginative territory of Greece as a site of H.D.'s bisexuality, discussing her relation to Bryher and to Kenneth Macpherson; Gregory, "Rose," discusses Sappho as the muse of *Sea Garden*.

23. For commentary by Edmonds on the Berlin fragments of Sappho, see *Classical Review* 23 (June 1909): 99–104; 23 (August 1909): 156–8; 30 (August–September 1916): 129–33; on the Oxyrhynchus fragments, 28 (May 1914): 73–5; 30 (June 1916): 97–102; 33 (November–December 1919): 125–7. Later essays on new manuscripts from the Oxyrhynchus papyri appear after 1922 and 1927 in other journals.

24. In his third edition of Sappho's fragments (1895), Wharton (181) gives facsimiles of two such inches of palimpsest from Egyptian parchment, the Fayum fragments. H.D. in her essay surely has this image in mind, though she had knowledge of the newer discoveries as well.

25. Zilboorg quotes a letter from Aldington to Harriet Monroe, dated 12 November 1912, in which he explains this situation in order to indicate that the Greek from which he has translated the Sapphic fragment might not be accurate; see "Influence" 42 n8. The fragments transcribed by H.D. would have been those edited by Edmonds in the *Classical Review* in 1909.

26. *New Freewoman* 1 (September 1913): 114.

27. H.D. cites in a prose translation the following fragments (Bergk/Wharton numbering): 11, 12, 21, 22, 23, 31, 41, 44, 50, 63, 69, 70, 72, 77, 106, 115, 126. She alludes to these: 1, 2, 5, 9, 19, 26, 30, 32, 33, 40, 42, 46, 48, 51, 57a, 58, 60, 62, 64, 65, 66, 79, 85, 87, 89, 91, 94, 100, 108, 119, 135, 138, 142.

28. This fragment, first published in 1922, appeared in Lobel's edition of Sappho in 1925.

29. Translations of fragments by Michael Field (Katherine Bradley and Edith Cooper) appear in Wharton's edition, and H.D. was generally acquainted with the writing of this couple (one book is in her library at Yale, and Aldington features them prominently in his anthology of the Aesthetes). René Vivien published translations of Sappho in a decadent French tradition, following Baudelaire, Gautier, and Louÿs. Undoubtedly H.D. knew of these as well. See Gubar for a discussion of Vivien (47–53); see also DeJean for a discussion of Vivien in the context of French decadent poetry (279–86).

30. See Friedrich on the subjective erotic state of *aphrodite* and on Sappho's role of incarnating or making the goddess present through the poem (117–25). Segal, "Eros," discusses Sappho's participation in a tradition wherein the enchantment of poetry and incantation is related to the manifestation and taming of eros.

31. Both Gubar 55–6 and DuPlessis, *Career* 29, note that "Hymen" focuses much attention upon erotic ties between women. Guest (108) suggests that "Hymen" "may be a 'wedding song' for Bryher . . . reluctant at the marriage rites" (however, Bryher was not actually married until 1921). The presence of children in the processions may point to H.D.'s reflection on the child she had lost (in 1915) or that she was carrying. The dedication of the volume to Bryher and Perdita would encourage these last associations. Burnett (*Between* 32) indeed suggests that the dedication specifies the relationship between Bryher and H.D. as a "marriage."

32. I use this phrase loosely, as H.D. and her generation did, referring to a complex amalgamation of compilations of epigrams in Greek. Mackail, the editor/translator whom H.D. knew best, also included epigrams from sources other than the Renais-

sance manuscript taking shape for instance in the five-volume Loeb edition (1916) (Babcock, "Verses" 202–23).

33. Pound brought H.D. Thomas Mosher books in their early days – Lang's translation of the bucolic poets for sure, possibly also Lang's translation of *Aucassin and Nicolette* (*Hermione* 61); and Pound mentions Mosher in an early letter to William Carlos Williams. Hermione in *Hermione* mentions to Fayne Rabb "the Portland Maine shop" as though it were common knowledge among New England literati (61). Aldington in the introduction to his anthology of the aesthetes mentions in particular the popularity of Mosher's editions and their importance in the dissemination of aestheticism (4). One may get an overall sense of turn-of-the-century tastes by perusing the index to Mosher's *Bibelot* (1895–1915), which largely duplicated the publications in his editions; see also the checklist of the Mosher books by Hatch.

34. Foster provides a comprehensive survey of translations of Greek authors until 1918; on the importance of schoolbook texts, see, for instance, Stedman on texts of Theocritus available at Cambridge at the time that Tennyson matriculated there (208–9).

35. An early, very persuasive study of analogies between Tennyson and Theocritus is that of Stedman.

36. The first bracketed phrase in this sentence represents a manuscript addition to the carbon typescript, while the second bracketed phrase is crossed out in the typescript.

37. Friedman, *Penelope's Web* 51, speaks of the pastoral in *Sea Garden*, in terms of H.D.'s affiliation with Theocritus.

38. In dating these events I am indebted to Silverstein's unpublished chronology of H.D.'s life.

39. On page 1 of the essay, H.D. has crossed out *"Pacific* rock-pools," and on pages 4–5 has eliminated the phrase "under great pine-trees, *beside full breakers."*

40. See Gregory, "Rose" and "Scarlet," for a discussion of H.D.'s deliberate construction of poetic sequences in *Sea Garden* and *Hymen*.

41. Pound's correspondence with Harriet Monroe suggests that there were three or four months' lead time for publication in *Poetry*, so "Hermonax" was probably submitted in October or November 1913.

42. This idea was suggested to me by Babcock's essay, "Verses," in which he discusses the importance of Mackail's introduction to *Select Epigrams from the Greek Anthology* and calls attention to it as a primary text not only for H.D. but for early modernists in general (213–16).

43. "Little, but all roses" comes from Mackail's translation of the proem to Meleager's *Garland* (93); "Curled Thyme," the title of H.D.'s essay on Theocritus, comes from Mackail's translation of one of Theocritus's epigrams (137). The epigram of Simonides, when quoted by H.D. in her essay "People of Sparta" (419) and in *Hermione* (220–1), is given in Mackail's translation (150).

44. Another epigram by Philodemus (*Palatine Anthology* 6.349) seems also to come into play. Entitled in Mackail "To the Gods of Sea and Weather," it invokes, like H.D.'s poem, all sea gods, beginning with Palemon and Ino, under aliases, "O Melicerta son of Ino, and thou, sea-green Leucothea, mistress of Ocean." Ino and her son, Melicerta, are the names of mortals, transformed by Hera into the sea deities Leucothea and Palemon. H.D. refers to the mortal origin of Ino/Leucothea, evoking her gray-greenness, in the opening of her poem.

45. Pound wrote to Dorothy Shakespear in 1913, "The Dryad with no sense of moder-

nity has writ a poem to Tycho the god of little things" (*Pound and Shakespear* 238) – probably *Palatine Anthology* 9.334.

46. H.D.'s copy of the Greek text of books 1–12 of the *Odyssey* is in the H.D. Library at Yale.

47. For instance, H.D. in "Helios" refers to book 16 of the *Iliad*, when Phoebus Apollo strips Patrokles of armor on the battlefield; she refers in "Sea Heroes" to a specific passage from book 8 of the *Odyssey*.

48. This quotation appears written in H.D.'s hand between *Bacchae* and *Hippolytus* in an edition of Euripides from her library in the Beinecke Rare Book and Manuscript Library at Yale. The edition is that of Wilhelm Dindorf, *Euripidis opera omnia* [Oxford: Jacobus Parker et Soc., 1871–3].

49. H.D. notes the gift of a Greek edition of Pindar from F. L. Flint in a letter to him dated 17 May 1916. The first Pindaric poem appears in *Sea Garden*, published in October 1916.

50. Letter from Bryher to H.D., December 1918.

51. Letters indicate that H.D. sent Bryher an early draft of "Sea Heroes" – drawn from Homer's *Odyssey* – in December 1918 and a draft of the Homer translation in February 1919.

52. For a discussion of these interrelated themes in *Helen in Egypt* see Friedman, *Psyche* 256–72.

53. Friedman, *Penelope's Web* 386 n5. Spoo in his introduction to *Asphodel* (xv–xvi) takes the clue to the title from a Landor poem that is quoted, or misquoted, in the text. But the association of asphodel with the underworld is well known, and H.D. did read at least the first half of the *Odyssey* very closely.

54. The most extensive reading of H.D.'s critique of Western masculine hierarchies of war is given in Friedman, *Psyche* chap. 8.

55. For the connection with Freud, see *Collected Poems* (ed. Martz) xxv–vi; Burnett in his final chapter (*Between*) reads the poem as a response to Lawrence's novel.

56. H.D. makes the connection between "A Dead Priestess" and "Sigil XVII" with regard to the "love–death motif" in *H.D. by Delia Alton* 215.

6. Euripides: Dream Time and Dream Work

1. Two excellent recent considerations of the relation between H.D.'s hellenism and historical contingencies are Walker, "Women and Time: H.D. and the Greek Persona," in *Masks* 105–34; and Edmunds, who gives a New Historicist reading of *Helen in Egypt* (95–148).

2. "Hippolytus Temporizes" (1921), "Phaedra" (1919), "She Contrasts with Herself Hippolyta," and "She Rebukes Hippolyta" (1919) appeared in *Hymen* (1921). Other poems published during 1924–7 – "Leucadian Artemis" (1924) and "Songs from Cyprus" (1925) – were partially integrated into the play. Still other poems of this period seem coincident with the material of the play: "All Mountains" (1925) and "Calliope" (1924). See Lyon 58–80 for a discussion of these related poems.

3. It is difficult to date these efforts of translation, but choruses from *Ion* first appear in 1923, *Hecuba* in 1927, and *Bacchae* in 1930. H.D. notes in *H.D. by Delia Alton* that "I had been working, at about that time [in 1923, at the time of writing 'Hesperia'], on a translation of Euripides' *Helen in Egypt*, which I never finally assembled" (218–19).

4. H.D. projects a future translation of the *Helen* in correspondence with Bryher in 1935,

while working on the translation of the *Ion* (letters dated 1 August and 24 August 1935). Later, in January 1936, H.D. notes to Bryher that "I am simply doing the more conventional Greek plays and so on" (letter dated 20 January 1936).

5. This reading is indicated in a working notebook for *Helen in Egypt* in the Beinecke at Yale, published in Gregory, "Euripides."

6. On translation projects after *Helen in Egypt*, see "Compassionate Friendship" 19, 23. H.D.'s 1958 rereading of her essays is indicated in a manuscript note on p. 18 of a carbon typescript of her essay on the *Helen*.

7. In his 1920 review of Gilbert Murray's and H.D.'s translations, Eliot admires H.D.'s choruses, "allowing for errors and even occasional omissions of difficult passages" (*Selected Essays* 50). In speaking of "difficult passages," Eliot probably has in mind a notorious passage from the opening speech of Hippolytus (lines 78–81), one of many quasi-moral musings that H.D. chooses to omit in her translations.

8. Robinson has proposed a reading of *Iphigeneia* in which H.D. is seen as the victim of the men in her life (Hilda/Iphigeneia sacrificed to become H.D./Helen, the muse of her male contemporaries). In this biographical allegory, the Greek figures are un-equivocal masks for literal men, and H.D.'s creative efforts are seen merely in terms of an economy of sexual substitutions (100–6).

9. Demeter is called *semne* in the first line of the Homeric hymn to Demeter. Euripides in the beginning of *Hippolytus* alludes to the Eleusinian story. Aphrodite relates that Phaedra first saw and fell in love with Hippolytus when he came to Athens to participate in the rites of the holy mysteries (*semnon mysterion*) (*Hippolytus* 25). Dramatic parallels are immediately established between Hippolytus and Persephone in Hippolytus's insistence on the untouched, virgin meadow from which he picks flowers to give to Artemis (73–4); and he claims to his father to have a "virgin soul" (*parthenon psychen*) (*Hippolytus* 1006).

10. This essay can be dated with some certainty because the translations of the choruses are the same as those published in *Red Roses for Bronze*, which depend upon a French translation of the play first published in 1923, a copy of which is inscribed by H.D. "Spring 1924." This book, in H.D.'s library at Yale, is *Les bacchantes*, trans. Mario Meunier (French) (Paris: Payot, 1923). On the half-title page a note by H.D. indicates page numbers in this text corresponding to translations of the choruses of the *Bacchae* in *Red Roses for Bronze*.

11. The play is the subject of a monograph by Lyon, who approaches it with New Critical preoccupations; Walsh's insightful "Afterword" to the Black Swan edition attempts to see the poem in light of some of H.D.'s imaginal preoccupations. In an earlier essay ("Virginity") I first explored the play in terms of its hellenism; and most recently Laity ("Transgressive Sexualities") approaches it in terms of the iconography of decadent-romantic hellenism.

12. Lyon also discusses the distinct and yet confused imagery surrounding the two goddesses (15–21).

13. This is a central idea in Friedman's study of H.D.'s narratives; for a preliminary articulation of the argument, see *Penelope's Web* 80–99.

14. Freud writes to H.D. in July 1933, immediately after their first sessions, "I confidently expected to hear from you that you are writing, . . . I trust I shall hear so later on"; and again in March 1934, "I am sorry to hear you do not yet work but according to your own account the forces are seething" (*Tribute to Freud* 191–2).

15. Letter from H.D. to Bryher, 3 April 1937, quoted in Friedman, *Penelope's Web* 293.

16. Subsequent references in this chapter to H.D.'s letters to Bryher will be indicated in the text.

17. An advertisement announcing H.D.'s translations from the *Ion* in the Poets' Translation Series appears in the *Egoist* 3.1 (January 1916): 15. Thus she must have envisioned translating the play as early as 1915. Evidence of H.D.'s early work on the *Ion* in 1916 also comes from her unpublished "Autobiographical Notes." A summary of dates is given on a page proof of the first printing of *Ion* (1937): "*Ion*: 1935 – Assembled Vaud, Switzerland from rough notes begun in England 1915–1917 and Greece 1920 & 1932" (quoted by Walsh, "Afterword" 130). Other evidence given below indicates that she was also engaged with the play during 1918 and 1919.

18. H.D. indicates in "Autobiographical Notes" that she was working on the *Ion* in Devon in 1917 [1916], during the time of Aldington's officer's training and his first adultery. A letter to John Cournos dated 8 August 1916 confirms this effort at translation. H.D. mentions to Bryher in her 1935 letters that she had been working on the *Ion* during her pregnancy with Perdita and her first meeting with Bryher (summer 1918). She also mentions in these letters a recent episode involving a bird, which brings back memories of "bird auguries" during her pregnancy. Finally, in these letters she mentions associations with "Scilly/Corfu" as well as with Cornwall, where she first met Bryher. See letters of 9, 14, 24, 27, and 28 August 1935.

19. See letters of 14, 27, and 28 August 1935. Throughout these letters H.D. frequently refers to "fish" as a sign of the "un-c," or unconscious; and this aquatic imagery is lived out during this period in H.D.'s strict ritual of daily swimming, which, she figures, is connected to her "mother-fix" (27 August). See Friedman, *Penelope's Web* 293, for a quotation from one of these letters, pertaining to swimming, her mother, and the *Ion*.

20. I am indebted here as elsewhere to Vanderwielen's discussion of *Euripides' Ion*, as well as to the "Afterword" of Walsh – the only full-length studies of this book.

21. I am indebted in my reading of Euripides' *Ion* to the discussion of Whitman (69–103).

22. See Friedman, *Penelope's Web* 328–9, for a discussion of "the room of analysis" as "a modern shrine of Delphi." Chisholm elaborates the association of Freud with Hermes, hermeticism, and hermeneutics (26–36).

23. Murray, whose book *Euripides and His Age* H.D. quotes as an epigraph to *Euripides' Ion*, attempts to situate Euripides' life by imagining the events he must have undergone. He relates that Euripides as a young boy was forced to flee Athens with his family during the invasion of the Persians (36–7).

24. The most extensive treatment of *Helen in Egypt* as a neoepic is Friedman, "Gender and Genre," and *Psyche* 253–72; see also DuPlessis *Career* 108–15, who speaks of it as a "deconstructed" epic, a "displacement of the narrative of war" (108); see also Gelpi 74.

25. General references to the Homeric poems are everywhere. There are, however, specific identifiable references to Homer, distinct from derivative stories: the image of the funeral pyre, which begins book 1 of the *Iliad*; the image of winged ships, alluding to book 2 of the *Iliad*, though also the opening chorus of *Iphigeneia in Aulis*; Helen on the walls, from book 6 of the *Iliad*; Paris in the assembly ("*return the wanton to Greece*") from book 7; Achilles' withdrawal in his tent, after book 1. Athene's wrath at Cassandra's rape introduces the *Trojan Women*, but it is also prominent in the *Odyssey*, which is indeed quoted by H.D. at one point (*Helen in Egypt* 122).

26. This is the somewhat erroneous premise given in the argument introducing the play in Way's edition (1.463), which H.D. read during the composition of the poem.

27. Stesichorus and perhaps Hesiod in a lost work say that Helen was never at Troy, but neither indicates that she was in Egypt. Herodotus, a few years before Euripides' play, tells the story that Helen and Paris were forced ashore in Egypt on their way to Troy and that Proteus insisted on keeping Helen; the Greeks, after successfully destroying Troy, found that Helen was not there. Euripides combines these two traditions in his play as no previous writer appears to have done (Lattimore, "Helen" 261–2).

28. She here refers to line 81, also the basis of her 1923 poem "Helen."

29. There is no textual basis for Helen in Egypt as a title for Euripides' Helen, as there is, for instance, in the case of the variant title Iphigeneia in Aulis. H.D. may have had in mind adaptations of the play with this title in opera versions. On Helen in Egypt in relation to Hofmannsthal's Agyptishe Helena, see Clack.

30. To my knowledge there is no evidence of H.D.'s reading of Homer after around 1920. A Greek text of the Odyssey survives in her library at Yale, but there is no edition of the Iliad except a late translation by Robert Graves (1959).

31. For a discussion of Euripides' resistance to "mythological necessity," see the reading of Iphigeneia in Aulis by Dimock, to which I am here indebted.

32. H.D. read Verrall and Murray at the time of writing her early essays on Euripides; she reread Murray's Euripides and His Age and perhaps also Verrall in preparation for the Ion (the former indicated in letters, the latter in references in the text itself); and she read the commentary of Grégoire during the composition of Helen in Egypt ("Compassionate Friendship" 71–2).

33. Friedman briefly discusses H.D.'s variance from Euripides in the characterization of Helen (Psyche 255). The most extensive treatment of this textual relation is that of Chisholm (171–8). The quotation here comes from Chisholm 171.

34. H.D. notes her reading of The Divine Fire and her subsequent meeting with Sinclair in End to Torment 9–10.

35. Of all the many versions of the Helen story circulating during H.D.'s formative years, this one seems most pertinent to her later interests, especially because she came to know Sinclair very well and may have discussed the play with her. Other significant variations of the Helen myth in the late nineteenth century that H.D. would have known include several poems of Walter Savage Landor, especially "Achilles and Helena"; D. G. Rossetti's "Troy Town," often quoted by H.D. in her narratives; William Morris's "The Death of Paris," recounting the story of Paris's fruitless entreaty of Oenone; A. C. Swinburne, "Leuké"; Andrew Lang, Helen of Troy: Her Life and Translation (1892); and Maurice Hewlett (whom H.D. knew in London), Helen Redeemed (1913).

36. See H.D.'s letter to Francis Wolle, dated 25 September 1952: "Strange, that just recently, I went off the deep end, over Helen in Egypt. I have written no poems for more than five years, but the idea has been swimming for decades. I did a sketchy translation of Euripides' Helen in Egypt, but threw away the old script."

37. See Gregory, "Euripides," for a transcription of H.D.'s working notebook for Helen in Egypt, indicating the notes she took while reading Leconte de Lisle's French translation of these plays.

38. H.D. takes "pallinode" from the comments of many critics about the relation of the Helen to Stesichorus; she takes "Leuké" from the name given in Andromache and "l'isle blanche" from the translation of this play by Leconte de Lisle; she takes "Eidolon,"

very probably, from the use of the Greek word in the *Helen*. H.D. indicates these emphases in her working notebook on *Helen in Egypt* in the Beinecke, where she took notes on her rereading of Euripides' plays.

39. For critical investigation of these specific themes in Euripides' plays, see Zeitlin, "Power," on Eros in *Hippolytus*; Wilson on Eris and Eros in several late plays; Segal, "Two Worlds," on the opposition of illusion and reality in the *Helen* (224–7).

40. The headnotes to *Helen in Egypt* originated as explanatory glosses for H.D.'s audio recording of lyrics from the poem ("Compassionate Friendship" 15).

41. For readings of *Helen in Egypt* in terms of Freud, see Friedman, *Psyche* 256–7 and passim; and Chisholm 165–213.

42. See Michelini, chap. 1, for a comprehensive survey of the criticism of Euripides, in which, she argues, certain reductive lines of interpretation were established within German classicism that even now insistently recur.

43. See, for instance, Murray, *Euripides and His Age* 144–6.

44. H.D. records her response to Grégoire's commentary in her 1955 memoir "Compassionate Friendship," though she may well have read it earlier.

45. Grégoire's complex argument about the *Helen* and the *Iphigeneia* (which does not involve the *Ion*, except very tangentially) is this: Because of a conflict with regard to Iphigenia and Helen between the cultic worship of a goddess and the mythic figure of a mortal, the mortals were imagined in legend to have been magically removed to a nebulous country at the margins of the known world – Iphigeneia in Tauris, Helen in Egypt. But in its national self-consciousness, fifth-century Athens wanted to recover its mythic origins. This motive might explain the connection H.D. makes with Grégoire's reading of the *Ion*, a play about the original Attic ancestor.

Works Cited

Ackerman, Robert. "Introduction." *Prolegomena to the Study of Greek Religion*. By Jane
    Ellen Harrison. xiii–xxx.

The Myth and Ritual School: J. G. Frazer and the Cambridge Ritualists. Theorists of Myth.
    New York: Garland, 1991.

Aldington, Richard. "Anti-Hellenism: A Note on Some Modern Art." *Egoist* 1 (15
    January 1914): 35–6.

Images Old and New. Boston: Four Seas, 1916.

Letter to Amy Lowell. Houghton Library. Harvard University, Cambridge, Mass.

Life for Life's Sake: A Book of Reminiscences. New York: Viking, 1941.

Literary Studies and Reviews. London: Allen & Unwin, 1924.

Richard Aldington and H.D.: The Early Years in Letters. Ed. Caroline Zilboorg.
    Bloomington: Indiana University Press, 1992.

Aldington, Richard, trans. *Greek Songs in the Manner of Anacreon*. Poets' Translation Series.
    London: Egoist Press, 1919.

Latin Poems of the Renaissance. Poets' Translation Series. London: Egoist Press, 1915.

The Poems of Anyte of Tegea. Poets' Translation Series. London: Egoist Press, 1915.

The Poems of Meleager of Gadara. Poets' Translation Series. London: Egoist Press,
    1920.

Aldington, Richard, ed. *The Religion of Beauty: Selections from the Aesthetes*. London:
    William Heinemann, 1950.

Alfrey, Shawn. "Toward Intersubjective Knowledge: H.D.'s Liminal Poetics." *Sagetrieb* 11
    (Winter 1992): 33–46.

Apollonius of Rhodes. *Argonautica*. Ed. and trans. R. C. Seaton. Loeb Classical Library.
    London: William Heinemann; New York: Macmillan, 1912.

Appian. *Appian's Roman History*. Ed. and trans. Horace White. Loeb Classical Library.
    1912. Cambridge, Mass.: Harvard University Press; London: William Heinemann,
    1962. 4 vols.

Apuleius. *The Golden Ass (Metamorphoses)*. Trans. W. Adlington; ed. and rev. S. Gaselee.
    Loeb Classical Library. 1915. Cambridge, Mass.: Harvard University Press; London:
    William Heinemann, 1947.

Arac, Jonathan. "Afterword: Lyric Poetry and the Bounds of New Criticism." In Hošek and Parker. 345–55.

Arnold, Matthew. *On Translating Homer.* 2d ed. London: John Murray, 1905.

Arrian. *Anabasis Alexandri, Books I–IV.* Ed. and trans. E. Iliff Robson. Loeb Classical Library. 1929. Cambridge, Mass.: Harvard University Press; London: William Heinemann, 1967. 2 vols.

Arrowsmith, William. "Editor's Foreword." *Helen.* By Euripides. Trans. Mitchie and Leach. vii–xv.

"Editor's Foreword." *Iphigeneia at Aulis.* By Euripides. Trans. Merwin and Dimock. v–xiii.

Aske, Martin. *Keats and Hellenism: An Essay.* Cambridge University Press, 1985.

Auerbach, Nina. *Woman and the Demon: The Life of a Victorian Myth.* Cambridge, Mass.: Harvard University Press, 1982.

Babbitt, Irving. *The Masters of Modern French Criticism.* 1912. New York: Farrar, Straus, 1963.

Babcock, Robert G. "H.D.'s 'Pursuit' and Sappho." *H.D. Newsletter* 3.2 (Winter 1990): 43–7.

"Verses, Translations, and Reflections from 'The Anthology': H.D., Ezra Pound, and the Greek Anthology." *Sagetrieb* 14 (Spring–Fall 1995): 201–16.

Bachofen, J. J. *Myth, Religion, & Mother Right: Selected Writings of J. J. Bachofen.* Trans. Ralph Manheim. Bollingen Series. Princeton, N.J.: Princeton University Press, 1967.

Baker, Carlos. *The Echoing Green: Romanticism, Modernism, and the Phenomena of Transference in Poetry.* Princeton, N. J.: Princeton University Press, 1984.

Balzac, Honoré de. *Seraphità* [English]. 1889. Freeport, N.Y.: Books for Libraries Press, 1970.

Seraphità [French]. Paris: Calmann-Lévy, n.d.

Barlow, Shirley A. *The Imagery of Euripides: A Study in the Dramatic Use of Pictorial Language.* London: Methuen, 1971.

"Battle on Trojan Plain." [London] *Times* 30 April 1915, 11, col. 4.

Benét, William Rose, ed. *Fifty Poets: An American Auto-Anthology.* New York: Duffield & Green, 1933.

Bergk, Theodor. *Poetae Lyrici Graeci.* Leipzig: B. G. Teubner, 1878–82. 3 vols.

Bernal, Martin. *Black Athena: The Afroasiatic Roots of Classical Civilization.* Volume I: *The Fabrication of Ancient Greece, 1785–1985.* New Brunswick, N.J.: Rutgers University Press, 1987. 2 vols.

Berthold-Bond, Daniel. "Evolution and Nostalgia in Hegel's Theory of Desire." *Clio* (Summer 1990): 367–88.

Blake, William. *The Poetry and Prose of William Blake.* Ed. David V. Erdman. Garden City, N.Y.: Doubleday, 1970.

Bloom, Harold. *The Anxiety of Influence.* New York: Oxford University Press, 1973.

Yeats. New York: Oxford University Press, 1970.

Boughn, Michael. "Elements of the Sounding: H.D. and the Origins of Modernist Prosodies." *Sagetrieb* 6 (Fall 1987): 101–22.

Boughn, Michael, comp. *H.D.: A Bibliography, 1905–1990.* Charlottesville: University Press of Virginia, 1993.

Brombert, Victor. "T. S. Eliot and the Romantic Heresy." In *The Hidden Reader: Stendhal,*

Balzac, Hugo, Baudelaire, Flaubert. Cambridge, Mass.: Harvard University Press, 1988. 191–204.

Bruzzi, Zara. "'The Fiery Moment': H.D. and the Eleusinian Landscape of English Modernism." *Agenda* 25 (Autumn–Winter 1987–8): 97–112.

"Hieroglyphs of Landscape in H.D.'s Early Work (1916–1922)." *H.D. Newsletter* 4.2 (Winter 1991): 41–51.

Bryher, Winifred. Letters to H.D. Beinecke Rare Book and Manuscript Library. Yale University, New Haven, Conn.

West. London: Jonathan Cape, 1925.

Bryher, Winifred, trans. *The Lament for Adonis.* London: A. L. Humphries, 1918.

"Nine Epigrams of Zonas." *Nation* (22 February 1919).

Bullen, Barrie. "Walter Pater's 'Renaissance' and Leonardo da Vinci's Reputation in the Nineteenth Century." *Modern Language Review* 74 (1979): 268–80.

Burnett, Gary. "H.D. and Lawrence: Two Allusions." *H.D. Newsletter* 1.1 (Spring 1987): 32–35.

H.D. Between Image and Epic: The Mysteries of Her Poetics. Studies in Modern Literature. Ann Arbor, Mich.: UMI Research Press, 1990.

"The Identity of 'H': Imagism and H.D.'s *Sea Garden.*" *Sagetrieb* 8 (Winter 1989): 55–75.

"A Poetics Out of War: H.D.'s Responses to the First World War." *Agenda* 25 (Autumn–Winter 1987–8): 54–76.

Burstein, Janet. "Victorian Mythography and the Progress of the Intellect." *Victorian Studies* 18 (1975): 309–24.

Bush, Douglas. *Mythology & the Romantic Tradition in English Poetry.* 1937. Cambridge, Mass.: Harvard University Press, 1969.

Busst, A. J. L. "The Image of the Androgyne in the Nineteenth Century." In *Romantic Mythologies.* Ed. Ian Fletcher. New York: Barnes & Noble, 1967. 1–95.

Callimachus. *Callimachus and Lycophron.* Ed. and trans. A. W. Mair. With *Aratus.* Ed. and trans. G. R. Mair. Loeb Classical Library. London: William Heinemann; New York: Putnam, 1921.

Campbell, D. A., ed. and trans. *Greek Lyric.* Loeb Classical Library. Cambridge, Mass.: Harvard University Press, 1982–93. 5 vols.

Carne-Ross, D. S. "Translation and Transposition." In *The Craft and Context of Translation.* Ed. William Arrowsmith and Roger Shattuck. Austin: Humanities Research Center–University of Texas Press, 1961. 3–21.

Carpenter, Edward. "The Status of Women in Early Greek Times." *New Freewoman* 1 (1 August 1913): 68–9.

Carson, Anne. *Eros the Bittersweet: An Essay.* Princeton, N.J.: Princeton University Press, 1986.

Carter, Huntly. "The House the Set-Backs Built" [review of *Ancient Art and Ritual* by Jane Ellen Harrison]. *Egoist* 1 (16 March 1914): 114–16.

Cartledge, Paul. "The Importance of Being Dorian: An Onomastic Gloss on the Hellenism of Oscar Wilde." *Hermathena* 147 (Winter 1989): 7–15.

Casey, Edward S. "The World of Nostalgia." *Man and World* 20 (1987): 361–84.

Catullus. *Catullus, Tibullus, and Pervigilium Veneris.* Ed. and trans. F. W. Cornish. Loeb Classical Library. 1913. Cambridge, Mass.: Harvard University Press; London: William Heinemann, 1976.

Cavafy, C. P. *C. P. Cavafy: Collected Poems*. Ed. George Savidis. Trans. Edmund Keeley and Philip Sherrard. Rev. ed. Princeton, N.J.: Princeton University Press, 1992.

Chisholm, Dianne. *H.D.'s Freudian Poetics: Psychoanalysis in Translation*. Ithaca, N.Y.: Cornell University Press, 1992.

Clack, Jerry. "Helen in Vienna." *H.D. Newsletter* 4.1 (Spring 1991): 27–31.

Clay, Diskin. "The Silence of Hermippos: Greece in the Poetry of Cavafy." In Harvey. 157–81.

Collecott, Diana. "Images at the Crossroads: The 'H.D. Scrapbook.'" In *H.D.: Woman and Poet*. Ed. Michael King. Man and Poet Series. Orono, Me.: National Poetry Foundation (University of Maine at Orono), 1985. 319–67.

  "Memory and Desire: H.D.'s 'A Note on Poetry.'" *Agenda* 25 (Autumn–Winter 1987–8): 64–70.

Conlon, John J. *Walter Pater and the French Tradition*. Lewisburg, Pa.: Bucknell University Press; London: Associated University Presses, 1982.

Cournos, John. "The Death of Futurism." *Egoist* 4 (January 1917): 6–7.

  Miranda Masters. New York: Knopf, 1926.

Craig, Cairns. *Yeats, Eliot, Pound and the Politics of Poetry: Richest to the Richest*. Pittsburgh: University of Pittsburgh Press, 1982.

Cronin, Richard. *Colour and Experience in Nineteenth-Century Poetry*. London: Macmillan, 1988.

Culler, Jonathan. "Apostrophe." In *The Pursuit of Signs: Semiotics, Literature, Deconstruction*. Ithaca, N.Y.: Cornell University Press, 1981. 135–54.

  "Changes in the Study of the Lyric." In Hošek and Parker. 38–54.

Davis, Dale. "Heliodora's Greece." *H.D.: Woman and Poet*. Ed. Michael King. Man and Poet Series. Orono, Me.: National Poetry Foundation (University of Maine at Orono), 1985. 143–56.

DeJean, Joan. *Fictions of Sappho, 1546–1937*. Women in Culture and Society. Chicago: University of Chicago Press, 1989.

Delcourt, Marie. *Hermaphrodite: Myths and Rites of the Bisexual Figure in Classical Antiquity*. Trans. Jennifer Nicholson. London: Studio Books, 1961.

Dellamora, Richard. *Masculine Desire: The Sexual Politics of Victorian Aestheticism*. Chapel Hill: University of North Carolina Press, 1990.

de Man, Paul. *Blindness and Insight: Essays on the Rhetoric of Contemporary Criticism*. Minneapolis: University of Minnesota Press, 1983.

  "Lyric and Modernity." In *Interpretation: Theory and Practice*. Ed. Charles Singleton. Baltimore, Md.: Johns Hopkins Press, 1969. 173–209.

  The Rhetoric of Romanticism. New York: Columbia University Press, 1984.

Dembo, L. S. "Imagism and Aesthetic Mysticism." *Conceptions of Reality in Modern American Poetry*. Berkeley: University of California Press, 1966. 10–47.

  "Norman Holmes Pearson on H.D.: An Interview." *Contemporary Literature* 10 (1969): 435–46.

Derrida, Jacques. "Structure, Sign, and Play in the Discourse of the Human Sciences." In *Writing and Difference*. Trans. Alan Bass. Chicago: University of Chicago Press, 1978. 278–93.

Desonay, Ferdinand. *Le rêve hellénique chez les poètes parnassiens*. Paris: Librairie Ancienne Honoré Champion, 1928.

Dictionary of Wars. Comp. George C. Kohn. New York: Facts on File Publications, 1986.

Dijkstra, Bram. *Idols of Perversity: Fantasies of Feminine Evil in Fin-de-Siècle Culture*. Oxford: Oxford University Press, 1986.

Dimock, George E., Jr. "Introduction." *Iphigeneia at Aulis*. By Euripides. Trans. W. S. Merwin and George E. Dimock, Jr. New York: Oxford University Press, 1978. 3–21.

Diogenes Laertius. *Lives of Eminent Philosophers*. Trans. R. D. Hicks. Loeb Classical Library. 1925. Cambridge, Mass.: Harvard University Press; London: William Heinemann, 1979. 2 vols.

Doty, Mark. *My Alexandria*. National Poetry Series. Urbana: University of Illinois Press, 1993.

Dowling, Linda C. *Hellenism and Homosexuality in Victorian Oxford*. Ithaca, N.Y.: Cornell University Press, 1994.

   Language and Decadence in the Victorian Fin de Siècle. Princeton, N.J.: Princeton University Press, 1986.

Duncan, Robert. "Beginnings, Chapter 1 of the H.D. Book, Part I." *Coyote's Journal* 5–6 (1966): 8–31.

   "From the H.D. Book, Part II, Chapter 5." *Stony Brook* 3–4 (Fall 1969): 336–47.

   "From the H.D. Book, Part II, Chapter 5." *Credences* 1 (July 1975): 50–94.

   A Great Admiration: H.D./Robert Duncan Correspondence, 1950–1961. Ed. Robert J. Bertholf. Venice: Lapis Press, 1992.

   "The H.D. Book, Part 2, Chapter 3." *Io* 6 (Summer 1969): 117–40.

   "The H.D. Book: Part II, Nights and Days, Chapter 4." *Caterpillar* 2 (April 1969): 27–60.

   "H.D.'s Challenge." *Poesis* 6.3–4 (1985): 21–34.

   Selected Poems. Ed. Robert J. Bertholf. New York: New Directions, 1993

   "Two Chapters from H.D." *TriQuarterly* 12 (Spring 1968): 67–98.

DuPlessis, Rachel Blau. *H.D.: The Career of That Struggle*. Key Women Writers. Bloomington: Indiana University Press, 1986.

   "Romantic Thralldom in H.D." In Friedman and DuPlessis. 406–29.

Eagleton, Terry. *Criticism and Ideology: A Study in Marxist Literary Theory*. London: NLB; Atlantic Highlands, N.J.: Humanities Press, 1976.

Edmonds, J. M. [The Berlin Fragments]. "Three Fragments of Sappho." *Classical Review* 23 (June 1909): 99–104.

   "More Fragments of Sappho." *Classical Review* 23 (August 1909): 156–8.

Edmonds, J. M., ed. and trans. *Lyra Graeca*. 2d ed. Loeb Classical Library. London: William Heinemann; New York: Macmillan, 1928. 3 vols.

Edmunds, Susan. *Out of Line: History, Psychoanalysis, & Montage in H.D.'s Long Poems*. Stanford, Calif.: Stanford University Press, 1994.

Eliot, T. S. *After Strange Gods: A Primer of Modern Heresy*. The Page–Barbour Lectures at the University of Virginia, 1933. New York: Harcourt, Brace, 1934.

   "Classics in English" [review of Poets' Translation Series, I–VI]. *Poetry* 9 (November 1916): 101–4.

   "A Commentary" [by "Crites"]. *Criterion* 2 (April 1924): 231–32.

   "The Function of Criticism." *Criterion* 2 (October 1923): 31–42.

   The Letters of T. S. Eliot. Volume 1: 1898–1922. Ed. Valerie Eliot. New York: Harcourt Brace Jovanovich, 1988.

Selected Essays. 2d ed. New York: Harcourt, Brace, 1950.

Selected Prose. Ed. Frank Kermode. New York: Harcourt Brace Jovanovich; Farrar, Straus & Giroux, 1975.

Engel, Bernard F. "H.D.: Poems That Matter and Dilutations." *Contemporary Literature* 10 (Autumn 1969): 507–22.

Euripides. *Electra.* Trans. Emily Townsend Vermule. In *Euripides V. The Complete Greek Tragedies.* Ed. David Grene and Richmond Lattimore. Chicago: University of Chicago Press, 1959. 1–66.

Euripide. Ed. and trans. Henri Grégoire et al. Paris: Société d'Edition "Les Belles Lettres," 1948–50. 5 vols.

Euripide. Trans. Leconte de Lisle. Paris: Lemerre, n.d. [188–]. 3 vols.

Euripides. Ed. and trans. Arthur S. Way. Loeb Classical Library. 1912. Cambridge, Mass.: Harvard University Press; London: William Heinemann, 1988.

Euripides: Ten Plays. Trans. Moses Hadas. New York: Bantam, 1960.

Helen. Trans. James Mitchie and Colin Leach. The Greek Tragedies in New Translations. New York: Oxford University Press, 1981.

Helen. Trans. Richmond Lattimore. In *Euripides II. The Complete Greek Tragedies.* Ed. David Grene and Richmond Lattimore. Chicago: University of Chicago Press, 1956. 189–264.

Iphigeneia at Aulis. Trans. W. S. Merwin and George E. Dimock, Jr. The Greek Tragedy in New Translations. New York: Oxford University Press, 1978.

The Iphigeneia at Aulis of Euripides. Ed. E. B. England. 1891. Salem, N.H.: Ayer, 1986.

Orestes. Trans. William Arrowsmith. In *Euripides IV. The Complete Greek Tragedies.* Ed. David Grene and Richmond Lattimore. Chicago: University of Chicago Press, 1958. 105–208.

Rhesos. Trans. Richard Emil Braun. The Greek Tragedy in New Translations. New York: Oxford University Press, 1978.

The Tragedies of Euripides. Trans. Theodore Alois Buckley. London: Bell & Daldy, 1871. 2 vols.

Faderman, Lillian. *Cloe Plus Olivia: An Anthology of Lesbian Literature from the Seventeenth Century to the Present.* New York: Viking, 1994.

Farnell, Lewis Richard. *The Cults of the Greek States.* Oxford: Oxford University Press, 1907. 5 vols.

Fletcher, John Gould. "H.D.'s Vision" [review of *Sea Garden*]. *Poetry* 9 (February 1917): 266–9.

Foley, Helene P. *Ritual Irony: Poetry and Sacrifice in Euripides.* Ithaca, N.Y.: Cornell University Press, 1985.

Forster, E. M. *Pharos and Pharillon: A Novelist's Sketchbook of Alexandria Through the Ages.* New York: Knopf, 1961.

Foster, Finley Melville Kendall. *English Translations from the Greek: A Bibliographic Survey.* New York: Columbia University Press, 1918.

Foucart, Paul. *Les mystères d'Eleusis.* Paris: Auguste Picard, 1914.

Fowler, R. "'On Not Knowing Greek': The Classics and the Woman of Letters." *Classical Journal* 78 (April–May 1983): 337–49.

F.R.A.I. "The Eclipse of Woman. IV. The Earth Goddess." *New Freewoman* 1.4 (1 August 1913): 69–70.

Fraistat, Neil. *The Poem and the Book: Interpreting Collections of Romantic Poetry*. Chapel Hill: University of North Carolina Press, 1985.

Fraser, Robert, ed. *Sir James Frazer and the Literary Imagination: Essays in Affinity and Influence*. New York: St. Martin's Press, 1990.

Frazer, Sir James George. *The Golden Bough: A Study in Magic and Religion*. Abridged. New York: Macmillan, 1922.

Freud, Sigmund. "Leonardo da Vinci and a Memory of His Childhood." In *Five Lectures on Psycho-Analysis, Leonardo da Vinci, and Other Essays*. Volume 11 of *The Standard Edition of the Complete Psychological Works of Sigmund Freud*. Ed. and trans. James Strachey and Anna Freud, with Alix Strachey and Alan Tyson. London: Hogarth Press and the Institute of Psycho-Analysis, 1964. 24 vols. 57–137.

Friedman, Susan Stanford. "Exile in the American Grain: H.D.'s Diaspora." *Agenda* 25 (Autumn–Winter 1987-8): 27–50.

"Gender and Genre Anxiety: Elizabeth Barrett Browning and H.D. as Epic Poets." *Tulsa Studies in Women's Literature* 5 (Fall 1986): 203–29.

"Hilda Doolittle (H.D.)" *Dictionary of Literary Biography: American Poets, 1880–1945*. Vol. 45. Detroit: Gale Research, 1983. 115–49.

Penelope's Web: Gender, Modernity, H.D.'s Fiction. Cambridge Studies in American Literature and Culture. Cambridge University Press, 1990.

Psyche Reborn: The Emergence of H.D. Bloomington: Indiana University Press, 1981.

"Serendipity: Finding a Draft Manuscript of H.D.'s 'Helen.'" *Sagetrieb* 14 (Spring–Fall 1995): 7–11.

"Who Buried H.D.? A Poet, Her Critics, and Her Place in 'The Literary Tradition.'" *College English* 36 (March 1975): 801–14.

Friedman, Susan Stanford, and Rachel Blau DuPlessis, eds. *Signets: Reading H.D.* Madison: University of Wisconsin Press, 1990.

Friedrich, Paul. *The Meaning of Aphrodite*. Chicago: University of Chicago Press, 1978.

Frischer, Bernard D. "*Concordia Discors* and Characterization in Euripides' *Hippolytos*." *Greek, Roman, and Byzantine Studies* 11 (1970): 85–100.

Fussell, Paul. *The Great War and Modern Memory*. New York: Oxford University Press, 1975.

Gardiner, Jeffrey. "Dionysian Presences." *American Poetry* 6 (Spring 1989): 2–14.

Gelpi, Albert. "H.D.: Hilda in Egypt." In *Coming to Light: American Women Poets in the Twentieth Century*. Ed. Dianne Middlebrook and Marilyn Yalom. Ann Arbor: University of Michigan Press, 1985. 74–91.

Gilbert, Sandra M., and Susan Gubar. *The Madwoman in the Attic: The Woman Writer and the Nineteenth-Century Literary Imagination*. New Haven, Conn.: Yale University Press, 1979.

No Man's Land: The Place of the Woman Writer in the Twentieth Century. Volume 1: The War of the Words. New Haven, Conn.: Yale University Press, 1988.

Golffing, Francis. "The Alexandrian Mind: Notes Toward a Definition." In *Harvey*. 115–26.

Golsan, Richard J. *René Girard and Myth: An Introduction*. Theorists of Myth. New York: Garland, 1993.

Greenwood, E. B. "H.D. and the Problem of Escapism." *Essays in Criticism* 21 (October 1971): 365–76.

Gregory, Eileen. "Euripides and H.D.'s Working Notebook for *Helen in Egypt*." *Sagetrieb* 14 (Spring–Fall 1995): 83–109.

——. "Falling from the White Rock: A Myth of Margins in H.D." *Agenda* 25 (Autumn–Winter 1987–8): 113–23.

——. "Ovid and 'Thetis' (*Hymen* Version)." *H.D. Newsletter* 1.1 (Spring 1987): 29–31.

——. "Rose Cut in Rock: Sappho and H.D.'s *Sea Garden*." In Friedman and DuPlessis. 129–54.

——. "Scarlet Experience: H.D.'s *Hymen*." *Sagetrieb* 6 (Fall 1987): 77–100.

——. "Virginity and Erotic Liminality: H.D.'s *Hippolytus Temporizes*." *Contemporary Literature* 30.2 (Summer 1990): 133–60.

Gubar, Susan. "Sapphistries." *Signs* 10 (Autumn 1984): 43–62.

Guest, Barbara. *Herself Defined: The Poet H.D. and Her World*. Garden City, N.Y.: Doubleday, 1984.

Hall, Nor. *Those Women*. Dallas: Spring Publications, 1988.

Harari, Josué. "Nostalgia and Critical Theory." In *The Limits of Theory*. Ed. Thomas M. Kavanagh. Stanford, Calif.: Stanford University Press, 1989. 168–93.

Harrison, Jane Ellen. *Ancient Art and Ritual*. The Home University Library of Modern Knowledge. 1913. London: Oxford University Press, 1947.

——. *Epilegomena to the Study of Greek Religion and Themis: A Study of the Social Origins of Greek Religion*. New Hyde Park, N.Y.: University Books, 1962.

——. *Mythology*. Our Debt to Greece and Rome. 1924. New York: Cooper Square, 1963.

——. *Prolegomena to the Study of Greek Religion*. 3d ed. 1922. Mythos: The Princeton Bollingen Series on World Mythology. Princeton, N.J.: Princeton University Press, 1991.

——. *The Religion of Ancient Greece*. Religions Ancient and Modern. London: Archibald Constable, 1905.

Harrison, John R. *The Reactionaries*. London: Victor Gollancz, 1967.

Harrison, John Smith. "Pater, Heine, and the Old Gods of Greece." *PMLA* 39 (1924): 655–86.

Harvey, Denise, ed. *The Mind and Art of C. P. Cavafy*. Athens: Denise Harvey, 1983.

Haskell, Francis, and Nicholas Penny. *Taste and the Antique: The Lure of Classical Sculpture, 1500–1900*. New Haven, Conn.: Yale University Press, 1981.

Hatch, Benton L., ed. *A Checklist of the Publications of Thomas Bird Mosher of Portland, Maine, 1891–1923*. Amherst: University of Massachusetts Press, 1966.

H.D. *Asphodel*. Ed. Robert Spoo. Durham, N.C.: Duke University Press, 1992.

——. "Autobiographical Notes." TS. H.D. Papers. Beinecke Rare Book and Manuscript Library. Yale University, New Haven, Conn.

——. *Bid Me to Live: A Madrigal*. 2d ed. Redding Ridge, Conn.: Black Swan, 1983.

——. *Choruses from the Iphigeneia in Aulis of Euripides*. London: Egoist Press, 1915.

——. *Collected Poems, 1912–1944*. Ed. Louis L. Martz. New York: New Directions, 1983.

——. "Compassionate Friendship." TS. H.D. Papers. Beinecke Rare Book and Manuscript Library. Yale University, New Haven, Conn.

——. *End to Torment: A Memoir of Ezra Pound*. Ed. Norman Holmes Pearson and Michael King. New York: New Directions, 1979.

——. *Euripides' Ion*. 2d ed. Redding Ridge, Conn.: Black Swan Books, 1986 [New title: *Ion: A Play after Euripides.*]

——. *The Gift* [abridged]. [Ed. Griselda Ohanessian.] New York: New Directions, 1982.

——. *H.D. by Delia Alton*. *Iowa Review* 16 (Fall 1987): 174–221.

Hedylus. 2d ed. Redding Ridge, Conn.: Black Swan, 1980.

Helen in Egypt. New York: New Directions, 1961.

Hermetic Definition. New York: New Directions, 1972.

Hermione. New York: New Directions, 1981.

Hippolytus Temporizes. 2d ed. Redding Ridge, Conn.: Black Swan, 1985.

Letter to F. L. Flint. Harry Ransome Humanities Research Center. University of Texas at Austin.

"Letter to Norman Pearson, 1937" ["A Note on Poetry"]. Ed. Diana Collecott. *Agenda* 25 (Autumn–Winter 1987–8): 71–6.

Letter to Francis Wolle. University of Colorado at Boulder.

Letters to Winifred Bryher, Havelock Ellis, and Norman Holmes Pearson. Beinecke Rare Book and Manuscript Library. Yale University, New Haven, Conn.

Letters to John Cournos and Amy Lowell. Houghton Library. Harvard University, Cambridge, Mass.

Letters to Marianne Moore. Rosenbach Foundation, Philadelphia.

Nights. New York: New Directions, 1986.

"A Note on Poetry." In *The Oxford Anthology of American Poetry.* Ed. William Rose Benét and Norman Holmes Pearson. New York: Oxford University Press, 1938. 1287–88.

"Notes on Euripides, Pausanius, and Greek Lyric Poets." TS. H.D. Papers. Beinecke Rare Book and Manuscript Library, Yale University, New Haven, Conn. [Given here in the order of their arrangement in the typescript.]

    Part I. "Euripides." Excerpts published in *Euripides' Ion* 132–33.

    "Helen in Egypt."

    "The Opening Scenes of Ion." Published in *Euripides' Ion* 134–48.

    "The Bacchae."

    Part II. "Pausanius."

    "People of Sparta." Published in *Bookman* 60 (December 1924): 417–20.

    "God or Hero."

    "From Megara to Corinth."

    "Those Near the Sea."

    Part III. "Garland."

    "Curled Thyme."

    "A Poet in the Wilderness. Songs of Anacreon."

    "The Island. Fragments of Sappho." Published as "The Wise Sappho" with *Notes on Thought and Vision.* 55–69.

    "Winter Roses." Review of *The Poems of Sappho.* Ed. and trans. Edwin Marion Cox. *Saturday Review of Literature* 14 March 1925, 596.

Notes on Thought and Vision & The Wise Sappho. San Francisco: City Lights, 1982.

Paint It Today. Ed. Cassandra Laity. The Cutting Edge: Lesbian Life and Literature. New York: New York University Press, 1992.

Palimpsest. 2d ed. Carbondale: Southern Illinois University Press, 1968.

Paris Diary. MS. 1912. H.D. Papers. Beinecke Rare Book and Manuscript Library. Yale University, New Haven, Conn.

"Responsibilities" [review of *Responsibilities and Other Poems* by W. B. Yeats]. *Agenda* 25 (Autumn–Winter 1987–8): 51–3.

Review of *The Farmer's Bride* by Charlotte Mew. *Egoist* 3 (September 1916): 135.

Review of *Five Stages of Greek Religion* by Gilbert Murray. *Adelphi* 3 (October 1925): 378.

Review of *Goblins and Pagodas* by John Gould Fletcher. *Egoist* 3 (December 1916): 183–4.

Selected Poems. New York: Grove Press, 1957.

Selected Poems. Ed. Louis L. Martz. New York: New Directions, 1988.

Tribute to Freud. 1956. Boston: David R. Godine, 1974.

Herodotus. *Herodotus*. Ed. and trans. A. D. Godley. Loeb Classical Library. 1920. Cambridge, Mass.: Harvard University Press; London: William Heinemann, 1946. 4 vols.

Hesiod. *Hesiod, the Homeric Hymns, and Homerica*. Ed. and trans. Hugh G. Eveyln-White. Loeb Classical Library. 1914. Cambridge, Mass.: Harvard University Press; London: William Heinemann, 1982.

Hillman, James. "Salt: A Chapter in Alchemical Psychology." In Stroud and Thomas. 111–37.

Homans, Margaret. *Bearing the Word: Language and Female Experience in Nineteenth-Century Women's Writing*. Women in Culture and Society. Chicago: University of Chicago Press, 1986.

Homer. *Iliad*. Ed. and trans. A. T. Murray. Loeb Classical Library. 1925. Cambridge, Mass.: Harvard University Press; London: William Heinemann, 1963.

Odyssey. Ed. and trans. A. T. Murray. Loeb Classical Library. 1919. Cambridge, Mass.: Harvard University Press; London: William Heinemann, 1984.

Odyssey. Trans. Richmond Lattimore. New York: Harper & Row, 1967.

Horace. *The Complete Works of Horace (Quintus Horatius Flaccus)*. Trans. Charles E. Passage. New York: Frederick Ungar, 1983.

Horace: Satires, Epistles, and Ars Poetica. Ed. and trans. H. Rushton Fairclough. Loeb Classical Library. 1926. Cambridge, Mass.: Harvard University Press; London: William Heinemann, 1961.

Hošek, Chaviva, and Patricia Parker, eds. *Lyric Poetry Beyond New Criticism*. Ithaca, N.Y.: Cornell University Press, 1985.

Hulme, T. E. *Speculations: Essays on Humanism and the Philosophy of Art*. Ed. Herbert Read. 2d ed. The International Library of Psychology Philosophy and Scientific Method. London: Routledge & Kegan Paul, 1936.

Huyssen, Andreas. *After the Great Divide: Modernism, Mass Culture, Postmodernism*. Bloomington: Indiana University Press, 1986.

Jackson, Brendan. "'The Fulsomeness of Her Prolixity': Reflections on 'H.D., "Imagiste."'" *South Atlantic Quarterly* 83 (Winter 1984): 91–102.

Jenkyns, Richard. *The Victorians and Ancient Greece*. Cambridge, Mass.: Harvard University Press, 1980.

Johnson, Barbara. "Translator's Introduction." *Dissemination*. By Jacques Derrida. Trans. Barbara Johnson. Chicago: University of Chicago Press; London: Althone Press, 1981. vii–xxxiii.

Jung, C. G. *Mysterium Coniunctionis: An Inquiry into the Separation and Synthesis of Psychic Opposites in Alchemy*. Trans. R. F. C. Hull. 2d ed. Princeton, N.J.: Princeton University Press, 1970. Volume 14 of *The Collected Works of C. G. Jung*. Ed. William McGuire et al. Bollingen Series. 20 vols. 1953–79.

Kammer, Jeanne. "The Art of Silence and the Forms of Women's Poetry." In *Shake-*

speare's Sisters: Feminist Essays on Women Poets. Ed. Sandra M. Gilbert and Susan Gubar. Bloomington: Indiana University Press, 1979. 153–64.

Keeley, Edmund. *Cavafy's Alexandria: Study of a Myth in Progress.* Cambridge, Mass.: Harvard University Press, 1976.

Kenner, Hugh. *The Pound Era.* Berkeley: University of California Press, 1971.

Kermode, Frank. *The Sense of an Ending: Studies in the Theory of Fiction.* Oxford: Oxford University Press, 1967.

Kissane, James. "Victorian Mythology." *Victorian Studies* 6 (1962): 5–28.

Kloepfer, Deborah Kelly. *The Unspeakable Mother: Forbidden Discourse in Jean Rhys and H.D.* Ithaca, N.Y.: Cornell University Press, 1989.

Knight, Philip. *Flower Poetics in Nineteenth-Century France.* Oxford: Clarendon Press, 1986.

Koestenbaum, Wayne. *Double Talk: The Erotics of Male Literary Collaboration.* New York: Routledge, 1989.

Kramer, Lawrence. "The Return of the Gods: Keats to Rilke." *Studies in Romanticism* 17 (1978): 483–500.

Laity, Cassandra. "H.D., Modernism, and the Trangressive Sexualities of Decadent-Romantic Platonism." In *Gendered Modernism: American Women Poets and Their Readers.* Ed. Margaret Dickie and Thomas Traverssno. Philadelphia: University of Pennsylvania Press, 1996 45–67.

    "H.D. and A. C. Swinburne: Decadence and Modernist Women's Writing." *Feminist Studies* 15 (Fall 1989): 461–84.

    "H.D.'s Romantic Landscapes: The Sexual Politics of the Garden." In Friedman and DuPlessis. 110–28.

    "Lesbian Romanticism: H.D.'s Representations of Frances Gregg and Bryher." Introduction to *Paint It Today.* By H.D. xvii–xliii.

Lang, Andrew, trans. *Theocritus, Bion, and Moschus.* 1880. 2d ed. Golden Treasury Series. London: Macmillan, 1901.

Larrabee, Stephen A. *English Bards and Grecian Marbles: The Relationship between Sculpture and Poetry Especially in the Romantic Period.* New York: Columbia University Press, 1943.

Lattimore, Richmond. "Euripides as Lyricist" [review of *Euripides' Ion* by H.D.]. *Poetry* 51 (December 1937): 160–4.

    "Introduction to *Helen.*" In *Euripides II.* 261–4.

Lawrence, D. H. *Aaron's Rod.* London: Martin Secker, 1922.

    The Letters of D. H. Lawrence. Ed. George J. Zytaruk and James T. Boulton. Cambridge ed. Cambridge University Press, 1981.

    The Lost Girl. Ed. John Worthen. Cambridge ed. Cambridge University Press, 1981.

    St. Mawr & The Man Who Died. New York: Vintage, 1953.

Layard, John. "The Incest Taboo and the Virgin Archetype." In Stroud and Thomas. 145–84.

Lee, Vernon [Violet Paget]. *Althea: Dialogues on Aspirations and Duties.* London: Lane, 1910.

Lefkowitz, Mary R. "Critical Stereotypes in the Poetry of Sappho." *Greek, Roman and Byzantine Studies* 14 (1973): 113–23.

Levenson, Michael H. *A Genealogy of Modernism: A Study of English Literary Doctrine, 1908–1922.* Cambridge University Press, 1984.

Liddell, Henry George, and Robert Scott. *A Greek–English Lexicon.* Rev. Sir Henry Stuart Jones. 9th ed. Oxford: Oxford University Press, 1968.

Lloyd-Jones, Hugh. *Blood for the Ghosts: Classical Influences in the Nineteenth and Twentieth Centuries*. London: Duckworth, 1982.

Lyon, Melvin E. *H.D.'s "Hippolytus Temporizes": Text and Context*. University of Nebraska Studies. Lincoln: University of Nebraska, 1991.

Mackail, J. W. *Lectures on Greek Poetry*. 2d ed. London: Longmans, Green, 1911.

"A Note on the Classical Revival." *Times Literary Supplement* 4 May 1916, 210.

Mackail, J. W., ed. and trans. *Select Epigrams from the Greek Anthology*. New York: Longmans, Green, 1911.

Maeterlinck, Maurice. *La vie des abeilles*. Paris: Charpentier, 1902.

Maika, Patricia. *Virginia Woolf's "Between the Acts" and Jane Ellen Harrison's "Con/spiracy."* Ann Arbor, Mich.: UMI Research Press, 1987.

Makin, Peter. *Provence and Pound*. Berkeley: University of California Press, 1978.

Martz, Louis L. "Introduction." *H.D.: Collected Poems, 1912–1944*. xi–xxxvi.

"Introduction." *H.D.: Selected Poems* (1988). vii–xxvi.

McDiarmid, Lucy. *Saving Civilization: Yeats, Eliot, and Auden Between the Wars*. Cambridge University Press, 1984.

McEvilley, Thomas. "Sapphic Imagery and Fragment 96." *Hermes* 101 (1973): 257–78.

McGrath, F. C. *The Sensible Spirit: Walter Pater and the Modernist Paradigm*. Tampa: University of South Florida Press, 1986.

McKnight, Stephen A. *Sacralizing the Secular: The Renaissance Origins of Modernity*. Baton Rouge: Louisiana State University Press, 1989.

Meisel, Perry. *The Absent Father: Virginia Woolf and Walter Pater*. New Haven, Conn.: Yale University Press, 1980.

The Myth of the Modern: A Study in British Literature and Criticism after 1850. New Haven, Conn.: Yale University Press, 1987.

Michelini, Ann Norris. *Euripides and the Tragic Tradition*. Madison: University of Wisconsin Press, 1987.

Middleton, Peter. "Nature and Culture: Reading and Readers in H.D.'s *Helen in Egypt*." *Textual Practice* 5 (Winter 1991): 352–62.

Monsman, Gerald Cornelius. *Pater's Portraits: Mythic Pattern in the Fiction of Walter Pater*. Baltimore: Johns Hopkins Press, 1967.

Walter Pater. Boston: Twayne, 1977.

Walter Pater's Art of Autobiography. New Haven, Conn.: Yale University Press, 1980.

Moody, A. D. "H.D. 'Imagiste': An Elemental Mind." *Agenda* 25 (Autumn–Winter 1987–8): 77–96.

Morris, Adalaide. "The Concept of Projection: H.D.'s Visionary Powers." In Friedman and DuPlessis. 273–96.

"A Relay of Power and of Peace: H.D. and the Spirit of the Gift." In Friedman and DuPlessis. 52–82.

"Science and the Mythopoeic Mind: The Case of H.D." In *Chaos and Order: Complex Dynamics in Literature and Science*. Ed. N. Katherine Hayles. Chicago: University of Chicago Press, 1991. 195–220.

"Signaling: Feminism, Politics, and Mysticism in H.D.'s *War Trilogy*." *Sagetrieb* 9 (Winter 1990): 121–33.

Mosher, Thomas B., ed. *Bibelot: A Reprint of Poetry and Prose for Book Lovers*. Portland, Me.: Thomas B. Mosher, 1895–1915.

Müller, K. O. *The History and Antiquities of the Doric Race*. Trans. Henry Tufnell and George Cornwall Lewis. 2d ed. London: John Murray, 1839. 2 vols.

Murray, Gilbert. *Euripides and His Age*. Home University Library of Modern Knowledge. New York: Henry Holt; London: Williams & Norgate, 1913.

    Four Stages of Greek Religion. New York: Columbia University Press, 1912.

    "Jane Ellen Harrison Memorial Lecture." In Harrison, *Epilegomena and Themis*. 559–77.

Murray, Gilbert, trans. *Euripides*. London: George Allen & Unwin; New York: Longmans, Green, 1902.

New, Elisa. *The Regenerate Lyric: Theology and Innovation in American Poetry*. Cambridge Studies in American Literature and Culture. Cambridge University Press, 1993.

Nietzsche, Friedrich. *The Birth of Tragedy and The Case of Wagner*. Trans. Walter Kaufmann. New York: Vintage–Random House, 1967.

Ong, Walter, S. J. "Latin and the Social Fabric." In *The Barbarian Within and Other Fugitive Essays and Studies*. New York: Macmillan, 1962. 206–19.

Ostriker, Alicia. "The Poet as Heroine: Learning to Read H.D." *Writing Like a Woman*. Ann Arbor: University of Michigan Press, 1983. 7–41.

Ovid. *Fasti*. Ed. and trans. Sir James George Frazer. 2d ed., rev. G. P. Goold. Loeb Classical Library. 1931. Cambridge, Mass.: Harvard University Press; London: William Heinemann, 1989.

    Heroides and Amores. Ed. and trans. Grant Showerman. 2d ed., rev. G. P. Goold. Loeb Classical Library. 1914. Cambridge, Mass.: Harvard University Press; London: William Heinemann, 1986.

    Metamorphoses. Ed. and trans. Frank Justus Miller. 3d ed., rev. G. P. Goold. Loeb Classical Library. 1916. Cambridge, Mass.: Harvard University Press; London: William Heinemann, 1977. 2 vols.

Oxford Companion to Classical Literature. Ed. M. C. Howatson. 2d ed. Oxford: Oxford University Press, 1989.

Oxford Companion to Ships and the Sea. Ed. Peter Kemp. New York: Oxford University Press, 1976.

Oxford English Dictionary. Ed. J. A. Simpson and E. S. C. Weiner. 2d ed. Oxford: Clarendon Press; New York: Oxford University Press, 1989. 20 vols.

Padel, Ruth. "'Imagery of the Elsewhere': Two Choral Odes of Euripides." *Classical Quarterly* 24 (1974): 227–41.

Palatine Anthology. In *The Greek Anthology*. Ed. and trans. W. R. Paton. Loeb Classical Library. Cambridge, Mass.: Harvard University Press; London: William Heinemann, 1916. 5 vols.

"Palimpsest of War, The." [London] *Times* 17 April 1915, 9, col. 5.

Parry, Hugh. *The Lyric Poems of Greek Tragedy*. Toronto: Samuel Stevens, 1978.

Pater, Walter. *Gaston de Latour: An Unfinished Romance*. 1896. Library ed. London: Macmillan, 1910.

    Greek Studies: A Series of Lectures [reprint of the Macmillan 1st ed., 1897]. Prophets of Sensibility: Precursors of Modern Cultural Thought. New York: Chelsea House, 1983.

    Imaginary Portraits. Library ed. London: Macmillan, 1910.

    Marius the Epicurean: His Sensations and Ideas. Library ed. London: Macmillan, 1910. 2 vols.

    Miscellaneous Studies: A Series of Essays. Library ed. London: Macmillan, 1910.

    Plato and Platonism: A Series of Lectures. Library ed. London: Macmillan, 1910.

The Renaissance: Studies in Art and Poetry. 4th ed. London: Macmillan, 1893.

Paton, W. R., ed. and trans. *The Greek Anthology*. Loeb Classical Library. Cambridge, Mass.: Harvard University Press; London: William Heinemann, 1916. 5 vols.

Pausanias. *Description of Greece*. Ed. and trans. W. H. S. Jones. Loeb Classical Library. 1926. Cambridge, Mass.: Harvard University Press; London: William Heinemann, 1954. 5 vols.

Payne, Harry C. "Modernizing the Ancients: The Reconstruction of Ritual Drama, 1870–1920." *Proceedings of the American Philosophical Society* 122 (June 1978): 182–92.

Pearson, Norman Holmes. Letter to Thomas Burnett Swann. Collection of American Literature. Beinecke Rare Book and Manuscript Library. Yale University, New Haven, Conn.

Perl, Jeffrey M. *The Tradition of Return: The Implicit History of Modern Literature*. Princeton, N.J.: Princeton University Press, 1984.

Pinchin, Jane Lagoudis. *Alexandria Still: Forster, Durrell, and Cavafy*. Princeton, N.J.: Princeton University Press, 1977.

Pindar. *The Odes of Pindar, Including the Principal Fragments*. Ed. and trans. J. E. Sandys. Loeb Classical Library. London: William Heinemann; New York: Macmillan, 1915.

Plato. *The Dialogues of Plato*. Trans. Benjamin Jowett. 4th ed. London: Oxford University Press, 1953. 4 vols.

Plutarch. *Plutarch's Lives*. Ed. and trans. Bernadotte Perrin. Loeb Classical Library. 1914. Cambridge, Mass.: Harvard University Press; London: William Heinemann, 1985. 11 vols.

Pound, Ezra. *The ABC of Reading*. New York: New Directions, 1934.

———. "The Caressibility of the Greeks." *Egoist* 1 (16 March 1914): 117.

———. "Elizabethan Classicists." *Egoist* 4 (September 1917): 120–2; 4 (October 1917): 135–6; 4 (November 1917): 154–6; 4 (December 1917): 168; 5 (January 1918): 8–9.

———. *Guide to Kulchur*. New York: New Directions, 1970.

———. "H.D.'s Choruses from Euripides." *Little Review* 5 (November 1919): 16–20.

———. ["Hellenist Series"]. *Egoist* 5 (August 1918): 95–7 ("Early Translators of Homer I. Hughes Salel"); 5 (September 1918): 106–7 ("Early Translators of Homer II. Andreas Divas"); 5 (October 1918): 120–1 ("Early Translators of Homer III"); 5 (November–December 1918): 130–1 ("Hellenist Series IV. Sappho"); 6 (January–February 1919): 6–9 ("Hellenist Series V. Aeschylus"); 6 (March–April 1919): 24–5 ("Hellenist Series VI").

———. *Instigations of Ezra Pound Together with an Essay on the Chinese Written Character by Ernest Fenollosa*. 1920. Freeport, N.Y.: Books for Libraries Press, 1967.

———. *The Letters of Ezra Pound, 1907–1941*. Ed. D. D. Paige. New York: Harcourt, Brace, & World, 1950.

———. *Literary Essays of Ezra Pound*. Ed. T. S. Eliot. New York: New Directions, 1954.

———. *Lustra*. 1916. New York: Haskell House, 1973.

———. "The New Sculpture." *Egoist* 1 (16 February 1914): 67–8.

———. "On Criticism in General." *Criterion* 1 (January 1923): 143–56.

———. *Patria Mia*. Chicago: Ralph Fletcher Seymour, 1950.

———. *Selected Poems of Ezra Pound*. New York: New Directions, 1956.

———. *Selected Prose 1909–1965*. Ed. William Cookson. London: Faber & Faber, 1973.

———. *The Spirit of Romance*. 1910. New York: New Directions, 1968.

"Tagore's Poems." *Poetry* 1.3 (December 1912): 92–4.

"Vortex." *Blast: Review of the Great English Vortex* 1 (20 June 1914): 153–4.

Pound, Ezra, and Dorothy Shakespear. *Ezra Pound and Dorothy Shakespear, Their Letters: 1909–1914.* Ed. Omar Pound and A. Walton Litz. New York: New Directions, 1984.

Preminger, Alex, and T. V. F. Brogan. *The New Princeton Encyclopedia of Poetry and Poetics.* Princeton, N.J.: Princeton University Press, 1993.

Propertius. *Propertius.* Trans. H. E. Butler. Loeb Classical Library. 1912. Cambridge, Mass.: Harvard University Press; London: William Heinemann, 1976.

Rainey, Lawrence S. "Canon, Gender, and Text: The Case of H.D." In *Representing Modernist Texts: Editing as Interpretation.* Ed. George Bornstein. Ann Arbor: University of Michigan Press, 1991. 99–123.

Rajan, Tilottama. "Romanticism and the Death of Lyric Consciousness." In Hošek and Parker. 194–207.

Rawson, Elizabeth. *The Spartan Tradition in European Thought.* Oxford: Clarendon Press, 1969.

Reid, Richard, ed. "Introduction." *Elektra.* By Ezra Pound and Rudd Fleming. Princeton, N.J.: Princeton University Press, 1989. ix–xx.

Retallack, Joan. "H.D., H.D." [review of several books by and about H D]. *Parnassus* 12.2–13.1 (1985): 67–88.

Reynolds, L.D., ed. *Texts and Transmission: A Survey of the Latin Classics.* Oxford: Clarendon Press, 1983.

Riddel, Joseph. "H.D. and the Poetics of 'Spiritual Realism.'" *Contemporary Literature* 10 (Autumn 1969): 447–73.

Riding, Laura, and Robert Graves. *A Survey of Modernist Poetry.* 1927. St. Clair Shores, Mich.: Scholarly Press, 1972.

Robbins, Bruce. "Modernism in History, Modernism in Power." In *Modernism Reconsidered.* Ed. Robert Kiely and John Hildebidle. Harvard English Studies. Cambridge, Mass.: Harvard University Press, 1983. 229–45.

Robinson, Janice S. *H.D.: The Life and Work of an American Poet.* Boston: Houghton Mifflin, 1982.

Roessel, David. "H.D.'s Troy: Some Bearings." *H.D. Newsletter* 3.2 (Winter 1990): 38–42.

Roethke, Theodore. "The Poetry of Louise Bogan." *On the Poet and His Craft: Selected Prose of Theodore Roethke.* Ed. Ralph J. Mills, Jr. Seattle: University of Washington Press, 1965. 133–48.

Rosen, George. "Nostalgia: A 'Forgotten' Psychological Disorder." *Psychological Medicine* 5 (1975): 340–54.

Rosenthal, M. L., and Sally M. Gall. *The Modern Poetic Sequence: The Genius of Modern Poetry.* Oxford: Oxford University Press, 1983.

Ross, Andrew. *The Failure of Modernism: Symptoms of American Poetry.* New York: Columbia University Press, 1986.

Rosset, Clément. "Reality and the Untheorizable." In *The Limits of Theory.* Ed. Thomas M. Kavanagh. Stanford, Calif.: Stanford University Press, 1989. 76–118.

Ryan, Charles J. *H. P. Blavatsky and the Theosophical Movement: A Brief Historical Sketch.* San Diego, Calif.: Point Loma Publications, 1975.

Ryan, Judith. *The Vanishing Subject: Early Psychology and Literary Modernism.* Chicago: University of Chicago Press, 1991.

Sappho. *The Fragments of the Lyrical Poems of Sappho.* Ed. Edgar Lobel. Oxford: Clarendon Press, 1925.

    Poems and Fragments of Sappho. Trans. Edward Storer. London: Egoist Press, 1915.

    The Poems of Sappho. Ed. and trans. Edwin Marion Cox. London: Williams & Norgate; New York: Scribner's, 1924.

    Poetarum Lesbiorum Fragmenta. Ed. Edgar Lobel and Denys Page. Oxford: Oxford University Press, 1955.

    Sappho. Ed. and trans. Henry Thornton Wharton. 3d ed. London: John Lane, 1896.

    Sappho and Alcaeus. Volume 1 of *Greek Lyric.* Ed. and trans. D.A. Campbell.

Schuchard, Ronald. "Eliot and Hulme in 1916: Toward a Revaluation of Eliot's Critical and Spiritual Development." *PMLA* 88 (1973): 1083–94.

    "T. S. Eliot as an Extension Lecturer, 1916–1919." *Review of English Studies* n.s. 25 (1974): 163–73.

Segal, Charles. "Eros and Incantation: Sappho and Oral Poetry." *Arethusa* 7 (1974): 139–60.

    "The Two Worlds of Euripides' *Helen.*" *Interpreting Greek Tragedy: Myth, Poetry, Text.* Ithaca, N.Y.: Cornell University Press, 1986. 222–67.

Shelley, Percy Bysshe. *The Complete Poetical Works of Percy Bysshe Shelley.* Ed. Thomas Hutchinson. London: Oxford University Press, 1952.

Skinner, Marilyn B. "Classical Studies, Patriarchy and Feminism: The View from 1986." *Women's Studies International Forum* 10 (1987): 181–6.

Silverstein, Louis H. "H.D.: A Chronological Account." Unpublished TS.

    "Nicknames and Acronyms Used by H.D. and Her Circle." *H.D. Newsletter* 1.2 (Winter 1987): 4–5.

Sinclair, May. *The Divine Fire.* New York: A. L. Burt, 1904.

    "The Poems of H.D." [review of *Hymen* by H.D.]. *Dial* 72 (February 1922): 203–7.

Smyers, Virginia. "H.D.'s Books in the Bryher Library." *H.D. Newsletter* 1.2 (Winter 1987): 18–25. "Errata," *H.D. Newsletter* 2.1 (Spring 1988): 25–6.

Snyder, Jane McIntosh. *The Woman and the Lyre: Women Writers in Classical Greece and Rome.* Carbondale: Southern Illinois University Press, 1989.

Spoo, Robert. "Introduction." *Asphodel.* By H.D. ix–xxi.

Starobinski, Jean. "The Idea of Nostalgia." *Diogenes* 54 (Summer 1966): 81–103.

Stauth, Georg, and Bryan S. Turner. *Nietzsche's Dance: Resentment, Reciprocity and Resistance in Social Life.* Oxford: Basil Blackwell, 1988.

    "Nostalgia, Postmodernism and the Critique of Mass Culture." *Theory, Culture & Society* 5 (1988): 509–26.

Stead, C. K. *The New Poetic: Yeats to Eliot.* New York: Harper & Row, 1966.

    Pound, Yeats, Eliot and the Modernist Movement. New Brunswick, N.J.: Rutgers University Press, 1986.

Stedman, Edmund Clarence. "Tennyson and Theocritus." In *Victorian Poets.* Boston: Houghton Mifflin, 1903. 201–33.

Stern, Bernard Herbert. *The Rise of Romantic Hellenism in English Literature, 1732–1786.* 1940. New York: Octagon Books, 1969.

Stewart, Jessie. *Jane Ellen Harrison: A Portrait from Letters.* London: Merlin Press, 1959.

Stigers, Eva Stehle. "Retreat from the Male: Catullus 62 and Sappho's Erotic Flowers." *Ramus* 6 (1977): 83–102.

Storer, Edward, trans. *Poems and Fragments of Sappho.* Poets' Translation Series. London: Egoist Press, 1915.

The Windflowers of Asklepiades and Poems of Poseidippos. Poets' Translation Series. London: Egoist Press, 1919.

Strabo. *The Geography of Strabo.* Ed. and trans. Horace Leonard Jones. Loeb Classical Library. 1917. Cambridge, Mass.: Harvard University Press; London: William Heinemann, 1949. 8 vols.

Stroud, Joanne, and Gail Thomas, eds. *Images of the Untouched: Virginity in Psyche, Myth and Community.* Dallas: Spring Publications, 1982.

Surette, Leon. *A Light from Eleusis: A Study of Ezra Pound's Cantos.* Oxford: Clarendon Press, 1979.

Swann, Thomas Burnett. *The Classical World of H.D.* Lincoln: University of Nebraska Press, 1962.

Swinburne, Algernon Charles. *The Poems of Algernon Charles Swinburne.* London: Chatto & Windus, 1904. 6 vols.

Symonds, John Addington. *Studies of the Greek Poets.* 3d ed. London: Adam and Charles Black, 1893. 2 vols.

Symons, Arthur. "The Decadent Movement in Literature." *Harper's New Monthly Magazine* 87 (November 1893): 858–67.

Thatcher, David S. *Nietzsche in England, 1890–1914. The Growth of a Reputation.* Toronto: University of Toronto Press, 1970.

Theocritus. *The Greek Bucolic Poets.* Ed. and trans. J. M. Edmonds. Loeb Classical Library. 1912. Cambridge, Mass.: Harvard University Press; London: William Heinemann, 1960.

Theocritus, Bion, and Moschus. Trans. Andrew Lang. 1880. 2d ed. Golden Treasury Series. London: Macmillan, 1901.

Theophrastus. *Theophrastus: Enquiry into Plants and Minor Works on Odours and Weather Signs.* Ed. and trans. Sir Arthur Hort. Loeb Classical Library. 1916. Cambridge, Mass.: Harvard University Press; London: William Heinemann, 1961.

Turner, Frank M. *The Greek Heritage in Victorian Britain.* New Haven, Conn.: Yale University Press, 1981.

Turner, Victor. *The Ritual Process: Structure and Anti-Structure.* Symbol, Myth, and Ritual Series. Ithaca, N.Y.: Cornell University Press, 1977.

Tuveson, Ernest Lee. *The Avatars of Thrice Great Hermes: An Approach to Romanticism.* Lewisburg, Pa.: Bucknell University Press; London: Associated University Presses, 1982.

Tylor, Edward Burnett. *Anthropology: An Introduction to the Study of Man and Civilization.* The International Scientific Series. New York: D. Appleton, 1899.

Vanderwielen, Betty. " 'No Before nor After': Translating the Greek Tradition." *Classical and Modern Literature* 13 (Fall 1992): 63–74.

Van Gennep, Arnold. *The Rites of Passage.* Trans. M. B. Vizedom and G. L. Caffee. Chicago: University of Chicago Press, 1960.

Verrall, A. W. *Essays on Four Plays of Euripides.* Cambridge: University Press, 1905.

Viatte, Auguste. *Les sources occultes du Romanticisme: Illuminisme – Theosophie, 1770–1820.* 2 vols. Paris: Librarie Ancienne Honoré Champion, 1928.

Vickery, John B. *The Literary Impact of "The Golden Bough."* Princeton, N.J.: Princeton University Press, 1973.

Walker, Cheryl. *Masks Outrageous and Austere: Culture, Psyche, and Persona in Modern Women Poets.* Bloomington: Indiana University Press, 1991.

The Nightingale's Burden: Women Poets and American Culture Before 1900. Bloomington: Indiana University Press, 1982.

Wallace, Emily Mitchell. "Athene's Owl." *Poesis* 6.3–4 (1985): 98–123.

——. "Hilda Doolittle at Friends' Central School in 1905." *H.D. Newsletter* 1.1 (Spring 1987): 17–28.

Walsh, John. "Afterword: Dawn Drove the Stars Back." *Ion: A Play after Euripides.* By H.D. 120–31.

——. "Afterword: The Flash of Sun on the Snow." *Hippolytus Temporizes.* By H.D. 139–51.

Wheelwright, Philip. *Metaphor and Reality.* Bloomington: Indiana University Press, 1962.

Whitman, Cedric H. *Euripides and the Full Circle of Myth.* Cambridge, Mass.: Harvard University Press, 1974.

Wigram, W. A. *Hellenic Travel: A Guide.* London: Faber & Faber, 1947.

Wilamowitz-Moellendorff, Ulrich von. *Greek Historical Writing and Apollo: Two Lectures Delivered before the University of Oxford, June 3 and 4, 1908.* Trans. Gilbert Murray. Oxford: Clarendon Press, 1908.

Wilde, Oscar. *The Portable Oscar Wilde.* Ed. Richard Aldington. New York: Viking, 1946.

Wilson, John R. "Eris in Euripides." *Greece and Rome* 26 (1979): 7–20.

Winckelmann, Johann Joachim. *Reflections on the Imitation of Greek Works in Painting and Sculpture.* Trans. Elfriede Heyer and Roger C. Norton. La Salle, Ill.: Open Court, 1987.

Wind, Edgar. *Pagan Mysteries in the Renaissance.* Rev. ed. New York: Norton, 1968.

Woolf, Virginia. "On Not Knowing Greek." *The Common Reader: First Series.* 1925. New York: Harcourt, Brace, 1953.

——. *Orlando: A Biography.* New York: Harcourt, Brace, 1928.

Wordsworth, William. *The Prelude: A Parallel Text.* Ed. J. C. Maxwell. Harmondsworth: Penguin, 1971.

Wright, F. A. *The Poets of the Greek Anthology.* Broadway Translations. London: Routledge; New York: Dutton, 1923.

Wright, F. A., trans. "Introduction." *The Girdle of Aphrodite: The Complete Love-Poems of the Palatine Anthology.* Broadway Translations. London: Routledge; New York: Dutton, 1923. vii–xxxvii.

Yates, Frances A. *Giordano Bruno and the Hermetic Tradition.* Chicago: University of Chicago Press, 1964.

——. *The Rosicrucian Enlightenment.* London: Routledge & Kegan Paul, 1972.

Zeitlin, Froma I. "The Dynamics of Misogyny: Myth and Mythmaking in the *Oresteia.*" In *Women in the Ancient World: The Arethusa Papers.* Ed. John Peradotto and J. P. Sullivan. SUNY Series in Classical Studies, ed. John Peradotto. Albany: State University of New York Press, 1984.

——. "The Power of Aphrodite: Eros and the Boundaries of the Self in the *Hippolytus.*" In *Directions in Euripidean Criticism: A Collection of Essays.* Ed. Peter Burian. Durham, N.C.: Duke University Press, 1985. 52–111, 189–208.

Zilboorg, Caroline. "H.D.'s Influence on Richard Aldington." In *Richard Aldington: Reappraisals.* Ed. Charles Doyle. English Literary Studies Monograph Series. Victoria, B.C.: University of Victoria Press, 1990. 26–44.

——. "Joint Venture: Richard Aldington, H.D. and the Poets' Translation Series." *Philological Quarterly* 70 (Winter 1991): 67–98.

Index

Achilles, 52, 174, 222, 243; as fatal lover, 176, 178, 185, 221; in H.D.'s writing, 176, 185, 242, 220–1, 228–31; in the *Iliad*, 242, 281n25; in Landor, 282n35; in Sinclair's *The Divine Fire*, 220; and Thetis, 101–2, 104, 117, 221, 242, 244

Ackerman, Robert, 111, 271n1, 272n5, 272n6, 272n7

"Acon," 235

Adlington, William, 250

"Adonis," 135–6, 147, 236

A.E., pseud. (George Russell), 174

"Aegina," 252

Aeschylus, 15, 22–5, 39, 141, 145, 219, 249; and Eliot, 23–4, 260n19, 260n20, 260n22; versus Euripides, in modern classicism, 22–8; and H.D., 25, 261n23; and Nietzsche, 22, 24; and Pound, 23–6, 260n19, 260n20, 260n21, 260n22; *Agamemnon*, 23, 24, 26, 187, 260n20, 261n21, 261n22; *Eumenides*, 261n22; *Libation Bearers*, 201; *Oresteia*, as a paradigm in modern classicism, 22–4, 27, 261n22

aestheticism, 5, 42–3, 77–8, 84, 153, 161, 163, 277n29, 278n33. *See also* decadence; Pater, Walter

Agamemnon, H.M.S., 23

alchemy: and *ascesis*, 78; *conjunctio*, and the androgyne or hermaphrodite, 93–4, 270n31; *nigredo*, 89; *opus*, 78, 80–1, 88, 89, 180, 207, 212, 270n31; and the Renaissance artist, in Pater's writing,

78, 80–1; and salt, 89–90; and the Uroboros, 215

Alcibiades, 224

Alcman, 107

Aldington, Richard, 32, 45, 54, 55, 109, 129, 161, 166, 171, 259n6, 267n2, 276n13; letters, 261n25, 262n29, 268n4, 271n48, 277n25; "Anti-Hellenism," 44; "The Days Pass," 262n39; *Greek Songs in the Manner of Anacreon* (trans.), 139, 172; "Hyella," 235; *Latin Poems of the Renaissance* (trans.), 139, 172; *Life for Life's Sake*, 24; *The Poems of Anyte of Tegea* (trans.), 139, 234, 236; *The Poems of Meleager of Gadara* (trans.), 139, 172, 243, 244; *The Religion of Beauty* (ed.), 163, 277n29, 278n33; "Theocritus in Capri," 164–5; "To Atthis," 139, 150. *See also* aestheticism; Anacreon; Anyte of Tegea; Greek Anthology, the; H.D.; hellenism, romantic; Meleager; Poets' Translation Series; Sappho; Theocritus

Alexander the Great, 59, 60, 62, 65, 266n42

Alexandria, hellenistic: aesthetic principles of, and Callimachus, 47–8, 264n17; as an analogue in fin-de-sieclè decadence, 3, 46–7, 51; versus Athens, 47, 4; and Cavafy, 3, 47–8, 50–1, 264n15, 264n18; as figured by H.D. in Meleager, 50–1; and the Greek diaspora, 40–1, 48–51, 65; H.D.'s Alexandrian project, 48–50, 65, 136, 161; and *Hedylus*, 49–50, 58–9;

and "Hipparchia," 49–50, 58–9, 62,
140; and homoeroticism, 51; in
Nietzsche, 46, 110; in Pound, 45,
264n13. *See also* decadence; Greek
Anthology, the; Helen; hellenism,
H.D.'s; hermeticism; Meleager;
Theocritus
Alfrey, Shawn, 275n1
Alington, Rev. C. A., 274n16
"All Mountains," 248, 279n2
Althaia, 245–6
Althea: in H.D., 107; in Lee, 94; in
Swinburne, 270n35
Amalteo, Giovanni Battista, 235, 252
"Amaranth," 248
Anacreon, 48, 67, 68, 139, 156, 171–2,
264n19, 266n52
"Ancient Wisdom Speaks," 252
Anderson, Margaret, 45, 259n5
"And Pergamos," 185, 262n30, 275n5
androgyne, or hermaphrodite, 93–4, 96,
99, 102, 107, 154, 174, 211, 270n31,
270n32. *See also* alchemy; Balzac,
Honoré de, *Seraphità*; hermeticism;
statue
anthropology. *See* Cambridge ritualists;
Frazer, Sir James George; Harrison,
Jane Ellen; Nietzsche, Friedrich
Antiope, 101, 242
"Antipater of Sidon," 168, 250
Antipater of Sidon, 48, 60, 61, 63–4, 65,
149, 168, 169–70, 233, 237, 250, 253,
265n35, 266n46
Anyte of Tegea, 48, 139, 149, 167, 169,
234, 236, 253
Aphaea (Britomaris), 251
Aphrodite, 135, 242, 244, 248, 251,
274n14; and divine mania, 114; in
Dorian hellenism, 92, 93, 99, 105–6; in
Euripides, 143, 145, 188, 189, 221,
280n9; figural place of, in H.D.'s
hellenism, 72, 94, 95–6, 105–7, 116–17,
122, 188–90; in Harrison, 115, 198; in
Helen in Egypt, 230; in *Hippolytus
Temporizes*, 195–8; in Sappho, 106, 149,
154, 157; and the Venus de Milo, 96;
Anodymene (title), 115; Aphrogenia
(title), 115; Corinthian (title), 72;
Cyprian (Kupris) (title), 92, 143, 145,
149, 189, 196–8, 200; Cytheraea (title),
228; Ourania (title), 115. *See also* Venus
Apollo, 23, 71, 87, 95, 167; and *ascesis*,

86, 87, 94; and divine mania, 50, 83,
96, 98, 114, 121, 193, 196, 205, 211; in
Euripides, 26, 201, 202, 205, 212, 213;
figural place of, in H.D.'s hellenism,
50, 96–8, 107, 198–9; and the *hieros
gamos*, 121, 160; in *Hippolytus
Temporizes*, 195–9; and homoeroticism,
94, 96–8; and immolation, in H.D., 64,
71, 83, 96–8, 114, 188, 190, 193, 194,
202; in Nietzsche, 109–10, 121; in
Orphism, 118, 121–2; and paternal
authority, in H.D., 188, 193, 194, 200–
2; Delian (title), 138, 237, 251; Delphic
(title), 87, 138, 193, 237; Hyacinthia
(festival of), 71, 187, 240, 270n37;
Hyperborean (title), 138, 237;
Leucadian (title), 235; Loxias (title),
211; Oulios (title), 176, 251; Paeon
(title), 199; Phoebus (title), 94, 96, 243,
244; Sitalkas (title), 138, 237, 276n12.
See also Delphi; statue
Apollonius of Rhodes, 246, 253
Appian of Alexandria, 48, 62, 266n46
Apuleius, Lucius, 250, 253
Arac, Jonathan, 130, 131, 275n3
Arctinus, 176, 250
Arethusa, 142, 143, 144
Argestes, 137, 138, 237–8, 276n12
"Ariadne," 148, 176, 249
Aristogiton, 247
Aristomenes, 69–70
Aristotle, 60, 237, 266n42, 276n12
Arnold, Matthew, 25, 39, 40, 54, 68, 75
Arrian (Flavius Arridnus), 48, 62, 266n46
Arrowsmith, William, 202, 225, 226,
276n20
Artemis, 72, 116, 167, 189, 208, 237,
240, 248, 251; and *ascesis*, 85, 87; and
divine mania, 94, 102, 189; in Dorian
hellenism, 94, 95, 100–1, 106, 107; in
Euripides, 145, 184, 188; and female
homoeroticism, 95, 107, 154, 189,
196, 271n43; figural place of, in H.D.'s
writing, 107, 116; in *Hippolytus
Temporizes*, 195–7, 199; and
immolation, in H.D., 114, 187, 189;
and paternal authority, in H.D., 188,
200; as virgin mother, 100–2, 107, 189,
280n9; Brauronia (title and festival of),
94, 240; Daphnaia (title), 246;
Daphnephoria (festival of), 240;
Leucadian (title), 279n2